Pastor Nichols' *Lift Up Your Eyes* ad
the Pasadena Citizen. Succinct an
the heart of the message and make

The Citizen
Pasadena, Texas

As a community newspaper editor/publisher for more than 50 years, I appreciate the art of language but also the art of brevity. Clyde always delivers a beautiful, insightful and inspiring message and his style is an editor's dream—well crafted and concise.

J.W. "Bill" Cooke, Editor & Publisher
The Rockdale Reporter
Rockdale, Texas

I have known Pastor Nichols for many years, and have had an opportunity to read an assortment of his writings. His strong Christian leadership has had a lasting positive effect on family, friends, and community. This book continues his mission to lift us all up in His goodness.

Drayton McLane
Chairman and CEO of the Houston Astros
Chairman and CEO of the McLane Group

From the pulpit, in countless visits to our home, in his letters to a lonely soldier, and in his published writings, this humble man of God has provided spiritual direction and comfort to four generations of my family. Whether listening to his message in Church or reading his columns, I've always felt it was just Clyde and Sammy, the two of us, in God's presence. In "Lift Up Your Eyes," Clyde is again at my side. And as I reflect on each devotional, I feel the love of Christ.

Samuel W. Floca Jr.
Colonel, Field Artillery, Retired

Having been the Head Football Coach and Athletic Director at Temple High School for twenty eight years, I have become a huge fan of Rev. Clyde Nichols. His weekly columns have been an integral part of my life. I have used many of his columns when speaking to young people at athletic banquets across the state. This book, taken to heart, will make you a better person. It will help you to more easily deal with life's challenges. Reverend Clyde is definitely one of God's very special people.

Bob McQueen
Coach, Retired

Rev. Clyde E. Nichols is the pastor's pastor! He not only provided pastoral care for First Christian Church (Disciples of Christ) for 23 years, he was and is pastor to the community of Temple, Texas. It is only fitting that his collective works are here presented in book form. His writing continues to be an encouragement for many in our area. Now the book provides an opportunity to deepen the devotional life of hungering people in a much broader way. *Lift Up Your Eyes* will allow us to do what Clyde Nichols has done for years. Let this work be a blessing to you.

Pastor Don Lynn
First Christian Church
Temple, Texas

Lift Up Your Eyes is an earthy book of daily devotions. With his feet planted firmly on the earth, Rev. Nichols addresses the issues we all find ourselves facing every day—issues of fear and trust, hatred and forgiveness, weariness and strength, loneliness and hope. With our feet planted on the earth—mired in the mud of fear, hatred, weariness, loneliness, and a myriad of hungers for something *more*—we lift up our eyes. And there, in God's grace, we find our hope.

Pastor Pat Dietrich
First Lutheran Church
Temple, Texas

The Lord said, "I came that you might have life and have it more abundantly." In *Lift Up Your Eyes*, Rev. Nichols makes us realize that life is a gift from God and what we do with our lives is our gift to God.

Pastor Roscoe Harrison, Jr.
Eighth Street Baptist Church
Temple, Texas

This book is thoughtful and inspirational. I highly recommend it for all Christians.

Dr. S. A. Sanchez, M.D.
Temple, Texas

This book of daily devotions will indeed touch your heart for Rev. Nichols writes from his heart. Each daily reading is a selection that pertains to our daily lives and reminds us of things we need to do. He presents each page in such a way you can hear God speaking to you.

Doris Kirkley
Temple, Texas

Lift Up Your Eyes

I lift up my eyes to the hills.
From whence does my help come?
My help comes from the Lord.
Psalms 121: 1-2

Clyde E. Nichols

Cover photo of Mount Sinai by Berthold Werner
Creative Commons License BY-SA 3.0

ISBN-13: 978-1517465209
ISBN-10: 1517465206

First printing 2011 (AuthorHouse)
Revised 2015 for second printing (CreateSpace)
Printed in the United States of America

DEDICATION

To my faithful readers whose words of appreciation
and encouragement keep me ever striving to make
my *Lift Up Your Eyes* columns half as good
as they are kind enough to say they are.

FOREWORD

One day in 1986, my father presented me with a wooden box. In it were twenty-one file folders, each containing fifty-two clipped newspaper articles. They were devotional columns that had appeared in our city's newspaper for over two decades.

During all these years, these interpreted stories have lifted the eyes of thousands upon thousands of individuals toward Heaven. That is what these columns continue to do when they are read and shared.

I was once told by a church executive, "There is no shortage of ministers; there is a shortage of good ministers." In today's book market, there is no shortage of Christian devotional books; there may be a shortage of *good* devotional books. In this book, you will find an author who, over a lifetime of ministry, has come to know the hungers and hurts, the hearts and hopes of humanity.

Over the years, Clyde has received hundreds of letters with such words of appreciation and encouragement as:

"Your column which appears in the Telegram each week is read by thousands of people. We at the paper continue to hear compliments about the column and the inspiration it brings to many lives."

"I want to compliment you on your excellent column in the Temple Telegram each week. It always deals with some thought-provoking idea. Thank you for the contribution you are making to life in Temple."

"I am writing to tell you how much we appreciate your articles in the Temple paper. My husband's niece sends them to us. Your writings bear fruit here in Aurora, Missouri."

"I want you to know how special your newspaper column is to us. Would you ever consider publishing them in book form? If so, reserve 5 copies for us!"

Finally, don't overlook the Scripture verses. If you will memorize one verse from each week, at the end of the year you will have 52 verses at your command. Most Christians I know can't quote half that many.

Now, you are invited to open this book, discover its rich messages, and lift up your eyes.

Rev. Dr. Gregory L. Nichols
Disciples Minister

INTRODUCTION

In 1965, when the *Temple Daily Telegram's* managing editor, Larry Ingram, told the Rev. Clyde Nichols, pastor of Temple's First Christian Church, he would run his inspirational column and "see how it goes." Little did he know that he was opening the door on a 30-plus year fixture on the *Telegram's* Saturday editorial page.

Right from the start, Clyde Nichols' *"Lift Up Your Eyes"* made an impact on readers. The professionally and inspirationally written column became such a part of the *Temple Daily Telegram* that the paper continued to run the column after the Rev. Nichols retired.

First appearing on May 8, 1965, the column has failed to run only twice throughout the years. Just two weeks after it first appeared, the *Telegram* simply forgot to run it. Then on July 9, when a desperate Larry Ingram called him at home to tell him they could not find his column, Clyde realized he had forgotten to write it.

Soon the column became a habit for both the *Telegram* and the Rev. Nichols, and a welcome bright spot for Telegram readers who always find it uplifting, refreshing and inspirational.

When the Christian Church was mentioned around town, it was commonplace to hear, "Oh that's the church where the minister who writes the Saturday column for the *Telegram* preaches."

The column obviously touches many lives based on the notes and letters received by the Rev. Nichols and the *Telegram's* Letters to the Editor.

The name of the column comes from Psalms 121: 1-2, "I lift up my eyes to the hills. From whence does my help come? My help comes from the Lord..."

Because of our long association with the Rev. Clyde Nichols' *"Lift Up Your Eyes"* column, we at the *Temple Daily Telegram* know readers young and old will find comfort, inspiration and joy in this book of daily devotions taken from columns which originally appeared in the *Temple Daily Telegram.*

Sue Mayborn, Editor and Publisher
Temple Daily Telegram
Temple, Texas

ACKNOWLEDGEMENTS

These daily devotions are taken from columns which have appeared on the Saturday editorial page of the *Temple Daily Telegram* over the past twenty some-odd years. I would like to thank the following people who helped make the column and this book of devotions possible.

The late **Larry Ingram**, managing editor, whom I approached with the idea for the column was very frank in stating up front: "I am very skeptical of a religious column in a daily paper." But he had the courage to give it a try, and made it possible for me to minister to thousands of people beyond my own congregation. It was also Larry who first suggested in a letter, "At some point soon I think you ought to consider a book compiling your best between permanent covers."

Sue Mayborn, Publisher and Editor, for her kindness in looking over the proposed book and giving permission for the columns to be published.

Jerry Prickett, assistant managing editor, who receives my columns each week, keeps my mistakes and typos at a minimum and is always a faithful friend.

All of my fellow-workers on this project: My wife, **Marianne**, my daughter, **Lori Russell**, and **Doris Kirkley** for hours and hours of proofreading and helpful suggestions, my sister, **Carolyn Beach**, encourager and patron extraordinaire. **Greg**, my son, fellow craftsman and comrade of the unending quest, who helped select the Scriptures and designed the cover. To them I am forever indebted. There would have been no book without them. God Bless!

And time would fail me to say all I would like to say about my faithful readers. When I requested that they send me their favorite Bible verses to be used as texts for the daily devotions, I was swamped. Most of these verses are to be found in this book.

Clyde E. Nichols
Temple, Texas

Clyde E. Nichols, Senior Minister
First Christian Church, Temple, Texas
1963-1986

x

I WAS MADE A MINISTER

I was made a minister by the grace of God. There was no Damascus Road with a light shining round about me from heaven. There was no burning bush with a voice commanding, 'Put off your shoes.' There was no seraphim crying one to another, 'Holy, holy, holy.' That God has called others in such dramatic fashion I do not question, but his call came to me in a far less spectacular way.

I was made a minister by my mother and father. I was made a minister by the example of their lives; by their love and devotion to God; by our family worship at the close of each day; by their love and their prayers which have followed me. I was made a minister by parents who took me to Sunday school and church and led me to love the house of God next to my own home.

I was made a minister at the feet of a Sunday school teacher, a teacher who caused the Old Testament prophets, the Master of men, and the Apostle Paul to live again for me. After all these years I can still see a face and hear a voice which gave witness to the consecrated life of one who loved God and desired more than anything to share it with those to be the men and women of tomorrow.

I was made a minister by my own minister whose life was a demonstration of what God can do with a consecrated man. In his efforts I saw the power of God to transform and change the lives of men.

I was made a minister by those who listened to my first sermons and offered encouragement, by countless people who have touched my life and helped in so many ways, people, I know now, who were used by God to bring help in time of need.

I was made a minister by the multitudes unfed, gaunt, starving for the Living Bread. Amidst the crying needs of life, I have come to know that the supreme need of every life and the life of the world is God revealed to us through Jesus Christ, our Lord.

I was made a minister, and how do I feel about it? I am persuaded that if my life were to be lived a thousand times, that along the way there would come the call. Just as before, there would be 'many a conflict, many a doubt, fightings and fears within, without,' but at last the surrender—My life is little to offer; my talents are few, and these are small; but if I am needed, if I can serve; 'Here am I, Lord; send me!'

If I Were In His Place

It was late one afternoon during the first week of the New Year. I had come downtown to exchange a Christmas gift and was returning to my car. The hard misting rain was turning to sleet, and it was growing colder as darkness fell.

I stopped at the corner and waited for the traffic light to change. As I lowered my face to protect it from the sharp east wind, I overheard two people in front of me talking. A voice said very distinctly, "Well, I know one thing; if I were in his place... ."

At that moment the light changed, and the roar of moving traffic drowned out the conversation. But as I returned to my car and drove home, I kept wondering—in whose place, and if he were, just what was it he would do?

Of course, I know it is impossible for one person to enter the life of another and think and act for him, but on the threshold of the New Year, it poses a very fascinating question. Just suppose another person could come into your life and assume control. What kind of changes do you think he would make?

If you know of changes that might be made, why don't you make them? You see, you know more about your life and the changes that are needed than anyone else could ever know.

It is no easy thing to do. For one thing, it is hard for us to see our own faults. And even when we recognize them, the battle is far from won. How many times—especially on New Year's—have we made heroic resolutions, only to see them broken. Heroic efforts ending in despair! Why try again?

Someone else coming in may be the answer. It sounds strange at first, but this is really what the Christian faith is all about. It is Christ coming into a life and bringing hope, where there was no hope. It is Christ doing for us what we could never do for ourselves.

This was the secret that the Apostle Paul discovered and that caused him to exclaim triumphantly: "It is no longer I who live, but Christ who lives in me."

Listen as Christ speaks to you and me, "Behold, I stand at the door and knock. If any man will hear my voice and open the door, I will come in."

The Master Musician

One winter a number of years ago, Dr. F. B. Meyers made a trip through Norway. For a week he was a guest at a very exclusive inn. Also staying at the inn that week was a little girl of some six years of age whose favorite pastime was playing on the big piano which stood in the large downstairs parlor.

It wasn't exactly what you would call playing. Banging was more descriptive. You know—picking out tunes with your index finger. And she wasn't content to play just any time. She liked to get up early in the morning and play before anyone else was awake. Day after day, her playing awakened everyone.

One night there came to the inn one of the most famous pianists in all Norway. But this didn't stop the little girl. Early the next morning, she was down in the parlor as usual banging away.

Her playing awakened the great pianist. He slipped on his robe, went to the head of the stairs, and was ready to shout down angrily when he saw it was only a little girl.

The expression on his face changed. He walked down the stairs and over to where the little girl was. When she turned and looked up at him, smiling, he said, "I know the piece you are playing. Could I play with you?"

Overjoyed, the little girl moved over on the bench. He sat down beside her, and they began to play—the little girl with her pecking and the pianist as only a great artist can play.

For a while they played along together; then, the little girl began to listen. Her finger moved slower and slower, came to rest on one of the keys, and then slid down into her lap, as she sat there spellbound by the wonderful music.

That is a parable of your life and mine. How often we go along through life banging, banging, banging away. We produce a lot of discord and noise, and that is about all, but it doesn't have to be like that.

If we want to—really want to—we can invite the Master Musician to come in, and he can sit down at the keyboard of our soul and produce the kind of music we were intended to produce.

Look Up at the Light!

She got on the elevator at the fifteenth floor of the big hotel. The eight of us, who were already on, had been in a conference meeting all afternoon. We were tired and hungry and wanted to get home to our families.

Impatiently, we shuffled back a little to make more room. The lady was pretty. She was dressed in black that seemed to add poignantly to a touch of grief that lay in her eyes.

Along with her came a little girl. I suppose she must have been about four years of age. She wore a blue coat that matched her eyes, and blonde curls showed from beneath her little cap.

Again we all shuffled back and made more room. Little girls who aren't very tall can't reach up where there is lots of air. That is why they require even more space than is required for a grownup.

Then we stood as the elevator door clanged shut and we started down. And just as we did, there came a cry of "Oh!" in a frightened tone from the little girl. She caught on to her mother and hid her face against her mother's skirt.

The mother understood. Tenderly, she reached down and picked her up in her arms. For a few moments, she held her close. Then she whispered, "Darling, you must not be frightened—just open your eyes and look up at the light."

And the little girl did. Very slowly, she raised her head and looked up at the bowl-like globe in the top of the elevator, and all the way down, she kept her eyes fastened on the big white light.

Finally, the elevator reached the main floor, and the eight of us waited as the mother and her little four-year-old daughter stepped off and went on their way. It was a small incident, and rather insignificant, I suppose. We saw them but for a little while, and were to see them never again, but somehow I can't forget.

At times, through changeful season and scene, alone or on a crowded street, I see a mother with her little girl, and I hear those never-to-be-forgotten words: "You must not be frightened—just open your eyes, and look up at the light!"

Help From On High

Late one afternoon I was making pastoral calls out in Western Hills when a little model car came out into the street up a ways in front of me, made a U turn and went back into the driveway. No one was pulling or pushing it. This was something I had to investigate.

In the driveway, the young owner, Chris Hotchkiss, showed me his new toy. It was an Audi Quattro Sports car, and he was operating it with a remote control. I fell in love with it. I'm going to get one for my grandson's birthday so I can play with it.

Two things came to the little car from the remote control—guidance and power—help from on high. God does that for you and me. The psalmist says, "I lift up my eyes to the hills. From whence does my help come? My help comes from the Lord, who made heaven and earth."

God gives us guidance. One of my favorite songs says, "All the way my Savior leads me, what have I to ask beside? Can I doubt his tender mercy, who through life has been my guide?" That guidance comes from many sources—from time alone in prayer, from the reading of God's Word, from the counsel of friends, but there is always guidance from on high in our time of need.

God also gives us power. Jesus told his disciples to wait until they were armed with "power from on high." That power is available today for anyone who wants to follow and serve him.

To a certain hospital a little boy was brought for surgery, and they prepared to administer the anesthetic. It wouldn't hurt at all, the nurse explained; he would just go to sleep.

"Before I go to sleep, I always say my prayers. Could I say my prayers?" Yes, he could say his prayers. So in the operating room, while the men and women in white stood by, a little boy of five clasped his hands, closed his eyes and prayed. "Now I lay me down to sleep, I pray thee, Lord, my soul to keep. If I should die before I wake, I pray thee, Lord, my soul to take."

The prayer over, the masks adjusted, and the operation was underway, but the doctors and nurses there that day had witnessed something they would not soon forget. Through the eyes of a little boy, they had looked up into the face of God. They had witnessed firsthand what it means to receive help from on high.

Learning to Forgive

It was 1947 and Corrie ten Boom had come from Holland to speak to a defeated Germany, to assure them of God's forgiveness. It was the message they needed to hear: "When we confess our sins," she said, "God casts them into the deepest sea."

Solemn faces stared back at her, not daring to believe. In silence they stood up and began filing out. It was then that she saw him, a balding man in a gray overcoat, a brown felt hat in hand. In a brief moment she relived it all—the large room, their clothes piled in the corner, and the shame of walking naked past this man. She remembered her sister Betsie—so pathetically thin.

Standing in front of her he said, "It is so good to know that, as you say, our sins are at the bottom of the sea." Corrie ten Boom, who had spoken so glibly of forgiveness, looked away from his outstretched hand. He didn't remember her. How could he remember one single prisoner among thousands? But she remembered him, and her blood ran cold.

"You mentioned Ravensbruck," he said, "I was a guard there." No, he didn't remember her. "But since that time," he continued, "I have become a Christian. I know God has forgiven me for the cruel things I did, but I would like to hear it from you." Again with hand out-thrust, he said, "Will you forgive me?"

She stood there—she whose sins had again and again needed to be forgiven—and could not forgive. Betsie, her sister, had died there! It was only a few seconds that he held out his hand, but it seemed like hours. It was the hardest thing she ever had to do, but she had to do it. "If you do not forgive men their trespasses," Jesus had said, "Neither will your Father forgive you."

Still she stood there with coldness clutching her throat, but forgiveness is not an emotion. Forgiveness is an act of will. She prayed, "Jesus, help me. I can lift my hand. You supply the feeling." Woodenly she held out her hand, "I forgive you;" she cried, "with all my heart I forgive you!"

For a long minute they grasped each other's hands, the former guard and the former prisoner. As she did so, an incredible thing happened. A current sprang into their joined hands and healing warmth flooded Corrie ten Boom's being. Healing warmth had brought tears to her eyes.

You Be The Miracle!

In the book of Acts the disciples were asked, "Why do you stand looking into heaven?" Commissioned to be his witnesses, they stood gazing up into the sky looking where they thought Jesus ought to be rather than in the place where he promised he would be. Staring up, where Jesus was not, they were unable to go where Jesus was and is today.

The movie *Bruce Almighty* is about a man disillusioned with God. Things have not gone well at work, and Bruce blames God. He screams and curses and accuses God of being unjust. Then God appears, gives Bruce almighty power and says, "OK, let's see you do it better!"

Bruce tries out his newly given power by parting the tomato soup in his bowl at lunch. Great fun! But then prayer requests start coming in thick and fast. He uses the e-mail to respond, but the prayers keep piling up. Finally, he programs the computer to answer all the prayers with a yes.

Chaos ensues. Just as quick as he possibly can, Bruce gets back in touch with God. He tries to explain, "There were so many voices coming from every direction! I thought saying yes to all of them would be a good thing." God explains, "You can't do that. People don't know what they really want. They are all looking up expecting God to do it for them."

That's the problem, isn't it? We want God to do things FOR us; God wants to do things THROUGH us. Doing it FOR, cuts us out. Doing it THROUGH is what being a disciple of Jesus Christ is all about.

God says to Bruce, "Don't think for a minute that parting the tomato soup in your bowl was a miracle, because it wasn't. Parting the tomato soup was nothing more than a magic trick. A single mother working two jobs and still getting her kids to soccer practice—that's a miracle. A teenager saying no to drugs and yes to an education—that's a miracle." Then God says to Bruce, "You be the miracle!"

You and I know that the only way any of us could ever be a miracle is for God to work through our lives, but we spend our time doing exactly what the disciples did—staring up into heaven expecting God to do it for us rather than inviting God's Spirit to be at work through us.

God is waiting to work through you. Why are you gazing up into heaven?

When, If Not Now? Who, If Not You?

Jane Addams was a Christian social worker. One hundred years ago she changed the way the church does business in America forever. Before she began her work the churches were islands of holiness surrounded by cities of despair and poverty. Wrapped up in their own little isolated lives, it never occurred to the churches of America that it was their business to help.

Born to a wealthy industrialist family in Chicago, why should she care about needy families? Then one night that all changed. On the way home from a party her chauffeur took a wrong turn, and instead of going directly back to their wealthy Chicago mansion, they drove into the slums of Chicago.

For the first time in her life that young woman saw what it was like to be poor. The streets through which they drove that night were unpaved and half of them were impassable. The chauffeur could hardly find his way through the morass of that part of town. Finally, after a seeming eternity they made their way out, but Jane Addams had had an up-close, personal view of how most of the people of Chicago lived.

When she got home, she was so upset she was shaking. She sat down with her parents, good God-fearing, church-going people, looked them in the eye and said, "How can this be!?" They had no answer. She asked, "Well, what is Chicago doing?" They had no answer. She said, "We go to church. What is our church doing?" They had no answer. She said, "What should we as individuals be doing?" They had no answer.

She went up stairs, lay down on her freshly-ironed sheets and cried herself to sleep. In the middle of the night she was awakened by a voice speaking with power to her heart, saying, "When, if not now? Who, if not you?"

The next morning she got up and began preparing for her life's work. Of course, Jane Addams didn't solve the whole problem, but her work has made the solution more and more and more possible.

Never has there been a greater need for caring Christians to make a difference in the lives of the homeless and needy of our nation. God is calling you and me and Christians of our land to look and listen. When we do, we will hear the voice of God calling to us, saying, "When, if not now? Who, if not you?"

January 8   **Jeremiah 29: 13**
Life's Greatest Discovery

"He is their strength in time of trouble." Those words from the Book of Psalms come to my mind as I remember the story of Lt. James C. Whitaker which he told about in his book, *We Thought We Heard The Angels Sing.*

In October of 1942, a plane was forced down in the Pacific, and eight men were left stranded in three rubber rafts. Without food and water, with the burning sun beating down on them, for three weeks they were tossed on a sea churned by sharks and high waves.

At dawn on the twenty-first day, Lt. Whitaker was awakened by one of the airmen. "Jim," he said, "I think I see something." About twelve miles away were to be seen palm trees.

Exhausted and spent, Lt. Whitaker got out their aluminum oars and for almost eight hours rowed toward the shore. They had almost reached land when a wind arose and a perverse current carried them back out to sea.

Thirty minutes more he rowed. It was evident that he was making little or no progress against the current. Then an offshore wind sprang up, and the raft was swept out to sea again.

In despair and ready to give up and quit, he cried out above the rising wind, "Oh, God, all of my strength is gone. You have got to help me!" And God heard his cry for help and came to his rescue.

Jim Whitaker held the oars, but as he said later, "I didn't do it. I didn't have enough strength to bend a pin. I was not conscious of exerting any effort. It seemed to me that the oars worked automatically. My hands were merely following their motion. There were other hands than mine on those oars."

At two o'clock on that twenty-first day they touched the island. Kneeling down, they gave thanks to God. Later, Lt. Whitaker wrote in his diary, "During those twenty-one days on a raft, I made the greatest discovery any man can make—I discovered God."

That is the greatest discovery any one can make, and when we make the discovery, we will find with Isaiah that "they who wait for the Lord shall renew their strength, they shall mount up on wings like eagles, they shall run and not be weary, they shall walk and not faint."

8

Homeless

The movie *Planes, Trains and Automobiles*, starring Steve Martin and John Candy, is a hilarious comedy about an ad exec stranded on his way home for Thanksgiving who meets up with an unlikely co-traveler.

Driving late at night, they enter an exit ramp by mistake and are heading toward the oncoming traffic of the interstate. A driver on the other side sees what is happening and begins shouting frantically, "Hey! You're going the wrong way! You're going the wrong way!" John Candy turns to Steve Martin and says, "That guy must be drunk. How would he know where we're going?"

After dozens of unbelievable situations, in some of which they barely escape with their lives, they finally arrive in Chicago. In the train station, they hilariously recount all of their narrow escapes and harrowing experiences; say their goodbyes, wishing each other a Happy Thanksgiving and take leave to go to their respective homes.

Seated on the El train, dreaming of the happy reunion with his family for the holidays, Steve Martin begins to have second thoughts. He gets off, catches another train and goes back to the station house. There, sitting all alone, he finds his traveling companion.

"What are you doing here?" he asks, "I thought you were going home." Embarrassed, chagrinned, John Candy breaks down and tells him, "I don't have a home. My wife, Marie, died eight years ago."

The movie has an unforgettable, heartwarming ending with Steve taking John home with him for Thanksgiving and somehow we know everything turns out fine. It's a wonderful movie, filled with lots of laughs. But what I remember most, what I can't forget, is John's reluctant confession, "I don't have a home!"

We are seeing more and more homeless people across our cities and our nation. For anyone to come to the end of the day and have no home to go to is tragic. You and I—the followers of Christ— simply must do something about it.

It is even more tragic to come to the end of life's little day and have no home to go to. In the Gospel of John, we read these words of Jesus. "I go to prepare a place for you." That was the purpose of his coming to earth two thousand years ago. Through faith in him, you and I have "a house not made with hands, a home eternal in the heavens."

9

Do I Have To Go To Church?

It was a belligerent young man who said, "I can be just as good a Christian without going to church as I can by going!" I understood; I had felt the same way once. Instead of arguing and trying to persuade, I said, "Let me share a personal experience with you:"

"I was in seminary and was being plagued with headaches. When I mentioned it to the dean, he suggested I see Dr. Roy Gough, an optometrist who was a good friend of his who took an interest in 'preacher boys.'" "Dr. Gough checked my eyes and fitted me with glasses. 'I think this will clear up your headaches,' he said. But the next week I was back. 'They aren't helping,' I told him, 'My headaches are as severe as ever.' Puzzled, he asked, 'Are you wearing your glasses all the time?'

"'Well, not really,' I admitted, 'I forget to put them on. That's something else—I can see just as well without them!' Rather amused, he said, 'You must wear your glasses regularly. I want you to put them on the first thing when you wake up in the morning and don't take them off until you go to bed at night.' I agreed to give it a try.

"Gradually, my headaches went away. One afternoon I was on the city bus seated by the open window when something struck my cheek. I took off my glasses and rubbed the side of my face. I vividly recall looking down and seeing the green grass a blur beside the road. As I replaced my glasses, the grass suddenly came into focus.

"Surprised and somewhat in doubt, I removed my glasses. The grass blurred. Replacing them, the grass came back into sharp focus. There was no room for doubt, my glasses made all the difference in the world.

"Later I went by to share the news with Dr. Gough. He listened, smiling. 'You know, in a way you were right,' he said. 'You were able to see just as well without your glasses, but you were straining your eyes to do so and that was the thing causing your headaches.'"

My friend smiled and nodded in agreement as I continued, "It's true, I can be a good Christian without going to church, but it puts a strain on my life, a strain of which I am completely unaware until I go to church regularly for a while and then miss a Sunday."

Augustine stated a great truth when he wrote at the beginning of his *Confessions*: "Lord, you have made us for yourself and our hearts are restless until they find their rest in you."

Running Away From God

Fred Craddock tells the story about an old woman, a scavenger on the streets of London. Rolling drunks was about her only source of income. She found one who had fallen off the sidewalk into the gutter.

With great effort, she finally got him on his feet. Taking her time, she hauled him up the rickety stairs to her drab room over a store. Then she put a little coffee in him while she rifled his pockets. She couldn't believe it! Not a dime, not a penny, not a thing!

What was this—a dirty, worn, crumpled piece of paper. She went over to the kerosene lamp, smoothed out the paper, and held it under the dim light and read:

> I fled him down the nights
> and down the days.
> I fled him through the arches
> of the years.
> I fled him through the labyrinthine
> ways of my mind.
> Under the mist of tears,
> Under running laughter—

She looked at him, puzzled. "What are you running from?" she asked. The man looked at her with a vacant stare. She repeated the question, "Who are you running from, the police?" He answered, "God."

You can't run away from God. Nobody can. But people try. The pages of history are filled with them—Adam and Eve disobey God and then try to hide "from the presence of the Lord." God commands Jonah to go to Nineveh. Instead he takes a ship bound in the opposite direction "away from the presence of the Lord."

The prodigal son, thinking home and family "a drag," leaves his father and goes to a far country. His older brother stays at home, but in reality he is just as much, if not more, outside the fellowship and love of his family as if he had run away with his brother. In all these cases, it wouldn't work.

In Jesus' story we read, "But while he was yet at a distance, his father saw him." God is like that. We may run away to some far country, but our heavenly Father ever "stands on the portals, waiting and watching" for our return.

Against the Storm

Sometimes in memory I see my mother seated by the window sewing, listening to her favorite soap on the radio. I never listened to the storyline but as though it were yesterday I can hear the words that opened every episode: "Against the storm keep your head low; that's common sense, but keep your heart high. That's better still. And remember that the longest storm the world has ever known, and the worst, came to an end one bright morning."

Storms come to the lives of everyone and perhaps it is then, as no other time, that prayer becomes a reality for each of us as we cry out, "Oh, God, I need your help!" I know it is true of my life. Haven't you found it to be so?

In the sunshine we may debate if there is a God and if there is does he hear and answer our prayers, but when the storms break in all their fury, debating ends, and we lift voices in prayer for God's help.

Recently I heard about a woman who was lost in a blizzard. She didn't know what to do. In her fear she began to panic. She visualized Jesus seated beside her in the car, the best thing she could have, and said to him, "Lord, I am scared and don't know what to do. Please help me!"

She heard Jesus say to her, "Follow." She replied, "Jesus, there is no one to follow," but the voice said again, "Follow." Then looking up she saw a tow truck in front of her car that she hadn't seen before. She followed the tow truck all the way into the heart of town where the lights were burning and she was safe.

She got out of the car in the cold winter air intent on thanking God. As she looked around, she suddenly realized that she was standing all alone in the street. She looked in front of her car for the tow truck she had been following. No truck was there. She glanced down and saw to her amazement that there were no tire tracks in front of her automobile.

She walked around behind her car. The only tracks were the tracks of her car, no tracks of the tow truck she had followed for the 20 miles through the blizzard. Falling on her knees in the snow she said, "Lord, it's true. You really do guide us through the storm!"

Soon or late storms come to every life. When the storm breaks in your life, lift up your eyes and pray. God wants to help you. Give him a chance!

On The Beach

The words were emblazoned on the page, the motto of a service group that is making a difference today: "Changing the world, one person at a time."

That has always been the secret. The Man from Galilee, the greatest life ever lived, gave us the blueprint 2000 years ago. Jesus Christ was a great teacher. He spoke to multitudes. From his lips came what has been called the greatest sermon ever preached.

But Jesus' best work was done with individuals—Peter, Andrew, James, and John, the woman at the well, Mary, Martha and Lazarus, the blind Bartimaeus, Mary Magdalene, the tax collector, Matthew, the thief on the cross—and you could go on and on.

He lived this way of life and pointed the way for you and me as recorded in the Gospel of Matthew with the words, "to one of the least of these."

The Apostle Paul followed in the footsteps of the Master. He was a preacher of power, but his chief work was with individuals. Turn some time to his letter to the Romans, a major statement of Paul's theology. In the last chapter, as he closes, Paul listed 25 individuals by name whose lives were entwined with his.

Paul wrote lots of letters, powerful writings that make up half of the books of our New Testament. But have you noticed that he closed each one with greetings to individuals?

There is a story about an old man who walked the beach at dawn. Just ahead, he noticed a young woman picking up starfish and flinging them back to the sea.

Catching up with her, he asked, "Why are you doing this?" She replied, "The stranded starfish will surely die if left beneath the noonday sun." "But the beach goes on for miles," he said, "And there are millions of them. How can your efforts make any difference?"

The young woman looked at the starfish she was holding in her hand, then, threw it safely behind the approaching wave. Turning to the old man, she replied, "It made a difference to that one."

Each and every day you and I walk the beach beside the Sea of Life.

Formula For A Miracle

Dr. John Maxwell gives this biblical formula for a miracle: "When there's a need sensed by a few and each individual understands his responsibility and gives his all, regardless of the odds, then Jesus works a miracle."

What is required for God to perform a miracle? Prayer? Faith? Yet people have received miracles who didn't pray, and people have received miracles who had no faith at all. Miracles in the Bible have this in common: They all begin with a need. Anyone who has a need is a candidate for a miracle.

There is one miracle that is found in all four gospels. It is about a little boy who left home one morning going to hear Jesus, carrying a lunch of five small rolls and two fish his mother had quickly prepared for him. Little did he dream that on that very ordinary day God would use his life to produce a miracle.

As they listened to Jesus, it grew late. The disciples suggested that Jesus send them away so they could go get something to eat. But Jesus said, "You give them something to eat." Strange, isn't it, when God does miracles he always involves people. When we refuse to do our part we don't really want a miracle; we want God to do magic.

"What?" the disciples exclaimed, "You want us to spend a fortune to feed this crowd?" Jesus said, "Go and see how much food you have." They began to inquire. No one had food. As they got closer and closer to the little boy, I think he must have hid his lunch.

It's hard to care for others when you are comfortable yourself. He had food; he didn't need anything. Besides, it didn't make sense. The disciples said Jesus wanted to take it and feed 5,000 people! I can understand. Many times Jesus has asked for my lunch and I have not given it to him because—well, it didn't make sense.

But this little boy gave his lunch, and Jesus took it, multiplied it, and fed 5,000 people. The lesson: Nothing multiplies in our hands. Nothing! Lunches multiply only when Jesus gets hold of them.

The little boy never got over that day. He told his mother when he got home and years later told his children and his children's children how on a very ordinary day, against all the odds, he gave his lunch and Jesus took it and fed 5,000 hungry people.

Hey, I'm A Minister, Too!

There is a story told about a certain minister who became so discouraged that one Monday morning he decided to leave the ministry. It wasn't easy finding another job, but finally he accepted a position at the local zoo.

It seems the big gorilla had died and they planned to dress the minister in a gorilla costume and put him in the cage until they could find another live gorilla. Dressed in his costume, his only responsibility was to jump around in the cage, make guttural noises, and entertain all the people who walked by.

It was a great life. He was getting more attention than he ever got in the pulpit. He had all the food he could eat, and if he grew tired he could lie down in the warm sunshine and take a nap.

One day he was swinging on the trapeze. The children were excitedly cheering as he swung higher and higher. Then suddenly, he lost his grip, went flying over the bars, and landed in the adjoining cage.

Staggering to his feet and seeing a ferocious lion coming toward him, he started yelling for help. Quickly the lion put a paw to its mouth and said in a loud whisper, "Hey! Be quiet, I'm a minister, too!"

Dr. Elton Trueblood says the great need of the church in our day is to take seriously the fact that every member of the congregation is a minister. He gets this model for ministry from the book of Ephesians: "(Christ's) gifts were that some should be apostles, some prophets, some evangelists, some pastors and teachers, to equip the saints for the work of ministry."

In other words, the task is not for the minister to do all the work but for him/her to teach and train the members of the church so they can do ministry. But, as Rick Warren points out in *The Purpose Driven Church,* all too often the very opposite is the case—the minister does all of the pastoral calling, the preaching, and evangelizing while the membership watches to see if he/she is doing what he/she was called to do and, if and when it is needed, offer their "helpful criticism."

Perhaps you have never thought of yourself as a minister, but the New Testament says if you are a member of the church that is what you are. What kind of a minister are you and what kind of church is your church becoming because of your ministry?

Proverbs 22:6
It's Easier When You're Taught

"Train children in the right way, and when old, they will not stray." Read those words over again. They are from the Book of Proverbs.

The eleven-year-old boy was doing what he liked best—fishing with his father in the middle of a beautiful lake in New Hampshire. It was the evening before the bass season opened, and they were catching sunfish and perch using worms for bait.

On a whim, he decided to try casting with a silver lure to get ready for the bass season that opened at midnight. He cast and immediately his rod almost bent double—there was a whopper on the end of his line.

His father watched with pride as his son battled the big fish, worked it alongside and into the net. It was the biggest fish the boy had ever caught, and the largest bass he or his father had ever seen.

They stared in amazement. Then his father lighted a match and looked at his watch. It was ten o'clock—two hours before bass season opened. His eyes slowly met those of the boy. Reluctantly, he spoke, "Son, you know you will have to put it back." "But, Dad—," the boy exclaimed. "There will be other fish," said the father. "But not like this one, Dad; this is the catch of a lifetime!"

The boy looked around the lake. Not a boat, not a single person was in sight. No one else would ever know what time it was. He looked again at his father, but he already knew that the decision was non-negotiable.

With an ache in his heart, he removed the hook and lowered the incredible bass back into the water. A sudden powerful swish and it was gone. Somehow he knew he would never again see such a fish.

That was thirty years ago. The little boy is grown and is a successful architect in New York City. The family's cabin is still on the island and he takes his own son there to fish from the dock. However, he was right. Over the years he has caught lots of fish, but never again a fish like the one he put back.

He sees that bass, again and again, every time he comes up against a big ethical decision. You see, his father taught him the difference between right and wrong. It still isn't easy. Even when the decision is clear, the doing is difficult, but it is a lot easier when you have been taught to put the fish back.

A Faith To Live By

Theirs was about the finest Christian family I have ever known. It was my privilege to serve as their minister. They were a part of everything that went on in the church, the school, and the community.

They had bought their own business and were working hard to make a go of it. The nature of the business forced him to work on Sunday. But he always went down early in order to be through in time for church. He usually came in during the singing of the opening hymn and hurried down to join his wife and two boys in the pew where they always sat.

Then came the Korean War, and he was called back into the service. To the amazement and joy of all of us, they kept their business. With the help of a friend, the wife took over the management and did an unbelievably fine job.

With a growing business and two little boys, her hours were long and hard, but she did it, and every Sunday found them in their places in Sunday school and church.

None of us can ever forget the day we received the news: "Killed in action." What could any of us do? What could we say to a mother and two little boys who through the long weeks had worked, and hoped, and prayed?

"Our God is able . . . ." "I will never leave you . . . ." "The Lord is my shepherd . . . ." We tried so hard, but the words seemed so empty!

The next Sunday we gathered for worship. The call to worship, and we stood for the opening hymn. As we began the second stanza, a mother entered the sanctuary from the foyer with two little boys, and they walked down the aisle to their accustomed places.

There were few dry eyes in the house of God that day, and you will understand when I say that, in my opinion, the most powerful sermon ever preached in that church was preached unknowingly by that young mother and her little boys.

I believe the words now; I know they are true. "I am sure that neither death, nor life, nor angels, nor principalities, nor things present, nor things to come, nor powers, nor height, nor depth, nor anything else is all creation, will be able to separate us from the love of God in Christ Jesus our Lord."

God Loves Me, But Does He Like Me?

In Brennan Manning's book *The Wisdom of Tenderness*, the question is asked, "Does God like me?" Not does God **love** me, but does God **like** me?

The Bible assures us of God's love. In his first letter John writes: "In this is love, not that we loved God but that he loved us . . . ." And in John 3: 16, we read the reassuring words: "For God so loved the world that he gave his only Son, that whoever believes in him should not perish but have eternal life."

As children we sang the little chorus, "Praise him, praise him, all you little children. God is love, God is love." It's true—God is love and so, by his very nature, God loves each and every one of the children created in his image. No, the question is not does God love me? The question is does God like me?

I know of a couple that have a routine they go through every year on their wedding anniversary. It began on their first anniversary when at the breakfast table the young husband asked his bride of one year, "Well, how do you like me now?"

She replied, "I love you, darling. You know that." He continued, "No, I don't mean that. I know you love me, but how do you like me? I want you to be frank and honest. What bugs you about me? What changes can I make? What can I do to become the kind of person you would like for me to be?"

Following that young husband's example could you and I, standing in the presence of God, ask, "Lord, how do you like me?" There can be no doubt as to what God's answer would be, is there? He would say, "I love you. You know that. I love you so much I gave my only Son to die for you."

But suppose we pursued our quest further. Suppose we said, "Yes, Lord, I know that you love me, but how do you like me? What changes in my life can I make? What can I do with your help to become the kind of person you want me to be?" What would God say to us then? What would his answer be?

If somehow we can find the courage to pray like that, God will have the opportunity he needs to speak to our hearts, open our eyes to the needs and possibilities of our lives, and change them, and with enough such courageous prayers, God can change the world!

Give The World A Smile!

One afternoon two little girls were busy playing house when one asked her playmate, "Does your father have a den?" The second little girl thought for a moment and then replied, "Oh, no, he just growls all over the house." Are you ever a growler like that? If so, what can be done to remedy the situation?

Do you remember this little chorus? "You can smile; when you can't say a word, you can smile. When you cannot be heard, you can smile. When it's cloudy or fair, any time, any place, anywhere."

That's good advice—and good theology. Recently I saw the painting "The Smiling Christ." It was wonderful! I believe Jesus must have smiled a lot, when he was with the twelve, when he blessed the little children, during all of the dinners to which he was invited, when the paralytic picked up his pallet and walked—and many more occasions.

Mother Teresa worked for years among the poor of India. Toward the end of her life, she was recognized and honored for all her work. During the interview someone asked her, "Mother Teresa, what can we, the common, everyday people, do for the cause of peace in the world?" She paused, and then answered, "Smile."

That is where we are so prone to fail. When we are overly serious we give people the impression that our Christian faith is one of gloom and doom. Many times in the gospels we hear Jesus saying, "Be of good cheer."

Smiles of understanding and encouragement can make a tremendous difference in our world. I remember being in an oratorical contest as a student in high school. I was seated on the stage with seven other contestants, the auditorium was crowded with people I did not know, and I was so keyed up I could actually feel my heart pounding in my chest.

Looking out into that sea of faces, I saw Miss Jessie Sims, one of my teachers in junior high, who gave me the most reassuring smile you ever saw. I will remember that smile as long as I live. It's true, "A smile takes but a moment, but the memory of it can last forever."

One thing more—sometimes you meet people who are too busy, too tired, too worried, too discouraged to give you a smile. When that happens give them one of yours. No one needs a smile so much as someone who has no smiles left to give.

The Lifting Power Of God

During the annual Minister's Week on the campus of Texas Christian University, Dr. Charles Allen, minister of First United Methodist Church in Houston, who was the Wells Preacher, told about visiting a lovely little park just outside Florence, Alabama.

He was there for a revival meeting, and one afternoon the minister of the church took him to the park that is on top of a bluff overlooking the Tennessee River. It was a wonderful experience to sit there watching the river below. High above them could be seen the great hydroelectric dam built by the Tennessee Valley Authority.

As they were enjoying the view, they saw a tugboat, heavily loaded, coming up the river, huffing and puffing against the swift current. Dr. Allen asked where the little boat would turn around. His host replied, "It won't turn around. It will go on up to the lake above."

"Now that is something I have to see," Dr. Allen said to himself, "I've never known of a tugboat that could fly, and there is no other way for it to get over that great concrete dam and onto the lake above."

Then as they continued to watch, the little tugboat pulled into a lock built on the side of the dam and cut off its motor. Huge gates came down behind it, and water began to pour in from above. Gradually, the boat began to rise.

Then it moved into a second lock and was raised to a higher level. The procedure was repeated for the third time. Now it was on a level with the lake. The motor was started and under its own power, it moved on up the lake and out of sight.

The story is highly reminiscent of Psalms 121 from which we get the name for our weekly column: "I lift up my eyes to the hills. From whence does my help come? My help comes from the Lord . . . ."

As Dr. Allen pointed out, "Life is like that. Our little crafts make their way up the River of Life. We go huffing and puffing along against the swift currents. Then, often without warning, our progress is halted. It is impossible to go forward under our own power.

"Many times when barriers block our way the wisest and most effective thing for us to do is to turn aside, stop our huffing and puffing, and experience the lifting power of God."

20

January 21   **Mark 5:19**
The Drunk Under The Bed

It happened in 1972. He was an alcoholic whose life was clear out of control. At the insistence of a friend, he accompanied him to church one evening to a meeting of an Alcoholics Anonymous group.

Through the AA program, his life was changed, and he made a vow that whenever and wherever he had an opportunity, he would tell others about Christ and how Christ transformed and revolutionized his life.

One evening at the AA meeting, there was a telephone call. A member of the group who had fallen off the wagon was calling for help. Would somebody go?

One of the group finally raised his hand and when no one else offered, the young man who had made the vow volunteered to go with him. They arrived to find the place a mess. They didn't have to knock; the door was standing open. A man dressed in a very expensive suit, lay sprawled across the bed on a mattress without sheets reeking with alcohol and filth.

There was nothing they could do. The man was too drunk to understand. He would have to sleep it off. But as they prepared to leave, the young man remembered his vow and said to his friend, "Go on down to the car. I will be with you in a few minutes."

Standing over the sleeping drunk, he told how Christ had changed his life and given him power over alcohol. Then he invited the man to turn his own life over to Christ. Leaving, he felt it was an utter waste of time.

The next week at AA, when they asked, "How did it go?" he was ready to say, "He was too drunk for us to do anything," when across the room a man stood and said, "It went real well." The young man looked at him, "Who are you?" The man replied, "I heard your witness. That's why I'm here. I want to go to church Sunday and become a Christian."

"Wait a minute!" the young man said, "I saw the drunk I was talking to on the bed, and you aren't that man. He was at least thirty years older than you." The man replied, "That's right. You were talking to the drunk on the bed. I was the drunk under the bed."

"You shall be my witnesses." They are the words of Christ to his followers. Whenever and wherever we answer Christ's call and speak, miracles follow. Think about it! Pray about it! Do it!

21

The Devil Is A Grizzly Bear

Down through the years and centuries, Satan has been pictured in many ways. In the book of Genesis, he is portrayed as a serpent. In his first letter, the Apostle Peter, depicted him as "a roaring lion, seeking someone to devour," but Loren Young contends that "the devil is a grizzly bear."

Grizzly bears grow to a length of nine feet and often weigh as much as a thousand pounds. Yet, in spite of their size, they are known for their swiftness. On a straight stretch of ground, they can outrun a horse. The grizzly is different from other bears. Other bears eat herbs and berries. Grizzlies are meat eaters.

A friend of Loren's was once chased by a grizzly bear. The roaring beast overtook him in no time and was ready for the fatal lunge when something happened. His friend tripped over the root of a tree extending across his path.

He pitched forward striking his head on a rock which knocked him unconscious and left his limp and seemingly lifeless body at the mercy of the ferocious bear.

For a brief moment, the snarling grizzly hovered over his victim. Then in one quick motion, he flipped him over with his sword-like claws. Then, while growling deeply, the ferocious beast turned and reluctantly walked away.

The fall, which seemed to be a tragic accident at the time, was the thing which miraculously saved his life. It is a known fact that a grizzly bear will not eat meat that he doesn't kill himself. The grizzly thought the man was dead, left him, and walked away.

Even so, the devil is a grizzly bear. Satan doesn't waste his time tempting Christians who are spiritually dead. He goes after Christians who are alive, those who are a threat to his cause.

When you find yourself overwhelmed with temptation, you may know that there is something in your life which is valuable to Christ and an asset to his kingdom.

In the midst of temptation and trial, stand firm in your faith, looking to him who is able to keep you from stumbling and to present you at last before his throne with exceeding great joy.

Mark 4: 39-40
Hurricanes Of The Heart

For twenty years, Marianne and I lived near Galveston Bay southeast of Houston, a part of Texas very prone to hurricane activity. People there still talk about the 1900 hurricane that killed some 6,000 persons in Galveston. The season lasts from June to November. We were never in one; we always traveled inland but friends who have weathered them say, "Never again!"

Hurricanes originate in the western Caribbean. A low pressure forms, and wind begins to whirl around it blowing in a counter-clockwise direction. Moving westward, it grows in size and strength and follows a curving path toward the North Pole.

Towering cloud masses produce torrential rains, and powerful winds build up waves fifty or more feet high. Landfall may be anywhere along the Gulf coast from Florida to Brownsville—it's anyone's guess as to when and where.

Wherever it rips into the coastal area, boats are carried inland and dumped on dry land. Trees and telephone poles are uprooted, literally twisted out of the ground. The 100 mile-an-hour winds demolish buildings, tear off roofs, shatter windows, and leave behind unbelievable wreckage, millions in damage, and hundreds of thousands of people homeless.

Just as real, destructive and devastating are hurricanes of the heart. They begin as low-pressure hassles of life—little things that disturb and annoy—we all have them. Then they build to a new level—hurts of life that cut into mind and heart—we all have these too.

Then comes the final burst of fury, landfall, bringing the heavy stuff of life—the unexpected crisis of health, employment, home and family—it happens to all of us, too. All that saves us is the eye of the storm. That is the center of the hurricane. It measures about 20 miles across and is an area of calm; the fury begins at the edge of the eye. Even so, at the center of the hurricanes of the heart, there is a place of refuge where God himself resides.

Are you in the midst of a hurricane today? No emergency aid can help. Move to the center of your hurricane where God is. There you will find a place of calm. Listen to his words: "Be strong and of good courage, I will not fail you or forsake you."

Three Rules For Living

I want to suggest three rules for living that just might change your life.

Hold on! One afternoon two little girls were playing beside a stream when one of them fell into the water. Terrified, the other little girl reached down and seized her by the hair. Holding her head above the water, she began shouting for help.

Her arm grew numb and ached from fatigue, but she kept saying to herself, "I've got to hold on; I've just got to hold on!" Finally, help arrived and the little girls were carried home. It was a lesson they never forgot—don't let go; hold on!

Don't run! A farm family was sitting before the fireplace one evening; the mother was rocking the baby to sleep. When she rose to lay the baby in his crib, she leaned too close to the fire. Suddenly, her hair was ablaze.

The father saw what was happening and shouted, don't run! don't run!" as he threw a coat over her head smothering the flame. Sinking in a chair, he exclaimed in relief, "I'm so glad you didn't run." Don't try to run away from life. You don't have to run away if you depend on God.

Take another step! Some years ago in South America, there was a plane crash. William Guilmet, the lone survivor, battered and bruised and with a shoulder crushed, made his way for miles down the treacherous mountain to the village below. When he was asked by the press how he ever made it, he thought for a moment, and replied, "I simply took a step, and then I took another." How important it is to take another step.

Christ showed us the way. During that last week, as the cross loomed before him, Greeks came with an invitation for him to come away with them, but Christ didn't run.

In Gethsemane he went a little farther. While the disciples slept, he took another step and found the strength to say, "Thy will, not mine, be done."

Finally, there in the darkness, suspended between heaven and earth, he cried out, "My God, my God, why?" But he didn't let go. He held on, and at last the words came, "Father, into thy hands I commend my spirit."

Making A Difficult Life Less Difficult

After searching all over the store, he finally found what he was looking for—a box of Duz detergent. Checking him out, the clerk asked, "Son, what are you going to do with a box of Duz?" He replied, "I am going to wash my little dog."

The clerk, thinking about it, said, "Well, I don't know; Duz is pretty strong stuff for washing a little dog. You will want to be real careful. You just might hurt your puppy."

About a week later, the little boy was back in the store. The clerk recognized him and asked, "How did you get along washing your little dog?" The youngster answered, "It didn't go so well. My little dog is dead." "Oh, I'm so sorry," the clerk sympathized. "I was afraid of that. Duz is pretty strong." The little boy shook his head, "Nah, it wasn't the Duz. I think it was the rinse cycle that did him in."

Do you ever feel like you have been through the rinse cycle? Let me suggest some ways to help make a difficult life less difficult.

1. Learn to view life from a larger background. I heard a man remark recently, "A hundred years from now, we won't know the difference." The long run, keep your eyes on that.

2. Enlarge your circle of friendships. Friends are one of life's greatest assets. Just remember: "To have a friend, you must be one."

3. Remember that life fluctuates. The old African American spiritual says, "Sometimes I'm up, sometimes I'm down." When you're down in the dumps, look on the bright side. You will be back on top of things before you know it.

4. Don't look back regretfully. John G. Whittier wrote, "Of all sad words of tongue or pen, the saddest are these—it might have been." Don't look back.

5. Don't look forward apprehensively. Someone has said, "All of my life I have worried about troubles—most of which never happened."

6. Have faith in God. In his farewell at Springfield, Abraham Lincoln said, "Without the assistance of the Divine Being, I cannot succeed. With that assistance, I cannot fail." Listen to God saying to you, "Fear not, for I am with you, be not dismayed, for I am your God."

January 26

Philippians 4:9

The Story Of Two Men

I want to tell you a couple of stories about two men. Butch O'Hare was from Chicago. He was a navy pilot during World War II. In the Pacific his squadron had taken off from its carrier on a mission. A few minutes away from the carrier, he realized his plane had not been serviced. His fuel was too low to make it to the target. Radioing his squadron leader, he turned back.

On his way, he spotted fifty Japanese bombers flying straight for the American fleet. Nobody knew they were coming. The American fleet would be devastated. All the planes had been sent off. Butch O'Hare remembered his father who had chosen God and honor first over all. He whispered a quick prayer and then dived toward the fifty Japanese bombers.

When his machine guns ran out of ammunition, he began suicide dives disabling as many planes as he could. He disorganized the entire Japanese flight, until the other American planes he had radioed turned and came back to help.

Later, he learned that he had shot down five Japanese bombers and heavily damaged any number of others. He was the first navy aviator ever to receive the Congressional Medal of Honor.

When you fly into Chicago today, you land at O'Hare Airport, named after the young man who that day saved thousands and thousands of American sailors.

Easy Eddie was also from Chicago. He was part of Al Capone's mob. The lawyer who kept the mob out of jail, he never got his hands dirty. Everybody thought well of Easy Eddie. Even after Al Capone went to jail, the mob kept going because Easy Eddie kept it going.

One night a friend gave him a Bible. Putting his feet up, he read. Before long he realized that he was going to hell and that everything he was living for was the work of Satan.

That night he gave his heart to Christ. The next morning he walked into the FBI headquarters and turned state's evidence. It brought down the mob. Within a year, Easy Eddie was gunned down in the streets.

What do these two stories have in common? Easy Eddie's last name was O'Hare. He was Butch O'Hare's father.

Stumbling On The Kingdom

In his book, *What's So Amazing About Grace?* Phillip Yancey tells about a vagrant who lived near Fulton's Fish Market on Manhattan's lower east side. The smell of fish was almost unbearable, and he hated the delivery trucks that noisily arrived before daylight.

But midtown got crowded, and the cops harassed him there. Down on the wharves, no one paid any attention to a grizzled man who kept strictly to himself and slept on a loading dock behind a Dumpster.

Early one morning when the truckers were slinging halibut and eel, yelling at each other in Italian, he roused from sleep and started poking through the Dumpsters behind the tourist restaurants. Such an early start insured good pickings: last night's uneaten garlic bread, French fries, untouched ripe and green olives, celery and carrot sticks, and a big wedge of cheesecake.

He ate all he could hold and stuffed the rest into a brown paper bag. Then he put all the cans and bottles he could find in separate plastic bags and stashed them in his rusty shopping cart.

The morning sun, pale through the harbor fog, was finally making it over the buildings by the wharf when he saw a mayonnaise-smeared ticket from last week's lottery half-buried in a pile of wilted lettuce. He almost ignored it but, out of force of habit, he picked it up and jammed it in his pocket. He remembered that in the old days he used to buy a ticket every week, but never more than one.

It was past noon when suddenly he remembered the ticket stub. He located a newspaper and held the ticket up to the box to compare the numbers. Three numbers match, the fourth, the fifth—all seven! This can't be true. Nothing like that ever happens to him. Bums don't win the New York Lottery.

But it was true. Later that day, he squinted into the bright lights as television crews presented to the city and nation the latest winner, the unshaven, unkempt, baggy-pants vagrant who would receive $ 243,000 per year for the next twenty years.

In the Gospel of Matthew, we are told that we stumble on the kingdom of God that way—the discovery of a lifetime. We fully expect there to be a catch somewhere. But there is no catch. No loophole to disqualify us from God's love and extravagant grace.

God's Appointments

Years ago, in the state of Illinois, there lived a little Swedish boy, who more than anything wanted to learn to be a photographer. One day, looking through a magazine, he came across an advertisement for a book. It was entitled, *How To Be A Photographer.* Entertaining all kinds of dreams, he saved his money and ordered it.

When it came in the mail, it wasn't what he had ordered at all. The book he received was *How To Be A Ventriloquist.* When he realized what had happened, he broke down and cried.

He said later of the incident, "I was heartbroken. I didn't even know what the word 'ventriloquist' meant. It didn't occur to me that I could send it back, and even if I could have, I didn't have money for the postage."

Then, one day he picked up the book out of curiosity, started reading it and became interested. He began to practice throwing his voice, and became quite proficient at it. He carved out a wooden dummy, modeled after a little Irish newsboy he knew, and named him "Charlie McCarthy."

So it was that Edgar Bergen began a wonderful career and a wonderful life. He is not only a great entertainer; he is an outstanding Christian as well.

It makes you stop and wonder. Did a worker in a mail order house make a mistake and send the wrong book, or did God have a hand in it? Of course, you could never prove it either way, but still you wonder.

I firmly believe that some tomorrow we will find out that God had far more to do with the things that happened to us along life's way than we ever dreamed.

All the way my Savior leads me;
What have I to ask beside?
Can I doubt his tender mercy,
Who through life has been my guide?

Heav'nly peace, divinest comfort,
Here by faith in Him to dwell!
For I know whate'er befall me,
Jesus doeth all things well.

Leading With The Heart

Sam Rayburn was from Texas. He served 49 consecutive years as a member of the United States House of Representatives and as Speaker of the House for 17 years, longer than any other man. He was one of the most powerful men in Washington and the world.

One morning his phone rang and his secretary said, "Mr. Rayburn, I'm sorry to wake you, but one of the congressmen has lost his daughter in a terrible car wreck, and I thought you would want to know."

Sam Rayburn thanked her and in twenty minutes was on the doorstep of that man he barely knew. The man opened the door, "Mr. Rayburn!" Sam Rayburn said, "Please, I just want to tell you how sorry I am."

The man said, "Well, won't you come in, Sir?" Sam Rayburn entered. He was in his shirtsleeves, hat in hand, hadn't shaved, hadn't done anything. He had gotten over as fast as he could.

He asked, "What can I do?" The man said, "Really nothing, Sir; your just being here means more than you can know." Sam Rayburn said, "Tell me what happened," and the man started talking about his daughter and about the accident. When the man got through, Sam Rayburn, with tears running down his face, gave him a big Texas bear hug and said, "Now, you just take care of the other people coming in and I will see you later."

Looking around, Sam Rayburn realized there was a large group of people there and that nobody had eaten. He went into the kitchen and made a fresh pot of coffee. Then he rolled up his sleeves and was soon frying bacon, scrambling eggs and making toast—feeding everybody in the house.

When the phone rang, the congressman came rushing back, "Mr. Rayburn, it's the White House. You have a breakfast meeting with the president." Sam Rayburn went to the phone, "Mr. President, I am sorry, but a more pressing engagement has come up. I'll phone you as soon as possible later today."

Years afterward when that family was asked how they were able to get through the dreadful loss of their daughter, they mentioned many things. But the one thing that stood out was when Sam Rayburn walked into their home and brought Jesus himself in the process.

God's Mysterious Ways

William Cowper's first writings were total failures. No one would have anything to do with his poetry. Out of money with no chance at a job, he hailed a horse-drawn cab. "Take me to the River Thames," he said. There he planned to jump off London Bridge and drown himself.

They had barely started when one of those fogs for which London used to be famous rolled in. You couldn't see your hand in front of your face. For one hour the horse-drawn cab wandered through the streets of London trying to find the Thames River, normally only a ten-minute ride away.

Finally, the driver stopped and said, "I'm sorry, I don't know where we are; we are completely lost. If I give the horse the reins I think he can find the way back to the barn. I'm sorry to let you off here for I don't know where I am leaving you, but I can't find the Thames. I can't find anything. The horse and I are going home. Goodnight."

Can you imagine William Cowper? He can't sell his poetry, a relationship won't work, he can't get a job and now he can't even kill himself! Upset and frustrated, he got out of the cab and stepped up on the curb. As he did, his knee brushed a hitching post he recognized as being in front of his flat. After an hour of traveling lost through the fog of London, not having a clue as to where they were, the taxi driver had deposited him, unknowingly, right back where he had started.

William Cowper was shaking like a leaf. He got down on his knees and said, "Oh, God, forgive me for what I was about to do. I had given up on my life, but you had not given up on me. You have given me a second chance. Here and now I give you my life, and I ask you to lead."

So it was that William Cowper moved from being Christian in principle to being Christian in fact and gave Christ full control. It was the turning point in his life. He went on to become a great poet, a great human being, and a great follower of Jesus Christ.

That night William Cowper wrote a poem telling what happened to him. Here is a part of that poem:

> God moves in a mysterious way
> His wonders to perform;
> He plants his footsteps in the sea,
> And rides upon the storm.

This Boomerang World

> There are loyal hearts, there are spirits brave,
> There are souls that are pure and true;
> Then give to the world the best that you have,
> And the best will come back to you.

So goes a poem by Madeline S. Bridges, and it's true. I vividly remember my first boomerang, that strange looking little curved piece of wood. My dad told me about them one morning at breakfast. I couldn't believe you could throw it, and it would sail out, curve around, and come back to you.

After breakfast, we went out to the workshop and dad made a boomerang. It took a little practice learning to throw it, but it worked. I would play hours on end, throwing it into the air and watching in amazement as it curved around and came back to fall at my feet.

We live in a world like that—a kind of "boomerang" world. Whatever we "throw" out, comes back to us. You know what I am talking about. If not, the next time you pass someone smile. Ninety-nine times out of a hundred they will smile back at you.

That should afford you enough courage to take the experiment a step further. Greet someone with a "hello" and you will receive a greeting in return. When you are kind, people tend to be kind to you. When you help others, you receive help in your hour of need. When you give love, love comes back, usually many times over.

It is especially true of our giving, though most of us are afraid to try it. If you need money, give some away. It was the Master Teacher who said, "Give and it will be given to you, good measure, pressed down, shaken together and running over."

It really is a "boomerang" world. What you throw out, circles around and comes back to you. You need to decide what you want coming back. If happiness, throw happiness. If joy, throw joy. If love, throw love and watch it miraculously come back. Yes, miraculously. You will find that you get back more than you give away.

> You and I live in a "boomerang" world,
> It's just what we are and do;
> Then give to the world the best that you have
> And the best will come back to you.

February 1   **Isaiah 11:6**
Mud Puddles And Dandelions

Each Sunday morning as the children come forward for the Children's Sermon, our organist plays "Jesus loves the little children, all the children of the world." He does you know. "Red and yellow, black and white, they are precious in his sight."

Once when the people were bringing children to Jesus that he might touch them, the disciples stopped them, but when Jesus saw it he was indignant, and said to them, "Let the children come to me, do not hinder them; for to such belongs the kingdom of God."

Jane Williams, who directs children and family ministries at St. Luke's Methodist Church in Houston, shares the following: "When I look at dandelions I see a bunch of weeds taking over my yard. My kids see flowers for Mom, and blowing white fluff you can wish on.

"When I look at a homeless person who smiles at me, I see a person who probably wants money, and I look away; my kids see someone smiling at them, and they smile back.

"When I hear music I love, I know I can't carry a tune so I just sit self-consciously and listen; my kids feel the beat and move to it. They sing out the words, and if they don't know the words they make up their own.

"When I feel wind on my face, I brace myself against it. I feel it messing up my hair and pulling me back when I walk. My kids, on the other hand, close their eyes, spread their arms and fly with the wind until they fall to the ground laughing.

"When I pray, I say 'Thee' and 'Thou' and 'give me' a lot. When my kids pray, they say, 'Hi, God, thank you for my toys and my friends. Please keep the bad dreams away, tonight. Sorry, I don't want to come to heaven yet; I would miss Mommy and Daddy too much.

"When I see a mud puddle I step around it; I see muddy shoes and dirty carpets. My kids sit in it; they see dams to build, rivers to cross, and worms to play with.

"I sometimes wonder—are we given kids to teach or to learn from?"

Oh, my friends enjoy the little things in life. Someday you may look back and realize that they were the big things. I wish for you big mud puddles and sunny yellow dandelions!

32

A Man Like That

Liz Curtis Higgs was one of the most famous disk jockeys in North America; also one of the wildest. She and Howard Stern, who was recently taken off the airways in a number of markets for indecency, were a tandem team on a radio show. Liz was getting so reckless that Howard Stern took her aside and said, "Liz, you are going way too far."

Liz had been hurt badly by things that had happened to her as a child. She had been hooking up with the wrong kind of men and burned by some she had become involved with. By the time she became a DJ, she was quite angry with men, and it came out in all she said and did.

But she had a Christian girl friend who cared about her and kept inviting her to church. Finally, Liz agreed. She said, "O. K., I will come once," and so it was that this hard-edged, angry, burned, bitter, hurt woman came to worship. Her girl friend was praying, "Jesus, you've got one shot. She's coming this Sunday."

Sad to say, that Sunday the preacher took as his text this verse from Ephesians: "Wives submit to your husbands!" Now it's in the Bible and so it's true, but if you were trying to win someone like Liz Curtis Higgs, would you have picked that text? I don't think so! (By the way, if you are interested, a ministerial friend of mine says the Greek word "submit" in that verse has the connotation of "put up with!").

When Liz heard the words of that verse, she became disturbed, angry, and upset. But she kept listening and heard the second half of the sentence that almost nobody ever quotes: "Husbands be willing to sacrifice yourselves for your wives like Jesus Christ did for the church, dying for her."

Liz was intrigued. Leaning over to her friend, she whispered, "If I could ever meet a man like that who would be willing to sacrifice for me, I would go with him anywhere." The friend leaned back to her and said, "Liz, the man has already done it. His name is Jesus, and he laid down his entire life for you on the cross that you might have life and have it abundantly."

Tears began to roll down her cheeks, and her defenses began to melt. Four months later, Liz Curtis Higgs accepted Christ and went on to become an outstanding Christian leader, speaker, and author of over twenty books. Her third novel, *Thorn In My Heart*, was on the Christian Historical Fiction best-seller list for seven months.

One Strike Left!

One of the great truths of this life is the fact that no matter how dark the night, there is a glimmer of light. When all seems lost, there is still hope. It is illustrated in a baseball game that Bill Smith tells about.

"Things hadn't gone well. The visiting team scored two runs in the first inning, and it stayed that way to the last half of the ninth. We were at bat for the final time.

"A runner got on with a single, and after a couple of outs the pitcher tired and walked the batter, but when we saw who was on deck, we gave up. He was the worst. He never hit safely.

"The fans began calling out to the manager about what he might do, could do, or ought to do, but no changes were made.

"The first ball came over the center of the plate. The umpire called out, 'Strike one!' The second pitch, and the umpire shouted, 'Strike two!' It was a hopeless situation. The score two to nothing, two men on base, two outs and now two strikes!

"We began gathering up our things. Then it happened. The pitcher delivered, we heard the crack of the bat and looked up to see the ball sail out over the pitcher, over second base, over the center fielder and out of the park—a home run! We had won three to two."

It happens over and over. What the manager should, could, or might do, what the batter had or had not done, the ninth inning, the two outs, the two strikes, everything about the game dwindled into insignificance when, with the one strike that was left, the batter hit a home run.

No matter how dark the day, how bad things look, you still have a chance. The bottom of the ninth, two outs, two strikes gone, but you still have one strike left.

Some two thousand years ago at Calvary, the Son of God died upon a cross. "There was darkness over all the earth." It looked like all was lost. His disciples had fled. They even "took his garments." It was, indeed, earth's darkest day, and yet, God took what was left and used it to redeem the world.

This is God's message for you and me: There is always something left— use it!

Where Do You Go To Church?

According to the book of Acts, Jesus' last words before his ascension were, "You shall be my witnesses." To be a witness simply means telling the good news that through Jesus Christ we have forgiveness of sins and new life.

It isn't always easy for us to be witnesses. What do you say? How do you get started? Jesus gave us a pattern. One day at high noon, he met a woman beside a well in Samaria and soon realized she needed what he could give. He did a very simple thing; he asked her for a drink of water. Soon they were deeply involved in dialogue. She forgot all about the water. Excited, she left her water jar and hurried back to the village to tell everyone about Jesus—"Come, see a man!"

Years ago, Steve, a ministerial friend of mine, taught me how to witness. A ministerial friend had taught him. He told about being in New York for a meeting when they caught a cab one morning to the convention center.

They had been in the cab but a very short while when Steve was surprised to hear his friend say to the driver, "Where do you go to church?" The cabbie answered, "To tell the truth, I don't. I used to go all the time, but I have gotten out of the habit. I know I should, but for some reason, I just don't."

In a few minutes they were at their destination. As they were getting out of the cab, the driver said to Steve's friend, "Thank you for asking about my church attendance. I appreciate your interest and concern."

Later Steve admitted his surprise at what had happened. His friend said, "This has been a habit of mine for a number of years. It's the easiest way I know to be the evangelist I believe God wants me to be."

When Steve returned home, he decided to try it. He even practiced in front of the bathroom mirror, "Where do you go to church?" It sounded strange at first but soon it was an integral part of his life. It is a part of my life, too. Soon or late, I ask everyone I meet, "Where do you go to church?"

There is an old hymn we sing which declares, "Jesus, paid it all; all to him I owe." It's true. We call it "Amazing Grace," and you are called to be a witness, to tell this good news. It isn't hard. In fact, it is **as easy as asking**, "Where do you go to church?"

February 5   **Proverbs 20:22**
Our Help In Time Of Need

In the book of Isaiah are to be found these words: "They who wait for the Lord shall renew their strength, they shall mount up with wings like eagles, they shall run and not be weary, they shall walk and not faint."

On May 25, 1787, a group of men charged with the responsibility of drawing up a constitution for the United States of America met in the State House in Philadelphia. Almost without exception they were men of outstanding ability. Among the group were such distinguished Americans as General George Washington, James Madison, Alexander Hamilton, and Benjamin Franklin.

Because of bad roads practically all of the delegates arrived late. Only 29 of the 55 representatives were present for the opening session. This created a problem since decisions reached were constantly being reversed by the arrival of new votes.

They faced the challenging task of constructing a government that would be democratic and at the same time protect the rights of the minorities. But the biggest decision was in regard to representatives. The large states wanted it based on population. The small states demanded that each state have the same number.

The air was charged with tension. Debate and discussion turned to bitter wrangling. The entire effort seemed doomed to failure and, if so, there would probably never be a union. Just when all seemed lost, a gray-haired man, the eighty-one-year-old delegate from Pennsylvania, Benjamin Franklin rose to speak.

"Gentlemen," he said, "I have lived a long time and am convinced that God governs in the affairs of men. If a sparrow cannot fall to the ground without his notice, is it probable that an empire can rise without his aid? I, therefore, move that prayers imploring the assistance of heaven be held every morning before we proceed with business."

The assembly adopted Benjamin Franklin's motion, compromises were worked out, and the document that ever since has been used as a model by seekers of freedom all over the world was born.

Let us give thanks to God for their faith and for all they gave to us as an inheritance. Following their example, let us consider and heed these words of counsel from the book of Proverbs: "Wait for the Lord, and he will help you."

February 6   **Hebrews 11:1**
                    What Do You Expect?

In the Gospel of Mark we are told about a father who brought his son to Jesus to be healed. He said to the Master, "If you can do anything, help us!" Jesus answered, "If I can? If you can! All things are possible to him who believes."

Lewis Timberlake tells about a group of 11th-grade boys in Harlem. All had police records, and 80 percent had experimented with drugs. Incorrigible, they had had eight different teachers in seven weeks time. In desperation, the principal called a 67-year-old lady out of retirement to take the class. To his surprise, she accepted. "Give me those boys," she said, "I can handle them."

That evening at home, she went over the list of names. She had been given the usual run of information—ages, addresses, etc. Suddenly, there it was! The thing all the others had missed, Billy Blackman 146, Jimmy Jones 139, Tommy Stone 143. These boys were brilliant, almost geniuses. Everybody had labeled them stupid, asking for mediocrity. She went to class next day dedicated to making them live up to their potential.

At the close of the school year, every boy in the class was promoted to the 12th grade. At the closing assembly, the president of the school board was there to present this remarkable teacher with a beautiful achievement plaque.

"I can't accept a plaque," she said, "It should go to the principal." The principal was taken back. "Why," he asked, "What did I do?" "Don't you remember?" she said, "The day you gave me the list of students you were thoughtful enough to give me their IQ numbers."

For a brief moment, the principal was dumbfounded. Then he remembered, broke into laughter and exclaimed, "Goodness! Those weren't IQ's. Those were their locker numbers!"

Do you happen to remember the little chorus, which contains these words? "Only believe, only believe, All things are possible, only believe."

It's true; so much of what we achieve depends upon what we anticipate. Our lives are going to be successful in direct proportion to what we expect. It was the Carpenter from Nazareth who put it in these words: "Your reward shall be equal to your faith."

With Only Three Strings

Itzhak Perlman is one of the world's greatest violinists, a marvelous musician, but it is painful watching him come onto the stage. You see, he had polio as a boy and has heavy braces on both feet. Customized crutches enabled him to shuffle onto the stage, and he kind of throws each leg forward as he walks.

Applause rises as he walks slowly across the stage and is sustained by an audience that evidently doesn't know what else to do. After what seems like an eternity, he reaches his platform. He gradually eases himself up and then just plops down.

Reaching down, he puts his crutches on either side. An assistant hands him his violin, and he begins to play. It is sheer magic. Passion and power flow through him; the beauty of the music enriched and enhanced by his commitment.

A few years back, Itzhak Perlman was playing a concert at Lincoln Center in New York City with the New York Philharmonic when all of a sudden one of his strings broke. It sounded like a gunshot.

He stopped and the conductor shut down the orchestra. Everyone thought somebody would bring another violin; maybe the second violinist will hand him his. Nothing!

Itzhak Perlman sat there in deep thought for a moment. Then, taking up his violin, he nodded to the conductor to start again. How in the world do you play a symphonic piece with just three strings? I have no earthly idea, but he did.

Those there that evening said you could almost see his mind at work as he modulated and transposed in order to make the whole thing work. At the conclusion, people sat in stunned silence. Then the place exploded with applause.

Itzhak Perlman, wiping perspiration from his brow, turned to the audience and said, "Sometimes it is the artist's task to find out how much music you can play with what you have left."

It was Justice Oliver Wendell Holmes who once said, "Most of us die with the music still in us." That is not God's will for you and me. Before each of us is the challenge: Go to work and see how much music you can play with what you have left.

Moving Past Your Past

Some years ago on New Year's Day, Georgia Tech was playing the University of California in the Rose Bowl. Just before the half, Tech fumbled and a University of California player, Roy Regals, picked up the ball.

Now Roy was a little directionally challenged and started running the wrong way. Being a man, of course, he didn't stop to ask directions! He kept going for 65 yards toward his own end zone. Finally, one of his teammates tackled him to prevent his scoring for the other team.

Pinned against the end zone, California punted on fourth down. Georgia Tech blocked the kick and recovered for a safety. It looked like it might cost California the game.

In the locker room, Roy Regals was beside himself. Wrapped in a towel, he sat crying like a baby. No one on the team knew quite what to say, so they said nothing.

An official came in and announced that the second half would begin in three minutes. The coach spoke, "Men, the same team that started the first half will be starting the second."

Everybody got up and started out—all except Roy Regals. He was still in his towel, sobbing. The coach walked over and said, "Son, I said the team that started the first half is starting the second half." Roy said, "I can't do it, Coach. I've ruined you. I've ruined the University of California, and I've ruined myself. I couldn't face the crowd in that stadium to save my life." The coach reached out, put his hand on Roy's shoulder, and said, "Roy, get up and go on back. The game is only half over."

Three centuries ago on the west side of the wilderness in Midian, a man by the name of Moses was keeping a flock of sheep. Happening to look up, he saw a bush burning that wasn't consumed, and out of the bush God called to Moses, instructing him to return to the land of Egypt and lead the Israelites out of bondage.

Moses was terrified. He could have said, "There is no way I would dare show my face in Egypt! I killed a man there," but he found the courage to move past his past. What about you? Isn't it time for you to let the past be the past? Listen and you will hear the Great Coach saying to you, "Get up and go back. The game is only half over!"

A Spirit Of Power

It took place in a small town in the Deep South. There had been oppression and injustice there for years. Something happened on Friday afternoon, an incident between the races, and Friday night they got together, all the African American men on one side of town and all the White American men on the other. Individually these two groups decided it was time to fix this problem.

Saturday morning they were down on Main Street. One group at one end, the other group at the other, walking toward each other carrying baseball bats, rocks, bricks, and some guns brought from home.

Just off Main Street, a little old lady was going through her Saturday morning ritual—frying sausage and singing hymns. She had grown up in that town. She knew everybody and everybody knew her. Hearing the ruckus, she stepped out on the porch. The men had stopped just a few feet apart and were yelling at each other. There was going to be a violent riot.

Without batting an eye, she dashed out between them and just stood there. They were ready to kill each other, but they didn't know what to do with her. She had known these men since they were boys. She knew their families. Still in her bathrobe, her hair up in curlers, holding her spatula like the cross of Jesus, she wasn't sure what she was going to do.

She had been frying sausage and singing hymns, so she decided to sing. Standing between these two groups ready to kill each other, she began singing, "Amazing grace, how sweet the sound." Then she started directing with her spatula, "That saved a wretch like me." And those men, not knowing what else to do, started singing, "I once was lost, but now am found; was blind but now I see."

The singing stopped and those men, looking at that woman, that hymn ringing in their ears, put the baseball bats on their shoulders, dropped the sticks and clubs, put the pistols back in their pockets and slowly walked back each to his own home. On Sunday morning, every church in that little town was packed.

In the years to come, there was violence throughout the South. But in that little town, they made all the changes they so desperately needed to make to take care of all of God's children. They made sure everybody got treated the same, right way, and they did it without a single future incident.

As A Man Thinks

As the father was finishing his breakfast, he spied his 16-month-old son with his car keys. The youngster would never give them up willingly. A battle was in the offing for sure. Searching for a solution, the father came up with an idea. Taking a ring of aluminum spoons from the kitchen cabinet, he held them down within the boy's reach and jingled them. His young son hesitated for a moment, then reached out for the new play thing. As he did, the car keys fell down into the playpen.

In psychology, this is called sublimation, replacing a given value with a higher value, and because so much depends on making the right choices in life it is one of the laws of life we need to remember.

Starr Daily tells how he discovered this law for himself while in prison. His guards, determined to break his rebel spirit, locked him in a room so small he could neither sit nor stand. In no time at all, the pain and discomfort were terrible.

However, Starr Daily found that he could think about only one thing at a time. By concentrating on pleasant ideas, he crowded out the thoughts of suffering. Pain no longer dominated him and, at last, the guards gave up and set him free.

We are all aware of the desirability of thinking positive thoughts, yet how often negative thoughts fill our minds. We can do something about this. Unwanted thoughts can be replaced, and replacement is a must. You don't get rid of a thought just by saying, "I'm not going to think about it." For example, you may say, "I don't want to think about money. I'm not going to think about money." And what are you doing? You are thinking about money.

Just as the little boy automatically dropped the keys when he took the spoons, so can we rid our minds of unwanted thoughts when we concentrate on desirable ones.

It is a little thing and quite simple, but it has the power to transform one's life. This is the key to Christian growth that Paul gave us when he wrote, "Whatever is true, whatever is honest, whatever is just, whatever is pure . . . think on these things."

It is as true as night following day—what we DO and what we eventually BECOME begins with the way we think.

Trust And Obey

The prophet Isaiah was reflecting on his high calling, mission and destiny. It seemed to him that, like the prophets of God before him, he had been a failure. With an aching heart he whispered to himself, "I have labored in vain. I have spent my strength for nothing."

Have you ever felt that way about your life in service to God? Before you pass judgment you need to read the fine print: "Trust in the Lord with all your heart, and do not rely on your own understanding. In all your ways acknowledge him and he will make your paths straight."

You do not know where you will eventually wind up. This is a journey without maps. As it was with Abraham of old, this is a matter of going, not knowing. No doubt there will be times in your life when you will find yourself in places of defeat and failure.

At such times the book of Numbers might help you. It describes how God guided the Israelites. There was a cloud over the tabernacle. At night it looked like fire. When the cloud moved—day or night—the Israelites set out. When the cloud stayed, the people stayed. God not only tells us where, he tells us when. As Christians, we move according to God's timing.

A ministerial friend of mine says you can't make a mistake before you are forty. Before forty, it's all experience. But let me tell you about a man who fell flat on his face long before he reached the age of forty. Here are some of the milestones of his life:

    He failed in business - Age 22
    He failed running for office - Age 23
    He failed in business again - Age 24
    His sweetheart died - Age 26
    He had a nervous breakdown - Age 27
    He was defeated in another election - Age 29
    He was defeated for congress - Age 34
    He was elected to congress - Age 37
    He was defeated in his bid for reelection - Age 39
    He was defeated for the Senate - Age 46
    He was defeated for Vice President - Age 47
    He was defeated again for the Senate - Age 49

Tomorrow marks the anniversary of this man's birth. On March 4, 1861, at the age of 51, he was sworn in as the 16th president of the United States. His name was Abraham Lincoln.

42

Lincoln Goes To Gettysburg

There it was. His most famous speech. He was mistaken when he said, "The world will little note, nor long remember what we say here." What he said there that day was more important than the battle itself.

Edward Everett, the orator of the day, spoke for two hours. The president waited patiently in the sweltering heat before he rose to deliver his address. Before the photographer could set up his camera for a photograph, the speech was over.

The Chicago Times reported, "The cheek of every American must tingle with shame as he reads the silly, flat, and dish-watery utterances of the man who has to be pointed out to intelligent foreigners as the President of the United States."

But there it was, engraved in marble on the south wall of the Lincoln Memorial, a great beacon of light and hope:

"Four score and seven years ago our fathers brought forth on this continent, a new nation, conceived in Liberty, and dedicated to the proposition that all men are created equal.

"Now we are engaged in a great civil war, testing whether that nation, or any nation so conceived and so dedicated, can long endure. We are met on a great battle-field of that war.

"We have come to dedicate a portion of that field, as a final resting place for those who here gave their lives that that nation might live. It is altogether fitting and proper that we should do this. But, in a larger sense, we can not dedicate—we can not consecrate—we can not hallow—this ground. The brave men, living and dead, who struggled here, have consecrated it, far above our poor power to add or detract. The world will little note, nor long remember what we say here, but it can never forget what they did here.

"It is for us the living, rather, to be dedicated here to the unfinished work which they who fought here have thus far so nobly advanced. It is rather for us to be here dedicated to the great task remaining before us -- that from these honored dead we take increased devotion to that cause for which they gave the last full measure of devotion -- that we here highly resolve that these dead shall not have died in vain -- that this nation, under God, shall have a new birth of freedom -- and that government of the people, by the people, for the people, shall not perish from the earth."

The Waiting Father

It was a tradition. All the family gatherings were held at their home because they had a large front room and everybody loved to dance. They would have a big potluck meal and then move back all the furniture and dance. Her father was a terrible dancer, but he loved to dance the Beer Barrel Polka with his daughter. When she was very small, she would put her feet on his and move around the room.

That day, years ago, she was having a rotten day. She was a teenager, a tough time in life for all of us. She didn't know what it was, but it seemed everything in her life was hurting. She was upset with the world, angry and afraid all at the same time.

Everybody was there and they were dancing the Beer Barrel Polka. Her father came up, touched her shoulder and said, "Come on, doll, and let's dance those blues away!" She slapped his hands away. There was a look of horror and hurt on his face as she said in front of everybody, "No! And don't you ever touch me again!"

She would never forget the look on her father's face. She had told him not to touch her, and he didn't. He loved her, was always there for her, but she had set a boundary, and he never crossed it.

Over the years the distance between them grew. He became like a stranger, a loving stranger, but still a stranger. Since she didn't talk to him, he didn't talk with her. She didn't know how to break the distance.

It was years later. Everybody was there. She hadn't been home for a long time. The meal was over and she was visiting, but all the time wondering how she could reconnect with her father.

They had put on the music and were dancing the Beer Barrel Polka. Her father looked much older now and was stooped. She knew what she had to do. Walking across the floor, she tapped him on the shoulder, and said, "Excuse me, sir; I believe this dance is mine." He turned with a smile on his face, as he said, "I've been waiting!"

Oh, my friend, you have a God who waits for you. Coming back, however you have separated, can seem very hard at times, but once you have done it, you will wonder why you waited so long. Take one step and he will run out to meet you and throw his arms around you. And as he does, all heaven will cheer for you with a joy resounding for all eternity!

Isaiah 65:24
Before They Call

The words are found in the book of Isaiah. "Before they call I will answer." Out of Africa comes the story. But let the medical missionary tell it in his own words:

"I worked so hard to help the young laboring mother, but in spite of our efforts she died leaving a tiny premature baby and a two-year-old daughter crying for her mother. In the West there would have been an incubator, but we had no incubator, and even if we had an incubator, we had no electricity to run it.

"Our hospital is on the equator, but the nights are bitterly cold. A student midwife brought a box and wrapping for the baby. Another, going to fill a hot water bottle, returned in distress. The only bottle we had burst as she filled it (Rubber doesn't last long in tropical climates). 'Ok,' I said, 'Put the baby close to the fire and keep it warm.'

"At noon, having prayers with the orphanage children, I told them about the tiny baby, the problem of keeping it warm, about the hot water bottle and the little sister crying because her mother had died.

"Ruth, a ten-year-old, prayed with 'Please, God, send a hot water bottle today; tomorrow will be too late.' I gasped inwardly as she added, 'And while you are at it, send a dolly for the little girl.' I was on the spot. Could I honestly say, 'Amen?' I know that God can do everything; the Bible says so; but there are limits, aren't there?

"That afternoon, unexpectedly, a twenty-two pound parcel arrived and some forty pairs of eyes watched as I lifted out knitted jerseys, bandages for the leprosy patients, a box of raisins, and on and on. Then I felt it, and pulled it out—a brand new hot water bottle!

"I heard Ruth cry out, 'If God sent the bottle, he must have sent the dolly, too!' Rummaging down, I pulled out a beautifully dressed doll. Ruth's eyes shone; she had never doubted! That parcel had been on the way for five months. Packed up by my former Sunday school class, whose leader had heard and obeyed God's prompting to send a hot water bottle, even to the equator; and, someone had put in a doll for an African child—five months before, in answer to the believing prayer of a ten-year-old to send it 'that very afternoon.'"

Listen again to God's promise. "Before they call I will answer."

Our Steadfast Friend

In the 1930's in a small town in East Texas, there were two teenagers, seventeen and sixteen, very much in love. They didn't mean for anything to happen, but things got out of control and did happen.

When the town doctor told her she was pregnant, she was not the only one who was told. The office nurse thought the whole town should know. The doctor called her parents so they could be prepared when she got home. Unfortunately, they were prepared in the wrong way.

Her father started beating her, calling her shameful names as her mother stood there crying. Finally, she got away and ran to her boy friend's home. He had heard, decided he wasn't ready to be a father and jumped a freight train out of town. All alone, she ran to Aunt Sally, an old lady in a shack on the edge of town.

Adults didn't approve of Aunt Sally. She chewed tobacco and could spit further than anyone. But the kids adored her. She fell into Aunt Sally's arms sobbing her heart out, and Aunt Sally just held her, stroking her hair.

When she ran out of tears, Aunt Sally said, "Honey, one of the hardest things in life is to discover that the people we love the most and need the most are just not there for us when we need them. But remember that you have one thing that no one can take from you and that's the love of Jesus. That's whatcha got! Whatcha gonna do?"

Looking at Aunt Sally, she said, "I love you." Then she walked out of that East Texas town and through the next three towns. She walked until she came to a place where they had never heard of her. A Methodist pastor and his wife took her in, got her into a home for unwed mothers, her baby was adopted by a loving Christian couple and she started walking again—all the way to Tennessee.

With the help of a scholarship, she worked her way through college, got a degree, went to medical school, graduated at the top of her class, and became one of the leading pediatricians in Tennessee, specializing in the care of unwanted babies.

When people ask how she has been able to achieve so much, all her years of education drop away and she says, "I always remember I don't need nothing save the love of Jesus. That's the one thing folks can't ever take away." What do YOU need?

Black Rock Bend

Black Rock Bend! It was a boy's paradise, or so it seemed to me as a boy of twelve. Maybe it was because it was declared off limits by all of our parents. That made it all the more exciting and a constant invitation to adventure.

It nestled in the curve of the T & P Railroad line. The huge boulder had been rolled aside when the tracks were laid and, over the years, had gathered soot from the passing locomotives, and had acquired the name.

You can understand why the spot was forbidden. A railroad track is a dangerous place for children to play. Also, after an hour at Black Rock Bend, mothers were never able to get clothes back to normal.

But time and again, we slipped away and went back. We continued to believe we could go and our mothers not know. But it never worked. The black evidence was all over us when we got home.

I outgrew the desire to play at Black Rock Bend years ago, but I find that there are other forbidden playgrounds to which I am urged to return. Especially in moments of restlessness when a coaxing voice whispers, "No one will ever know."

But to listen is to deceive ourselves. Even if we succeed in hiding it from others, it is never hidden from God—or from ourselves! The dark marks are upon us. Not outwardly, perhaps, at least not at first. But deep inside we see the telltale traces. Disobedience always leaves its mark.

The Master comes to all who have been caught up at their Black Rock Bend—whatever it may be. For those of us so caught up, Robert Freeman has written the following prayer:

> White Captain of my soul, lead on;
> I follow Thee, come dark or dawn.
> Only vouchsafe three things I crave:
> Where terror stalks, help me be brave!
>
> Where righteous ones can scare endure
> The siren call, help me be pure!
> Where vows grow dim, and men dare do
> What once they scorned, help me be true!

Romans 5: 8
Now Much Do You Love?

> "I love you a bushel and a peck,
> A bushel and a peck
> And a hug around the neck."

Those are the lyrics of a popular song of some years ago. How do you measure your love? In his little book, *Three Kinds of Love,* Masumi Toyotome lists three different kinds of love. As you read, it becomes a mirror in which you see yourself and just how much you love.

The first kind is "if" love. "I will love you, if—." It is a declaration of love to which is attached a requirement. Parents say to their children, "I will love you if you are good." Children say to their parents, "I will love you if you buy me the toy I want." Wives say to husbands or husbands to wives, "I will love you if you will change into the kind of person I want you to be." "If" love has strings attached.

The second kind is "because" love. "I love you because you are beautiful." "I love you because you arc rich." "I love you because you let me have my way." "Because" love is love that has to be earned. One who is loved "because" lives in constant fear—fear that another will come along who is more beautiful, richer, or more indulgent. As insecurity creeps in, we try to hide the unacceptable side of ourselves. After all, we are loved "because."

The third kind of love is "in spite of" love. You don't have to earn it; you don't have to deserve it. You are loved—that's all. Regardless of whatever, in spite of anything and everything, you are loved.

This is God's kind of love. "For God so loved the world that he gave his only Son, that whoever believes in him should not perish but have eternal life."

It is Christ's kind of love, too. He doesn't say to us, "I will love you if you are good, if you go to church." Nor does he say, "I love you because you are good, because you go to church." Christ simply says, "I love you. Period." No conditions, no requirements, no strings attached. We need only to accept his love.

How do we know we have accepted his love? He gives us the ability to love others. As God's word tells us, "We love, because he first loved us." No "ifs," no "becauses." In spite of what they are or are not, we love everybody. Period.

Like Hinds' Feet

In the second book of Samuel are to be found these sometimes puzzling words from a song written by King David: "He makes my feet like hinds' feet, and makes me tread secure upon my high places."

Glenn Clark, founder of "Camps Farthest Out," and one of the most widely published authors on the life of prayer in the 20th century, tells how this Bible verse became clear to him.

He was spending a few weeks one summer on a ranch in Wyoming. The horse assigned to him for his private use was the fastest on the range, and he felt very honored.

But he was to discover that while speed may be something to be reveled in on the plains, there is something far more important to be desired on the mountains.

Five of them were riding on the mountainside one day when they came to a dangerous, slippery, craggy place where a misstep would send them all to eternity. The men advised Glenn to take a longer, less dangerous, route to the mountaintop.

The foreman explained, "Your horse is a great horse, but he is not dependable on the hills. Our horses are true climbers. Their rear feet track exactly where their forefeet are planted. When they place a forefoot upon a safe ridge, their rear foot will follow unfailingly.

"Your horse," he continued, "Unfortunately, has spent several years in the city and has lost the gift. His rear feet miss the front tracks by several inches. On these trails, a miss of even an inch can mean sudden death."

All at once the meaning of David's words became clear. As the feet of the hinds are to the mountains, so is the mind to the heights of life. Jesus once said, "Have faith in God. Whatever you ask in prayer, believe that you have received it, and it will be yours." Our lips are able to speak the thoughts of our conscious mind, but only the heart can speak the thoughts of our subconscious.

When the mind and the heart are aligned, when they track together, nothing is impossible. "Let the words of my mouth and the meditations of my heart be acceptable in thy sight, O Lord, my rock and my redeemer."

Love Is Patient And Kind

It was 2:30 a.m. when he stopped his cab and checked the address. The building was dark. Most drivers would have honked, waited a minute and left. But he knew the passenger might need assistance, so he walked to the door and knocked.

"Just a minute," answered a frail, elderly voice. The door opened and a small woman in her 90's stood there. The apartment looked empty. In the corner, he noticed a cardboard box filled with lots of photos and glassware.

"Would you carry my bag?" she said. She took his arm and they walked out to the curb. When they were in the cab, she gave him an address and asked, "Could you drive through downtown?" "It's not the shortest way," he answered. "Oh, I don't mind," she said. "I'm in no hurry. I'm on my way to hospice." He glanced in the rear-view mirror. Her eyes were glistening. "I don't have any family left," she continued, "The doctor says I don't have very long."

He reached over and shut off the meter. For the next two hours, they drove. She showed him where she once worked, where she and her husband had lived as newlyweds, a warehouse that had once been a ballroom where they had gone dancing. It was toward dawn when she said, "I'm tired. Let's go now."

They drove in silence to the address she had given him. It was a small convalescent home. Two orderlies, solicitous and intent, were waiting. They must have been expecting her. He handed them her suitcase.

"How much do I owe you?" she asked, reaching into her purse. "Nothing," he said. "You have to make a living," she answered. "There are other passengers," he responded. He gave her a hug. She held onto him tightly as she said, "Thank you." As he got back into the cab, he heard a door shut. It was the sound of the closing of a life.

For the rest of the day he wondered. What if she had gotten a driver impatient to end his shift? What if he had honked only once and driven away? It gradually dawned on him that he had never done anything more important in all of his life.

As we journey along life's way, we are tempted to believe that our lives revolve around great moments—and sometimes they happen; but great moments are often beautifully wrapped up in small ones.

February 20   **Acts 4:19-20**
                        What Do You See?

The Big Dipper is a group of 7 bright stars, 3 of which form a handle, and 4 which form a bowl. It is a part of the constellation Ursa Major, or Great Bear. You have probably seen it many times in the north sky. The two outmost stars of the bowl point toward Polaris, the North Star.

All seven stars have names. The second star from the end is not a star but two stars. The ancients used it as a test of good eyesight. You might want to take the test the next time you are looking at the Big Dipper. Of our seven senses, sight is the most treasured. Above all else, we want to see, and we pity blindness. That is why a man in dark glasses posing as blind can easily relieve us of all our change. But there is another kind of sight that is even more important.

There is recorded in Luke an interesting story of Jesus asking a man, "Do you see this woman?" Jesus asked the question because though the man had looked at the woman, he had not really seen her at all.

What do you see when you look at people? In the rambunctious kid down the street, do you see a juvenile delinquent, winding up in prison, or do you see one who with understanding and guidance can become a teacher, a coach, a doctor, a leader of our nation and world?

In a refugee, do you see a threat to our way of life or a person capable of enriching America? Many such persons who have come to our shores and attained greatness number in the thousands.

The ability to see with our minds and hearts is a precious talent that is acquired. Who could see in George Washington, who quit school to become a surveyor, the making of the first president of our country? Who could see in Abraham Lincoln, the rail-splitter, the great leader who would save our nation in the time of its greatest crisis?

George Albert Coe, famous American author and philosopher, contemplating the vastness of outer space, once made this statement in one of his research papers: "Astronomically speaking, man is insignificant." However, the spiritual sight of Harry Elmer Barnes, the great American sociologist, was much keener. He wrote in a response to Coe's paper, "Astronomically speaking, man is the astronomer!"

Tonight, why don't you take a look at that next to the end star and test your physical eyesight? Then, tomorrow, take a good look at all the people around you and test your spiritual sight.

Makers Of Miracles

How would you like to be a maker of Miracles?

In her bedroom, the little girl of seven picked up a jelly jar, poured out the change, and counted—one dollar and eleven cents. Then putting the jar back she slipped out of the house and made her way to the Rexall Drug Store.

She waited as the pharmacist filled a prescription. When he finished, he smiled down at her, "And what can I do for you, little lady?" She cleared her throat. "I would like to buy a miracle, please."

"A miracle? You want to buy a miracle?" "Yes, Sir," she said, "It's for my little brother, Andrew. There is something real bad growing in his head and the doctor says unless he has surgery only a miracle can save him.

"Mommy and Daddy say there is no way they can afford to pay for the surgery so I want to buy a miracle. I have the money right here." The pharmacist stood helpless, not knowing quite what to say.

A well-dressed man standing in line had overheard their conversation and said, "Perhaps I can help. What kind of miracle does your brother need?" "I'm not sure," the little girl replied, "I just know he is really sick." "How much money do you have?" the stranger asked. "A dollar and eleven cents," she said, "But I could get more."

"Well, what a coincidence," said the man who happened to be a famous neurosurgeon from a hospital in Chicago, "That's exactly the price of a miracle for little brothers. Let's go see your little brother and talk with your parents."

The surgery was completed without charge, little brother was back home doing well, and Mom and Dad were happily telling all their friends and neighbors about the amazing chain of events.

It's a wonderful story about a little boy in need, parents who knew not where to turn, a little girl willing to give all she had, and an alert doctor in the right place at the right time willing to help.

Maybe it just happened. You know—a lot of coincidences that just fell into place. Maybe. But I think God had a hand in it, don't you? He is generally there for any of us if we would like to be a maker of miracles.

I Timothy 4: 14
Use It Or Lose It!

Recently my son Greg introduced me to the world of aqueducts. It's a fascinating field. There are many aqueducts in our nation today, and aqueduct engineering dates back as far as 312 B.C.

Aqueducts were one of the Romans greatest accomplishments. Nine of them were built in 97. They brought some 85 million gallons of water a day from mountain springs to the baths and fountains of Rome.

In 112 the Emperor Trajan constructed an elaborate aqueduct that was connected to a spring near the present day city of Segovia, Spain. It should have easily qualified as the eighth wonder of the world.

Around the turn of the century, a group of concerned citizens, realizing its historical value, decided to preserve it for posterity. Modern pipes were laid, and the ancient water flow was re-channeled. Then an unexpected thing happened, the aqueduct disintegrated.

Hot weather dried the mortar, the masonry blocks fell away, and one by one the sections crumbled to the ground. The Segovia aqueduct rendered useful service century after century and then was destroyed by a few years of standing idle!

The same thing can happen to the human body. Arms and legs thrive on exercise, but place an arm in a sling and fail to use it and it atrophies and becomes useless. A mind that is not engaged and challenged slips into senile behavior. The various parts of our bodies are wonderfully made and they can withstand a lot; but there is a law that says, "Use it or lose it."

This law also applies to our spiritual lives. In one of her poems, May Richstone tells how in need of spiritual power she returned to the church of her fathers, confessing as she did so that "the years away had been long." There she watched humble, devout folk lifting transfigured faces up, drawing strength from prayer. Her poem concludes:

> But no fund of faith was there for me,
> Only emptiness and doubt;
> For years I had put nothing in—
> What could I hope to draw out!

Whether it is our physical bodies, our talents, or our immortal souls, the law applies: "Use it or lose it." It's as simple as that.

The Guiding Light

One stormy winter evening, in days long gone and dead, my father said to me, "Son, I think we need to go out to the barn and check on the livestock."

Through our living room window, when lightning flashed, I could see the trees waving and things being buffeted by the wind. I said, "Dad, I don't want to go out there; it's dark and scary!"

My dad was already moving toward the kitchen. As he came up to me, he put his hand on my shoulder and said, "There's nothing to be afraid of. Come, I'll show you how it works."

We went into the kitchen, and he reached up on the shelf and took down the kerosene lantern and lighted it. I looked at the lantern and then out the window and said, "I still can't see. The light is here, but I still can't see out there. Dad, it's scary and I don't want to go!" But he took my hand, opened the door, and the gusting wind struck us full force as we walked out into the scary darkness.

I will never forget it. Step-by-step, as we moved forward, the darkness moved back. We couldn't see very far ahead, but we could see step-by-step. Step-by-step, we made our way to our destination. Step-by-step, we were safe. Step-by-step, we were never out of the light.

My friends, many of us are facing futures filled with lots of dark and dreadful shapes. We can't control the darkness around or before us, but if we want to, we can live in Jesus who is the Light of the World.

In that light, step-by-step, we will go forward with him; and as we go forward, the darkness will move back; and we will arrive safely at our destination.

> Lead, kindly light,
> Amidst the encircling gloom,
> Lead Thou me on;
> The night is dark,
> And I am far from home;
> Lead Thou, me on:
> Keep Thou my feet;
> I do not ask to see
> The distant scene—
> One step enough for me.

February 24   **II Corinthians 5:15**
A Bucket Of Shrimp

Every Friday morning the old man went out to the beach carrying a bucket loaded with shrimp. The seagulls would see him coming and swoop in surrounding him. One by one, he would feed them, a shrimp at a time, until all had been fed. Then, with the birds swarming around him, he would walk back to his house. His name: Eddie Rickenbacker.

In October 1942, newspapers across the nation carried the headlines that Eddie Rickenbacker's plane was lost out over the Pacific. He and his crew were carrying a very special message to General Douglas McArthur, a message that couldn't be trusted to radio.

Their B 17 was attacked and shot down by enemy planes. Their radio and navigation equipment was knocked out, and they were forced to ditch in the ocean. Eddie Rickenbacker and seven crewmembers survived the crash and took to life rafts. They were hundreds of miles from land under a blistering Pacific sun. Their life raft was surrounded by sharks, and nobody knew where they were.

Every day began and every night ended with prayer to God, as day by day they grew weaker and weaker. Finally, realizing they were at the point of death, they had a very special prayer service asking God to receive them to himself if that was his will. If not, "we could surely use a miracle!" Then, too weak to stay awake, they drifted off to sleep.

Eddie Rickenbacker was awakened by a seagull that had landed on his head. Asking God for strength, he reached up with both hands and seized it. Using it for bait, they fashioned a hook out of metal and caught fish that kept them alive until they were found and rescued.

Later, they wondered where that seagull came from. They were hundreds of miles from land and seagulls never go out that far. Only God knew, but Eddie Rickenbacker knew what he had been given, and so it was for the rest of his life. After he got out of the service, as a civilian and as a retiree, every Friday morning he would walk to the beach with a bucket full of shrimp and a heart full of thanks. There he fed the birds and gave thanks to God for the sacrificial visitor that had given them life.

My friends, you and I have received a Sacrificial Visitor who has given us life—for this world and for the next—to all who would claim it. May our hearts be open to receive the peace, the light, and the life angels of God would bring to us through that gift.

No Hands But Our Hands

On January 20, 1961, John F. Kennedy in his inaugural address challenged all America with these stirring words: "With a good conscience our only reward, with history the final judge of our deeds, let us go forth to lead the land we love, asking His blessing and His help, but knowing that here on earth God's work must truly be our own."

He stated anew a great truth. I don't know why—except that God has willed it so—but it seems that everything God wants done must be done by you and me. He has placed the task of building a better world in our hands.

In one of his books, Alexander Irvine tells about their neighbor, Eliza. She lost her only son and came over to their house to talk with Alexander's mother for consolation and help.

Anna Irvine listened as the neighbor poured out her heart through heartbreaking sobs. When at last Eliza's sobbing let up a bit, Anna Irvine spoke to her quietly and then they prayed.

Anna asked God to help and strengthen her friend. "Oh, God," she said, "Lay your hand upon her weary head and comfort her."

Suddenly Eliza spoke up excitedly, "Anna, He has done it! God has done it! A wonderful peace came over me. And you know, Anna, His hand is just like your hand."

"Eliza, the hand was mine," Anna told her, "But it was God's hand too. God takes a hand wherever he can find it and uses it. He takes the hand of a minister and lays it upon the head of a little child in benediction.

"He takes the hand of a doctor and uses it to heal the sick. And sometimes He takes the hand of an old woman like me and uses it to bring comfort to a neighbor like you."

That's it. Hands of common people—people like you and me. God takes them, wherever He can find them, touches them with His Spirit, and uses them in His work. Let us never forget—God has no hands but our hands.

President Kennedy was right. "Here on earth God's work must truly be our own."

The Hour Of Decision

Stepping off the plane at International Airport, we found the concourse so crowded we could hardly move; everyone jostling and pushing their way through the jam of people. Just then we heard the beep, beep, beep of the airport tram. Over the heads of the crowd, we could see the little blue light of the tram as it moved down the middle of the crowded concourse aisle.

We were thinking there was no way the tram could get through that crowd! But it kept coming, slowly, carefully, right down the middle of that group of people, splitting it like a hot knife going through butter.

Some people moved to the right; others moved to the left. Some were not sure which way to go. They just stood there. The tram kept coming slowly, inexorably. At the last moment, sensing that they could be run over, some jumped to the right and others jumped to the left. Everybody there, whether they wanted to or not, had to make a choice—no middle ground.

Like that tram, moving down that crowded concourse aisle, Jesus Christ for centuries has divided humanity into two groups—those who decided he was the Son of God and   those who decided he was not—no middle ground.

The decision is not about whether or not he lived. The Encyclopedia Britannica confirms that fact. Nor is it about his teachings. Even non-Christians agree he was a great teacher. Rather the divisiveness of Christ has to do with who we say that he is.

C. S. Lewis, in *Mere Christianity*, spells out these three possible options: 1. Jesus was the Son of God. 2. He was a liar. 3. He was a lunatic.

Psychologists, like William James, have lifted up Jesus as the model of emotional health. He was not crazy. At his trial his enemies could find no ground for accusing him of falsehood. He was not a liar. That leaves but one option; he was who he said he was, the Son of God and Savior of the world.

If Jesus was who he said he was, your eternal destiny and mine hangs upon the decision we make. When Jesus asked the twelve, "Who do you say that I am?" Peter answered, "You are the Christ, the son of the living God." Today, Christ asks the question of you and me, "Who do YOU say that I am?"

Putting Things In True Perspective

Dr. Charles Allen, longtime minister of First Methodist Church, Houston, used to tell the story about a letter a college freshman wrote to her parents. She hadn't written for months. She wrote: "Dear Mom and Dad, I'm sorry I have neglected writing, but I will bring you up to date. I'm getting along pretty well now. The skull fracture and concussion I got when I jumped out of the window of my dorm as it burned to the ground shortly after I arrived is almost healed. I only get these sick headaches once a day.

"Fortunately, an attendant at a gas station near the dorm witnessed the fire and my jump and called 911. He visited me in the hospital and since I had nowhere to live because of the fire, he was kind enough to invite me to share his apartment with him. He is a fine boy, and we have fallen deeply in love and plan to be married.

"We haven't set the exact date, but it will be before my pregnancy begins to show. Yes, Mom and Dad, I am pregnant. And I know how much you are looking forward to being grandparents. I know you will welcome the baby and give it the same love and devotion you gave me when I was a child.

"The reason for the delay in our marriage is that my boy friend has this silly minor infection that prevents us from passing our premarital blood test and I carelessly caught it from him. I know though that you will welcome us home when we move back to live with you.

"Now that I have brought you up to date, I want to tell you that there was no dormitory fire. I did not have a concussion or skull fracture. I am not in the hospital and I am not pregnant. I am not engaged, and I am not infected. There is no boy friend in my life. However, I am getting a D in history, and I wanted you to see those marks in their true perspective."

All of us, at times I think, need to see things in their true perspective. So often we get caught up in the moment and lose sight of the fact that life is for the long haul. One failure, whatever it may be, doesn't mean that your whole life is a failure. One success, no matter how wonderful it may seem, doesn't mean that you have it all made.

John Mark deserted Paul and Barnabus on their first missionary journey, deserted them and went back home. Later he wrote the Gospel of Mark. Benedict Arnold, a success in every way, seemed to have it made. He became the most famous traitor in United States history.

Taking Baby Steps

There is an old hymn that expresses this longing: "Be like Jesus, this my song, In the home and in the throng; Be like Jesus all day long, I would be like Jesus." God's good news is that we can be like the Master.

What About Bob? is a hilarious movie about a young man who is able to overcome his psychological problems using the program prescribed in his psychiatrist's new book, *Baby Steps.*

The secret is to set small reasonable goals one day at a time. Or, as Bob expresses it, "By taking one little step at a time, I can do anything."

Some 2000 years ago, God came into our world in the human form of the baby Jesus. God's divine miracle calls for human responsibility. He calls us to share all the words of this life, words of encouragement, faith, hope, and love with those around us.

He is the bright and morning star, but he calls us to be the light of the world. He is the true vine, but we are the branches. He is the bread of life, but he calls us to feed the hungry. He is the Good Shepherd, but he calls us to seek the lost.

He is the Alpha and Omega, the first and the last, the beginning and the end, but he calls us to live in the here and now, doing the little things we are able to do.

Some years ago Erma Bombeck, on New Year's Day made the following resolutions:

1   I'm going to clean this dump as soon as the kids grow up.
2   I'll go to no doctor whose office plants have died.
3   I'm going to follow my husband's suggestion to put a little excitement into my life by living within our budget.
4   I'm going to apply for a hardship scholarship to Weight Watchers.
5   I will never loan my car to anyone I have given birth to.
6   And finally, just like last year, I'm going to remember that my children need love the most when they deserve it least.

Do you want to be like Jesus? YOU CAN BE. Start with the baby steps. Commit to doing the small things of life well. If you will do that, God will help you grow and soon you will be doing all the things you were intended to do.

February 29 (Leap Year)   **Luke 12: 15**
                    What Are You Living For?

The greatest danger any of us face is that of giving our lives for something too small. Billy Rose pointed this out once in his column in the *New York Herald Tribune* with a very striking example.

In 1923, an important meeting was held at the Edgewater Beach Hotel in Chicago. Present at the meeting were: The president of the largest independent steel company, the president of the largest utility company, the greatest wheat speculator, the president of the New York Stock Exchange, a member of the president's cabinet, the greatest "bear" on Wall Street, the president of the Bank of International Settlements, and the head of the world's greatest monopoly.

Certainly all of these men were living for something. Together, they controlled more money than was in the U. S. Treasury. Look at them twenty-five years later.

The steel company president, Charles Schwab, lived on borrowed money the last years of his life and died broke.

The utility company president, Samuel Insull, died a fugitive from justice, penniless in a foreign land.

The wheat speculator, Arthur Cutten, died abroad, insolvent.

The president of the New York Stock Exchange, Richard Whitney, died after he had just been released from Sing Sing Penitentiary.

The cabinet member, Albert Fall, was pardoned from prison so he could die at home.

The greatest "bear" on Wall Street, Jesse Livermore, committed suicide.

The president of the Bank of International Settlements, Leon Fraser, committed suicide.

The head of the world's greatest monopoly, Ivar Krueger, committed suicide.

All of these men lived for something. The great tragedy of their lives was that they lived for things far, far too small.

What are you living for? For what are you giving your life?

Matthew 11:28
Burdens

An old African American spiritual declares, "I'm gonna lay down my burdens, down by the riverside." We all know what burdens are.

There are burdens of the body. Jack was stricken with arthritis at the age of six. Now at 36, his body is turning to stone. He has to speak through his teeth. He said to me once, "I can't remember a single day in all my life when I was not in pain."

There are burdens of the mind. Harry was in the war in the Pacific. Their Jeep hit a land mine, and his three buddies were blown to bits. He was thrown clear and after months in the hospital returned home. "They were all men with families," he said one day through tears, "I was single; why couldn't it have been me?"

There are burdens of the heart. Phillip and his young wife were returning from vacation when a drunk driver struck their car, and she was killed. I spent a lot of time with Phillip in the months that followed. He said one evening, "Preacher, I know I am not very good company. I'm still having a rough time. My heart is buried out there with her."

Burdens. How do we deal with them? Is there any word from the Lord? Yes, there is. The first word is in the book of Galatians: "Everyone shall bear his own burdens." Paul is saying to each of us, "Bear your burdens with courage."

Paul tells us to "Bear one another's burdens and so fulfill the law of Christ." Over the door of a wayside chapel are found these words: "Pause here, kneel down, and pray; then go refreshed to lift your brother's load and find your own made light."

The final word is from the Psalms. "Cast your burden on the Lord, and he will sustain you." Yesterday is gone; it can't be recalled. Tomorrow is in the future; nothing can be done until it arrives. Live today at its highest and best and leave the results to God.

Howard Thurman, watching Haley's comet as a boy, cried out to his mother, "What if the stars fall on us?" His mother answered, "Don't be afraid, whatever happens God will take care of us."

He never forgot her words. She didn't promise the stars wouldn't fall on them. She offered no magic. She simply said, "Whatever happens, God will take care of us."

No Failure Has To Be Final

In 1738, a ship sailed from America taking back to England a distraught and discouraged young man. He had come to the American colonies to serve as a missionary to the Indians and had failed so miserably he questioned his faith.

But he didn't quit. He wrote in his diary, "I went very unwillingly to a society in Aldersgate Street. About a quarter before nine, while the leader was describing the change which God works in the heart through faith in Christ, I felt my heart strangely warmed. I felt I did trust in Christ alone for salvation; and an assurance was given me that He had taken away **my** sins, even **mine**, and saved **me** from the law of sin and death." John Wesley later founded the Methodist Church.

In 1841, a young man went to the Black Hawk War as a captain. Ninety days later he was a buck private, his military career a failure, but he didn't quit. That man was Abraham Lincoln.

In 1854, up in Michigan, a pupil was sent home with a note saying he was "too addled to ever learn." Three months were all the formal education he ever received, but he didn't quit. Thomas Edison patented over 1,100 inventions and changed the lives of millions.

In 1883, a couple in England placed their son in military school because of what they considered to be his "limited intelligence." He failed the entrance examinations twice before passing them, but he didn't quit. That young man was Winston Churchill.

In 1902 the Atlantic Monthly sent a rejection slip to a 28-year-old writer ridiculing his "vigorous verse," but he didn't quit. He kept on writing. That poet was Robert Frost.

The little boy had been looking over the greeting cards for some time. Finally, a sales clerk asked, "Just what are you looking for—a birthday card? Get well card? Anniversary card for Mom and Dad?" "No, not exactly," he said. Then he ventured, "Do you have anything in the way of blank report cards?"

Greeting card companies don't make them—but God does. And we fill them out by the way we respond to the D's and F's of life. All of us, soon or late, experience failure. Lift up your eyes. No human failure—large or small—ever needs to be final. With the help of Christ, you can rise above it. It's up to you!

Unlikely Benefactors

God has no hands but our hands to do his work. I don't know why but I know it's true, whenever God wants something done he looks for men and women, boys and girls he can count on, who are willing to help.

Those he has chosen in the past are a very strange, unlikely group. Turn sometime to the eleventh chapter of Hebrews—the faith chapter of the Bible—and see if it isn't so.

"Noah was a drunk, Abraham and Sarah were too old, Isaac was a daydreamer, Jacob was a liar, Leah was ugly, Joseph was abused, Moses couldn't talk and Rahab was a prostitute.

"Gideon was afraid, Samson had long hair and was a womanizer, Ruth was a penniless widow, David had an affair and was a murderer, Solomon was a polygamist, Elijah was suicidal, Isaiah preached naked, Jeremiah was too young, Jonah ran away from God and Job went bankrupt.

"John the Baptist ate insects, Peter denied Christ, the disciples fell asleep while praying, Martha was a born worrier and Mary Magdalene was demon possessed.

"The Samaritan woman—divorced five times—was living with a man who wasn't her husband, Zacchaeus was too short, Paul was a dangerous religious fanatic, Timothy had an ulcer, and Lazarus was dead."

For us Christians, that's our family tree! They were very much similar to the folk who gathered for your last family reunion. They were people just like you and me.

But they all had one thing in common—they were willing to let God use them, let God command them; and God not only used them to bless others, he transformed their own lives beyond anything they could have imagined.

God is able to do unbelievable things with broken lives if we are willing to give him all the pieces.

There is work to be done and loads to lift, and God has no hands but our hands. Let him take control and direct your life. He will make you a blessing and take you places you have never dreamed of!

The Nail Scarred Hands

Once upon a time a certain man was taking a shortcut across a muddy field. All of a sudden he slipped and fell into a deep pit. He struggled and struggled, trying to get out. It was no use; the pit was far too deep.

In the midst of all his endeavors, a pop psychologist happened to pass by that way. He said to the poor man, "I feel your pain; I empathize with you." So saying, he went on his way.

A very short time later, a TV talk show host came by. He said to the man, "I very seriously doubt if you will ever get out, but if you should happen to make it, here is my card. Come by and I will try to give you a spot on my show."

A religious fanatic happened by. When he saw his predicament, he said, "You must be a very wicked person. You had to have committed a terrible sin to be in such a fix." Next, a lawyer tried to persuade him to file a lawsuit and an IRS agent came by to see if he had paid his taxes on the pit.

A neurotic stopped and said, "You think your pit is bad; you ought to see mine!" An optimist passing by said, "Things could be a lot worse." And a pessimist said, "Just wait, things will get a whole lot worse!"

Then another person came by. He reached down with both hands, took the man's hands and pulled him up out of the pit. In gratitude the man thanked the stranger and ran into town to tell everyone the good news as to what had happened.

"How did you get out?" the people asked. "A man came by and helped me out," he said. "Who was the man?" they wanted to know. "It was Jesus," he told them. "How do you know it was Jesus?" they asked. The man replied, "There were nail prints in his hands."

Once a father and his son went mountain climbing. There were some steep and treacherous places on the path and at one dangerous point someone called out to the little boy, "Do you have a good hold on your father, lad?" To which he replied, "No, but he has a good hold on me."

The prophet Isaiah has reminded us of a wonderful promise: "I am the Lord your God who holds your hand; fear not, I will help you." We can't always depend on our own grip, but we can count on his. No matter what happens, he will never, never let us go!

"Who Do YOU Say I Am?"

Sometime ago there was an article in the *Milwaukee Courier* about the event at Caesarea Philippi when Jesus asked his disciples, "Who do you say I am?" Paraphrasing the encounter, the writer said that if Jesus came today and asked some of our theologians the question, the answer would probably go something like this:

"You are the eschatological manifestation of the ground of being and of the faith community, the Kerugma manifested in conflict, the self-realization of personhood, and the motivational encounter for the process of humanizing and socializing mankind."

To which Jesus would reply, "I am what?" Then he would straightway instruct his disciples, "Tell no one who I am for I can't recall the formula or repeat it myself!"

Dan Jones is the minister of the First Christian Church in Garland, Texas. He was my associate in Temple just before my retirement in 1986. In one of his church newsletters, he told about something that took place in a ministerial study group to which he belonged.

It was the Lenten season, and they were talking about Jesus and one of the members wanted to know: "Who was He really?" One after another, they proceeded to tell him: "Jesus was the incarnation, the Son of Man, the Messiah, the Crucified One, the Suffering Servant, the Pre-existent Christ, incomprehensibly both human and divine."

"But who was Jesus, really?" the man persisted. They all fell silent. Theological explanations were not enough. Jesus was more to them than that, and Jesus demanded more. He wanted heartfelt confessions—"Who do YOU say I am?"

Then, one by one, they told their stories: "When my father died and my whole world fell apart, Jesus was my light in the darkness." "When my daughter was diagnosed with cancer and the doctor didn't think she would make it, Jesus was my strength." "When I had back surgery there were complications; Jesus was my courage and hope." "When my husband left me and the kids and we had only a few dollars to live on, Jesus was my very present help in trouble."

Who was Jesus, really? He asks each of us, "Who do you say I am?" So many people are wondering and asking. What is your answer? Perhaps if you just told them your story, they would come to know.

A Message From God

Find a penny; pick it up,
All day long you'll have good luck.

I was reminded of that couplet when I heard Arlene's story. She and her husband were invited to spend the weekend at the home of his employer and were quite excited about it. The boss was very wealthy, with a fine home and a car that cost more than their house.

They were delighted to have this rare glimpse into how the very wealthy live. The employer proved to be an extremely generous host. He was taking them to a very swank and exclusive restaurant, and they were walking toward the entrance. The boss suddenly stopped and looked down at the pavement. There on the ground, they saw a single darkened penny. Silently, the man reached down and retrieved it. He held it up smiling, and then put it in his pocket as if he had found a valuable diamond. "How absurd!" Arlene thought "What did this rich man need with a penny? Why would he take the time and go to the trouble of picking it up?"

For some reason she couldn't get the incident off of her mind. During dinner she casually mentioned that her daughter had a coin collection and asked if the penny he had found was of some value. Smiling, the man took out the penny and held it out for her to look at. She had seen thousands of pennies. What was the point?

"Look at it," he said. "Read what it says." She read the words aloud, "United States of America." "No, not that," he said. "Read further." "One cent?" she asked. "No, keep reading." "In God we trust?" "Yes." "And so?"

"Those words are on every United States coin," he said, "For years I never even noticed them! But there they are, right in front of me—God telling me to trust in him. I think it is God's way of starting a conversation. Lucky for me, God is patient and pennies are plentiful!"

A few days ago I went grocery shopping. As I stepped out of my car in the parking lot of the supermarket, I spotted a darkened penny on the pavement. I picked it up and read the inscription, "In God we trust."

All at once I realized that a problem I had been worrying about for days was one I could do nothing about. As I put the lucky penny in my pocket, I whispered, "Yes, Lord, I get the message. Thank you!"

March 7   **Romans 8: 18**
A Goodly Heritage

In the Sermon on the Mount Jesus asked, "Are grapes gathered from thorns, or figs from thistles?" He was saying we produce what we are. Alcoholics produce alcoholics, negative people beget negative people, parents with low self-esteem most likely will have children with low self-esteem.

Today, if you are battling to overcome some temptation, trying to break some kind of bad habit, if you look back you will generally find it somewhere in your family line. Back there somebody gave in to it, and now you are having to deal with it.

In 1874 a member of the New York Prison Board noticed that six people from the same family were serving in one of the New York prisons. Intrigued by it, he decided to do a study. He traced the family line back to a man by the name of Max Jukes who was born in 1720. Known as the town troublemaker, he was an alcoholic with no integrity, no character; a man who didn't believe in God.

Max Jukes married a woman who was just like him. They had six daughters and two sons. Approximately 1,200 of their descendants were closely looked at in the study that was made. Among them, 310 were homeless, 180 wrecked their lives through drug and alcohol abuse, 160 were prostitutes, 150 were criminals that spent time in prison, 7 of them for murder. They ended up costing the state over twenty million in today's dollars and not one of them made a contribution to society.

Around that same time, another study was made of the Jonathan Edwards family. Born in 1703, he was an ordained minister and president of Princeton University, a devoted family man who loved and served God. He and his wife Sarah had eleven children. Approximately 1400 of his descendants were studied. Among them 13 were college presidents, 65 were professors, 100 were attorneys, 32 were state judges, 85 were authors of classic books, 66 were physicians, and 80 held public office including three governors, three United States senators, and one vice president of the United States.

All of us, I think, want to hand down to our children and our children's children a noble worthwhile heritage; and as someone has aptly said, "We cannot give what we do not have any more than we can come back from where we have not been." What kind of legacy are you and I leaving to those we love and to our world?

It Is Well with My Soul!

The Katrina hurricane along with its aftermath touched the lives of all of us. In the face of such devastation and senseless tragedy, our natural tendency is to question, to doubt, to blame, and accuse God. Let me tell you about a man who showed us another way.

Horatio G. Spafford was a very successful attorney who lived in Chicago in the 1870's. He was a sincere Christian, quite active in the Presbyterian Church, and a loyal friend and supporter of Dwight L. Moody, who was doing great things.

In 1870, everything started going downhill for Mr. Spafford. His business interests took a nosedive. His only son contracted scarlet fever and died at the age of four. Then in 1871, came the great Chicago fire. His businesses burned down; everything he owned was destroyed.

With what little he had left, he decided to take his family to Europe. "Our family has got to get away. We will make it a holiday, and we will also help Mr. Moody, who is on a crusade over there."

However, he was unexpectedly detained in Chicago due to urgent business concerns. But he wouldn't let it stop the vacation. He put his wife and four daughters aboard the S.S. Ville du Harve as scheduled.

Midway through the trans-Atlantic voyage, there was a shipwreck and all four of his children perished. His wife said later, "I have to live with the memory of the waters ripping my baby out of my arms." She sent her husband the heartbreaking telegram: "Saved alone."

Horatio Spafford immediately sailed for England to join his grief-stricken wife. He asked the captain to let him know when they reached the place where the shipwreck had occurred. Arriving at the approximate location, the captain pointed to a spot on the waters and said, "There is where all your children died."

In deep sorrow, mingled with an unwavering faith in God's goodness, he returned to his cabin. There he wrote these words that later became the song:

> "When peace like a river attendeth my way,
> When sorrows like sea billows roll,
> Whatever my lot, Thou hast taught me to say,
> "It is well, it is well with my soul."

Philippians 2: 14-15
A Power For Good

Paul was writing to the Christians at Rome. These are his words: "None of us lives to himself, and none of us dies to himself." In other words, for good or bad, all of us are living lives that are affecting the lives of those about us.

Robert is a manager in a national corporation that brought all their managers together for a wilderness excursion. They were to do teambuilding during the day—canoeing, mountain climbing, etc. and at night around the campfire have meaningful conversation.

However, Robert got put in with nine who were completely secular. Around the campfire, all the nine did was drink, curse, and tell dirty jokes. At the end of the first evening Robert was saying to himself, "This is not how this is supposed to work. I'm not going to get much out of it professionally, plus my minister said I am supposed to be a light. How am I supposed to do that? If I start standing up, reading from the Bible, I don't think it's going to fly. They won't listen. What should I do?"

This is what happened. By the end of that ten-day experience, all those men were sitting around the campfire talking about God, sharing things about their marriages, their dreams, their hopes and fears, thinking about real issues, life issues. At the end of the camp, they covenanted to keep in touch as together they searched for answers.

What made such a difference? At the end of the first day, seeing the difficulty, Robert prayed, "Lord, what can I do to change things?" And God gave him the answer. After every meal, he took the dirtiest pot to clean. On the hikes he picked up the heaviest pack. Whatever had to be done, he took on the hardest part.

After three days, one of the men came to him and said, "I want to know what makes you tick!" As Robert answered, talking about the fact that he worshipped a God who loves servants, the conversation moved from the superficial to the soul-searching.

The Lesson? If you want to be a power for good, don't be a goldbrick. As you take your share of the work and more than your share, you will establish credibility as a hard worker people can depend on, listen to, and follow

Listen again to Paul as he writes to the Christians at Rome. "None of us lives to himself, and none of us dies to himself."

Life's Real Worth-Whiles

In one of his poems Lucien Lewis has pointed out one of our most glaring weaknesses—that of overlooking the real worth-whiles of life. He compares us to knights and kings of old, saying, "With eyes fixed on some distant star, we seek the Holy Grail afar. And the dross of ore in some far-off land, blinds us to jewels close at hand." I think he is right.

Years ago, when I was a minister in West Texas, Glynn Adsit was a fellow minister and a close and treasured friend. We attended church conferences and assemblies together, and our families were very close.

Glynn, who had served as a missionary in China, shared with me how they, along with other Christian missionaries, were chased out of China in 1940. For months he was under house arrest. He and his family didn't know what was going to happen.

Then, one day, soldiers of the People's Republic came with the surprising news that they were free to leave, to return to America. You can imagine their relief, their excitement and joy at such good news.

They were informed that they could take only two hundred pounds with them. That wasn't such good news. They had been living in the province for years and had acquired a lot of stuff.

Each member of the family had his favorite things. This vase, my books and papers, the typewriter that was brand new, keepsakes and toys—on and on; how would they ever be able to decide?

Glynn said, "We got out the scales and began to choose and weigh. We weighed and subtracted, weighed and subtracted until finally we had it right on the money, two hundred pounds."

The soldiers impatiently inquired, "Are you ready to go?" "Yes, we are all packed and ready." "Did you weigh everything?" "Yes, we have weighed everything—two hundred pounds exactly." Then came the question that shocked them. "Did you weigh the two children?" "The two children?" "Yes, the two children!"

Glynn said, "It was in that moment that we discovered what was of real value. Books, vases, typewriters—they all became trash, worthless junk!"

What are the real worth-whiles in YOUR life?

An Answer To Prayer

In his book *Your Other Vocation* Dr. Elton Trueblood voices the opinion that the great need of our day is for the church to realize and take seriously the notion that every member, man or woman, boy or girl, is a minister of Jesus Christ.

The Man Who Played God is the story of a great pianist who while on a concert tour was involved in a terrible accident that destroyed his hearing. His career was ended.

In despair, he moved to New York and secluded himself on the tenth floor of a fashionable Park Avenue apartment. He was persuaded by a friend to take up lip-reading and became very proficient at it, but his zest for living was gone. He was a very cynical young man.

One fall day, standing at his window, he noticed the autumn leaves in the park below and picked up his binoculars for a closer look. Gazing upon the red and gold panorama, his heart was stirred.

Just then his glasses picked up a young couple that seemed greatly disturbed. Gradually he gleaned the story. With their wedding a week away, the young man had learned that he had tuberculosis and must have medical treatment. It would cost a thousand dollars and they had nothing.

The man watched as they talked and then as they prayed together for God's help. He smiled derisively at their faith that God would help. Then he thought, "I have plenty of money; I will do it myself."

Calling his valet, he sent him with the money to the couple in the park below. Then he watched through his binoculars. "Where did it come from? Who sent it?" the couple wanted to know. "Let's just say that God sent it," the valet answered.

It was the beginning of a new life for the great pianist. Many hours were spent reading the lips of people in the park below, learning their needs and answering their prayers. A wonderful thing happened in his life. The cynicism, hardness and doubt gave way to faith, hope, and love.

Today, Christ is speaking to each of us: "As the Father has sent me, so send I you." Who knows how much depends upon the response we decide to make!

Adopted Daughter Of The King

When Mattie was eight months old, her father shot and killed her mother. Her maternal grandparents adopted and raised her. Of course, she had no memory of that terrible event, but it hounded her all the time she was growing up.

Mattie pushed it aside, refusing to deal with it. She finished high school and college and feeling a call to teach Bible in seminary was working on a degree in biblical studies when she heard God say, "Mattie, you need to come to terms with your father being a murderer now." With the help of a Christian counselor, Mattie at last was able to say, "Yes, that is a part of me and my story."

A lot of good things happen to students in seminary. Mattie met a young man named Chad. They fell in love and decided to get married. She was seated at a table addressing envelopes, sending out wedding invitations, when the Lord nudged her and said, "Mattie, why don't you send wedding invitations to some of the people on your father's side?"

She had had no contact with them from the moment that terrible thing had happened, but with fear and trembling she called, got addresses, sent some wedding invitations, and in the midst of her wedding celebration met an aunt and uncle and a paternal grandmother. The grandmother said to her, "Oh, Mattie, I have wondered about you so often. Over the years I have prayed night and day for you and now there you are!"

Six months later Mattie did another great thing. She went to the prison where her father is still incarcerated and sat across the table from the man who had brought so much pain and suffering into her life.

Today, Mattie is in Cambridge, England, working on a Ph. D. in Old Testament, becoming the person God wants her to be. Recently she said, "The thing by which I never wanted to be identified has become the hallmark of God's powerful grace. Indeed, I am the daughter of a murderer, but much more am I the ransomed, healed, restored, and forgiven adopted daughter of the King of Kings. Indeed, "by his stripes we are healed."

At the foot of the cross, Mattie found release, and there you and I are invited to come. Many of us brought our sins there, but we have never brought our hurts and suffering. Christ waits to touch our wounds with his wounds, take what was meant for evil, and work it for good.

Sadhu Sundar Singh

Sadhu Sundar Singh, a truly great Christian, lived in India and did his work among the people of Tibet. Once while traveling through the Himalayas, he and a companion were caught in a driving snowstorm. From time to time, the blizzard would let up for a moment, only to blow even harder afterward.

During such a brief lull, they found themselves on the edge of a steep slope and thirty feet below them lay the body of a traveler who had obviously fallen from the path. Sundar Singh began making preparations to clamber down and rescue him. His companion couldn't believe it, "We have all we can do to take care of ourselves. Ranget is a long way off. If we try to save this stranger, we will all perish."

"We can't go off and leave him here to die," Sundar Singh pleaded, "The two of us can save him; I know we can." His companion shook his head, "It is impossible. If you are foolish enough to risk your life, that is your business, but I am going to save myself." So saying, his companion walked away, and Sundar Singh was left alone.

Descending the mountainside, he dragged the fallen man back to the path. Then placing him on his shoulders, he began the long slow trek to the city of Ranget.

It was growing colder. Was it a mistake? Should he have tried to save only himself? The man on his shoulders was almost frozen to death. If Sundar Singh fell, they both would perish in the blizzard. Only if he kept moving could they hope to survive.

Hours passed. Sundar Singh noticed that he was no longer aware of the cold. In fact, the exertion of carrying the man on his shoulders was warming his body and causing him to perspire. On and on, he slowly made his way. As darkness was falling, he saw the gates of the city in the distance. He had made it; they were saved!

In that moment he noticed a prostrate form half-buried in the falling snow. It was his earlier companion who had gone on without him. Overcome by the cold, he had frozen to death. Suddenly Sundar Singh realized the truth—saving the stranger he had saved himself!

It was the Carpenter from Nazareth who said, "Whoever would save his life will lose it; and whoever loses his life for my sake and the gospel's will save it."

The Lamb Of God

Anyone who has ever attended a Billy Graham Crusade can never forget the hymn of invitation sung at the close of the message, "Just as I Am." The closing words of each of the six stanzas are "O Lamb of God, I come, I come." What do those words mean?

Some years ago a man up in eastern Washington State, driving a Volkswagen, was forced to slow down and stop for a flock of sheep crossing the road. As he sat there in his parked car waiting and watching, he found himself humming that hymn.

He came to the closing phrase "O Lamb of God, I come, I come." Suddenly he stopped. He had sung those words many times. They referred to Jesus he knew, but what did it mean? He didn't have a clue. He asked himself again, "What do those words mean?"

On an impulse he leaped from his car and stopped the shepherd, "Tell me," he said, "As a shepherd, what does 'Lamb of God' mean to you?" The shepherd to whom he spoke was taken back in surprise, but looking at this stranger he realized that he was sincere.

"Yes, I know exactly what 'Lamb of God' means. Each year at lambing time there are lambs and ewes that don't make it. Inevitably, on one side of the field is a ewe whose lamb had died. She's full of milk, but she won't nourish any lamb that she doesn't recognize as her own.

"Inevitably, on the other side of the field is a lamb whose mother has died. That lamb is going to starve to death because no other ewe will accept and feed it.

"So the shepherd takes the dead lamb, slits its throat and pours its blood over the body of the living lamb. Then the living lamb is taken to its new mother. The ewe recognizes the blood and accepts, welcomes and nurses the living lamb.

"Through the gift of the blood of the lamb that has died, the living lamb is recognized and is accepted and nourished and saved. That is the 'Lamb of God.'"

My friends, you and I are in the fold of God today because we have been washed in the blood of the lamb. Looking at us through rose- colored glasses—blood-tinted glasses—God sees us as his beloved children. It is called redemption.

Do You Have A Trouble Tree?

Most of us, I think, can deal with today. It is when we add the regrets of yesterday and the anxieties of tomorrow to today that we lose heart and are tempted to give up, to not even try.

Recently I read about a man who decided to restore an old farmhouse. He knew it was too big an undertaking for one person, so he looked up a plumber and contracted his help.

From day one everything seemed to go wrong for the plumber. On his way driving out to the farm a flat tire caused him to lose an hour of work. Next his electric drill quit on him, causing further delays. Then at quitting time as he prepared to call it a day and go home, his ancient one-ton truck refused to start. He tried and tried but it wouldn't go.

Out of sympathy the man who hired him volunteered to drive him home. They drove all the way in stony silence, but when they arrived the plumber invited him in to meet his family. Let him tell you in his own words what happened:

"As we walked toward the front door, the plumber paused briefly at a small tree. Reaching out he touched the tips of the branches with both hands. Then, when he opened the front door he underwent an amazing transformation. His tanned face was wreathed in smiles as he hugged his two small children and gave his wife a kiss. I was deeply touched by the love and affection displayed. Afterwards, as he walked me to the car, we passed by the tree and my curiosity got the better of me. I asked about what I had seen him do earlier.

"'Oh, that!' he said, rather embarrassed, 'That's my trouble tree. I know I can't help having troubles on the job, but those troubles don't belong in the house with my wife and the children. So I just hang them on the tree when I come home and ask God to take care of them. Then in the morning I pick them up again. You know, it's a funny thing, when I come out in the morning to pick them up, there aren't nearly as many of them as I remember hanging up the night before.'"

Sir William Osler, the famed Canadian physician, used to give this advice to his students: "Live compartmentalized lives. Live neither in the past nor in the future, but let each day's work absorb your entire energies." In the Sermon on the Mount Jesus counseled us, "Let the day's own trouble be sufficient for the day." Maybe a trouble tree is something you would like to try.

Caring Is What Matters Most

A few days ago I received a note from a friend of mine. It contained the philosophy of Charles Schultz, the creator of the *Peanuts* comic strip, who is just about my favorite theologian as well as my favorite cartoonist.

Over the years I have clipped and saved any number of these strips. Charlie Brown and his gang have taught me a lot. Some of them have been too subtle for me, but all of them have given me something to think about.

In the article I received, you are asked to do the following:

1. Name the five wealthiest people in the world.
2. Name the last five Heisman Trophy winners.
3. Name five winners of the Miss America Pageant.
4. Name five Pulitzer Prize winners.
5. Name the last five winners of the World Series.

How did you do? Frankly, I racked my brain and couldn't name a single one of the people.

The point being made is that none of us remember the headlines of yesterday. These are no second-rate achievers. They are the best in their fields. But the applause dies. Awards tarnish. Achievements are forgotten. Accolades and certificates are buried with their owners.

Then you are asked to do the following:

1. List a few teachers who aided your journey through school.
2. Name three friends who helped you through difficult times.
3. Name five people who taught you something worthwhile.
4. Name a few people who have made you feel appreciated.
5. Think of five people you enjoy spending time with.

How did you do with these? I had no trouble naming three or four people for each of these. I'll bet you didn't either.

These two quizzes teach a valuable lesson: The people who make a difference in our lives are not the ones with the most credentials, the most money, or the most awards. They are the ones who care about us.

Who do YOU care about?

Who Are You And Where Are You Going?

Cornelius Vanderbilt in his day was one of the richest men on earth. One day, walking through the woods, he got lost. He was worried over a lot of problems in his life—problems in his business, problems in his family life, problems in his heart.

Not paying any attention to where he was going, he got lost. Totally disoriented, he didn't know what to do. Finally, in desperation he just sat down, leaned back against a tree, closed his eyes and went to sleep.

He woke up a little while later as he felt someone's foot kicking his. Opening his eyes, he looked up. Before him was a big bear of a man with a big black beard looking down at him. The man said, "Who are you and where are you going?"

Later, remembering that moment, Cornelius Vanderbilt said, "As soon as I figured out he wasn't a bear those two questions were like ice water in my mind, clearing my thoughts in a most amazing way. They had not been so cleared for weeks and months.

"Right then and there I offered that forest ranger a job. He wouldn't take it, but I offered him a job doing nothing but moving back to the city and waking me up every morning with those same two questions: "Who are you?" and "Where are you going?"

There is a lesson there for all of us I think. If we will take time every day to pray and read God's word, we will be asking those same two questions, "Who am I?" and "Where am I going?" and if Jesus Christ is the Lord and leader of our lives, the answer is "We belong to him, not to the world, and we are going to heaven, not because we are so good but because God is so faithful."

As we remember that every day, it can help us keep our perspective in this world, remembering that all we experience through the day is not final, but just the preparation for the life that God is going to give us.

So fortified, we can look through the lie of worldly wealth, see it for what it is and begin using it to build up real wealth where it counts.

In the Gospel of Luke there is a parable that Jesus told which speaks to this issue. It is about a certain steward who looked into the future, saw what was in store for him and decided to use his money to change that future and make it secure. May God grant us that kind of wisdom.

The Shimabuku Experiment

On the Island of Okinawa there is a village called Shimabuku. There was a trouble spot there toward the end of World War II, and American forces were closing in upon it.

As they approached the village, they fully expected to be fired on. Imagine their surprise when, instead, they were met by two very dignified men. Coming forward, they greeted the GI's. Bowing low, the two men welcomed the soldiers as "fellow Christians." Unable to believe what they were seeing and hearing, the soldiers called their chaplain.

Together they entered the village. They had not seen anything like it. The other villages of the island had been filthy and dirty. The natives lived in poverty and ignorance. Shimabuku was neat and clean, and the inhabitants were prosperous and happy.

Later that day, they learned the story. Thirty years before, an American missionary on his way to Japan had stopped there. His stay was very brief, but during that short time, he won Shosei Kina and his brother Mojon to Christ.

The missionary gave them a Bible and went on his way. During all the intervening years, they saw no other Christians, yet from reading the Bible they had deepened their commitment to Christ and had found a pattern for the life of their village.

Mojon was the teacher of the village, and through his influence everyone in Shimabuku became a Christian.

Shosei Kina became the headman and governed his people by the principles he found in the Bible.

As a result, the life of the village was changed. Each one counted as much as another, and they all called one another brother.

One of the soldiers, a battle-scarred sergeant, shook his head in amazement, "How could a village like this come about merely because of a Bible and two men who wanted to live like Jesus?"

Then with great conviction, he said to the men gathered about him, "They tell us we are in this war to make the world different. You know, it just might be that we are using the wrong kind of weapons!"

March 19   **Psalms 62:6**

He Cares For His Children

In his book, *The Road Less Traveled*, Dr. M. Scott Peck contends that to experience the grace of God is a common phenomenon. John Newton referred to it in his hymn as "amazing."

Years ago in downtown Denver, two young men, Scott and a friend, saw something tiny and insignificant that changed the world. No one else even seemed to notice. The sun was shining bright and there wasn't a hint of a breeze as they made their way to an outdoor eatery.

They finished lunch and started back to work. Coming out of the restaurant, they noticed a mother and her young daughter coming out of a card shop toward the street. The mother was holding her daughter by the hand while reading a greeting card. She was so engrossed in the card she didn't notice a shuttle bus moving rapidly toward them. She and her daughter were one step away from disaster.

Scott tried to yell a warning, but no sound came from his lips. At that very moment a breeze blew the card out of the mother's hand over her shoulder. She spun and grabbed at it, nearly knocking down her little daughter. By the time she picked up the card and turned back around the shuttle bus had whizzed by. Neither mother nor daughter ever knew what almost happened.

Scott and his friend still recall and talk about the incident. Two things continue to perplex them: First, where did that one spurt of wind come from to blow the card out of the mother's hand? It was perfectly still and calm that day.

Secondly, if Scott had been able to get his words out, the mother might have looked up at them and continued to walk into the bus. The wind caused her to turn back to the card in the one direction that saved her life and that of her daughter.

The passing bus didn't create the wind. On the contrary, the wind came from the opposite direction. Scott said later, "I have no doubt it was a breath from God protecting them both, but the awesomeness of this miracle is that neither mother nor daughter ever knew."

How often do you suppose it happens that God acts in our lives when the difference between life and death is a very little thing and without our even being aware of it? It is what theologians refer to as the grace of God. Amazing Grace!

79

Patience And Kindness

In the 13th chapter of Corinthians the Apostle Paul tells us that the greatest thing in the world is love, and he defines love as patience plus kindness. Dr. Steve Wende, minister of the First Methodist Church in Houston, tells how he discovered the incredible power of such love as a college student back in the sixties when there were lots of marches and demonstrations going on all across our nation.

He had a dormitory friend who took part in every one that came along. Most of the time his friend didn't know what they were about, didn't care what they were about. He was a bright young man but a very angry young man, a rebel lashing out at all the world. He didn't trust anyone over thirty and not very many under thirty.

One day there was a demonstration in the student union that turned into a riot. The police were called out, tear gas was fired, windows were broken out. The rioting students were herded out through the broken glass, loaded into vans and taken off to jail. Dr. Wende's friend was a part of the riot, probably helped start it. The next Sunday morning he was in church. Why? Not from being in jail—he had been in jail many times before. It was something far, far more.

This is how his friend explained it: "As I stumbled out of the student union, half blinded, losing the sandals I was wearing, a policeman with hands like a vice grabbed my arm. I fully expected a night stick to the head; instead I heard him say as gently as he could, 'Careful son, don't cut your feet on the glass.'

"He guided me to one of the vans. When it was full he got in to ride with us. Stunned that he would be so kind, I began a conversation. At the jail, as we were booked and put in cells, the conversation continued—outside the bars, through the bars and eventually inside the bars. Throughout the long evening we talked. Finally, at two o'clock in the morning he said to me, 'Son, at some point don't you think you ought to ask God to help you? Help you with your decisions; help you with your dreams; help you with your life?' Sunday morning I was in church."

Dr. Wende says, "Two months later he walked down the aisle to the altar and accepted Christ as his Lord and Savior, and to think that for months I had invited him to church using every theological and philosophical argument I could muster to no avail. What turned the tide? A policeman with patience plus kindness. You will never find anything greater!"

Why Didn't You Tell Me?

Martin Niemöller was a German pastor who opposed Adolf Hitler. In 1937, preaching to an overflowing church, he declared, "No more are we ready to keep silent when God commands us to speak . . . we must obey God rather than man." His sermon angered Hitler and three days later Martin Niemöller was arrested and imprisoned. He was finally freed by American GI's in 1945, two days before he was to be executed.

After the war Martin Niemöller and others of the anti-Hitler movement gathered in a conference to ask the question, "Was there anything more that we could have done that we didn't do to stop Hitler?" After two days they decided, "No, we did all we possibly could have done."

That night, at three o'clock in the morning, Niemöller was awakened by a voice. It was a voice coming from a great distance across a great chasm, filled with an agony. The voice was crying, "Martin, why didn't you tell me? Martin, why didn't you tell me?"

He tried to figure out what the dream meant. Then, he remembered, the voice he had heard was the voice of Adolf Hitler. He had heard it in a conversation he had had with Hitler just after Hitler came to power.

Before all the negative things had begun, Hitler had asked Martin Niemöller as one of the key leaders of the nation to come and meet with him. They talked about many important things. For an hour they talked one on one.

Then, to his horror, Martin Niemöller realized that never once in that entire hour had he asked Adolf Hitler, "Where do you stand with the Lord, Jesus Christ?" Now he understood that voice filled with all the anguish of hell, "Martin, why didn't you tell me?" He spent the rest of that night on his knees in repentance and confession.

The next morning at the third and final conference, he stood up before the others and said, "My friends, we have been kidding ourselves. I, at least, did not do all that I could!"

If Jesus Christ is your Lord and Savior, you are going to heaven. My question is, "What voices will you hear as you spend eternity?"

You cannot save others; that's between them and Jesus. But you can so share the good news that you do not have to spend eternity listening to them crying out, "Why! Why didn't you tell me?"

Radiance Amidst Our Tears

Between Lake Erie and Lake Ontario, with the United States on one side and Canada on the other, flow the waters of the Niagara River. This waterway is one of the most beautiful natural regions of the world. Compared with other rivers the Niagara is not a great river. It is only 34 miles long, less than a mile wide and seldom over 21 feet deep. The thing that makes the Niagara River significant is Niagara Falls.

The river flows along quietly at five miles an hour. Then, six miles below Buffalo there is a break in the even flow of the stream. At this point the Niagara plunges 158 feet. Each minute 500,000 tons of water pours into the steep-walled gorge below. As the raging waters are shattered on the rocks, there is cast up into the sunlight the beautiful rainbow of the Niagara. A breathtaking sight!

Life is like that, isn't it? You and I go along for years in a contented flow of experience. We have good health, our friends, our work, our faith. Then suddenly there's an unexpected tragedy—a breakdown in health, the loss of a loved one or maybe even a moral disaster.

We are forced to take a blind leap into an overwhelming abyss of suffering. Completely shattered on the cruel rocks of reality, our emotions are churned into a seething foam of bewilderment.

But out of our distress there is cast up into the sunlight of God's love a rainbow of penitence, hope and trust, a radiance in the midst of our tears so that what could have been our destruction is transformed into a glorious Christian testimony.

Herein lies the unique greatness of our Christian faith. As George Matheson expresses it in his hymn:

O Love, that will not let me go,
I rest my weary soul in Thee;
I give Thee back the life I owe,
That in Thine ocean depth its flow
May richer, fuller be.

O Joy, that seekest me through pain,
I cannot close my heart to Thee;
I trace the rainbow through the rain,
And feel the promise is not vain,
That morn shall tearless be.

Making Pancakes

Saturday morning six-year-old Brandon decided to make breakfast for his mother and dad. What could he fix that they liked? Pancakes were the answer. They would be a sure hit.

He pulled a chair up to the counter, opened the flour canister; and as he scooped flour with his hands into a big bowl, watched in dismay as a shower of white fell to the floor.

Getting milk from the refrigerator he filled the large measuring cup. It overflowed onto the counter and down onto the floor where his kitten began lapping it up. As he poured a cup of sugar he noticed that his pajamas were covered with flour and sugar and soaked with milk. What should he do next? He wasn't sure. Put it in the oven? Then it dawned on him that he didn't know how the oven worked! This was to be something special for mom and dad and things weren't going well at all.

The kitten was up on the counter licking from the mix. Reaching to push it away, he knocked the carton of eggs to the floor. He clambered down to clean up the monumental mess, slipped on the broken eggs and down he went in the white and yellow sticky stuff in his brand new blue pajamas.

He looked up. Towering above him, he saw his dad looking down. Tears welled up in his eyes. Wanting to do something good, he had made a terrible mess. A scolding was coming for sure, maybe a spanking.

But his dad reached down, picked up his tear-stained son and hugged him tight, ignoring his own pajamas being smeared with the white and yellow gooey mess. Snuggling there on his dad's shoulder, somehow Brandon knew that everything was going to be all right.

That is how God deals with us. We try to do something good and it turns into a mess. We fail at our job, our marriage goes on the rocks, our children go astray, we alienate a friend, and on and on and on—.

We stand there in tears not knowing what else to do. That's when God picks us up, loves and forgives us, even though some of our mess gets all over him.

Keep that ever in mind. And whatever you do, don't ever stop making pancakes!

True Contentment

Recently my son Randy received from a friend a little story with a big message. He shared it with me and now I would like to share it with you. As with so many worthwhile writings, the author is unknown.

One day a boat docked in a tiny Mexican village and the American tourist complimented the Mexican fisherman on the quality of his fish and asked how long it took him to catch them. "Not very long," answered the Mexican. "Then, why didn't you stay out longer and catch more?" asked the American.

The Mexican explained that his small catch was sufficient to meet his needs and those of his family. "But what do you do with the rest of your time?" the American asked. "I sleep late, fish a little, play with my children, and take a siesta with my wife. In the evenings, I go into the village to see my friends, play the guitar, and sing a few songs. I have a full life."

The American interrupted, "I have an MBA from Harvard, and I can help you! You should start by fishing longer every day. You can then sell the extra fish you catch. With the extra revenue, you can buy a bigger boat." "And after that?" asked the Mexican. "With the extra money the larger boat will bring, you can buy a second one and a third one and so on until you have an entire fleet of trawlers. Instead of selling your fish to a middleman, you can negotiate directly with the processing plants and maybe even open your own plant. You can then leave this little village and move to Mexico City, Los Angeles, or even New York City! From there you can direct your huge new enterprise."

"How long would that take?" asked the Mexican. "Twenty, perhaps twenty-five years," replied the American. "And after that?" "Afterwards? Well my friend, that's when it gets really interesting," answered the American, laughing. "When your business gets really big, you can start selling stocks and make millions!"

"Millions? Really? And after that?" asked the Mexican. "After that you'll be able to retire, live in a tiny village near the coast, sleep late, play with your children, catch a few fish, take a siesta with your wife and spend your evenings doing what you like and enjoying your friends."

In his Sermon on the Mount, Jesus counseled us: "Be on guard against greed. Even when a man has more than enough, his wealth does not give him life."

Enjoy Your Age

Texas poet Karle Wilson Baker in her poem "Growing Old" has written: "Let me grow lovely growing old; so many fine things do." It is, indeed, "a consummation devoutly to be wished." The Psalmist prayed, "So teach us to number our days that we may get a heart of wisdom." If we could do that, we would be content and happy at any and every age.

Luke Bolen was a close friend of mine. He was minister of Lakewood Christian Church in Waco when I was minister in Temple. He used to say, "I have enjoyed every year of my life. I was happy as a teenager in high school. I was happy during my college days. I was happy becoming engaged and getting married. I have been happy watching my children grow up. It has been fun facing the challenges of middle age and solving some of them, and I look forward to being sixty, seventy, eighty, ninety and who knows, maybe one hundred and ten."

You know, I feel the same way. I think the trick is to stop wishing you were older or younger and love the age where you are.

From the pen of some unknown author comes this prayer:

"Lord, you know better than I myself that I am growing older and will someday be old. Keep me from the fatal habit of thinking that I must say something on every subject and on every occasion.

"Release me from craving to straighten out everybody's affairs. Make me thoughtful, but not moody, helpful but not bossy. With my vast store of wisdom, it seems a pity not to use it all. But you know, Lord, that I want a few friends in the end.

"Keep my mind free from the recital of endless details; give me wings to get the point; seal my lips on my aches and pains; they are increasing, and love of rehearsing them is becoming sweeter as the years go by.

"I dare not ask for improved memory, for a growing humility, and a lessening cocksureness when my memory seems to clash with the memories of others. Teach me the glorious lesson that occasionally I may be mistaken.

"Keep me reasonably sweet, for a sour old person is one of the crowning works of the devil. Give me the ability to see good things in unexpected places and talents in unexpected people, and give me, Lord, the grace to tell them so. Amen."

As For The Master

In the Gospel of Matthew Jesus paints a haunting picture of the final judgment. The Son of man is seated on his throne and all the nations are gathered before him. He separates them, placing some on his right and some on his left.

He says to those on his right, "Come into the kingdom prepared for you. I was hungry and naked and you fed and clothed me." In amazement they ask, "When did we see you hungry and feed you or naked and clothed you?", and he says to them, "When you did it to these my brothers you did it to me."

Then he says to those on his left, "Away with you! I was hungry and naked and you didn't feed or clothe me." In a dilemma they ask, "When did we ever see you hungry and not feed you or naked and not clothe you?", and he says, "When you refused to feed and clothe the least of these my brothers, you were refusing to feed and clothe me."

A number of years ago Jerry Brown was the governor of California. After he left the governor's office he went to work for Mother Teresa in Calcutta. Each morning at 6 a.m. Mother Teresa would give the workers a pep talk. She would say, "Always remember that Jesus is found in the distressing guise of the poorest of the poor. What you do to them you do to him." Then she would hold up her hand and touching each finger would say, "What you do to him; what you do with him; what you do for him."

Jerry Brown was assigned to wait on the dying men in the mission. Most of these men had tuberculosis and coughed constantly, spitting up phlegm in a cup that had been given them. He also had to clean up patients after they soiled themselves.

The soiled blankets, covered with phlegm and excrement, had to be washed constantly. It was Jerry Brown's job to dip these blankets in and out of a big brick vat full of disinfectant.

Recalling it he said, "It was impossible to pull out the blankets without splashing water in my face. Keeping my lips as tightly closed as possible I kept reminding myself of Mother Teresa's words: "What you do to him; what you do with him; what you do for him." Those words must also be your motivation and mine as we go to touch our community and the world for Jesus Christ.

　　　　　　　　　　　　　　　　Proverbs 25: 21-22
If Your Enemy Is Hungry

The Book of Romans says, "If your enemy is hungry, feed him." The John Champ family ran across that verse one day during their family Bible reading. The two boys, seven and ten at the time, were especially puzzled.

"Why would anyone want to feed an enemy?" they wondered. The only reason they could come up with for heeding it was "because the Bible says so." Soon they were going to learn why from experience.

John, Jr. came home from school complaining about a classmate seated behind him. "Bob keeps hitting me in the back when the teacher isn't looking. Some day on the playground, I'm going to smack him good!"

As a family, they talked about the problem of Bob—obviously a spoiled brat—and what could be done. During the conversation, the younger brother spoke up, "Maybe John ought to feed his enemy."

The words startled them. An enemy isn't in the fifth grade. An enemy was someone far off. But the Bible says, "Feed your enemy," so that is what they would do. "What does Bob like to eat? Might as well make it something he likes." John, Jr. thought for a moment. "Jelly beans!" he shouted, "Bob just loves jelly beans!"

And so jelly beans were purchased, and a strategy worked out. The next time Bob jabbed him in the back, John, Jr. turned and put the jelly beans on his enemy's desk.

When the yellow school bus let them off that afternoon, the boys made a dash for the front door. John, Jr. called out ahead, "Mom, it worked! It really worked!"

All the while, his younger brother was reminding them that he was the one who thought up the whole thing. "What did Bob do?" the mother asked. "He didn't do or say anything, but he didn't hit me again the rest of the day."

In the days and weeks that followed, Bob and John, Jr. became the best of friends. And all because of a bag of jelly beans!

Years later, John, Jr. and his brother became missionaries. In foreign lands, when they encountered "enemies" of the faith, they knew what to do—they invited them into their homes to eat!

Encourage One Another

One day a teacher asked her students to list the names of the other students in the room, leaving a space between the names. Then she said, "Think of the nicest thing you can say about each one of your classmates and write it down." The class completed their assignment, and as they left the room handed in the papers.

That weekend the teacher wrote the name of each student on a separate sheet of paper and listed what everyone else had said about that individual. On Monday she gave each student his or her list. Soon the entire class was smiling in astonishment, surprise and disbelief.

Those papers were not mentioned in class again. She never knew if they discussed them with each other or with anyone else, but the project had accomplished its purpose. The students were happy with themselves and with one another. At the end of the semester they moved on.

Last year one of the students, Mark, was killed in Iraq and the teacher attended his funeral. The church was filled with his friends. One by one they passed by his casket. She was the last. As she stood there, one of the soldiers acting as a pallbearer asked, "Were you Mark's math teacher?" When she nodded, "Yes," he said, "Mark talked about you a lot."

After the service Mark's mother and father came up to his teacher. "We want to show you this," his father said, holding out a wallet. "They found this on Mark when he was killed. Opening it he took out a sheet of notebook paper that had been taped, folded and refolded. She knew without looking that it was the list of good things Mark's classmates had said about him. "Thank you for doing that," his mother said, "As you can see, Mark treasured it."

All of Mark's classmates were looking on. One said, "I still have mine; it's in the top drawer of my desk." Another said, "Mine is in my diary." Still another took from her handbag a worn and frazzled list, "I carry mine with me at all times. I think we all saved our lists." A poet has said:

> "If you have a word of cheer
> That may light the pathway drear,
> Of a fellow pilgrim here,
> Tell him so."

Mark 8: 34
Two Crosses

Almost every institution and organization has its distinctive symbol. Nations have flags, schools have mascots, Masons have the square and compass, Rotarians have the wheel, Kiwanis has the K.

The Christian faith has its symbol—the cross. Crosses are to be seen everywhere—on church spires, on altars, in chapels, on the lapels of men, on necklaces worn by women. The cross symbolizes Christianity. And what a meaningful symbol! It was on the cross that the life of Christ reached its highest meaning for mankind. It was there that he suffered and died to redeem us from sin. It is in the cross that we find the entire gospel of God revealed. Paul was right when he said of the cross, "It is the power of God." That is why he exclaimed, "God forbid that I should glory save in the cross of Christ."

Little wonder that our best loved hymns are centered in the Cross. Our hearts thrill to the words, "On a hill far away stood an old rugged cross, the emblem of suffering and shame." We express a deep conviction when we sing, "When I survey the wondrous cross on which the Prince of Glory died, My richest gains I count but lost, and pour contempt on all my pride." They are great songs on a great theme.

However, there is more to this matter of the cross than at first meets the eye. The truth is Christianity has not just one, but two crosses. This other cross is the one Christ referred to when he said, "If anyone would come after me, let him deny himself and take up his cross daily and follow me."

God's Word has a great deal to say about love and sacrifice exemplified in an act of God on the cross of Christ. It also has a great deal to say about the love and sacrifice which must be exemplified in the life of one who would take up his cross and follow Jesus.

Today, as we think on Calvary, let us remember another hymn of the church:

> Must Jesus bear the cross alone,
> And all the world go free?
> No, there's a cross for everyone,
> And there's a cross for me.

Let us never forget that the Christian faith has two crosses—His cross and mine!

God's Transforming Power

In the city of Copenhagen, Denmark in the Protestant Cathedral there stands what is perhaps the most impressive statue of Christ ever sculptured. The great Bartel Thorvaldsen sculpted it. It portrayed Christ with strong arms extended, raised high in gesturing command. The head was thrown back in triumph. It was indeed "the powerful, majestic Christ."

Contented and pleased, he left the clay to set. Days later he returned to stare at his statue in disbelief. There had been a rainstorm and the dampness had altered it. The arms were no longer outstretched; now they fell low. Moisture had caused the triumphant head to bend. Gone was the triumphant Christ. In its place stood a defeated Christ.

For weeks Thorvaldsen went around as in a daze. He had no heart for anything. Then one day at the insistence of a friend he went with him to see if somehow the damage could be repaired.

Entering the studio they looked upon the statue in awe. Bathed in shimmering light, the lowered arms no longer depicted defeat. Now they reached out in compassion, waiting to enfold the brokenhearted. The head no longer drooped; instead, it bowed low as though to say, "I understand all you are going through."

Thorvaldsen was convinced that what had happened was an act of God, that a far greater power had transformed his ruined statue. It was no longer the majestic Christ, nor was it a defeated Christ. Now it was the Christ of the Gospels. God does indeed work like that. Haven't you found it to be so? Over and over he takes the ruined things of your life and mine and somehow manages to change them into things of beauty and worth.

More and more we come to know with the Apostle Paul "that in everything God works for good with those who love him, who are called according to his purpose."

> Have you got any rivers
> They say are uncrossable?
> Have you got any mountains
> You can't tunnel through?
> God specializes
> In the wholly impossible
> Doing what nobody else can do.

John 17: 11
Our Hope For A United Church

Dr. Graham Frank was the minister of the Central Christian Church in Dallas. In 1938, he represented the Christian Church (Disciples of Christ) at the Congregational Church at Utrecht, Holland, for the drafting of the constitution of the World Council of Churches.

On the way, he and his wife spent three never-to-be-forgotten weeks in Palestine, going up and down that country with an Arab guide and an interpreter, both of whom were Christians.

It was Easter Sunday, and the guide asked them to come to their home. He had told them that his wife was in deep sorrow for her brother who had been killed. They hesitated about going, but the guide insisted.

When they arrived, they found that she had invited fifteen neighbors and friends. They visited as long as they thought they should and then Dr. Frank said to their host, "Mr. Nijem, I would be glad to have prayer with your wife and family and your friends if Mrs. Nijem would like it."

As the guide conveyed the message to his wife, a wistful smile came upon her face. Dr. Frank said later, "In that moment, I learned that a broken heart is a broken heart anywhere in the world." He indicated that they would have prayer, and then it dawned on him that outside of the interpreter and Mrs. Frank no one could understand what he was saying!

In the only language he could speak, he lifted his voice and prayed for the heartbroken woman and all who were gathered there. Only two people knew what he was saying, but they all understood what he was doing. There came over the little group, a feeling of the Presence of One who came to another group, in the same setting years before, when the doors being shut, He came and stood in their midst.

Across the barriers of language and race, color and culture, their hearts were made one before God. Later, speaking of the experience, Dr. Frank said, "I should not want to belong to a church which would deny membership to those people, and I want to go to no heaven where they would be excluded."

Christ prayed for the unity of his church—"that they all may be one." The answer to his prayer lies mainly in our coming to know and love one another. When we surrender our stubborn wills and realize we are one, God will give us the unity we seek.

Mark 16: 15
What Are Your Marching Orders?

Over the years and centuries, our world has attached a great deal of importance and validity to a person's last words. They are usually about things closest to the heart—things that mean the most to the individual. According to the gospel records, we discover that the parting words of Jesus had to do with the worldwide mission of his church. "Go," he said, "And make disciples of all nations."

Jack Sutton, in his book, *Witness Beyond Barriers*, wrote: "When people tell me they don't believe in missions, I get sick inside because I know they don't believe in Jesus Christ. Jesus was the very first missionary. He left his home in heaven and came farther to be a missionary to you and me than anyone else has ever gone."

The world mission of the Christian faith came from the lips of Jesus. In his recorded words "all nations" and "world" occur over and over again. Dr. George Buttrick was of the opinion that the world venture is a part of our human nature. He pointed out that our language is the bequest of many lands, music knows no one nationality, and the foods we eat come from the ends of the earth.

Christian missions place upon the followers of Christ a strong moral obligation. In 1953, Dr. Jonas Salk discovered a vaccine for the prevention of poliomyelitis. Soon a wide scale program of inoculation was underway. But what if Dr. Salk had refused to share his discovery with the millions who faced crippling and possibly death without it? As Christians, we stand under just such a judgment. God's Word tells us that we are bound in the bundle of life. No one lives to himself or dies to himself. When we seek to live little self-centered lives, we destroy ourselves. As Edna St. Vincent Millay has so graphically pointed out:

> The world stands out on either side
> No wider than the heart is wide;
> Above the world is stretched the sky,
> No higher than the soul is high.
> The heart can push the sea and land
> Farther away on either hand;
> The soul can split the sky in two,
> And let the face of God shine through.
> But East and West will pinch the heart
> That cannot keep them pushed apart;
> And he whose soul is flat—the sky
> Will cave in on him by and by.

Be A Star In Someone's Sky!

The book of Daniel tells us about the reward of those who influence others for good. We are told that they will shine like the stars. Have you ever thought about the possibility that you might be like a star to someone? You can be. In this dark world you can be a shining light in someone's life.

Today in the Bridge Street Cemetery on a windswept hill in Northampton, Massachusetts is the grave of David Brainard. A graduate of Yale University, David Brainard gave up the opportunity for a successful and profitable career to serve as a missionary to the North American Indians who had been so wronged by his people. He became known among fur trappers as the man who trapped Indians with love.

It was a very grueling existence filled with hardships and suffering. In five years David Brainard was dead from overwork and exposure. He never so much as dreamed of being a star in anyone's sky, but Jonathan Edwards was so touched that he wrote the story of his work and heroic sacrifice.

One day a young man by the name of Henry Martyn chanced to read the story and it changed his life. At the age of twenty-five he went as a missionary to India. There he burned out his life in service, dying at the age of thirty-one.

A star in somebody's sky? It never occurred to Henry Martyn. But a young man by the name of David Livingstone read about his life and was so moved that he went to darkest Africa to take the message of Jesus Christ to "a thousand villages where no missionary had ever been."

It is an unending line of splendor. For 200 years this one solitary life of David Brainard's has touched the lives of thousands. Today that star still shines challenging all of heroic heart and will.

It was the Man from Nazareth who said, "Let your light so shine on the lives of others." Our light comes from Him who is the Light of the World. With his help, you, too, can be a star in somebody's sky.

> "Lives of great men all remind us
> We can make our lives sublime,
> And, departing, leave behind us
> Footprints on the sands of time."

April 3   **Romans 14:8**
Abiding Friendship

It is God's promise found in the book of Hebrews. "He has said, 'I will never fail you nor forsake you.' Hence we can confidently say, 'The Lord is my helper, I will not be afraid.'"

George Matheson was born in Glasgow, Scotland, in 1842. While still an infant, he developed a serious eye infection. For 17 years, he waged a relentless battle, but all in vain. He had barely begun his college career when darkness fell. He was to be blind for the rest of his life.

With indomitable courage, memorizing the assignments read to him, George Matheson continued his education. In 1861, he graduated from the University of Glasgow with honors and began to prepare himself for the Christian ministry.

His accomplishments as a minister in Glasgow and later in Edinburgh are almost unbelievable. Preparing and memorizing every sermon and address, he became a preacher of influence and power.

To many ministers who feel overworked, the daily schedule of George Matheson is a constant challenge. Throughout his life, he continued his studies in French, German, science, history, philosophy, and theology. He wrote and published a dozen books while handling the responsibilities of his pastorate and a heavy program of preaching and pastoral calling.

What was George Matheson's secret? What was the source of his strength and power, courage and daring? Perhaps the key is found in a poem he wrote. It was set to music and is one of the great hymns of the church to this day.

According to the story, George Matheson was in love with a beautiful young girl. When she learned of his impending blindness, she decided it was a burden greater than she could share and broke off their engagement. Heartbroken and alone, he sat down and penned the words that expressed his confidence and trust in another love that would never fail:

> O Love that will not let me go,
> I rest my weary soul in Thee;
> I give Thee back the life I owe
> That in Thine ocean depths its flow
> May richer, fuller be.

94

Beneath The Cross Of Jesus

Through the centuries, many theories have been advanced to explain the cross. There is mighty truth in each of the theories; otherwise, they could not have survived.

There is the Ransom Theory. "Jesus gave his life a ransom for many." To be a Christian is to be set free—free from habits that hinder, free from sin that enslaves. John tells us, "If the Son makes you free, you will be free indeed." Christ did that for you and me. And to be set free is to be "ransomed" indeed.

Another is the Moral Influence Theory. The Cross says to all mankind: "Look, and behold how much God loves you and what he is willing to do to make you realize the greatness of that love."

There is also the Substitutionary Theory. Barabbas saw this. You remember in the play "Give us Barabbas," Barabbas is constantly saying to himself, "He died for me . . . He is taking my place." Christ sets us free by taking our place.

There is the Reconciliation Theory. Paul said it this way: "God was in Christ reconciling the world to himself." It is through the cross that God draws men back into his fellowship and purpose.

But all the theories ever advanced have not been able to fathom the depth of the cross. Just what happened at Calvary, we do not know. But we know that something happened, and we are persuaded that it was for us he suffered there and died.

On May 12, 1937, King George VI was crowned king of Great Britain. The CBS Radio Network was there to carry the coronation to the world. Just before they were to go on the air, it was discovered that a wire on the equipment was broken. There wasn't time to repair it, and millions were waiting to hear. Then one of the engineers, Walter Vivian, stepped up and took hold of either end of the wire. With the current surging through his body, Walter Vivian held on until the broadcast was finished.

That is a picture of what happened at Calvary. With one hand Christ reached up to his heavenly Father and with the other he reached out to man. Then came the words—"It is finished." Atonement was complete. At-one-ment. Man was at one with God.

The Place On Which You Stand

Moses was keeping sheep on the backside of the desert near Mount Horeb, thinking about his people in bondage, slaves in the land of Egypt. It was out of concern for them that he had struck and killed an Egyptian for beating a Hebrew and was forced to flee for his life.

As he sat musing, he saw in the distance a bush burning. When it continued to burn and was not consumed, Moses went to investigate. Suddenly, out of the bush there came the voice of God, "Put off your shoes from your feet, for the place on which you stand is holy ground."

God was not referring to the past, to Moses' ancestors, Abraham, Isaac, and Jacob. He was not talking about the future, Moses' successors, Joshua, Saul, and David. He was speaking about today, the here and now: This is holy ground.

As it was with Moses so it is with most of us. We are not impressed with the present. The past with its heroes is much more attractive. The future has great possibilities, but the present seems drab and hopeless.

However, it is the present that concerns God. That day out in the desert, God took hold of a man, broke the grip of Egypt and brought a nation forth to freedom. Today God speaks to you saying, "The place on which you stand is holy ground."

God created you for a purpose. Whether young or old, rich or poor, man or woman, boy or girl, "a butcher, a baker or candlestick maker," you are a part of God's plan if you will have it so.

She lives in a rest home now after a long life of service to God through her family, community, and church. She has lost her sight and suffers severe arthritis pain.

One afternoon when her minister was visiting with her, she reached out in her darkness and touched his arm. "Why does God keep me here?" she asked, "There is nothing I can do."

God gave her minister the words he needed: "Because you have a mind with which to think, and because you still can pray. There is a tremendous need for prayer in our world today."

Listen again to the voice of God as he speaks. "The place on which you stand is holy ground!"

April 6   **Matthew 28:6**
                    Questions From The Cross

On Easter Sunday, crosses in churches throughout the world are decked with flowers symbolizing victory and answering all the soul-searching questions that haunt the human mind.

On that Black Friday, hanging on the cross, the body of Christ was twisted into a giant question mark. Calvary asked the questions. The answers came with the Easter dawn.

Black Friday's cross asks, "How far can lies go?" The truth is they can go a long way. Lies won out some 2000 years ago and Christ was sentenced to death. Lies thrive today; they flourish profusely tomorrow, but on the third day lies fall away. The flower-decked cross of Easter proclaims their defeat by the stern reality of truth.

Black Friday's cross asks, "How strong is evil?" It was sin and evil that nailed Christ to the cross. There in the gathering gloom he cried out, "My God, my God, why have you forsaken me?" but there was no answer. On Friday and Saturday the heavens were silent, but the thundering dawn announced victory. The flower-decked cross of Easter proclaims that evil is always overcome by good.

Black Friday's cross asks, "Is there any hope for those who fail?" On Friday the disciples deserted Jesus and fled. Saturday was filled with despair and defeat. But as dawn broke the victorious Christ sent the message, "Go tell my disciples and Peter."

As followers we are not always faithful. Today we deny him. Tomorrow we desert him. We fail him over and over again. But he never fails us. The flower-decked cross of Easter gives the assurance to all who struggle in their own strength that they don't have to go on alone. The risen Christ waits to grant forgiveness and the power to become.

Black Friday's cross asks, "If a man dies, shall he live again? Just how powerful is death?" On Friday, Christ was dead and buried. On Saturday, all hope seemed gone, but the Easter dawn gave the victorious answer: "He is risen!"

This is our Christian faith. The flower-decked cross of Easter proclaims what in our heart of hearts we know: "If the earthly frame which houses us today should be demolished, we have a house not made by human hands, a building which God has provided, a home eternal in the heavens."

Lifesaving Stations

Back in 1953, Theodore Wedel told a modern day parable about a little lifesaving station that stood on a dangerous rocky seacoast where storms frequently raged and ships were wrecked. The building was a small rude hut, and there was one boat, but the members kept vigil and went out day or night to rescue shipwrecked seamen.

Many of those who manned the station were sailors who themselves had been rescued. In gratitude, they joined their rescuers in saving others. New boats were bought, crews trained, and the little lifesaving station grew.

Some new members thought the little building crude and poorly equipped. They felt a nicer place should be provided for those saved from the sea. So beds and nice furniture replaced the emergency cots.

Gradually it became a social center for members. Fewer were interested in going out on lifesaving missions, so they hired a captain and crew to do the work. They kept the lifesaving motif; in the meeting room was a small gold lifeboat.

Then one night, a large ship was wrecked off the coast. The hired crew brought in load after load of cold, wet seamen. They were exhausted, and many were sick. Some had dark skins. The beautiful clubhouse was really messed up.

At the next meeting, there was considerable discussion. Most members wanted to stop the lifesaving. It was unpleasant and interfered with their meetings and activities.

Some insisted that lifesaving was their purpose and number one priority, but they were voted down and told, if they wanted to do lifesaving and rescue perishing seamen, they could build a lifesaving station of their own. They did.

As time passed, the new station went through the same change. It became an exclusive club for the members, and another lifesaving station was started farther down the coast.

History continued to repeat itself. Today, there are many rescue stations on the beach, but there are not enough boats or personnel to do the work that needs to be done. There are still lots of shipwrecks, but most of the victims drown.

Where Would God Have You Serve?

There on the Damascus Road, intent on bringing back to Jerusalem any followers of the way he could find, blinded by a light from heaven, the Apostle Paul asked the question every follower of Jesus Christ is called on to ask: "Lord, what do you want me to do?"

She was a shut-in now. She could no longer attend church, but she still wanted to participate in her church's ministry, and so she prayed this prayer, "Lord, you know that I can no longer go to church, but I still want to be a part of the ministry of my church. What can I do to serve you where I am?"

God heard her prayer and gave her an idea. That happens quite often, you know. You may have experienced it. God answers our prayer by giving us an idea. When he does, we should not claim credit for it but give thanks to God who gave it.

God gave this shut-in widow a great idea and she acted on it. She decided to move past words and prayers to action. Today, if you should join that church you would receive a personal handwritten note from this dear little lady.

She is crippled with arthritis, and it hurts her to write, but she writes every one of them by hand to every member who joins the church. In the note, she simply tells them: "Welcome to our church. I can no longer be actively involved, but I want you to know that I am praying for you.

"I hope you will get involved in the Sunday school and volunteering ministries, serving Christ where you are. The day is coming, perhaps sooner than you think, when you will not be able to. You are going to miss it then, so you don't want to miss it now." The people who belong to that church say those letters are changing the face of their congregation.

My friend, God has a place of service for you—a place where you are needed. What do you suppose God could do through you in the network of relationships where he has placed you?

If you are serious about living a life of service for the Master, then just pray. Ask him, "Lord, what do you want me to do?" If you ask that question sincerely and in faith, he will answer your prayer and show you what he wants you to do.

Strength for Climbing

In her poem "Uphill," Christina Rosetti likens life to a mountain climb. You recall her words:

> Does the road wind uphill all the way?
> Yes, to the very end.
> Will the journey take the whole day long?
> From morn to night, my friend.

It makes a wonderful analogy, and each of us can fill it in from the foot to the glorious view at the top—but most of all, I think, our thoughts are on our Leader and our Guide.

In the Swiss Alps, there is an exceedingly high mountain known as Old Jungfrau. At a certain inn at the foot of the mountain, one evening a party of mountain climbers sat around the fireplace. Early the next morning they planned to scale that mountain.

Seated near the group, listening to every word, was a little boy who lived at the inn. Noting his keen interest, the guide asked, "Have you ever climbed Old Jungfrau?"

"No, sir," the lad replied, "I'm crippled. I've never climbed at all." The guide asked, "Would you like to?" The boy's eyes lit up, "Oh, yes sir!" Then the light faded, "But I couldn't, sir. I can't even walk."

The guide spoke with reassurance, "If you really want to, you shall. I will do your walking. You be ready to go at dawn."

At the break of day, they were on their way with the little cripple on the shoulders of the guide. All morning they climbed. Toward noon the little boy said, "I'm too much trouble. Leave me here, and you go on." The guide replied, "No, we will make it to the top together."

The hours passed and still they climbed up and up, higher and higher. Then, there they were. Standing at the summit, they looked down upon the scene spread out far below. Suddenly the little boy turned to the guide. "Oh, thank you, sir. I could never have made it without you!"

Someday, by his grace and power, perhaps I shall stand up yonder amidst the wonders unspeakable. And, if I reach it, my greatest joy will be to fall at the feet of him who has been my Guide and confess, "My Lord and my God, I could never have made it without you!"

To The Farthest Shore

One of our poets has written:

> Drop a pebble in the water,
> Just a splash and it is gone,
> But there's half-a-hundred ripples,
> Circling on and on and on.

Back more years than I care to admit, as a small boy I fished the pond on our farm. One afternoon I dropped a small stone. Almost before I could say Jack Robinson, it was gone. I caught a brief glimpse, and then it was out of sight on its way to the bottom.

Hardly aware, I watched the ripples spread from the center for a second or two, then I turned back to the task at hand of baiting my hook for the afternoon of fun ahead. Suddenly a faint noise in the distance caused me to look up just in time to see the ripples I had started lapping on the farthest shore.

All of that seems long, long ago, but over the years the scene has come before me many times. Abrupt, alone, or in a crowd, I have heard the plink of that stone and have watched in my mind's eye again and again the ripples circling out and out and out.

Life is like that, I think. We drop an unkind word, make a careless remark, and almost in an instant they are gone. Not really. They keep spreading and spreading, no way to stop them once they start. On the distant shore, they break a heart or cause a tear to fall.

We can also drop words of kindness and encouragement with the same results. At once, we forget, but the ripples circle out and far away and lives are transformed, changed, and made new.

Oh, yes, there's one other thing I noticed that summer afternoon so long ago. When the ripples reached the shore, they started coming back. You have seen the same thing happen, I am sure.

Edwin Markham sums it up for us in these words:

> There is a destiny that makes us brothers;
> None goes his way alone.
> All that we send into the lives of others,
> Comes back into our own.

April 11 **II Corinthians 6: 1**

Co-Workers With God

The great pianist, Ignace Jan Paderewski, wanted more than anything to spread the arts throughout his native Poland. He planned his concerts so they would take him into the most obscure towns and villages.

Such a concert was scheduled in an out-of-the-way village. There, a young mother, desiring to encourage her son, who didn't care all that much about his piano lessons, bought two tickets for the performance.

They arrived at the concert early, found their seats down front, and eyed the Steinway Grand waiting on the stage. The mother found a friend and began visiting.

Eight o'clock arrived. The houselights dimmed; the big spotlight came up and the audience grew quiet. It was then that they noticed the little 10-year-old boy. He had slipped away from his mother and was up on the stage. Seated at the big concert piano, he began picking out "Twinkle, Twinkle, Little Star."

The audience gasped in unbelieving amazement. The poor mother, her face burning with embarrassment, sat flabbergasted not knowing what to do. Stagehands went out to grab the boy, but suddenly from the other side of the stage Paderewski appeared and waved them away.

He quickly moved to the piano and standing behind the little boy whispered, "Don't quit now. Don't stop. Keep playing." Then leaning over, the great pianist reached around with his left hand and began filling in with a beautiful bass part.

Then he reached around on the other side with his right hand and produced an incredible running obbligato as a complement. Playing together, the old master and the young novice held the crowd mesmerized in what had to be a most magical moment.

It is so in all of our lives. There are hours of discouragement and doubt when we want to give up and quit, not even try anymore. In just such hours as that, there is One standing behind us who whispers, "Don't quit now! Don't stop! Keep going!"

If we will heed his words and not give up, he will weave into our novice ways his obbligatos and supplement our weak melodies with his great harmonies. What is created will be enhanced beyond our fondest dreams by the touch of the Master's hand.

102

As To One Of The Least

Sir Wilfred Grenfel was a medical missionary to Newfoundland and Labrador. The stories from his life thrilled and inspired me as a boy growing up. One of the stories he told, a true story, was about an army officer in World War I.

It was a bitter cold night at the front line trenches. The officer was touring the various sentry posts when he came upon one of the guards asleep at his post. Sleeping while on guard is the most serious of offenses, especially in wartime, and the young soldier was subject to general court-martial.

As he talked with the young man, the officer noticed that he was only a boy. Furthermore he noticed that the young sentry was so cold his teeth were chattering. Immediately he saw the reason why—the boy had no topcoat.

Taking off his own coat, he gave it to the lad and went on his way checking the other sentry posts. Sleet began to fall and the icy wind blew harder and harder. By the time he reached the guardhouse the officer was half-frozen. They put him to bed with chills. Later it developed into pneumonia. Delirious with a fever, he dreamed that he died.

He found himself walking down the street of the celestial city when suddenly he saw in the distance a man coming toward him. He thought it looked like Jesus. As he came closer, he realized it was Jesus, and he was wearing the officer's topcoat. There was a warm loving smile and then came the words: "As you did it to one of the least of these my brothers, you did it to me."

It is caring that matters most. It expresses itself in many ways. It may mean a kind word, a letter of encouragement, or a telephone call saying, "I was just wondering how you are doing?"

Bishop Fredrick Warnecke once told about a lonely man who felt so rejected and unloved that he decided to kill himself by throwing himself into the river. As he began the walk down to the river's edge, he said to himself, "If I meet someone who looks at me as if he cared one way or the other, then I will not take my life."

There the Bishop ended his story. Did the man meet someone? I don't know. But if he had met you or me, would he have turned back?

Flawed

He was a judge known for his wisdom and understanding. He tried to help everyone if he possibly could. The young man standing before him was a nineteen year old, in trouble with the law a number of times before. He had been arrested and was now on trial.

Looking at him, the judge recalled his own boyhood. He knew well that many things can happen to get a fellow into trouble. He realized too, that in life, as in a race, sometimes we can get off on the wrong foot.

"John," he said, "All of us have but one life to live. You haven't been doing very well with living yours. You have made some mistakes. We all do that, but, now, why don't you turn over a new leaf, start over and make a man of yourself?"

John was silent for a moment. Then he replied, "Yes, Sir, I know. I am sorry for what I have done. I wish I could make a new start, but it is too late."

"No, John," the judge said, "Things are never ruined completely. It is never too late to begin again and save them. Then the judge shared with him this story:

"Some four hundred years ago there lived in the city of Florence, Italy, a sculptor by the name of D'Antonio. One day he took a great block of marble and began work on a piece of sculpture, but the marble had a flaw. D'Antonio was not as careful as he should have been and the piece of marble was ruined. He carried it out back, threw it on the trash heap behind his shop, and it was forgotten.

"Forty years later, in 1501, a young man named Michelangelo came across the castoff piece of marble with its strange shape, weatherworn and covered with dirt and grime. After studying it carefully, he asked if he might have it, and from that old block of marble, ruined by an irreparable flaw and thrown aside, Michelangelo carved the famous statue of David."

> "When things go wrong, as they sometimes will,
> When the road you're trudging seems all uphill,
> When the funds are low and the debts are high,
> And you want to smile, but you have to sigh,
> When care is pressing you down a bit,
> Rest if you must—but don't you quit!"

You Can Always Begin Again

Thomas Carlyle was one of England's leading writers and a tremendous intellect. He spent years studying the French Revolution, what went right and what went horribly wrong. Living before the days of the typewriter, his entire manuscript had to be written by hand.

After five months of labor he completed the first volume and took it to his friend, John Stuart Mill. He said, "Will you read it and tell me what you think?" John Stuart Mill was honored. He took the manuscript home and that evening started reading.

He became so entranced by the book he sat up all night. As he read he laid the pages on the floor. When day dawned, he had read the entire book. He realized that Thomas Carlyle had written a masterpiece.

He got up and went down stairs to breakfast. While he was gone, the cleaning lady came in, saw the papers on the floor, thought it was trash and threw it into the fire. Can you imagine yourself in John Stuart Mill's position having to tell his friend what had happened?

When Thomas Carlyle received the news he was horrified. He screamed at the cleaning lady, at John Stuart Mill, he screamed at God. Finally, on the fourth day he regained control. Bowing his head he whispered, "Lord, forgive me. Years ago I gave you my life. Therefore the book was yours. Your book is gone. What would you have me do?"

Just then he heard a tapping outside his apartment. The tapping had been going on for days, but due to his screaming he hadn't heard it. Looking out across the street he saw a bricklayer building a wall.

He watched as the builder put a brick in the mortar and tapped it into place. Another brick and tapped it into place. As he watched the wall slowly rise, brick, by brick, by brick, he knew what he had to do.

That very day he sat down with a clean sheet of paper and began to write one word, one line, one page, one chapter at a time. When *The French Revolution* was published in 1837 Thomas Carlyle realized that the second writing was far superior to the first.

We live in a world of disappointments, times when all we've worked for goes up in flames. When it happens to you, my friend, lift up your eyes. God still rules and all is well. Take courage and with his help begin anew!

Start Me With Ten

Dr. James Cleland once told about a church that faced a problem with its choir, or rather with its lack of a choir. It was a large congregation of some 600 members, but the choir was pathetic. One Sunday there would be a choir of six, the next Sunday eight, the next four; and when only three showed up they went out and sat in the congregation.

The entire membership was aware of the problem. It was commonplace to hear on Sunday mornings and during the week such comments as "Why don't they do something about the choir!"

The choir director tried. He wrote some cute ads for the church newsletter. It was to no avail. The minister begged for support from the pulpit. No response. Things continued to go from bad to worse.

Then it happened. One beautiful Sunday morning as the choir and congregation were struggling through the processional hymn, an old man seated on the far side of the filled sanctuary moved out of his pew. Hymnal in hand, he walked down the aisle and took his place in the choir. The next Wednesday evening over 75 people were on hand for choir rehearsal. Today that church has three choirs and every Sunday and especially at Christmas and Easter, the music stirs the hearts of all who come to worship there. It all came about when an old man stopped complaining about the problem and did what he could to help.

It is a strange thing. Church growth experts tell us that a small, inadequate choir actually drives prospective members away. A small congregation is no problem. In fact, most people are attracted to a small congregation rather than a large one. But if the choir is not what it should be they look elsewhere for a church home.

It's true: "There's a place for every worker in the vineyard of the Lord." And so often all that is needed for those places to be filled is one person willing to lead the way. In Rudolf Friml's operetta, *The Vagabond King,* there is this rousing chorus:

> "Give me some men who are stouthearted men,
> Who will fight for the right they adore.
> Start me with ten who are stouthearted men
> And I'll soon give you ten thousand more."

Could it be that God is calling you?

Is There Someone You Can Help?

In the background I could hear music coming from the stereo. I recognized the voice of Bobby Vinton. I had heard the lyrics many times before:

Lonely, I'm so lonely,
I have nobody
To call my own.
I'm so lonely
I'm Mr. Lonely—

The song continued but my mind had gone elsewhere. I was thinking, those plaintive words speak for all of us some of the time and for some of us all the time.

It was 1930. A group of friends sitting in a restaurant were sharing stories about the Great Depression. A once-rich man, unable to face financial ruin, had taken his life. There had been another downsizing at the local factory. There was a homeless family sleeping in the city park.

Then the minister in the group confessed: "I have to preach a sermon on Wednesday evening before Thanksgiving, and I don't have a clue as to what I'm going to say. I want to say something to cheer people up, but what is there to be thankful for in the midst of a great depression?"

William Stidger was sitting with the group. He thought he heard God whisper, "Why not give thanks for people who have blessed your life?" Even as he spoke, he thought of someone to whom he should write.

That evening, taking pen in hand, he wrote to a minister who had meant very much to him. He thanked him for investing his time, his experience, his advice—so much of himself in others.

In two days he found a reply letter in his mailbox: "My Dear Will: Your letter was so beautiful, so real, that as I sat reading it in my study, tears fell from my eyes, tears of gratitude. Before I realized what I was doing, I rose from my chair and called my wife's name. Forgetting she was gone, I wanted to share your letter with her. You'll never know how much your writing has warmed my spirit."

There are a lot of lonely people in this world of ours. I'll bet if you think about it you will find that you know a few of them. Is there an e-mail you could send, a letter that you should write?

April 17

April 17   **Mark 12: 43-44**

All That I Am and Have

The name on the telegram read, "Matthew Sands." He tore it open with trembling hands. "We regret to inform you . . . your son . . . killed in action." The letters squirmed like snakes.

He swallowed hard, fighting the bitter rebellion building up inside him. He sat down at the desk, seized a pen, and wrote hastily, "All I am and have, I give to God and his service." It helped; he felt much better after he had written it.

Late that afternoon, he took a walk along a familiar country road. The son he loved was dead! He looked over toward a little chapel by the roadside. It had been deserted for years. Then, he saw the for sale sign. The building and site were being sold to the highest bidder.

Out of nowhere, the decision came. He would buy the little chapel, fix it up, and dedicate it to the memory of his son. He would make it into a beautiful place where people might come in hours of need to worship and talk with God.

He figured carefully how much he could afford to pay, wrote the amount on a piece of paper, and put it in his pocket. He would mail it later.

On the day the bids were to be opened, Matthew Sands arrived early and took a back seat in the little chapel along with other bidders. He waited anxiously. Suppose he had not bid enough; what if he didn't get it?

Unconsciously, he put his hand in his coat pocket. A feeling of panic swept over him; what was the paper in his hand? He drew it out and looked. What he feared was true—it was his bid. It had never been mailed!

He didn't have time to think about what went wrong. Someone was speaking at the front of the chapel. The bids had been opened and considered one by one. The highest bidder—one Matthew Sands. The man at the front was holding a piece of paper in his hand. For all assembled there to hear, he read the bid aloud: "All that I am and have, I give . . . ." Immediately, Mathew Sands realized what had happened. He had mailed the wrong piece of paper!

"All that I am and have, I give." You cannot give less and be a Christian, and no one can give more.

Mark 9: 35
To Give And To Serve

Henry P. Crowell was a powerful industrialist on the eastern seaboard of our nation quite a few years ago. At the age of fifty he was diagnosed with tuberculosis. In those days there was no treatment available. The doctors told him he was facing a long and lingering death.

He had read about the West—the plains and mountains. He decided he would gather up all he had and take a slow train westward. If he was to die he would die out there on the western prairie surrounded by the mountains.

But he never made it all the way to the mountains. As they were passing through one small town the train stopped to take on provisions. Getting out to stretch his legs, he found a town in despair. There was only one industry, a large mill. It had been mismanaged and was going out of business.

The whole town was going to be wiped out and the people had nowhere to go. Henry P. Crowell, the wealthy and successful industrialist, looked around and said to himself, "Well, I'm going to die somewhere. Might as well die here. Maybe before I die I can help these people."

He sent back east for his money, bought the mill and took over its management. He started hiring people, then more people, and the business boomed. The town became a city. Under his dedicated leadership, out of his love for them and his love for God, a spirit of community cooperation was born. The city was transformed.

Henry P. Crowell did die—at the age of 96! He wrote to his kids back east, "I'm fine; I just got too busy to die." The business he started he named Quaker Oats.

Like Henry P. Crowell, no matter what your circumstances, you still have the capacity to love and serve. As you give yourself in love and service, God's energy will begin to flow through you creating a new future, not just for you but also for all those whom you love and serve.

It was Sir Wilfred Grenfell, the great missionary to Labrador, who said, "The service we render to others is really the rent we pay for our room on this earth. It is obvious that man is himself a traveler, that the purpose of this world is not 'To Have and to Hold' but, 'To Give and to Serve.'"

Go Fly A Kite!

In 1847 Charles Ellet, Jr. was commissioned to construct a bridge across the Niagara River. His first task was to create a line of communication, followed by a solid line, in order to establish a link to the American side. Since the gorge was 800 feet wide it was too dangerous to attempt to establish this link by water.

It occurred to someone that kite flying might be the answer to this difficult problem. A five-dollar prize was offered to the person who could fly a kite across the Niagara Gorge. A young American boy named Homan Walsh flying his kite from the Canadian shoreline was the one who was able to accomplish the feat on the second day of the contest.

The string of the kite was fastened to a tree on the American side, and a light cord attached to it was pulled across. Next came a heavier cord, then a rope and finally a giant wire cable which was the beginning of the new bridge.

On July 26, 1848 the first Niagara Suspension Bridge was completed. It consisted of four massive towers 80 feet high, two on each bank connected by four giant cables each composed of 120 strands of number 10 wire. It was 762 feet long, 8 feet wide and the roadway was suspended 220 feet above the river below.

Edwin Markham in a poem said that our prayer life is much like the building of that bridge. The builder sends across the gulf his venturing kite carrying a slender cord. Unseen hands on the other side grasp it and draw a greater cord and a greater still. At last, across the chasm swings the cable and then the mighty bridge in air.

Even so, we are privileged to send our little thoughts across the void, out to God's reaching hands. We send out our love and faith to thread the deep again and again. At last, the little cord has become a mighty cable; and we are anchored to the Infinite.

Dwight D. Eisenhower believed firmly in the power of prayer. He once said, "A thousand experiences have convinced me beyond the shadow of a doubt that prayer multiplies the strength of the individual and brings within the scope of his capabilities almost any conceivable objective."

Now, how about it? Are you ready to go and fly a kite?

April 20

Matthew 7:21

Like A Mighty Army?

Dr. Halford Luccock of Yale Divinity School used to tell about a church that invited a returning serviceman to speak at the Sunday worship service. He finally agreed with one stipulation, that they sing "Onward, Christian Soldiers" before he spoke. They did—"Like a mighty army moves the church of God." Then their soldier boy got up. It was a sermon they never forgot.

He began, "I have been in the army quite a few years now, and I have never seen an army move like a church. What if the army accepted some of the feeble excuses church members use. Imagine this:

"Reveille 7:00 a.m. The sergeant barks, 'Count four! One! Two! Three! — Where is Private Smith?' Someone volunteers, 'Private Smith was too sleepy to get up. He was out late last night. He said he would be with us in spirit.'

"'That's O. K.' says the sergeant, 'I understand. Give him my regards. One! Two! —Where is Private Jones?' Another speaks up, 'Sir, Private Jones had a cold and didn't want to give it to the entire army.' 'There are a lot of colds going around,' says the sergeant, 'I will try to get by to see Jones this week. Where is Private Brown?'

"'Oh,' puts in a buddy, 'Private Brown is playing golf. It is hard for him to get away any other day and he feels that recreation is very important. Besides he says he can drill just as well on the golf course. He sent his best wishes and said to tell you that he would see you next Easter.'

"'That's perfectly all right,' says the sergeant, 'I hope he has a good game. We shall look forward to seeing him on Easter Sunday. Does anyone know about Private Roberts?' 'Private Roberts really hated to miss this morning,' another says, 'You see, his family came down this weekend and they plan to leave around noon. So he couldn't just go off and leave them, you know.'

"'Of course, I understand completely,' says the sergeant, 'There are some things that have to come first. I believe he was here last week, anyway.'"

"Like a mighty army?" the young soldier concluded, "If the church really moved like a mighty army, most of us would wind up with a court-martial!"

April 21   **Matthew 6: 12**
Forgiveness, Riches And A New Life

Do you ever stand in need of forgiveness? Do you know what it is like to be forgiven?

Fiorello LaGuardia was the mayor of New York for three terms from 1934 to 1945. A popular mayor, he led New York's recovery during the Great Depression. One evening a court judge in one of New York's poorest districts was surprised when Mayor LaGuardia entered his courtroom, dismissed him and sat at the bench.

The court was filled with many common criminals, and one old lady dressed in tattered clothing who had been charged with stealing a loaf of bread. With cheeks wet with tears she confessed in shame to her crime, "My daughter's husband has deserted her. She is sick, and her children are starving."

Every heart in the courtroom went out to the little old lady and the sad situation that had motivated her. Still, they understood the problem faced by the storekeeper who felt he had no choice but to prosecute the woman. "It's a bad neighborhood," he explained, "She has to be punished to teach other people a lesson."

Mayor LaGuardia faced a decision that called for the Wisdom of Solomon. He turned to the old woman and said, "I have got to punish you, the law makes no exceptions, ten dollars or ten days in jail."

The lady's face turned ashen. Humiliated and ashamed of her sin, she offered no protest. She didn't notice the mayor, who even as he was speaking reached in his pocket, took out a ten dollar bill and threw it into his hat.

"Here is the ten dollar fine which I now pay for you," he said, "And, furthermore, I am going to fine everyone in this courtroom fifty cents for living in a town where a person has to steal bread so that her grandchildren can eat. Mr. Bailiff, collect the fines and give them to the defendant."

The morning paper carried the story. In part it read, "Late last evening forty-seven dollars and fifty cents was turned over to a bewildered and frightened grandmother. She was arrested for stealing a loaf of bread to feed her starving grandchildren. Making the forced donations was a red-faced storekeeper, seventy petty criminals and a few New York policemen."

Matthew 13: 45-46
The Only Things That Really Matter

Her name was Sadie Virginia Smithson, and she lived in the little town of Johnson Falls in West Virginia just prior to World War I. After she graduated from high school, she earned a modest living sewing for the people of the town. More than anything she wanted to belong to the Laurel Literary Society, but she was never invited to join. She didn't belong to the upper social set of the town.

Dreams do not die easily. Sadie Virginia Smithson continued to hope and scheme. No one from Johnson Falls had ever traveled abroad. What if she saved her money and made a trip to Europe? In her reverie she could almost hear the polite applause of the ladies when she finished reading her paper, "My Trip To Europe."

So she saved the money she earned, dollar by dollar, year after year, and made the trip abroad with a professor and his wife. Shortly after they arrived the war broke out. They had to go from Belgium to Paris at night by automobile. In the darkness they lost their way.

Suddenly they found themselves crossing a field where minutes before a raging battle had been fought. The scene was terrible to behold. Before she realized what she was doing, Sadie Virginia Smithson was out of the car and in the big middle of the holocaust.

She found a spring nearby and brought water to the wounded soldiers. Tearing her skirt into strips, she made bandages. She scribbled messages for men who were dying to be sent to loved ones back home.

The long dark night slowly passed. Dawn brought an ambulance and two young medics. "Who are you and what in the world are you doing here?" one of them asked in amazement. "My name is Sadie Virginia Smithson," she heard herself saying, "and I have been holding back hell all night."

After she returned to the United States and Johnson Falls, West Virginia, a close friend said to her, "I'll bet the Laurel Literary Society will be glad to have you as a member now."

Sadie Virginia Smithson smiled. "Somehow after being face-to-face with war and death," she said, "everything has changed. The things I once considered important don't seem to matter anymore. In fact, the only things that really matter are God, and love, and serving as Christ served."

Holding Hands

The Cascade Mountains with their snowcapped peaks is one of the most beautiful sights I have ever witnessed. The range is some five hundred miles long. It receives its name from the great cascades of the Columbia River.

Recently I read about a place in Oregon where for years there was a great need for a footbridge across the Columbia. At first it seemed to be an impossible task, but finally some loggers working together were able to fell a giant fir tree directly across that mighty stream.

The giant evergreen made a fine crossing for lumberjacks, but most other people felt so insecure that they would not ever attempt a crossing. Constructing a handrail bolted securely along the side of the log solved the problem. It furnished those crossing with balance and support.

Life is a lot like that, don't you think? Sooner or later all of us are called on to make crossings where we need something that gives us firm support and balance, and there are times when we need even more than this.

Once while visiting Carlsbad Cavern in New Mexico we experienced a heartwarming and inspiring sight. As we stood in the Big Room of the canyon that is 4,000 feet long, 350 feet wide and a maximum height of 350 feet, a little boy looked up at his father and said, "Daddy, let me hold your hand." As his father took his hand, the little boy reached out to his little sister saying, "And you can hold my hand!"

A guide who takes visitors to the top of the tower at the University of Texas once said, "At that height everyone wants to hold on to something. Adults hold on to the guardrail, but children always prefer to hold on to people."

God gave each of us two hands and for good purpose. At the crossings of life when the going gets tough, we can reach up and take the hand of our heavenly Father. Then we can take the hand of a fellow traveler.

There are a lot of people all around us who are looking for an outstretched hand. You and I can offer the hand that is needed, but first we must take hold of the hand of God. We can depend on him. He will never fail or forsake us. Listen to his promise: "I, the Lord your God, have hold of your hand. Do not be afraid. I am your helper."

God's Challenge And Promise

William Colgate was the founder of the Colgate-Palmolive Soap Company. He was a mere boy of sixteen when he left home to seek his fortune. In his hand, tied up in a bundle, he carried all of his worldly possessions. Each member of his family took turns hugging him and wishing him luck. His mother waited to be last. Holding him close, she said, "My son, seek first the kingdom of God."

Trudging down the road he met an old neighbor, the captain of a canal boat, who asked where he was going. "I thought I would go to New York," he said, "Father can't afford to keep me at home any longer and says I must make a living for myself."

"No trouble there," said the captain. "Just start right and you will do fine." William Colgate explained that the only trade he knew about was soap making which he had learned at home from his father. "Well," said the old man, "Let me pray with you and then you can be on your way." After his prayer, he gave him this advice: "Be a good man. Give your heart to Christ. Make an honest soap and give the Lord all that belongs to him of every dollar you earn. God bless and keep you, my boy."

Finding work in New York wasn't easy. Lonesome and far from home, he remembered the words of his mother and united with the church. At last he secured a position as an apprentice to a soap maker. Recalling the words of the old captain, he gave a tithe, from his first paycheck and every one afterward, ten cents of every dollar he earned to the Lord.

In time he became a partner in the company, and when his partner died he became the sole owner. His first act was to instruct his bookkeeper to open an account with the Lord. Each week one tenth of his income was deposited to that account. He prospered. The business grew. His soap sold, and he grew wealthy—faster than he dreamed possible. He increased his giving to two tenths, then three tenths and then four tenths and five tenths. When he had educated his children and made plans for his life, he gave the whole of his company's income to the Lord.

William Colgate, founder of Colgate University, took God at his word, "Bring all the tithes into the storehouse, prove me, and see if I will not open the windows of heaven and pour out a blessing such as you will be unable to receive."

With God In Charge

Dr. Tony Campolo was speaking at a small Christian College up in Pennsylvania. The students all joined hands for prayer. When his turn came, he prayed, "Lord, whatever my agenda, I want you to take charge." It was a powerful moment for him. At the end of the prayer time someone prayed, "And Lord, we want to ask a special prayer for Bert Harris." When Dr. Campolo asked, "Who is Bert Harris?" the student said, "I don't know. I just felt led to pray for Bert Harris."

Dr. Campolo gave an outstanding speech that evening, got in his car and was driving home when just ahead he saw a man dejectedly walking down the street. He didn't know why, but all at once he decided to do something he rarely ever did; he pulled over and offered the man a ride.

"Where are you going?" he asked. The man replied, "Anywhere you want to go." "O. K.," Dr. Campolo said, "I can take you to the next town. By the way, my name is Tony Compolo, what's yours?" Imagine his amazement when the man said, "My name is Bert Harris."

Suddenly it dawned on Dr. Compolo that when he offered to make room in his agenda for God's agenda, God had taken him at his word. It was quite evident that a conversation was needed so they started talking, first about marriage, and then about Bert's marriage.

As they came to a wide place in the road, Dr. Campolo whipped the car around. "What are you doing?" the man shouted. "We're going back," Dr.Campolo said, "I don't think you really want to leave." As they drove back, Dr. Campolo talked to Bert Harris about the power of God to change things, to make a difference where a difference was needed.

Spotting the mobile home by the park, Dr. Campolo pulled up and stopped. Inside, he met Bert's wife and the three of them talked until three o'clock in the morning. When they finally had prayer and said good night, reconciliation had taken place.

Driving home, his heart strangely warmed, Dr. Campolo realized a great truth. No one can be used by God without being touched and blessed by God.

All of us want to be great. Jesus has told us how: Let the One who is great live inside you. Plug into God. Plug into the needs of this world. He wants to use you today.

Hearing And Doing

If you want to warm the heart of any minister all you have to say is "That was a good sermon; it was helpful and I enjoyed it very much." However, it would be a far greater compliment if you should say, "I liked your sermon very much and I am going to try to do the things you talked about." This is the real test of any sermon. Not the number of people who comment on it, but the number whose lives are helped and changed by it.

Perhaps the greatest weakness of the church in our day is the undisciplined lives the great majority of us live. At our best moments when we take time to consider, we realize that we are not the effective instruments of God we ought to be. What about you? Do you have a longing to be bigger and better than you are? Would you sincerely like for your life to count in a more constructive and powerful way for Christ and the kingdom of God? Here are some suggestions for a beginning:

1. I will make it a point in my life to be regular in my attendance at Church on Sunday. I recognize how important corporate worship is and believe if I am too busy to attend on Sunday, I am too busy.

2. At the same time I also recognize the value of private devotions. I resolve to make it a point in my life to spend some time each day alone in meditation, Bible reading and prayer. I will keep this time faithfully and allow nothing to crowd it out of my schedule.

3. I will spend at least five minutes each day in absolute silence. The "still small voice" can speak only to those who are calm and quiet. I will obey the scriptural command, "Be still and know that I am God."

4. I will do my very best to be of service each day to someone who needs help. If at all possible I will try to render this service with my hands and do it without anyone else knowing.

5. I will strive to live life simply. The needs of the world are such today that I dare not be extravagant in the possession of things for my own personal use. I will try to make my life, my influence, my talents and my money a dedicated response to the cause of Jesus Christ.

Someone has said, "Christianity is not so much for beginners as it is for beginners again." Today you can begin again. It is never too late to make a new start, and there is no limit to what God can do with dedicated and disciplined lives.

No Wider Than The Heart Is Wide!

Some years ago the trustees of the Denver zoo were given a polar bear. They were quite excited over the gift. The problem was they didn't have any place to put it. So they went on a financial crusade throughout the city of Denver to raise enough money to build it a home.

In time a state of the arts palace was planned and built. It was beautiful— ice water baths, rock-climbing, mountains, a waterfall. That polar bear was going to have a wonderful home.

However, the drive to raise the money and the time for the construction took three years. During the three year period they had to keep the polar bear in a little bitty cage with very limited space. In fact, there was only enough room for him to walk three steps this way, rise up, turn around and walk three steps that way.

So it went on all the daylong and into the wee hours of the night; three steps this way, rise up, turn around and walk three steps the other way. It was indeed a pathetic situation and a pitiful sight to watch.

Finally, after three years the new home was finished. Everybody who was anybody in the city of Denver; everybody who had worked on the project, everyone who had given money to the effort was there for the unveiling of the polar bear's new home. The stands were packed with the leading citizens.

The zookeepers made a major event of it. Ceremoniously they wheeled the little cage out into the brand new home, opened the door, and went outside and waited. The polar bear didn't budge an inch.

The zookeepers went back in and after quite a bit of effort pushed it out. Then they wheeled the cage away so everybody could watch as the polar bear explored its brand new home.

And you know what that bear did? He looked around, took three steps this way, rose up, turned around, walked three steps that way, rose up, turned around—why did the bear do that? Because it got a little bitty cage imprinted on its mind and its mind stayed caged even after the cage was removed.

Far too often your life and mine are like that. Somehow, like the polar bear, we get little bitty cages imprinted on our minds and our minds stay caged even after the cages have been removed.

For What Are You Giving Your Life?

Late one afternoon, a group of men and boys stood on the bank of a swollen and sullen stream. It had rained all night and all morning, and the river was cresting. The dark waters rushed by carrying all kinds of debris.

All at once, one of the men pointed excitedly toward something out in the water. A huge log being carried by the current had lodged against a treetop. There, sitting on the log was a little marooned rabbit.

One of the boys, some fifteen years of age, decided to catch it. Before anyone realized what he was doing, he had pushed a boat away from the shore and was rowing out to where the little bunny was stranded.

When he reached the log jam, he picked up the quivering little rabbit and held it aloft and waved it for everyone on the bank to see.

Then, tucking it inside his jacket, he started back. No one was sure just what happened next. Some heavy object, swirling below the surface of the water, struck his boat with a sickening thud.

There was a scream of terror, and those on the bank saw flailing arms and then he disappeared beneath raging waters. For hours their eyes scanned the river for some sign of life, but to no avail.

At the break of dawn, as soon as they could see, a searching party was formed. They combed the banks for miles downstream. Toward noon, they found the boy's body, half-buried in a backwash of driftwood.

As they stood over the body, waiting for the ambulance to arrive, one of the searchers bent down, reached inside the jacket and pulled out a little water-soaked rabbit. Holding it up, he said, "This is the thing for which he gave his life!"

Every person is called on to make a choice. Let's face it; a life can be wasted. It can be thrown away "for that which is not bread, for that which does not satisfy."

It doesn't need to be so. Christ says, "I came that you may have life, and have it abundantly." Your life can be meaningful. Your life can have purpose. It can count for things infinitely worthwhile. That is God's will for you, but you must make a choice. For what are you giving your life?

April 29   **Lamentations 3:25**
A Deed Of Simple Kindness

I remember the very first Bible verses I memorized in Sunday school as a child. "Be kind to one another." Kindness is the great hallmark of the Christian life.

In 1931 the Great Depression was at its height. Edison Marshall was traveling across the state of Mississippi in an old Ford sedan. On the outskirts of one of the little towns a stranger signaled for a ride. Edison pulled to a stop and picked him up, a youth in his teens who had nothing on his head and a coat that was ragged and worn.

As they drove away Edison spotted another youth standing on the opposite side of the road, hugging himself to keep warm. Speeding on down the highway the sight of the young man haunted him. Finally, he asked, "Did you notice that boy across the road from you?"

"Yeah," replied his passenger, "He's my buddy. We are going to Mobile. We have jobs waiting there. So many holdups lately nobody will pick up two hitchhikers. We agreed I would take the first car." Edison wanted to go back, but by now the boy was twenty miles behind so he went on, but he couldn't get the tall redheaded lad standing in the cold off of his mind. It was still bothering him when they arrived at an old-fashioned tollgate.

"Good morning," he called to the keeper who came out to collect the ten cents, "Really is cold isn't it!" The old man made no reply. His face was stern, his lips fixed in a grim line. In spite of his forbidding manner, Edison continued, "Listen, a hitchhiker will be along this way soon. He is tall and red-headed. He doesn't have shoes or a coat. Will you give him this money?"

It was two years before Edison Marshall was back that way. This time a kind, gray-haired lady took the toll. "Two years ago," he said to her, "I gave a man some money to give to a red-haired boy; do you know if he ever showed up?"

The woman's face lighted up. "Are you the one?" she asked, "My husband probably wasn't very friendly. We lost our son in the war and Jim never got over it. That morning he gave the young fellow your money and they got to talking. Jim invited him to stay, and he did. He lived with us and helped with the work up until Jim died. Roy made such a difference in our lives. Jim used to say that God sent him to heal our hurt. You will never know how much you did that day for all of us."

Giving Is Living

I want to tell you about a man named Sam Reeves. Some years ago the White House called a conference on small businesses. Sam Reeves was invited to attend. Sam was from the state of Michigan. Twenty years earlier, with a capital outlay of $1.50, he had started a service station.

The administration wanted to know the secret of his success. The puzzling part was there were three other service stations at the same intersection. Their products were just as good, but they had grown very little.

What was Sam Reeves' secret? Let him tell you in his own words: "I just tried to give away more than my competitors. It was that simple." But what was it that Sam Reeves gave away? It wasn't lottery tickets or a chance on a new sports car.

No, what Sam Reeves gave away was service. After every snowstorm Sam Reeves cleared dozens of driveways free of charge. If someone was without transportation, Sam Reeves would pick up an order of groceries or meet someone at the depot or at the airport.

Parents could leave their youngsters at his station for an hour or two when a sitter was unavailable. He would keep an eye on the home of people while they were away on vacation. He would drop by and water their flowers or feed and water their pets and on and on, ad infinitum.

On the desk in Sam Reeves' service station there is a much used Bible. One day he ran across these words in the gospel of Luke: "Give and it will be given to you; good measure, pressed down, shaken together and running over." That is when it all began.

First, he gave free parking to people shopping in that vicinity. Then free right to your door delivery—especially in rainy, cold weather. For over twenty years the secret of service to others has worked for Sam Reeves, and it will work for you.

The English poet Robert Browning declared, "All service ranks the same with God." What you do for others, you do for Him. It was the Man from Nazareth who said that whoever gave so much as a cup of cold water to one in need would not lose his reward.

Listen again to the words of the Apostle Paul: "In love serve one another."

121

Travelers On Life's Highway

It was Jesus who told the story. A certain man went down from Jerusalem to Jericho. On the way, he fell among thieves who stripped and beat him and left him half-dead.

There were others on the road that day. In their responses—from deadly indifference to compassionate concern—they became prototypes of all mankind—those who lived in that time and in all the years to come.

There was the hurt. "A certain man," Jesus said. It could have been anyone. Human suffering knows no bounds. In William Saroyan's novel, "The Human Comedy," Homer MacCauley, after his first day delivering telegrams, says to Old Grogan the operator, "There surely are a lot of people with troubles," and John Donne counsels, "I am a part of mankind. Every man's death diminishes me. Therefore, send not to know for whom the bell tolls. It tolls for thee!" The hurt.

There were the hurters—those with a knack for causing pain and suffering. There seems to be no limit to man's inhumanity to man. Open any newspaper and read the headlines: "Bandit Slays Two," "Temple Girl, 13, Shot," "Three Charged In Officer's Death." The hurters.

There were the heedless. Their byword in all ages has been and is "I don't want to get involved," and they don't! They turn their heads and act as though they cannot hear. They close their eyes and pretend they cannot see. They look upon people in pain and with problems and it makes no impression. With sorrow and suffering all around, they pass by on the other side. The heedless.

Finally there was the helper who stopped and rendered aid. Why? Because that was the kind of person he was. Helpers are people of compassion, and through their deeds of mercy fellow travelers behold the face of God. The Helper.

> "I showed men God," my Lord will say,
> When we come to the end of the King's highway.
> "I helped the blighted to be resigned,
> I showed the stars to souls gone blind.
> And what did you do?"
> My Lord will say,
> "As you traveled along the King's highway?"

Christ Calls Us To Care

Juliette Fowler Homes in Dallas is a home for the aged and offers a comprehensive program for children, youth and family services. They have a very unique motto: "Caring is the thing we do best." It is an excellent description of what it means to be a Christian.

Caring is what Jesus was talking about when he commanded, "Love one another as I have loved you." The greatest definition of love I have ever heard is this: "Love is the desire to give oneself in affirming the well-being of another."

Jesus not only talked about loving, he demonstrated it when he took little children up in his arms and blessed them, when he stopped and talked with a woman beside a well in Samaria, when he fed 5,000 hungry people, when he said to an adulteress, "Neither do I condemn you, go your way and sin no more," when he said to a dying thief, "Today you will be with me in paradise." That is what he calls us to do.

In the early days of my ministry, the late Ernest Fremont Tittle was my ideal. He was a great preacher, but I learned later in my life that the members of his church in Evanston, Illinois looked on him more as their beloved pastor.

Once a leading Illinois industrialist shared what Dr. Tittle meant to him. He said, "When my wife died, my whole world caved in. In a daze I left the hospital and started walking faster and faster through the night along the shores of Lake Michigan.

"For hours I walked, my darkness as thick as the black night around me. Every time I looked back, there was Dr. Tittle just a little way behind me, following. All night I walked, and all night he followed. Finally, as the dawn was breaking over the lake, I stopped. Dr. Tittle came up, placed his hand on my arm and said, 'Let's go somewhere and get some breakfast.'"

> Isn't it strange that princes and kings
> And clowns that caper in sawdust rings,
> And common people like you and me
> Are builders for eternity?
> Each is given a bag of tools,
> A shapeless mass, and a book of rules;
> And each must make, ere life is flown,
> A stumbling block or a steppingstone.

Wait A Minute!

Throughout the book of Psalms we are admonished, "Wait upon the Lord." Isaiah tells us that, "They who wait upon the Lord shall renew their strength, they shall mount up with wings like eagles, they shall run and not be weary, they shall walk and not faint," but hearing and heeding are two different matters. How do we learn to wait instead of rushing headlong into hurry and worry?

James Truslow Adams once made this suggestion: "Perhaps it would be a good idea, fantastic as it sounds, to muffle every telephone, stop every motor, and halt all activity for an hour some day to give people a chance to ponder for a few minutes on what it is all about; why they are living, and what they really want." That first, I think. If we would wait on the Lord we must learn to pause. Pausing can make a big difference.

To pray is to wait upon the Lord. Alfred Lord Tennyson in one of his poems tells us "More things are wrought by prayer than this world dreams of."

People who pray testify to this truth. Through your prayers and mine God accomplishes that which all of our anxiety and worry can never accomplish.

To practice patience is to wait upon the Lord. Patience is needed every day of our lives, whether it is painting a picture, rearing a son or daughter, building a happy marriage, or helping to bring peace to a troubled world.

Finally, if you would wait upon the Lord, learn to persevere. Jacob Reis was a social reformer who over a lifetime cleared the slums of New York. He often said that discouragement was his biggest obstacle.

He made it a practice when things were going from bad to worse to go to the masonry and watch the stonecutters at work. Sometimes a worker would strike as many as one hundred blows with no results.

Then with the one hundredth and one blow the stone would split in two. Then Jacob Reis would remind himself that it was not the final blow that did the job, but all of the hundred blows before it.

Wait upon the Lord as you pause, as you pray, as you practice patience. And you shall renew your strength, you shall mount up with wings like eagles, you shall run and not be weary, you shall walk and not faint.

May 4   **I Peter 5: 5**
God Just Ran Out Of Color

Robert Brough, in his poem, *The Tent Makers*, has written:

> Of all the lunacies earth can boast
> The one that must please the devil the most
> Is pride reduced to whimsical terms
> Of causing the slugs to despise the worms!

God has made of one flesh all men to dwell on the face of the earth, but we refuse to live as brothers. Marcus Bach tells about visiting Stanley Reser, a friend of his who lived on the island of Haiti. Stanley had lived on the island among the native people for over thirty years. He spoke Creole fluently and was an authority on the music, song and folklore of the Haitian peasants. Everyone respected and loved him.

It was a sultry afternoon. As the two men walked down one of the winding streets, they became aware that a gang of hostile blacks who did not know Stanley was trailing them. They were swearing and shouting in Creole, "You dirty whites!"

Stanley whispered to Marcus, "Don't look around; just keep walking," but they were getting closer and closer, and their voices grew louder and angrier. There were six of them in all, and one giant of a man who seemed to be the leader had a jagged scar across his right cheek.

Suddenly Stanley stopped, spun around and faced their antagonists. Calmly he raised his hand and spoke in Creole. His words stopped the gang dead in their tracks. The big fellow stepped back and fell on his knees, clasping his hands together in an attitude of prayer.

As the two friends turned and walked away, Marcus asked in amazement, "Stanley, what in the world did you say to them?" Stanley smiled, "I said to them, 'Why do you taunt me by calling me white? Can I help it if God ran out of color before he got around to making me?'"

Humility and a sense of humor had saved the day and won the battle. These are qualities all of us can use in the midst of life's emergencies. In the book of Proverbs are to be found these words: "Pride goes before destruction, and a haughty spirit before a fall."

The Apostle Peter advises: "Clothe yourself with humility, for God opposes the proud but gives grace to the humble."

I Would Be True

Growing up in our youth group, one of my favorite hymns was Howard Walter's "I Would Be True." The second verse has these words:

> I would be friend of all—the foe, the friendless;
> I would be giving and forget the gift;
> I would be humble, for I know my weakness;
> I would look up, and laugh and love and lift.

Having finished assembling the stereo amplifier and tuner kit he had received for his birthday, he turned it on. Nothing happened. He double-checked; everything was OK. Then he spotted the problem—it wasn't plugged in! Life, to be lived at its highest and best, needs the power that God alone can give. Look up!

Reader's Digest affirms that laughter is the best medicine. An American visiting in Russia wrote home, "I am struck by the absence of laughter and joy in their lives." Laughter is needed in our world. It can afford new outlook, hope and courage.

"A new commandment I give you," said Jesus, "that you love one another." And Paul wrote, "Three things last forever, faith, hope and love, and the greatest of these is love." Indeed, love is the Christian's secret weapon. It never fails.

Finally, "God has not put us here to dream, to drift; there is work to be done and loads to lift." Each of us has one life to live, one life to give. In Christian service to others we find the key to happiness.

Christ showed us the way. His was the upward look. He taught us to pray, "Our Father who art in heaven," and his promise was, "You shall receive power from on high." His life was filled with joy and laughter. Even as he was facing death on the cross, he said to his disciples, "Be of good cheer. I have overcome the world." He died for you and me, and God's Word tells us greater love has no man than this. His life was a life of endless service. He knew what it meant to lift. The greatest portrait of his life is found in the Gospel of John when, knowing that he came from God and was returning to God, he girded himself with a towel and washed the disciple's feet.

Great words for living, these! If you would follow in the Master's footsteps let them be your guide: "Look up, and laugh, and love, and lift!"

Isaiah 41:6

Builders Together

This is the church; this is the steeple;
Open the door and see all the people.

Do you remember that little finger game you learned as a kindergartner in Sunday school? It teaches a very valuable lesson:

The church is not a building.
The church is not a steeple.
The church is not a resting place.
The church is people!

It happened years ago in Vacation Church School. Everything had gone exceptionally well. Everyone was having fun and enjoying the study.

That morning the director brought a new student to the primary department. "Boys and girls," she said, "this is Davy." Looking up, they all saw it—his sleeve was pinned up. His left arm was missing. The teacher gave him a welcoming smile, "Come in, Davy."

She found him a seat as the children watched. Then a fear swept over her—a fear that someone in the class might say something about his handicap that would hurt his feelings. If she could but warn them! She just hoped no one would say anything.

Almost before she knew it class time was drawing to a close. Looking at her watch, she breathed a sigh of relief. Everything was going to be all right. "Come, children," she said, "Let's put up all of our things. It is time for our closing." Soon the room was cleaned up, and everything had been put away.

"Now, is everyone ready? Good, let's make our churches." The hands of the children went up as she continued to lead them, "Is everyone ready? All together, 'This is the church, this is the steeple—'". Her voice trailed off, and then stopped as stark terror gripped her.

She had done the very thing she had feared the children would do! There was no way she could go back and undo it. She just stood there not knowing what to do or what to say.

Then it happened. The little girl sitting next to him reached across with her left hand and put it against his right hand and said, "Davy, let's build our church together!"

Yes, You Can! God Will Help You!

A. J. Cronin in his day was one of the greatest medical minds in the British nation and a wonderful writer. No doubt, many of you have read some of his inspiring novels such as *The Citadel, The Keys Of The Kingdom,* and *Hatter's Castle.* He went off to medical school in London wanting to be a surgeon, but the professor, under whom he studied, took a dislike to him. He would glare at him and say sarcastically, "You will never make a surgeon!" By semester end, he believed the professor.

When he finished interning he took a job as a doctor in a small town in the western highlands of Scotland, but he couldn't forget the words of the professor. They haunted him. Speaking later of the experience, he said bitterly, "I was a pill peddler. I never dared to attempt surgery. I sent all of the serious cases to Edinburgh and Glasgow."

Then one cold winter day as the minister's son was walking under an ice-laden tree, a large branch broke and came crashing down on him. At the scene Dr. Cronin discovered that he was paralyzed from his waist down.

He told the father, "I'm afraid nothing can be done. Surgery is the only hope and all of the roads are blocked." "Then you will have to do it," the father said. Dr. Cronin tried to explain, "This is a dangerous operation, and I can't do surgery." The father smiled with confidence, "Yes, you can! God will help you."

The kitchen table was covered with a sheet, the minister's son was placed on it, the anesthetic was administered, and the young doctor set to work. As he picked up the scalpel, he seemed to hear the words of the professor, "You will never make a surgeon!" He paused and stepped back. Over that voice he heard another. It was the voice of the minister, "Yes you can; God will help you."

Hours later, the surgery had been successfully completed, and he knew that the boy would walk and run again. It was then that he realized he had been repeating over and over Philippians 4: 13: "I can do all things through Christ who strengthens me." Dr. Cronin went on to become an outstanding surgeon and a professor of surgery at the school where he almost flunked out. He received so many honors. He was knighted by the queen and became a great Christian writer, and it was all due to the words of that father—words that gave him courage and faith: "Yes, you can! God will help you!"

Flowers Or Weeds?

Once upon a time there lived a certain king who loved the subjects of his kingdom and was very sad because they were constantly criticizing and finding fault with one another.

One day he summoned them all together. Then calling a courier, he said to him, "Ride throughout the kingdom and gather all of the different kinds of flowers you can find. In a fortnight, come back and bring them to me."

When the courier had ridden away, the king called a second courier and said, "Ride throughout the kingdom and gather all the different kinds of weeds you can find. In a fortnight, come back and bring them to me."

As he rode forth, the first courier was amazed. There were beautiful flowers everywhere. He gathered flower after flower. There was no end to the many varieties, and their beauty was beyond belief.

Meanwhile, the second courier, too, was amazed. There were weeds, thorns, and thistles everywhere. He gathered one kind after another. There seemed to be no limit. At the end of the fortnight, the couriers returned. All the people of the kingdom had assembled in the courtyard of the palace. When the first courier had displayed his beautiful collection of flowers, the king asked, "Did you find any weeds?" The courier replied, "I don't recall seeing any; I was looking for flowers." Then the second courier displayed his collection of weeds. "Did you find any flowers?" the king asked. "No, my king," he replied, "I saw no flowers. I was looking for weeds."

Then the king spoke to the citizens of his kingdom: "So it is with our lives. We find in others that for which we seek. If we look for flowers, we find flowers. If we look for weeds, we find weeds." The lesson was not forgotten. From that day on, the kingdom was filled with happy, loving subjects looking for and finding the best in the lives of others.

Paul gave wise counsel when he wrote, "Whatever is true, whatever is honorable, whatever is just, whatever is pure, whatever is lovely, whatever is gracious, if there is any excellence, if there is anything worthy of praise, think about these things." When you and I look at the lives of others, what do we see?

Crippled Beggars

You will find the story in the New Testament in chapter three of the book of Acts. It happened at the gate of the temple where a man lame from birth lay on a pallet. Four friends, as they did every day, had just brought him there to beg from those coming to worship.

His heart was filled with gratitude for his friends, but suddenly without warning gratitude turned to bitterness. It was not that he didn't appreciate his friends, without them he would starve. It was just that after they had done all they could he was still a cripple.

Two men were coming toward him. From habit he lifted his tin cup and called out, "Alms." One of them said, "I have no money." He was ready to turn away, but there was something different about these men. They were still standing over him, and the one who had spoken continued, "But I will give what I have. In the name of Jesus of Nazareth rise up and walk!" Then reaching down he took him by the hand and lifted him to his feet.

Joy filled the beggar's heart. For the first time in his life he was able to stand and walk. Peter and John had done something far more than help keep him alive. They had changed and transformed his entire life.

It is this change that all mankind needs. When we are completely honest with ourselves we know that we, too, are cripples. In the name of Jesus Christ we could walk, but pride holds us back. We spend the days of our years pretending, trying to make others believe that we are not in the crippled class.

One night there came to Jesus a religious leader named Nicodemus. Here was a good man who could have helped. Yet, Jesus said to him, "No one can see the kingdom of God unless he is born again." In other words if one isn't born of God it doesn't matter how good he is. Goodness alleviates; only the power of God can save.

It begs the question: Have you and I ever made a total commitment of our lives to God, all that we are and have?

That's what being a Christian means, and until this is true of your life and mine, we are not really Christian at all. Remember, in our own strength we are cripples begging before the gate of the temple of life, crippled by self-will, self love, and self-pleasing, but in the name of Jesus of Nazareth we can rise up—and walk!

A Little Child Shall Lead Them

One day Jesus was praying and when he ceased, one of his disciples said to him, "Lord, teach us to pray." This has been the desire of Jesus' followers down through the ages.

A certain father gained great insight into prayer when his little boy, kneeling beside his bed at the close of day, prayed, "O God, help us to be good and to help other people. Amen."

No one could have prayed a better prayer. The youngster didn't pray, "Make us;" he prayed, "Help us." Prayer isn't so much getting God to do things for us as it is his enabling us to do things for ourselves.

He didn't pray, "Help me;" he prayed, "Help us." He was following the example set by the Master who taught us to pray, "Our Father," not "My Father, Give us this day our daily bread," not "Give me this day, my daily bread."

He prayed for help to be good. Goodness is the great need of every life, don't you think? When things are right on the inside, they will be right on the outside.

The lad didn't petition God to help others. He prayed, "Help us to help others." For our prayers to be effective, our work must match our words. It is mockery to pray for the aged and lonely without visiting them.

It is a sham to pray for those who are hungry and cold unless we are willing to share our food and clothing. Prayers for missions are meaningless unless they are matched with our money which makes it all possible. Prayer should never be a lazy substitute for thought and action.

In the book of Acts, Luke tells of the imprisonment of Peter and the prayers of the church for his release. During the night an angel appeared in the cell where Peter was sleeping, chained between two Roman soldiers.

"Get up quickly," the angel said, and the chains fell from Peter's wrists. Then the angel said, "Dress yourself, and put on your sandals." It teaches us two things about prayer we should never forget. First, God's help is always available in our darkest hours of need. Second, God will never do for us what we are able to do for ourselves.

Pay It Forward!

They are the words of Jesus. "Give and it will be given to you; good measure, pressed down, shaken together and running over."

It was bitterly cold and her car was stranded. A car pulled up and a man got out. She was scared. "Ma'am, I'll help. Why don't you wait in the car where it is warm? By the way, my name is Bryan Anderson."

It was only a flat tire. He crawled under the car in the mud to place the jack. As he worked, she rolled down the window, "I'm from St. Louis, just passing through. I can't thank you enough for coming to my aid."

At last the tire was changed. He stood up; his clothes were wet and muddy and he was exhausted. "What do I owe you," she asked. Any amount would be fine with her. She had been imagining all the awful things that could have happened to her if he had not stopped.

He never thought about being paid. This was helping someone in need. "Tell you what," he said, "The next time you see someone in need, help them and think of me." He waited as she drove off. It had been a long, cold and depressing day, but he felt good as he headed home.

Down the road the woman spotted a small café. She would stop and grab a bite to eat before driving home. The waitress gave her a sweet smile and brought a towel to dry her hair. She noticed that she was about eight months pregnant and was tired. How could anyone who had been on their feet all day be smiling? She remembered Bryan.

She finished eating and paid with a hundred dollar bill. The waitress hurried to get change, but when she returned the old lady was gone. There were tears in her eyes as she read the handwritten note: "You don't owe me anything. I have been there. Somebody helped me out the way I am helping you. If you want to pay me back, help someone in need and think of me." Under the napkin were four more $100 bills.

Soon the long day was over and she was home thinking about the money and what the lady had written. How could she have known how much she and her husband needed it? With the baby due next month, it was going to be hard.

She knew how worried her husband was as he lay sleeping next to her. She gave him a soft kiss on the forehead and whispered, "Everything is going to be all right. I love you, Bryan Anderson."

You're Never Too Young Or Too Old

During the Second World War Frank Loessar wrote a popular song entitled *They're Either Too Young Or Too Old*. It had to do with a GI who was concerned about the girl he loved and the competition back home. In the song she assures him he has nothing to worry about—"What's good is in the army; what's not will never harm me." She describes them as "either gray or grassy green," and concludes "I'm yours alone to have and to hold; they're either too young or too old."

I want to change the lyrics just a little to say, "You're never too young or too old." How true this is when it comes to living a worthwhile life. When it comes to achieving goals of value and making a contribution to the world in which we live, we're never too young or too old.

Byron, Keats and Shelley died at 25, 30, and 36, respectively. Yet, what great poetry they left to our world. Michelangelo sculpted his statue, *The Boy David* and painted the *Madonna and Child* when he was 26. William Shakespeare wrote ten of his greatest dramas before he was 32. Cyrus McCormick invented the reaper at the age of 22.

Jesus began preparing for his life's work at the age of 12 in the Temple. He began his ministry at 30 and it lasted for three short years. But no one has affected the life of mankind as much as has that "One Solitary Life." You're never too young.

Benjamin Franklin helped write the Declaration of Independence when he was 70 and served as a member of the Constitutional Convention at the age of 81. Golda Mier became the Prime Minister of Israel at 71 and served until she was 76. Grandma Moses lived to be 101. She took up painting when she was 78.

The legendary head coach at Penn State, Joe Paterno, is past 80. Recently he and his Nittany Lions won the Big Ten Conference. And we could go on and on. Avery Brundage headed up the Olympic Games until he was 85 and Col. Sanders began his fried chicken enterprise after he was 66. You're never too old.

Look and you will find the pages of history filled with the names of both young and old who have met life's challenges triumphantly. God created each of us for a purpose. He calls us to give of our best and to make our lives count for good. And it is never too early or too late to begin. It stands eternally true—you are never too young; you are never too old.

Thinking Can Make It So

The Happy Hypocrite by Max Beerbohm is the story of Lord George Hell who everyone agreed was one of the most wicked men who ever lived. His drinking, gambling and corrupt living made him a source of constant grief to his family and an embarrassment to all who knew him.

One evening at the theatre in London he saw on the stage a beautiful young actress, Miss Jenny Mere, and fell in love with her. That very evening he declared his love and asked her to be his bride, but she declined. Heartbroken, he cried, "My wealth, my rank, my love, my total devotion, I lay them at your feet. I will wait for you a year, a decade, if you but bid me hope!" Jenny said, "My love must be freely given, and I could give it only to a man with an honest and open face."

Confused, Lord George spent the night wandering the streets heartbroken. In the morning he stumbled upon a mask maker's shop. He bought a saint's face mask, custom made to bear the mark of true love and it was applied to his face with care. With the disguise, Lord George won the heart of his beloved and they were married.

Lord George made a total moral conversion. He returned all of his ill-gotten wealth, donated all of his excess wealth to those in need and was kind and helpful to everyone. He and Jenny bought a woodman's cottage and there lived a quiet and happy life together.

Then one day a strange woman of the streets who knew his secret came to their home. She had seen him enter and leave the mask maker's shop. There in the presence of Jenny she ripped the mask from his face. As she did, she stepped back in disbelief. Lord George's face no longer bore the ugly lines of his former self, reflecting his sinful and selfish ways. His countenance had taken on the features of the mask, reflecting goodness, purity and love.

Lord George fell at Jenny's feet and begged her to forgive him for deceiving her. "I don't understand," she said, "Why did you cover your face with a mask? You are far more handsome than the mask." It was true. The hard cruel lines were gone. Lord George with changed thoughts and deeds had changed his life—and his face!

Paul was talking about such changes, changes you and I can make in our lives, when he wrote, "Whatever is true, whatever is honorable, whatever is just, whatever is pure, whatever is lovely . . . think on these things."

II Corinthians 12:9
You Never Walk Alone

In her book, *How Can I Find You, God?* Marjorie Holmes tells the story of Barbie Hertel. Barbie underwent operation after operation that involved intense pain and suffering. The letters Barbie wrote to her family and friends are epics of faith and courage.

When she was fifteen she wrote: "In my room I prayed, 'God, forgive my anger at you and my discouragement. I know it's wrong, but I'm desperate. I give up fighting AGAINST having it, and fighting with you OVER it. I don't understand it, but I accept it.'"

At sixteen, after unsuccessful surgery, she wrote: "I was disappointed that the surgery failed, and angry that I was born that way with no hope of ever changing it. But finally I was able to pray, 'God grant me the serenity to accept the things I cannot change, the courage to change the things I can, and the wisdom to know the difference.'"

Barbie was almost nineteen when she wrote her final letter. She had hoped to attend college but now realized that God might have other plans for her. The letter read: "I am not afraid to die. If that is his ministry for me, then I am willing . . . I am totally, completely his to do with as he chooses."

Such courage as this in the face of pain and suffering, the impact of such gallantry, cannot be measured. But it is into all hearts like this that God can pour courage and faith beyond human imagination. And with God beside us to guide us, we are sufficient for anything; we are more than conquerors.

It was Helen Howland Prommel who wrote:

> I walked alone—or I thought I did—
> The day was dark, the sun was hid,
> A wild wind lashed against the shore
> And beat against my face and tore
> At coat and dress. The lightening split
> The day apart and frightened it
> And frightened me till I cried out—
> But rude wind carried off my shout—
> And then I heard a Voice I knew
> That said, "Have faith, I walk with you."
> And though the storm raged as before,
> I walked with faith and peace once more.

Of Such Is The Kingdom

Eight-year-old Danny Dutton, given a homework assignment to explain God, wrote the following:

"One of God's main jobs is making people. He doesn't make grownups, just babies. I think because they are smaller and easier to make. That way, he doesn't have to take up his valuable time teaching them to talk and walk. He can just leave that to mothers and fathers.

"God's second most important job is listening to prayers. An awful lot of this goes on, since some people, like preachers, pray at times beside bedtime. God doesn't have time to listen to the radio or TV because of this. Because he hears everything, there must be a terrible lot of noise in his ears, unless he has thought of a way to turn it off.

"God sees everything, hears everything and is everywhere. This keeps him pretty busy, so you shouldn't waste his time by going over your mom and dad's head asking for something they said you couldn't have.

"Jesus is God's Son. He did all the hard work while he was here on earth, like walking on water and performing miracles and trying to teach the people who didn't want to learn about God. They finally got tired of him preaching to them and crucified him, but he was good and kind and told his father they didn't know what they were doing and to forgive them and God said O.K.

"His dad (God) appreciated all he had done, so he told him he didn't have to go out on the road anymore. He could stay in heaven. Now he helps his dad out by listening to prayers and seeing which things God needs to take care of and which ones he can take care of himself without having to bother God. Like a secretary, only more important.

"You should always go to church on Sunday. It makes God happy, and if there's anybody you want to make happy, it's God!

"If you don't believe in God, besides being an atheist, you will be lonely, because your parents can't go to camp with you, but God can. It is good to know He's around when you're scared in the dark or when you can't swim and big kids throw you into real deep water.

"But you shouldn't just always think of what God can do for you. I figure God put me here and he can take me back anytime he pleases.

"And that's why I believe in God."

Amidst The Storm

On December 18, 1944 just north of Luzon a three hundred foot warship made ready for heavy weather. The hatches were fastened down and the gear secured. Whipped by howling winds, the rain came down in torrents, and giant waves rolled over the ship as the typhoon rushed forward.

In the wheelhouse the captain studied the situation, deciding what to do next. Even he became alarmed when his ship rolled seventy degrees to the starboard and righted itself.

How do you keep a vessel afloat against such odds? The captain was a master seaman. First, he reduced the speed. Then, keeping the propellers going and using the rudder as a guide, he headed the ship straight into the storm.

On board, a young seaman, Ernest Miller, watched the whole affair with keen interest. He learned a lot that day about ships and storms that he never forgot, and he later decided that the lessons applied not only to ships but also to the voyage of life.

Perhaps the greatest lesson he learned was this: Heading into the storm the ship is safe. Turned from it, the ship is doomed. When the storm heaved the ship around and beat broadside against the hull it almost capsized as two sister ships did.

Looking back on the experience later he wrote, "The voyage of life is like that, and the storms of life can be overcome in the same way. First of all, the storms of life must be faced if we are to cope with them. Half the battle is sizing up our problems and meeting them objectively. When we close our eyes, hoping that somehow they will go away, we are in big trouble. It is then that we capsize.

Reducing speed, that is important too. Slowing down gives us a chance to think clearly and to make wise decisions based on sound judgment.

Keep the propellers going—that steady push from within, faith in the goodness and love of God and confidence in his power to keep, makes all the difference in the world.

Finally, remember the rudder of prayer. At the height of the storm, it is prayer that keeps us steady. It is prayer that keeps us facing into the winds of adversity until they pass.

Armed With Blanks!

He had been assigned to a battleship moored in Pearl Harbor. Saturday night he and some shipmates were looking for something to do. Having grown up in the church they decided to go to a church social. It was a wonderful affair. There were cookies and punch, lovely young ladies, and new friends to meet.

As the evening closed, they formed a circle. The pastor said, "We are going to go around the circle. Share your favorite Bible verse." The young man went cold. He had gone to Sunday school and church all his life, but he couldn't think of a single verse. Racking his brain, he thought of John 3: 16. "God so loved the world—something."

But to his dismay the fellow next to him chose John 3: 16. "For God so loved the world that he gave his only Son, that whoever believes in him should not perish but have eternal life." Shamefaced, he mumbled to the person next to him, "I'm sorry; you go on!"

Back aboard ship part of him was saying, "I've got to do better than that next time." Another part was saying, "I'm going to stay away from there. I don't want to go through that ever again."

The next morning, December 7, a little before 8:00 a.m., bombs started dropping. With all the others he rushed on deck. It was being strafed by Japanese warplanes. Every ship at Pearl Harbor was fighting for its life. He went running to his assigned gun, pointed it and started firing.

But America was at peace. The day before they had been having training exercises so he was armed with nothing but blanks. Standing there amidst the enemy's withering fire he realized this was the most useless and ridiculous thing he had ever done in all his life.

In that moment a voice rose up inside him, "This is your whole life. An enemy is attacking and spiritually you are armed with nothing but blanks!" and there on that burning deck he made a vow, "Lord, if I get out of this alive, I will grow in God's Word. Never again will I meet the enemy with empty hands."

What about you? Are you armed for spiritual warfare? Memorizing one scripture verse a week, at the end of a year you will have at your command fifty-two verses. Most Christians I know can't quote half that many. Why not resolve to begin today? When your hour of crisis comes, be armed; don't be caught with nothing but blanks!

God's Miracle Drugs

Some years ago there was an article in *Reader's Digest* that I have never forgotten. It was entitled, *Our Greatest Miracle Drug.* It was the story of aspirin—the most widely used drug in the world.

Today we have many "miracle drugs" —penicillin, tetracycline, diazepam, erythromycin and many more. They have virtually eliminated many formerly fatal diseases, but no discovery in the field of medicine has equaled the discovery of aspirin.

One of the great mysteries of aspirin is its ability to reduce fever without affecting normal temperature. When taken for a fever, the temperature is quickly reduced. When it is taken for a headache, the headache is relieved, but the temperature remains constant.

But physical illnesses are minor when compared with those that plague minds and spirits. Anxiety, loneliness, hatred, fear and doubt are the great killers of our time, and the field of medicine knows no cures for these.

In Shakespeare's play, you remember, Macbeth pleads with his wife's physician, "Canst thou not minister to a mind diseased ... that perilous stuff which weighs upon the heart?", but the doctor is helpless. He answers, "Therein the patient must minister to himself." Human help falls short.

We cannot cure ourselves, but what man cannot do, God can. God has "miracle drugs" of his own for healing sin-sick souls. Forgiveness is one of God's miracle drugs. Over and over in the gospels we hear Jesus saying to those who are sick, "Your sins are forgiven."

A famous American physician has said, "Practically all of the patients in our mental hospitals could go home tomorrow if they knew they were forgiven!", and Christ can speak the miraculous words, "Go, and sin no more."

The greatest miracle drug is God himself in our lives. In pride we diagnose our need and prescribe various remedies, but in our saner moments, we know that our deepest need is not what God can give but the gift of God himself.

That gift was given some 2000 years ago when Christ was born in Bethlehem. If we will but ask, that gift can be ours.

Our Sure Guide

Some years ago a young couple packed up their belongings and moved to a lonely spot in the Maine woods. Later, the wife, Louise Dickinson Rich, wrote about their experiences in her book, *We Took to the Woods*. It is highly reminiscent of Henry David Thoreau's *Walden*.

One day the author went for a hike over the mountain to B Pond. It was not very far and normally the trail was well marked. However, a recent windstorm had blown trees down across the path and at times it was difficult to know for sure where it was. When she started back the ranger asked if she had brought a compass. He said, "If you have to use it, remember: The compass is always right."

She knew the way perfectly. There was no way she could get lost—but she did! It was a terrifying ordeal. When she finally looked at the compass, she was shocked. She knew that the river was somewhere to her left, but the compass said it was to the right.

She was on the verge of going to the left when she remembered the ranger's warning: "The compass is always right." Against her deep feelings, she went with the compass. After what seemed an eternity, she heard the flowing river. It wasn't where she knew it should have been, but it was right where the compass said it would be.

You know, our lives are like that. Right paths are not always plain to see but God is there to guide us, and we can depend on him to steer us in the right direction. In the book of Deuteronomy are to be found these words: "The eternal God is your dwelling place, and underneath are the everlasting arms." The writer is saying, "Remember, no matter what happens, you can count on God."

I know that there are times when we do not think so. When the cause of evil prospers and everything wicked seems to succeed, it is really confusing, but we must realize that many times appearances are deceiving.

So often we must look beyond what seems to be in order to find the truth. Moods and fancies simply cannot be trusted. Faith in God's direction is our sure guide.

Louise Rich trusted her compass that was dependent on God's universal law, and it guided her aright. Even so, God waits to guide your life and mine.

Taking Inventory

When I was a boy *Liberty* was a magazine second only to *The Saturday Evening Post* in popularity. It carried the work of many of the most important and influential writers of the time. One of its unique features I vividly remember was a "reading time" printed alongside each article.

There is one short story from *Liberty* that over the years I have never forgotten. It was about two navy men by the names of Tompkins and Jacklin. The destroyer vessel they were on was struck by a thorium bomb, and all aboard were killed except Tompkins. His body was blown to bits, but his soul was blown into the body of his buddy, Jacklin.

Days later he was picked up by a passing freighter and returned to the United States. He tried to explain what had happened to him, but no one would believe such an outlandish story. There was nothing to do but take over Jacklin's life.

As he got into the role of being his buddy Jacklin, he made a number of discoveries. Jacklin's business dealings were questionable. The company was doing well; no need for shady dealings. Tompkins put a stop to it. He discovered that Jacklin was having affairs with a number of women. He took one look at his wife, decided Jacklin was a fool and became faithful.

An annual physical checkup with his physician indicated some serious health problems. Jacklin had been burning the candle at both ends and was on the verge of becoming an alcoholic. He took control, slowed his pace, delegated some of the workload to his staff, cut out the heavy drinking and made some other changes—personal, business and social. In time, the changes revolutionized his life completely.

I know. It was just a science fiction story, but you know, one can't help being fascinated. Think about it! If someone else should come in and take over your life, what changes do you suppose that person would make?

And if there are changes that another would make in your life, why don't you make them? You see, you know about your life and the changes that need to be made more than anyone else could ever know.

Why don't you and I take an inventory of our lives, throw out what needs to be thrown out and add whatever Christ would have us add? I think it might make a world of difference for me. What about you?

The Lady in Red

In her little book, *Heaven In My Hand,* Alice Lee Humphrey tells about her school children and their day-to-day living in the classroom. They move across the pages one by one with light skipping steps. One of the most memorable is Billy. Listen as she reminisces about him.

"Today's tornado was two miles away, but its rumble brought to mind the big twister of years ago, and I remembered Billy, a born clown, whose days were filled with antics. On the day of the storm I said to the children, 'Let's sing until the cloud passes.'

"Billy, ever alert, spied a tear on the cheek of his best friend. The next minute, moving into the aisle, he caught the fearful one. Concealing his own fear, he began singing, 'Oh, the Lady in Red,' and as the buildings all around us were blown away, Billy sang louder and louder.

"In my reverie, I felt a touch on my shoulder by a young soldier. He had come with news of Billy, a captain in the breakthrough from Anzio to Rome. On the beachhead they had waited, bodies tense and lips dry. Before them lay a level of wasteland, unprotected, which they must cross.

"High above them they saw the camouflaged enemy guns. Just as the signal was given, Billy came to the rescue. With a swagger of defiance, he started toward the gunfire singing the hit tune, 'Oh, the Lady in Red.' Soon they were all singing, racing for the foothills which Billy never reached.

"The young soldier paused, choked with emotion. 'It was a great day when we entered Rome,' he said, 'If only Billy could have been there!' I wiped my eyes. 'You would have thought Billy was a Fire-Eater,' I said, 'but I knew better. Even at six he put on such an act. Did you happen to see him on the day of the tornado as he drew a terror-stricken youngster to his side?' The soldier managed a smile, 'I was that little boy!'

"I looked at the young soldier. Save for the uniform and the medals he might still be my first grade pupil, but his eyes were gazing far away, seeing strange and terrible things I can never hope to understand.

"As for me, my thoughts went not beyond the classroom. I saw a little boy named Billy dancing in the aisle with his frightened little friend singing, 'Oh, the Lady in Red.'"

I Thessalonians 5: 11

Great Expectations

In the Broadway musical, *Man of La Mancha*, Don Quixote, an honest and affable old man, sets out to do battle with evil. With a battered and rusty suit of armor, he goes forth as a medieval knight to right the wrongs of the world. At the rundown inn where mule traders stay, Don Quixote greets the slovenly innkeeper as "lord of the manor" and requests that he knight him in proper fashion.

He chooses to honor the inn's kitchen maid with the glory of his deeds. He addresses her as Dulcinea. She protests that she is not Dulcinea but Aldonza, used and abused by hundreds of men, but Don Quixote will have none of it. To him she is the beautiful Dulcinea, and he requests a token of her purity to take into battle with the forces of evil. This process of exalting the commonplace and lifting up the potential in the lives of those he meets continues throughout his adventures.

At long last, back home and dying, Don Quixote is again in his right mind. No longer is he under the illusion that he is a knight. Then in the most moving scene of the play, the people whose lives he has touched gather at his bedside and beg him not to change. Their lives have been transformed and made new through the power of his great expectations.

It is always so, I think. All of us are helped, not by those who point out our faults and failures—we know about them more than anybody else—but by those who, despite our shortcomings, still love and believe in us. The Apostle Paul wrote, "The love of Christ constrains us"—not the condemnation of Christ, not the judgment of Christ, but the love of Christ which sees in us all that we are capable of becoming.

For Christ, the possibility for good is far greater than the actuality of evil. Of weak, sinful man, he went so far as to say, "Be perfect even as your Father in heaven is perfect." An amazing affirmation!

What about you, what do you see when you look at others—your children, your wife, your husband, your friends, your neighbors— problems or possibilities?

Christ has not called us to underscore people's sins and failures; the Holy Spirit does that. He has given us the ministry of affirmation, reminding all of those we meet that they are of infinite worth in the eyes of God. It is as we fulfill this ministry that people behold the love and grace of God.

The Praying Hands

No doubt you have seen *The Praying Hands* in a painting on someone's wall or a plaque on a bedside stand, but have you heard the story of friendship behind this work of art?

Albrecht Durer was the son of a goldsmith in Nuremberg, Germany. He always wanted to draw and paint, but his family couldn't afford lessons. The only solution was for him to leave home and to work and study at the same time.

He found a friend who wanted to become an artist and they decided to help one another, but the struggle to earn a living and pay for lessons was too much. Finally, his friend made a suggestion. "As it is," he said, "we are neither earning a living nor mastering our art, but one of us could make a living for us both while the other continues to study. Then when the paintings begin to sell, the one who has worked may have his chance. You are the younger and have the greater talent, and since I already have a job in the restaurant I will be the first to work.

Albrecht wanted his friend to study first but finally agreed. His friend continued to work, washing dishes and scrubbing floors. The work was menial and hard, but he was happy helping his friend and looking forward to the time when he would take up palette and brush again.

The day came when Albrecht sold his first work, a beautiful woodcarving. The money would pay for food and lodging for a long time. "Now," he said, "I will be the bread winner, and you shall return to your art."

But during those long days of toil, hard work had so stiffened his hands and twisted his fingers he could no longer use a brush with an artist's skill. His dream was gone forever. Albrecht was heartbroken. He could take care of his friend, but the skill of his hands was beyond his power to replace.

One day Albrecht returned to his room unexpectedly and found his friend kneeling in prayer. As he stood silently beholding the toil-worn hands folded in reverence, he received an inspiration. "I can't give back the lost skill of those hands," he thought, "but I will show the world the love and gratitude I have in my heart for his noble sacrifice. I will paint his hands as they are now, folded in prayer, and when people look at the picture they will remember with love and devotion all hands that toil for others."

Practicing The Presence

In his little book, *Practicing The Presence of God*, Brother Lawrence said that God was as real to him in the kitchen as he scrubbed the pots and pans as during the Holy Communion. It can be so for you and me.

Dr. Leslie Weatherhead has written, "Christianity is the acceptance of the friendship of Jesus." That is what the early followers of Jesus did, and living in his presence found their lives transformed and changed.

How can we go about accepting the gift of Jesus' friendship? Think how a little child accepts it. When she kneels to say her prayers at the close of day she imagines someone tall and smiling in a white robe is there, perhaps with a hand on her head.

With her imagination she accepts the gift, and over the years it becomes a tremendous reality. Countless thousands have found it to be so. Faith is imagination in long trousers, imagination grown up.

F. W. Boreham told about an old Scotsman, very ill, whose minister came to visit him. As the minister sat down near the bedside, he noticed on the other side of the bed another chair placed at such an angle as to suggest that a visitor had just left.

Glancing at it, he said, "Well, Donald, I see you have had a previous visitor." The Scotsman looked up in surprise, so the minister pointed to the chair. "Ah," said the old man, "I'll tell you about the chair. Years ago, I found it hard for me to pray. I was so tired at the end of the day I fell asleep on my knees, and even when I was able to keep awake I couldn't keep my mind from wandering.

"I was so worried about it I went and talked with my minister about it. He told me not to worry about kneeling. 'Just sit down and put a chair opposite you. Imagine that Jesus is in it and talk to him as you would to a friend.' I have been doing that ever since."

A few weeks later, the old Scot's daughter came to the minister's home. "Father died during the night," she said through her tears, "I had no idea death was so near. He hadn't moved since I last saw him except that his hand was out on the empty chair at the side of his bed. Domine, do you understand?" "Yes," the minister replied, "I understand."

Not by intellect or will, but by imagination, the old Scotsman had accepted a friendship that made the Master real.

I Can Sleep When the Wind Blows

For years now when I visit with hospital patients I present them with the little booklet, *Upon The Rock,* a copy of the Sermon On the Mount. At the close of his sermon, you remember, Jesus told us that storms come to every life. It is not a matter of whether but a matter of when. Sooner or later storms come to all of us alike, but Jesus also tells us that preparation can be made. Wise are those who heed Jesus' warning and prepare for the storms while the skies are blue and the weather is fair.

Once upon at time there was a farmer who advertised for a helper on his farm. Bright and early the following day a young man came to apply for the position. "Can you run a tractor?" the farmer asked. "No, I'm afraid not," came the reply. "Can you handle a milking machine?" he asked. The young man replied, "No, Sir. I don't believe I have ever seen one." "Well, how about cultivators; can you run them?" the farmer asked. "I rather doubt it," the youth said, "I have never even heard of them before."

At the end of his rope, the farmer said, "Well, maybe you had better tell me just what you can do!" Then came these words from the would-be helper, "I can sleep when the wind blows." The poor farmer didn't understand at all, but desperate for help he gave him the job.

A few days later, a storm came up in the middle of the night. The wind blew, lightening flashed, followed by the rumble of thunder. Hurrying to the young man's room, the farmer found him fast asleep. Rather than trying to wake him, the farmer hurried to check on things.

He found the barn doors tightly closed and bolted and all of the animals safely in their stalls. Then remembering the stack of hay in the feed lot, he said aloud to himself, "The wind will scatter that hay everywhere!"

Grabbing a pitch fork he rushed out to find that the hay had been securely covered with a tarpaulin and tightly tied down. Everything had been taken care of. Greatly pleased and relieved, he made his way back to the house just as the rain began to fall. It was then that he remembered the words of his young hired hand: "I can sleep when the wind blows." and he understood.

Heeding the words of our Master, while it is yet day and the skies are clear, let us build our houses as he directs. Then there will be no panic in the twilight. When the storm breaks in all its fury we shall stand firm and unafraid having built upon the rock.

146

The Power To See It Through

It was a never to be forgotten night. Millions of basketball fans saw UCLA defeat Kentucky 92-85 for the NCAA championship. It was a most memorable evening for coach John Wooden, who closed out twenty- seven years at UCLA.

During that time, John Wooden posted a 620-147 record including three perfect seasons of 30-0. During his last twelve years at UCLA, his Bruins won ten national championships.

The morning after the game, one man expressed the feeling of most of America when he exclaimed, "What a tremendous finish for a fantastic career!"

We stress the importance of a good beginning in life through Operation Head Start, Scouting, Church School, and any number of other organizations. It is fitting that we do so. Quite often we come to know that had it not been for a good beginning there would have been nothing achieved, but sometimes we tend to forget that a good ending is what matters most.

Just take the time to look, and you will find the pages of history are filled with the names of people who had good beginnings but failed to see it through; people whose ultimate failures made their good beginnings meaningless.

Hartley Coleridge, expelled from Oxford for intemperance, returning to the campus years later and saying, "How could I have lived such a life in a place like this!" A good beginning, but he failed to carry through.

One thinks of Benedict Arnold whose name is forever synonymous with betrayal and treason, late in life, holding his American uniform to his heart and saying through tear-filled eyes, "It is the only uniform I ever loved. God forgive me for ever putting on another." A good beginning, but he failed to carry through.

It doesn't have to be so. There is one "who is able to keep you from falling and to present you without blemish before the presence of his glory with rejoicing," even Christ our Lord.

From that divine companionship may you draw replenished power— power to see it through. May your life, splendid at the beginning, be the very best at the finish.

Using What We Have

Paul wrote in the book of Romans, "The gifts we possess differ as they are allotted to us by God's grace." All of us are given talents, large or small, God who gave them expects us to use them.

On a summer day in 1777 a contingent of soldiers rode up to a blacksmith shop in a little village in Vermont. A voice called out, "Is there anyone here?" Limping out, fifteen-year-old Luke Varnum answered, "Yes, Sir, I am here." He explained, "I am the only one left. Father and all the other men and boys have gone to join General Stark. Being lame, they left me behind."

"I see," said the spokesman of the group, "We need a blacksmith. Is there anyone here who can set a shoe on this horse?" Young Luke answered confidently, "I blow the bellows for my father. If you will hold the horse's foot I will try to set the shoe."

He handed Luke the detached horseshoe. Measuring, Luke exclaimed, "This shoe is too large, it doesn't fit." The rider replied, "It will have to do." Luke said, "No, I think maybe I have a better one." The little blacksmith went to work over the lighted forge and completed the job quickly and well. Then the men mounted and thundered away.

To this day the village tells how the tide of battle had turned against them, and they were on the verge of giving up, when Colonel Seth Warner and his men came riding in to save the day. History books say Colonel Warner and his band won the battle. Others say it was young Luke Varnum, the cripple who was left behind, who made the victory possible.

It was John Oxenham who wrote:

> Is your place a small place?
> Tend it with care; —
> He set you there.

> Is your place a large place?
> Guard it with care! —
> He set you there.

> Whate'er your place, it is
> Not yours alone, but His
> Who set you there.

148

They Are All Precious To Me

Upon a hill, about a mile from the little rural church, lived the Harris family. Mr. and Mrs. Harris had been married close to fifteen years, and during that time they had had ten children—eight boys and two girls. None of them were twins.

On Sunday mornings the young minister stood close to the door with an eye on the road to see if the Harris family was coming. This was about 20 percent of the Sunday school and virtually all of the nursery, beginners, and primary classes.

They drove an old '37 Chevrolet—a two door—which was all they could afford. In the front seat would be the father and mother with two or three of the little ones, and in the back all the rest were stacked to the top. The parents would get out, throw forward the seat, and children would tumble out endlessly. One wondered when the line would stop.

The neighbors were forever asking, "How in the world do you keep up with ten children? Do you count noses at the table to be sure they are all fed? Before you latch the screen door at night do you count bodies to be sure they are all tucked in?"

One Sunday morning the young minister asked, "Mrs. Harris, do you ever by accident leave any of them behind?" Mrs. Harris' eyes grew soft and little lines of loving care crinkled as she replied, "Oh, no! I never miss a one of them. They are all precious to me." God's love for you and me is like that.

Jesus told a story once about a shepherd who had a hundred sheep. One was lost, and the shepherd left the ninety-nine in the wilderness and went in search of the one that was lost. Finding it, he called his friends and neighbors together saying, "Rejoice with me, I have found my sheep which was lost." God's love for you and me is like that.

It was Augustine who said, "God loves each one of us as if there was only one of us to love." God's love is not divided up so that each of the world's 6.65 billion people has a little of it. Rather, God's love is so multiplied that each one has as much love as if there were only one.

That is the gospel—the good news, God saying to you and me, "I never miss a one of you; you are all precious to me." John in his gospel said it like this: "God so loved the world that he gave his only son, that whoever believes in him should not perish but have everlasting life."

You Are Andrew!

For as long as he lived, Andrew would look back on that day as the greatest day of his life. John the Baptist, standing with two of his followers as Jesus walked by, said to them, "Behold, the Lamb of God!"

When John said this, they followed Jesus, and when Jesus saw them following, he asked, "What do you seek?" They replied, "Teacher, where are you staying?" and Jesus said to them, "Come and see."

They went with Jesus, and as it was very late in the day, they spent the night. They talked late into the evening, and when they finally said good night, the two realized their lives would never be the same again.

One of the two who heard John the Baptist speak and followed Jesus was Andrew. Early the next morning he was up and dressed. He had a mission to perform. He went in search of his brother, Simon Peter, and having found him said, "Come and go with me. We have found the Christ." Reading the story as told in the Gospel of John, we happen on these meaningful words: "He brought him to Jesus."

Andrew was the first of a great company who through the ages have been engaged in the great calling of soul winning—finding men and women, boys and girls and bringing them to Jesus. Their worth to the cause of Christ cannot be estimated.

Everyone who has read the history of Christian doctrine knows of Augustine the Great, but very few have heard of Monica. She was the mother of Augustine who brought him to Jesus.

All of us have heard of John Wesley, the founder of the Methodist church, and his brother, Charles Wesley, writer of hundreds of the hymns we sing. Not many of us recognize the name "Susanna Wesley." She was the mother who brought her two sons to Jesus.

Thousands have heard and read the books written by E. Stanley Jones, missionary to India, but have you heard of Robert J. Bateman? He was the fiery evangelist who brought E. Stanley Jones to Jesus.

Upon the scroll of history has been written in blazing letters: "You are Peter, and on this rock I will build my church." It is a wonderful and fitting tribute. Very little has been written in recognition of Andrew, but I like to think that in heaven there is a scroll bearing these words: "You are Andrew, the brother who brought Simon Peter to Jesus."

Running Scared

Dr. Steve Wende, senior minister of Houston's First Methodist Church, tells how as a little boy of seven his parents took him to the Texas State Fair. They explained that he mustn't get separated from them, but if he did, he was to stay put so they could come back and find him.

They had a great time at the fair with all the rides, cotton candy, and so much to see. But guess what. Steve got separated from them. All at once they weren't there, so he went running to find them.

Then, suddenly he remembered what they had said, "If we get separated, don't run," so he just stopped, and as he stood there, his heart pounding, a big policeman put his hand down on his shoulder and said, "Son, do you belong to anybody?" Steve's lips trembled. He couldn't answer.

The policeman said, "Let's go. I'll take you to a place where your parents can find you." It was a special place in the corner of a large assembly hall. There were a lot of lost children there and also ice cream. Steve loved ice cream, but he was so worried about being lost. He didn't want any.

He imagined his parents not being able to find him. Then another thought occurred to him. Maybe they hadn't missed him and would just get in the car and go home. Then weeks later they would look around and say, "Didn't a little boy used to live here?"

It was very foolish thinking by a little boy of seven, wasn't it? But how many times have you and I waked up in the middle of the night asking ourselves, "Does God know about me? Does he see? Does he care?"

Worried and upset he jumped up and started running. He would find his mother and dad. He was weaving his way through knees and once in a while a belt buckle. Then, all at once, he heard his father call his name.

He remembers it to this day. He stopped dead in his tracks and looked up to see his parents, frantic with worry, reaching out to grab him, to hold him, to lift him up, to put their cheeks against his, to surround him with love. Right when he felt most lost, he was found!

It is a terrible thing to feel lost, but every one of us has something inside of us running scared most of the time. In your dark hour of need remember: God sees. God knows. God cares!

Do You Know Where You're Going?

In January, 2000, leaders in Charlotte, North Carolina invited their favorite son, Billy Graham, to a luncheon in his honor. After many wonderful things were said about him, Dr. Graham stepped to the rostrum, looked at the crowd, and said, "I'm reminded today of Albert Einstein, the great physicist who this month has been honored by *Time Magazine* as the Man of the Century.

"Einstein was once traveling from Princeton on a train when the conductor came down the aisle punching the tickets of every passenger. When he came to Einstein, Einstein reached in his vest pocket. He couldn't find his ticket. He reached in his other pocket. It wasn't there. He searched through his briefcase. No ticket. Then reaching down, his hands feeling everywhere on the seat, he searched frantically. The ticket simply was nowhere to be found.

"The conductor said, 'Dr. Einstein, I know who you are; we all know who you are. I'm sure you bought a ticket. Don't worry about it. Einstein nodded appreciatively. The conductor continued down the aisle punching tickets. As he was ready to move to the next car, he happened to turn and saw the great physicist down on his hands and knees looking under his seat for his ticket.

"The conductor rushed back and said, 'Dr. Einstein, Dr. Einstein, don't worry, I know who you are. No problem. You don't need a ticket. I'm sure you bought one.' Einstein looked at him and said, 'Young man, I too, know who I am. I also know I bought a ticket. What I don't know is where I'm going!

Having said that Billy Graham continued, "See this suit I'm wearing? It's a brand new suit. My wife, my children, and my grandchildren are telling me I've gotten a little slovenly in my old age. I used to be a bit more fastidious. So I went out and bought a new suit for this luncheon and one more occasion.

"You know what that occasion will be? This is the suit in which I'll be buried, but when you hear I'm dead, I don't want you to immediately remember the suit I'm wearing. I want you to remember this: I not only know who I am—I also know where I'm going."

The Apostle Paul said it in these words: "We know if the earthly house of this tabernacle be dissolved, we have a house not made with hands, a building of God, a home eternal in the heavens."

Something Old, Something New

This is the month for weddings. Young couples plan with excitement. Said a bride-to-be recently, "It is going to be the most beautiful wedding ever! There will be 'something old, something new, something borrowed, something blue.'"

You know, it's true of every wedding, whether it is in June or January, there will always be something old, something new, something borrowed, and something blue.

Something old—the home. It is as old as creation. Having coffee with a couple recently, I read these words on a plaque hanging on the kitchen wall: "Christ is the head of this house, the unseen guest at every meal, the silent listener to every conversation." How fortunate is every home where this is true.

Something new—the family. A family that is united and joined in a very special way. Speaking of this mystical union, Jesus said, "For this reason a man shall leave his father and mother and be joined to his wife, and the two shall become one."

Then their joys are doubled, as the happiness of one is the happiness of the other. And their troubles are divided in half as they are shared together.

Something borrowed—the children. In her book, *Angel Unaware*, Dale Evans says that from the beginning she and her husband, Roy Rogers, realized that Robin was given to them by God, a little life for them to have and to hold for a little while. Every child is a trust from God— something new to bless and help build the marriage.

Finally, there is something blue. Marriage is happiness and joy, but it is not all sunshine and roses. There are also dark clouds in the sky and thorns among the blossoms. The wedding vows say, "For better or for worse, for richer or for poorer, in sickness and in health, to love and to cherish, till death do us part." But it is this that blesses most. It keeps the hand of each holding tightly to the hand of the other and to the hand of God.

To every couple in love—those who are married and those who are to be married: May God bless your life together and send to your marriage as he always does, "Something old, something new, something borrowed, something blue."

Don't Forget To Pray!

As children in Sunday school we learned to sing, "Don't forget to pray, don't forget to pray, don't forget to kneel and pray." This little chorus gives us counsel of paramount importance. Just as our physical lives need food to eat, water to drink, and air to breathe, our spiritual lives stand in need of prayer.

Bonsai is the art of dwarfing. Recently I saw a pine tree that had been dwarfed. It was a very strange sight. In the wild the pine tree grows to more than 200 feet in height, but now dwarfed it stood less than fifteen inches.

The owner explained to me how the dwarfing was accomplished. It all began when the pine was still a seedling; the taproot was sniped off. Without the taproot, the pine was unable to acquire proper nourishment. It never grew as nature intended. It was a mere semblance of its God-given potential.

Every person I know wants to live a meaningful life—a life of value and worth. I have never seen anyone who wanted to come to the end of life's journey and say, "I lived a little insignificant life. I accomplished nothing. I contributed nothing."

How often do you and I, like that bonsai pine, live only a few inches above the ground when all the time God has created us to live large abundant lives that make a difference? The Bible says that the only way we can learn to live large and useful lives is to put the root of our soul down deep into the soil of God's grace through prayer—talking to God and letting God speak to us, giving us our marching orders for the day.

When our nation went to war with Iraq the first thing our military did was sever the lines of communication between the Iraqi troops and their headquarters. Cut off from their command, the Iraqi troops were soon in disarray. Unable to communicate, they were lost, not knowing what to do.

This is true of our lives. The first objective of the enemy, Satan, is to cut off communication with our headquarters, God. He does it by convincing us that we don't have time enough to pray.

As we go into a busy and difficult day, the first thing we need is time with headquarters to be sure that our plan of action is according to God's plans. Take time to lift up your eyes!

Letter to An Aunt

In 1806, a little six-year-old boy named John Todd lost both parents and was taken to be reared by an aunt. He attended Yale and became a minister.

Years later, his aunt, now advanced in years fell seriously ill. In great distress, she wrote her nephew expressing her fear of death and asking what it might be like to die. Here is the letter that John Todd sent in reply:

"Dear Aunt, It is now nearly 35 years since I, a little boy of six, was left quite alone in the world. You sent me word you would give me a home, be a kind mother to me. I have never forgotten the day when I made the long journey of ten miles to your house in North Killingsworth. I can still recall my disappointment when, instead of coming for me yourself, you sent Caesar to fetch me.

"I can still remember my tears and my anxiety as perched on your horse and clinging to Caesar, I started for my new home. Night fell before we finished our journey, and as darkness deepened, I became more and more afraid.

"Finally, I said anxiously to Caesar, 'Do you think she will go to bed before we get there?' 'Oh, no,' he answered reassuringly, 'She will surely stay up for you. When we get out of these woods, you will see her candle shining in her window.'

"Presently, we did ride out into a clearing, and there, sure enough, was your candle. I remember you were waiting at the door of your home, that you put your arms around me and lifted me, a tired and frightened little boy, down from the horse.

"There was a fire on your hearth, a warm supper on your stove, and after supper, you took me up to my room, heard my prayers, and then sat beside me until I dropped off to sleep.

"You undoubtedly realize, dear Aunt, why I am now recalling these things to your mind. Someday soon, God may send for you to take you to a new home. Don't fear the summons, the strange journey, the dark Messenger of Death. At the end of the road, you will find love and a welcome. You will be safe, there as here, in God's love and care. For surely he can be trusted to be as kind to you as you were years ago to me!"

Matthew 14: 16
Finding Help In Time Of Need

There is a story coming out of New Orleans during a time of flooding, about a man who was stranded in his small cabin. When a Jeep drove up, warning him of rising waters and offering to carry him to safety, he said, "Thank you, but I have prayed, and God has promised to rescue me."

The water rose higher forcing him up on the roof. A motorboat offered him help and received the same answer, "God, himself, has promised to rescue me."

Finally, the swirling water forced him clear up on the chimney. But when a hovering helicopter lowered a rope ladder and called to him, it was waved away. "Thank you, but God has promised that he will save me."

Swept away by the raging waters, the man was drowned and found himself in heaven. He was as mad as a hornet and demanded an audience with God.

"How could you do that to me?" he fairly shouted. "I prayed to you, you promised to rescue me. I trusted you and you let me down!" God quietly replied, "I did all I could. I sent a Jeep, I sent a boat, I sent a helicopter . . . ."

That is how God works, it seems. Haven't you found it so? I ask God for help, and I am sure he could help me directly, but he generally helps me through others. Others need help, and I ask God to help them, but generally I hear a still small voice saying, "You help them."

The Bible speaks a great truth when it declares that we are all "bound in the bundle of life with the Lord." An unknown poet has said it this way:

> I met a stranger in the night
> Whose lamp had ceased to shine;
> I paused and let him light his lamp from mine.
> A tempest sprang up later on,
> And shook the world about;
> And when the wind was gone,
> My lamp was out.
> Back to me the stranger came,
> His lamp was burning fine;
> He held the precious flame and lighted mine.

Using What God Has Already Given

Dr. Tony Campolo was once the guest speaker at a mission rally in Philadelphia. During the meeting, the chairperson reported a prayer request from a missionary doctor in Venezuela. The demand for medical services was so great they were having to turn people away. They needed to raise $5,000 to add an extension to the medical facility.

The prayer request was shared with the assembly, and then the lady serving as chairperson asked Dr. Campolo if he would lead the meeting in prayer asking God that the $5,000 would be raised. Dr. Campolo politely refused, but he said he would offer a prayer of thanksgiving after the money was raised, and, if need be, ask God to make up the shortfall.

Then reaching into his pocket he took out all the money he had that day—two one dollar bills, a quarter and a dime—just $2.35—and placed it on the communion table. Touched by his gesture the chairperson said, "Thank you, Dr. Campolo, I think we all get the point."

"No," Dr. Campolo replied, "I don't think you do. I have put my $2.35 on the table. Now it's your turn." The startled and embarrassed lady opened her wallet, took out the $10 she had in it and placed it on the table.

In no time all the people there were searching their billfolds, purses, and pockets for money to give. By the time they finished, they had $8,000! Dr. Campolo concluded by saying, "The audacity of asking God for five thousand dollars when God has already provided us with more than eight thousand dollars. We should not be asking God to supply our needs. God already has. Let us pray."

Some years ago, an earthquake struck Alaska leaving thousands homeless and in need. The wife of the governor said later, "We were flooded with requests for help; there were few offers of aid.
But one letter from a little ten-year-old boy we never forgot. It contained two nickels and this note: 'Use this money to help all the people in need, and if you need more just let me know.'"

> "It's not what you'd do with a million,
> If riches should be your lot;
> But what you are doing at present,
> With the dollar and a quarter you've got."

June 6

Psalms 25: 4

The Master Teacher

He wasn't quite two-years-old the day he climbed up on the piano bench and struck the keys. A big smile spread over his face, and his little fingers began to pound out symphonies that satisfied his soul.

At the age of four, he watched on TV and added the mannerisms of the popular pianist, Liberace to his own artistry, but his "music" remained unchanged.

When he was five, his mother told him, "Johnny, if you are going to play the piano, there are some things you are going to have to learn." They got as far as middle "C" when he decided he didn't want further instructions. He was having too much fun "playing the piano" his way to be bothered with a lot of rules.

One Sunday afternoon when he was eight, his mother found him seated at the keyboard with a sheet of music before him. The expression on his face was saying, "A song comes out of this thing. Mother knows how it's done. Those funny looking marks mean something. I wish I knew what."

He called to the kitchen, "Mom, show me how to play the piano," but his mother was expecting company for the Sunday evening meal. She had a roast to carve, gravy to thicken, potatoes to mash, and a salad to toss. There was no way she could stop and give piano instructions.

"Not now," she said hurriedly, but she would never forget the look on his face or the sound of his voice when he begged, "Just one thing, Mother, show me just one thing."

Your life and mine are so much like that. We go along banging, banging away at living, making little sense and no harmony, scorning instructions, blithely accepting the results. Then one day—as if by magic, we become aware of our ignorance, our helplessness, and the futility of our way of life. Finally we are ready to live with a purpose, to come into fellowship with the Creator.

We can't do this alone, but if we want to, really want to, we can turn to the Master Musician and ask him to show us how. The wonderful thing is he is never like that mother, too busy. He is always and forever ready to show us, not "just one thing," but everything we are ready to learn. Under his direction and with his help, we can produce the kind of music we were created to produce.

Teach Us to Pray

"Lord, teach us to pray." As far as we know that is the only thing the disciples ever asked him to teach them. They didn't ask him to teach them to preach or to heal or to counsel. They seemed to know that prayer was the key to God's power, and that if they knew how to pray they could do all the rest.

In response, Jesus gave six simple guidelines that are as applicable today as they were when he gave them. God is indeed OUR FATHER WHO ART IN HEAVEN. When we pray those six words, truly pray them, we have prayed The Lord's Prayer. The rest is commentary.

To pray is to realize God's greatness. Our hearts proclaim, "How great Thou art!" In adoration we exclaim, HALLOWED BE THY NAME.

Recounting his manifold blessings, his goodness, his love, we give ourselves to him anew. Realizing more and more our world's deep need of Christ, we pray, THY KINGDOM COME, THY WILL BE DONE ON EARTH AS IT IS IN HEAVEN.

All that we are and have are God's gifts to us. We are totally dependent upon his love and care. Trusting in his providence, we petition, GIVE US THIS DAY OUR DAILY BREAD.

To stand before God in all his holiness is to be painfully aware of our sins. God can deal with sin; no one else can. In Calvary's cross we behold the thrust of his pardon and voice our deep need, AND FORGIVE US OUR DEBTS.

God's forgiveness is conditional. "If you do not forgive men their trespasses, neither will God forgive you," and so we complete the circle, AS WE FORGIVE OUR DEBTORS.

Finally, he teaches us to pray, LEAD US NOT INTO TEMPTATION BUT DELIVER US FROM EVIL. Soon or late, testing comes to all. Of what use is the ship if it cannot stand the storms? Praying for deliverance admits our need and brings God to our aid.

Jesus has an unbelievable confidence in us. Listen again to his words: "The works I do you will do also, and greater works than these you will do." What amazing faith! Assured of his confidence in us, we can face tomorrow unafraid. Triumphantly we can declare, FOR THINE IS THE KINGDOM, THE POWER AND THE GLORY FOREVER. AMEN.

The Worth of a Soul

Norman Cousins, long time editor of the *Saturday Review*, was visiting Albert Schweitzer at the hospital he established in Lambarene, French Equatorial Africa where thousands of Africans were treated yearly. They were engaged in a discussion about atomic weapons tests, the danger of radioactive fallout and other far-reaching matters.

A nurse apologized as she interrupted their discussion. One of the patients was having difficulty breathing, and she needed to know what to do. Excusing himself, Dr. Schweitzer went to take care of the matter. Returning, he said to Dr. Cousins, "In a world of such great social issues, it is well to remember that individuals still have problems."

Individuals do have problems, and they can only be dealt with one at a time. Great social issues consist of problems happening to individuals.

It is not only that individuals are important. ALL individuals are important. This is a basic premise of sound psychotherapy. Dr. Alfred Adler once overheard a fellow physician speak of a patient as a "worthless type." He said to his colleague, "There are no worthless types."

It was William Booth, founder of the Salvation Army, who said, "The first vital step in saving outcasts consists in making them feel that some decent human being cares enough for them to take an interest in the question of whether they live or die."

The first step in helping anyone is to make that person feel that he is of worth. This was a lesson that Matthew discovered. Jews never soft-pedaled their speech. They said everything with gusto. When they referred to the tax collectors of their day, they called them "dirty Gentile dogs." That is what they saw.

When Matthew wrote his gospel and recounted his call to become a follower of Jesus, he wrote, "As Jesus passed by, he saw a man called Matthew sitting at the tax office." The thing that impressed Matthew was the fact that Jesus looked at him and saw a man. Everyone else looked at him and saw a "dirty Gentile dog."

What do we see when we look at people in need? Do we see sinners we feel sorry for, look down on, or even despise because of what they are and what they do? Or are we able to see persons of worth for whom Christ died?

Christian Revenge

Years ago while traveling in India, a group of men found a man seriously wounded lying beside the road. They carried him to the Mission Hospital and asked if a bed was available. The physician saw at a glance that the wounded man was an Afghan, a member of the warring Patau tribe. "Bring him in;" he said, "For him we have a bed."

The doctor discovered that the man was in danger of losing his sight. The man, desperate with rage and fear, pled with the doctor to save his sight. "I must find my attacker and extract revenge. I must kill him," he screamed, "After that I don't care if I am blind the rest of my life!"

The doctor told him it was a Christian hospital, and Jesus had shown them how to love and forgive their enemies. The man was unmoved. "Jesus' words are nice," he said, "but they are meaningless. Vengeance is the only reality." The doctor had to go to attend to other patients, but that evening he returned to tell the patient about another who took revenge. "Long ago," he said, "The British government sent a man as an envoy to Afghanistan. On the way he was attacked by a hostile tribe, accused of espionage and thrown into prison. The prison was unbearably hot. The food was terrible, and he was beaten cruelly by the guards.

"His only comfort was a copy of the *Book of Common Prayer* his sister had given him when he left. He used it for his prayers and filled the margins with a journal of his suffering and faith. He simply disappeared and was never heard from again. Twenty years later the book turned up in a second-hand bookshop. The owner located the sister whose name was on the flyleaf and sent it to her.

"With deep heartache she read the entries. The last one, written in a different hand, said the prisoner had been publicly beaten and forced to dig his own grave before being executed.

"She knew what she must do. Her brother had been tortured and killed in an Afghan jail. She must exact revenge—but Christian revenge. She was not wealthy," the doctor continued, "but she marshaled all the money she could and sent it to this mission hospital. The money was to be used to keep a bed free at all times for a sick or wounded Afghan."

The wounded man was very quiet, silenced by the story of such strange revenge. "My friend," said the doctor, "You are now lying in that bed. Your care is her revenge."

The Twelve Steps

June 10, 1935 was the day, and Akron, Ohio was the place. An alcoholic, Bill W., sought out Bob S., another alcoholic, not to drink with but to stay sober with. It seemed to be a case of the blind leading the blind, but it worked, and Alcoholic Anonymous was born.

Each man found in the other the support he needed to break the hold of alcohol, and they discovered the power they had to help other alcoholics. It changed the way we look at and deal with addiction. Since then the Alcoholics Anonymous movement has covered the world and changed the lives of millions for good.

I was first introduced to the program in 1953 when I was invited to speak to an AA convention being held in the city auditorium in Big Spring, Texas. I came away convinced that the twelve-step program could be applied to any personal problem. What do you think?

1. We admitted we were powerless over alcohol—that our lives had become unmanageable.
2. Came to believe that a Power greater than ourselves could restore us to sanity.
3. Made a decision to turn our will and our lives over to the care of God, as we understood Him.
4. Made a searching and fearless moral inventory of ourselves.
5. Admitted to God, to ourselves, and to another human being the exact nature of our wrongs.
6. Were entirely ready to have God remove all these defects of character.
7. Humbly asked Him to remove our shortcomings.
8. Made a list of all persons we had harmed, and became willing to make amends to them all.
9. Made direct amends to such people wherever possible, except when to do so would injure them or others.
10. Continued to make personal inventory and when we were wrong, promptly admitted it.
11. Sought through prayer and meditation to improve our conscious contact with God, as we understood Him, praying only for knowledge of His will for us and the power to carry that out.
12. Having had a spiritual awakening as the result of these Twelve Steps, we tried to carry this message to alcoholics and to practice these principles in all our affairs.

Happy Birthday, AA!

Isaiah 6:8
God's Clarion Call

On Thursday, April 12, 1912, the largest ship that had ever been built set sail on her maiden voyage from South Hampton, England to New York with 2,201 passengers aboard. Believed to be unsinkable, she was due in New York in five days, the following Wednesday.

Sunday morning dawned clear and bright. At 9:00 a.m. the *Titanic* received a message from the steamship *Carpathia* saying, "West bound steamers report icebergs and field ice." The *Titanic* sped on. At 9:00 p.m. *The Californian* radioed, "We are completely surrounded by icebergs." The *Titanic* sped on.

It was later reported that the captain received five different calls that day warning him. The *Titanic* sped on. At 11:40 p.m. the lookout, high atop his tower, suddenly saw this big white monstrous shape immediately ahead. Frantically, he sounded three bells and called the captain, "Iceberg dead ahead!" It was too late. There was a dull thud. The iceberg had ripped a 300-foot gash in the hull.

Passengers were awakened, told to dress quickly, and come on board. Irritated at being roused they demanded, "Why! Why has the engine stopped running?" Then their anger turned to pandemonium. There were only half enough lifeboats and these were leaving partially filled. Many people jumped into the icy water trying to catch the lifeboats.

The band, which had been playing ragtime, began playing "Nearer My God To Thee." At 1:20 a.m. on that ill-fated Monday morning, with a great hissing sound as a final death sigh, the mighty *Titanic* plunged to the bottom of the sea and 1,490 passengers went down to a watery grave.

Through the centuries God has been calling people—groups, nations, and individuals. Abraham in Ur, Moses at the burning bush, the child Samuel in the Temple, Saul on the Damascus Road. You and me?

The clearest clarion call is from the Cross of Calvary that says we are loved with an everlasting love. In light of God's love, we should live our lives in service to others. We can do so, whatever our circumstances. For some it means hanging on and being strong, for some it means giving up, for some it means making a telephone call of encouragement. All of us can do something. Let us not ignore his call. We do so at our peril. Let us hear and heed and then be willing to be used as God's instruments in this his world.

June 12

Luke 6: 41

"It's Me, It's Me"

Simon Peter asked the question of Jesus. He had tried his best to do what he believed Jesus would do, but he had just about reached the end of his rope. "How often am I to forgive my brother if he goes on wronging me? Would seven times be enough?" "No," Jesus replied, "Not seven times but seventy times seven. Even if he wrongs you seven times in a day and says, 'I'm sorry,' you must forgive him."

Remember—Jesus practiced that kind of forgiveness. As he hung in agony on the cross, suffering and dying, he prayed, "Father, forgive them; they do not know what they are doing."

Such forgiveness is not easy. It can't be left up to our feelings. It is a matter of will. You don't feel like forgiving? Forgive anyway, as God in Christ forgave you.

One morning the woman left her suburban apartment to go downtown on the bus to go shopping. She put on her most fashionable outfit and her favorite perfume. Then as she left, she thought to pick up a small sack of garbage. She would toss it in the container at the curb on her way.

As she took her seat on the bus, she noticed this terrible odor. She became upset with the city and determined to write a letter to city hall and complain. She muttered, "City buses shouldn't smell like this."

She opened a window seeking relief. The odor seemed worse. She decided it was the neighborhood through which she was riding. "How can people live in such filth?" she muttered to herself, "Why don't they clean things up?"

When she arrived at the shopping district, she discovered there was a horrible smell in every single store she visited. "The whole world smells terrible," she complained, "Everything is going to the dogs!"

It wasn't until she returned home and opened her packages that she realized the terrible truth—she had forgotten to toss the garbage! Perhaps you and I would be more inclined to forgive others if we first recognized the garbage we are carrying around in our own lives.

The great African American spiritual puts it this way: "It's me, it's me, it's me, O Lord, Standin' in the need of prayer. Not my sister nor my brother, but it's me, O Lord, Standing in the need of prayer."

164

Acres of Diamonds

In 1870, Russell H. Conwell went with a group of travelers down the Tigris River. They hired a guide at Baghdad to show them Persepolis, Nineveh, and Babylon. The guide was well acquainted with the land and loved to entertain his patrons. One evening he told this story:

"There once lived near the Indus River an ancient Persian by the name of Ali Hafed who owned a large farm with grain fields, orchards, and gardens. He was a wealthy and contented man. Then one day a priest visiting in his home told him how the world was made.

"At first it was all a fog bank. Then God whirled the fog bank into a solid ball of fire. As the surface cooled, the internal fires threw up the mountains, valleys, hills, and plains of this wonderful world of ours. If the internal melted mass cooled quickly it became granite; that which cooled less quickly, silver; less quickly, gold; and after gold, diamonds.

"A handful of diamonds would buy an entire country," he was told. Where could he find diamonds? The priest said, "Look for a river running through white sand between two mountains. In those sands, you will always find diamonds.

"Ali Hafed sold his farm and for a lifetime looked, in vain. Coming to the bay of Barcelona, Spain, penniless and in rags, he cast himself into the incoming tide and was drowned.

"One day Ali Hafed's successor took his camel into the garden to drink. Seeing in the stream a dark stone reflecting light, he picked it up and later placed it on his mantel. The next time the priest came visiting, seeing the stone, he realized it was a diamond worth a king's ransom. Rushing out into the garden, they stirred up the white sand and found more diamonds, larger and more beautiful than the first.

"Thus was discovered the diamond mine of Golconda, the greatest diamond mine ever, excelling the Kimberly itself. Ali Hafed had spent a lifetime searching for wealth. All the time there were acres of diamonds right there where he lived."

So it is with us. Searching for the true riches of life—contentment, joy, happiness, and success—we feel sure they are to be found "out yonder somewhere." We could spend a lifetime in futile search; when if we opened our eyes, we would discover that there are acres of diamonds at our doorsteps.

Being Used For Good

The Bible speaks a great truth when it tells us that we are "bound in the bundle of life." All of our contacts have eternal significance when we are willing to be used as God's instruments in this his world.

Her name was Margaret Schultz. She lost her husband when she was only 33. Three years later their only child, a little girl, was killed in an accident. She had a terrible time with her grief, but she was a Christian, and she came through.

She decided she wanted to help children, so she went to the hospitals in Boston every week. She talked with children, read to them, held them. She always left with these words, "God loves you, and so do I."

When she learned about a psychiatric hospital for children, she went down and was welcomed by a staff desperately in need of help. One by one, they introduced her to the children. Then they said to her, "There is one child you will never be able to reach. No one can reach little Annie. Incorrigible, we have her locked up in a cage at the end of the corridor."

In time, she learned little Annie's story. She had been terribly abused and hadn't spoken in three years. Margaret went to see her every day, but there was no sign of recognition. She sat silently staring off into space.

On Valentine's Day, Margaret made brownies for all the children. She took some to little Annie. They were totally ignored. Little Annie continued to stare into space. Her heart aching, Margaret set them down just outside the door of the cage and left in tears.

To her surprise, the next day the brownies were not there. They had been eaten. Again, as she did every day, Margaret talked to little Annie who just sat and stared. But as Margaret was walking away, she heard a voice and the words, "Thank you."

It was a breakthrough. Annie got out of the hospital, grew up, and became a teacher. One day she heard that there was another little girl, a little girl who had suffered a severe illness when she was two. It had left her deaf and blind, unable to speak, totally shut off from the world. She needed a teacher, so little Annie—Anne Sullivan left Boston and went to minister to Helen Keller. In doing so, she blessed all of our lives and enriched the world.

Slow Down!

Jack took a long look as he slowed down. The speedometer registered 73 mph in a 55 mph zone. This was the fourth time in four months that he had been stopped. How in the world could a guy get caught so often! Slowly he pulled over.

The patrolman was Bob from the church. This was really embarrassing—getting caught by a cop from his own church! "Guess you caught me red-handed. I was rushing home to my family." Bob hesitated and Jack continued, "I've been working long hours lately. I guess I was in hurry to get home."

"Yeah, I know what you mean." Bob said, "I also know the kind of reputation you have in this precinct." Things weren't going in the right direction for Jack. He had to change tactics, "How fast was I going?" Bob answered, "I clocked you at seventy. Would you get back in your car, please?" Jack was irritated, "Now wait just a minute! I checked the minute I saw your flashing lights. I was going barely over 65." With every ticket, it seemed easier to lie.

Bob said again, "Please, Jack, get back in your car." Jack got in, slammed the door and stared at the dashboard. Outside the rolled-up window, he saw Bob scribbling away on the pad. Why hadn't he asked for a driver's license? A tap on the door brought him back to reality.

Bob was standing with a folded paper in his hand. Jack rolled down the window a mere two inches, just enough for Bob to hand him the slip. "Thanks," he said with a sneer in his voice.

Without a word, Bob turned and went back to his patrol car. Jack unfolded the paper, wondering how much it was going to cost. What was this? Startled and surprised, he began to read:

Dear Jack, Once upon a time I had a daughter. She was six when she was run over and killed. You guessed right—a speeding driver. After a fine and three months in jail, the man was free—free to hug his daughters—all three of them. I had only one, and I'm going to have to wait until heaven before I can ever hug her again. A thousand times I have tried to forgive that man. A thousand times I thought I had. Pray for me, and, Jack, please slow down. My son is all I have left."

Drive carefully and safely and remember: Cars are not the only things that can be recalled by their maker.

Some to Be Teachers

The first day of class she gave the speech teachers always give, "You are all special to me. I have no favorites." But teachers lie—they do have favorites, and there are other students they can't stand.

Teddy Stoddard was that boy. His clothes were unkempt, his hair disheveled and he always needed a bath. She took delight in marking his wrong answers and putting an F at the top of the paper. She should have known better. She had his records. First grade: "Teddy is a bright boy with a ready laugh, works hard and is a joy to be around." Second grade: "Teddy is an excellent student but has a sad look. His mother is terminally ill." Third grade: "Teddy is gloomy and withdrawn. His mother died this year." Fourth grade: "Teddy is deeply troubled and is falling behind. His father shows no interest."

Christmas came, and the children piled gaily-wrapped presents on her desk. Teddy's was done up in brown paper from a grocery bag and held together with scotch tape. Miss Thompson opened it to find a rhinestone bracelet with some of the stones missing and a bottle of cheap perfume.

The children began to giggle, but Miss Thompson said how pretty the bracelet was and put some perfume on her wrist. After school, Teddy came up to her desk, "Miss Thompson, you smell just like my mother. I'm glad you liked my presents." When he left, Miss Thompson got down on her knees and in tears prayed for God's forgiveness.

After that she was a new teacher. She wasn't just teaching reading, writing and arithmetic; she was teaching boys and girls. Before long Teddy Stoddard had caught up with the class and was ahead of some.

Years passed, and she got a note: "Dear Miss Thompson, I am graduating second in my senior class. I wanted you to be the first to know." Four years later: "Dear Miss Thompson, I will be graduating first in my college class. You are still the best teacher I ever had."

Four years later: "Dear Miss Thompson, As of today I am Theodore J. Stoddard, M. D. How about that! I am going to be married in July, and I wonder if you would come and sit where my mother would have sat."

Miss Thompson went and sat where Mrs. Stoddard would have sat, and she deserved it. Miss Thompson had become a real teacher, and real teachers affect eternity.

June 17   James 5: 14
                        Faith Healing

In the book of James are found these words: "And the prayer of faith will
save the sick, and the Lord will raise him up." He is talking about the
problem of illness and the responsibility of Christians for one another.

A lot of my ministry and also the ministry of the congregation I served was
in hospitals. I strongly believe that sometimes we can help people there
more than anywhere else. It is then, as at no other time, that people need
the help and support of those who make up the fellowship of the church.

James was giving instructions for a ministry of prayer and anointing
for the sick. In those days, anointing with oil was the most common of
remedies. The modern day equivalent I think would be —"Give him his
medicine in the name of the Lord." You see, James was saying that we are
never supposed to omit the ordinary remedies. By all means, they are to
be followed religiously, and then they are to be reinforced with prayer.

In the hospital room, I always have prayer. I pray for the doctors and
nurses, that they may be the means of God's healing power. Doctors and
nurses are important, but faith and hope are even more important and
real. I have seen prayers of faith work miracles, and in many cases prove
to be the difference between death or incurable healing, and healing and
health.

I am aware of the problem that not everyone is healed, and frankly I don't
know why. Paul left Trophimus ill in Miletus. Timothy, Paul's son in the
faith, suffered affliction all his life, and three times, Paul prayed for God to
remove the thorn in his flesh. Instead, God gave him the strength to bear
it.

We are almost always reluctant to accept such an answer to our prayers,
but it is help of the highest caliber. Strength of character to conquer self-
pity, and the power to face what we must face with quiet courage is God's
greatest gift.

I believe with all my heart that James was right, when he wrote, "The
prayer of faith will save the sick," not only the physically ill but the sick in
any situation of life, and it all depends on our faith. It was the Carpenter
from the plains of Galilee who said, "If you can believe! All things are
possible to him who believes."

                            169

Unbearable Burdens

In the book of Psalms are these words: "Cast your burden on the Lord, and he will sustain you." Corrie ten Boom, speaking to a church in Tokyo, said to the tiny congregation, "Do you know the feeling when your heart is like a suitcase with a heavy load?"

It was right after World War II. The atomic bomb had totally obliterated two of their largest cities. They nodded yes to her question. Corrie ten Boom proceeded to demonstrate. Placing her heavy suitcase on the table, she told them how weary she was from tramping all over the world carrying it and its heavy contents.

Then she took out two heavy objects and laid them on the table. "Lord, here are my two co-workers. They are so tired." Taking a large package from the suitcase and laying it down beside the first two, she said, "Here is my trip next week to Chicago. You know how anxious I get thinking about going there. I don't know anyone in Chicago. I give this care also to you, Lord."

"Here are my friends who are ill. Please heal them." She continued to take objects from the suitcase. One by one she named them. "This is my doubt, this is my pride, this is my fear, this is my self-seeking—and on and on until the suitcase was empty. Then closing it, she pretended to walk away, swinging the suitcase as though it were made of paper.

The light of understanding broke on the faces of those assembled there in that little church. Through the lips of his servant, Corrie ten Boom, God had spoken his message to their hearts.

God speaks the same message to your heart and mine. There simply comes a time when you've worried enough, you've prayed enough, you've done enough. As a minister I have people talk to me about their kids. They say, "You know they were raised in a Christian home. We did everything we knew how to do. Now look at them; they are a total mess! We don't know where to turn or what to do."

It is time for you to realize that you have done your best. They belong to the Lord. Maybe your job now is simply to love them and pray for them. Turn them over to the Lord and trust them to his care.

Along the pathway of life, when the load gets too heavy for you to bear, listen to the words of the Psalmist: "Cast your burden on the Lord, and he will sustain you."

June 19   **Ephesians 3: 20-21**

With Wings as Eagles

Mary Verghese is one of the truly great Christians of our day. Her story is told in Dorothy Clarke Wilson's book, *Take My Hands.* As far back as she could remember, Mary wanted to be a doctor—not just any branch of medicine, she wanted to be an obstetrician.

Medical school wasn't easy, but Mary made it. She completed her studies and received her degree from Vellore Medical College in her native India. It was a day for celebration. With a dozen other medical students, she planned a picnic.

On the way, there was a terrible accident. They were passing a bus when the driver of the station wagon in which they were riding lost control. It went off the shoulder of the road and rolled over three times.

Five days later, Mary regained consciousness, paralyzed from the waist down. Her dreams were shattered. Through her tears she whispered, "Oh, God, I will never feel warm squirming babies in my hands!"

Then there occurred what she later realized was a miracle of God's infinite grace. There came to her out of the blue the words of an old hymn, "Take my hands and let them be Consecrated, Lord, to Thee." Those words became for her a prayer from the bottom of her heart.

Moments later, into her hospital room came Dr. Paul Brand, one of the greatest surgeons in all India. He said, "Mary, I want you to be my assistant in surgery. We will build a ramp, and you can operate from your chair."

Today, Dr. Mary Verghese is a most skilful and expert surgeon. Her hands have become the ten fingers of God. The world is a better, happier place because of her life. She puts it this way: "I asked God for legs and he gave me wings."

Our God is a great God. He takes seeming tragedies and turns them into triumphs. In the words of Paul, "He is able to do far more abundantly than all that we ask or think," and because of his greatness we can say with the poet:

> "Many things about tomorrow,
> I do not understand,
> But I know who molds tomorrow,
> And I know who holds my hand."

171

The Treasures of Darkness

The promise is found in the book of Isaiah: "I will give you the treasures of darkness." They are strange words for most of us. We associate darkness with trouble, heartache, illness, and death. It is rather hard to believe that darkness could contain treasures, but it may well be that in turning away in disbelief, we are missing a valuable treasure, something of great value. For one thing, darkness teaches us to be cautious.

Driving our cars in daylight, we get up and move on, but when darkness falls our range of vision is limited. We are able to see no farther than the beams of our headlights reach. We are compelled to slow down and drive with caution.

Life is like that. We live happy-go-lucky lives giving very little attention to anything. Then, often without warning, darkness falls and we are forced to slow down, and it may be that for the first time, we give serious consideration to the meaning of life.

Secondly, there comes calmness at eventide. A minister friend of mine, carrying tremendous responsibilities, found himself facing a nervous breakdown. Hospitalized by his doctor, he voiced this conviction: "I think God put me flat of my back to make me look up."

Finally, we can see farthest in the dark. I know it seems that we see farthest in the day, but think about it. The most distant object we see during the day is the sun, which is ninety-three million miles away, but when it grows dark enough, we can see the stars, which are millions of light years away, and when we remember that light travels 186,000 miles a second, the distance staggers our imagination.

Christ discovered this truth. In the daylight of his life, he rejoiced in God who loves and cares for all of us. Seeing this, he taught us to call God "Father."

But on the cross, he saw the farthest. Hanging there in the darkness, his life ebbing away, he saw a God who could be trusted even in death. Then came the words, "Father, into your hands I commit my spirit."

Sooner or later darkness falls in every life. When that time comes for you, do not panic. God is still watching and caring. He waits to give you the treasures of darkness.

Father to Son

Father Forgets, by W. Livingston Larned, is a classic of American journalism. I would like to share it with fathers everywhere.

"Listen, son; I am saying this as you lie asleep. I have stolen into your room alone. Guiltily, I came to your bedside. I scolded you as you dressed for school. You gave your face merely a dab with a towel. I called out angrily when you dropped some of your things on the floor.

"At breakfast I found fault, too. You spilled things. You gulped down your food. You put your elbows on the table. As you started off to play you called, 'Goodbye, Dad!' I frowned and said, 'Hold your shoulders back!'

"When I came home from work I found you on your knees playing marbles. Your jeans were dirty. I humiliated you in front of your friends by marching you in the house ahead of me. 'Jeans are expensive,' I said, 'If you had to buy them you would be more careful!' Imagine that, son, from a father!

"Later, as I was reading in the living room, you came in timidly with a sort of hurt look in your eyes. I glanced up, impatient at the interruption. You said nothing, but ran and threw your arms around my neck and kissed me. Then you were gone, pattering up the stairs.

"What has been happening to me? The habit of faultfinding, of criticizing— this was my reward to you for being a boy. It was not that I didn't love you; it was that I expected too much of youth.

"Your little heart is as big as the dawn over the wide hills. Nothing else matters tonight, Son, I have come to your bedside in the darkness and knelt here, ashamed. It is feeble atonement; I know you would not understand these things if I told them to you.

"But tomorrow I will be a real Daddy! I will chum with you, suffer when you suffer and laugh with you when you laugh, and when impatient words come I will bite my tongue. I will remember to say to myself, 'He is just a little boy, nothing but a little boy!'"

The poet was speaking directly to fathers when he wrote: "I am your son. You hold in your hand my destiny. You determine, largely, whether I shall succeed or fail. Give me those things that make for happiness. Train me, so I may be a blessing to the world."

The Love Chapter for Children

For many the Thirteenth Chapter of I Corinthians is the most wonderful chapter in the New Testament. It describes perfectly the life of Jesus. Sometime, sit down and read this meaningful chapter putting your own name in place of the word love. You will be able to see how your life measures up to the life of the Master. In order for us to hear it in a fresh way, someone has written this paraphrase that they call *The Love Passage for Kids."*

"If I can speak beautifully and can sing like an angel, but don't love others, I sound like a child banging on a piano or a screeching radio.

"If I'm very smart, almost a genius, if I can figure out the hardest math problems and understand sentence diagrams, but don't love others, I am nothing.

"Love will stand in line and wait its turn.
Love looks for the good in others.
Love doesn't always want what others have, and it doesn't brag about what it does have.
Love is polite, even when the other person is rude.
Love doesn't always have to be first.
Love doesn't get angry over the small things, and it doesn't remember one reason after another to be hurt.
Love isn't happy when someone else fails but is happy with the truth.
Love will always protect others, especially those who are often picked on or teased.
Love always believes the best about others and is steady and true.

"Love never gives up. Preaching will stop someday. So will speeches. Knowledge will come to an end. Today we only know part of what there is to know. We can preach and speak only with a small part of understanding, but when perfection comes then what is imperfect will go away.

"I am now young, and so I talk and think and speak like a child. When I become an adult I will put childish ways behind me. Now we see only a poor reflection, like in a mirror; then we will see face to face. Now I only know part of what there is to know; then I will know fully and will be fully known.

"There are three things that last forever: faith, hope and love; but the greatest of these is love."

The Good Old Days

The 90th Psalm petitions, "Teach us to number our days." Wise counsel! Time flies, and the older you get the faster it goes. I've never heard a senior citizen say that time was passing slowly, have you? I read recently of a boy who asked his grandmother what it was like "in the good old days." This was her answer:

"Well, I was born before television, penicillin, polio shots, frozen foods, Xerox, contact lenses, Frisbees and the pill. There was no radar, credit cards, laser beams or ballpoint pens. We never heard of FM radios, tape decks, CDs, electric typewriters, yogurt or guys wearing earrings.

"We listened to the Big Bands, Jack Benny, and the President's speeches on our radios. If you saw anything with *Made in Japan* on it, it was junk. The term 'making out' referred to how you did on your school exam. Pizza Hut, McDonald's, Radio Shack and Wal-Mart didn't exist.

"We had 5 &10 Cent stores where you could actually buy things for five and ten cents—Ice cream cones, phone calls, rides on a streetcar, and a Pepsi were all a nickel. If you didn't want to splurge, you could spend your nickel on enough stamps to mail a letter and two postcards. You could buy a new Chevy for $600, but no one could afford one, and gas was 11 cents a gallon.

"We thought fast food was what people ate during Lent. A meaningful relationship meant getting along with your cousins and time-sharing meant time the family spent together in the evenings and weekends— not purchasing condominiums.

"Grass was mowed, coke was a cold drink, pot was something your mother cooked in, and rock music was your grandmother's lullaby. Aids were helpers in the principal's office, chip meant a piece of wood, hardware was found in a hardware store, and software wasn't even a word.

"Your grandfather and I got married first and then lived together. The Ten Commandments, good judgment and common sense governed our lives. We were taught to know the difference between right and wrong and to stand up and take responsibility for our actions.

"We actually believed that a lady needed a husband to have a baby. No wonder people call us 'old and confused' and say there is a 'generation gap.' "And how old do you think I am? I'm 58!"

Speaking Up and Speaking Out

He was a fine young Christian man and a dedicated churchman along with his wife and two children. In their Sunday school class they were talking about Christian witnessing. "I never talk with people about my Christian faith," he said, "I let my example speak for me."

In a way it sounds good, doesn't it? But it is wrong, dead wrong. Jesus commanded us to go into all the world and proclaim the good news. The Christian faith is something we are called to talk about.

Somewhere I read that, when William Wrigley, Jr. went into the chewing gum business in 1891, for every five-cent pack of gum he sold a penny went into advertising. It was probably true.

Doublemint ads are the most successful ever developed, and Doublemint chewing gum is available in over 140 countries. Sales are fantastic. Those ads speak out loud and clear for Doublemint. Where do you suppose Proctor and Gamble, Coca-Cola, and Kellogg's would be if they simply let their products speak for themselves?

The early Christians led exemplary lives but the church grew because the followers of Christ went everywhere telling the good news to others, and that was true from the very beginning. We read, "Jesus came into Galilee proclaiming the gospel of God and saying ..."

Andrew went and spoke to his brother, Simon Peter. Simon Peter spoke on the day of Pentecost and 3,000 accepted Christ as Lord and Savior. Phillip spoke to the Ethiopian. Paul and Silas spoke to the jailor at Philippi.

Peter and John were imprisoned. Because they were living examples? No, because they told the people about Jesus. The authorities would have said, "Be an example all you want but keep your mouth shut!"

There are no silent witnesses in our courts or for Christ, and can you imagine a silent auctioneer, a silent car salesman, a silent TV announcer? Words need lives to back them up to be sure, but first and foremost a Christian witness must speak up and speak out.

Jesus said, "You shall be my witnesses." That is what you and I are if we belong to him. The words Jesus spoke to a certain man of Gadera two thousand years ago are his words to us today: "Go home to your friends and tell them ..."

Windows of Gold

I would like to share with you an old legend. Legends are unverifiable stories handed down by tradition and popularly accepted as historical. They usually teach valuable lessons. This one may help make a difference in your life and in your world.

Once upon a time there was a boy who lived in a little cottage on top of a high mountain. Each morning, as the sun was coming up, he would go outside and look down into the valley below. There, he beheld in all their shining glory, cottages with windows of shining gold.

More than anything, he longed for such windows in the cottage where he lived. He didn't understand why it was that his windows were so drab and depressing.

One day, he decided that he would make a trip down the mountain and see firsthand the wonderful sight. The ice and snow and howling winds would make it a difficult trip, but it would be worth far more than the trouble.

The next morning as the sun rose, he began his journey. He took one last look at his cottage with its plain windows and turned his face toward the valley and the cottages with windows of gold.

Mid-afternoon found him exhausted and weary. His feet were bruised and bleeding. His face burned with the cobwebs broken across it, and one eye wept from a twig having lashed across it.

Just as the golden sun was setting, he reached the village below, but he had lost his guiding light. The windows of glistening gold were gone. In their place were windows dark, cold, and foreboding. Tears of disappointment welled up in his eyes. "What has happened to them?" he asked himself, "What has become of the windows of gold?"

Just then he heard a kind voice saying to him, "Look!" He lifted his eyes. There, high on the mountain from where he had come, were windows of gold—and they were his! The setting sun had burnished the windows of his little cabin.

All of life it seems is a quest, a search for the best. How prone we are, much like the little boy, to look ever afar. But for each of us, as for him, our windows of gold are not to be found in some distant place. Always, they are close at hand. They are as near as a whispered prayer.

How Many Loaves Do You Have?

The busy day was coming to a close. It had been an exciting day. With Jesus teaching and healing, no one had thought about food, but now it was quite late and everyone was hungry. The disciples suggested that the crowd be sent away into the villages so they could buy food for themselves.

However, Jesus said to them, "They do not need to be sent away. You give them something to eat." Then Jesus asked the disciples, "How many loaves do you have? Go and see." Andrew found a young lad who had brought a lunch of five barley loaves and two fish. No doubt, it was a small lunch that his mother had prepared for him that morning as he was preparing to leave. Andrew talked with him, and learned that he was willing to share.

Jesus took the little boy's lunch. He gave thanks for the food, and I think he must have thanked God for the little boy who was so willing to share. Then he gave the food to the disciples and they, in turn, gave it to the people who were present. Five thousand people were fed that day, and when they were finished eating, the disciples took up twelve baskets of leftovers.

Down through the centuries, Jesus has continued to ask, "How many loaves do you have?"

In the 19th century, William Booth was asked the question as he faced the slums of the East End of London. His answer: "Not much money— but courage, audacity, and a love for the least, the last, the lowest, and the lost." In 1878, he organized the Salvation Army.

Abraham Lincoln heard Jesus' question and answered, "Very few—a boyhood of poverty, no formal education, a life of continuous defeats, yet an unwavering faith in God, a love for all mankind and for America. Abraham Lincoln placed all he had in the hands of the Master, and the Union was preserved.

The question came to Albert Schweitzer. He answered, "An excellent education, a well-trained mind, a love for music, a dedication to medicine, and a passion for the world's oppressed." In 1913, he went to French Equatorial Africa as a medical missionary. His Christian impact on our world can never be forgotten.

Today, Jesus asks, "How many loaves do YOU have?"

Broken Dreams

James Russell Lowell in one of his poems wrote:

> "Life is a leaf of paper white,
> Whereon each one of us may write,
> His word or two, and then comes night."

One of life's great truths is that we start out to write one story and wind up being forced to write another? Paul wrote in a letter to the church at Rome, "When I go to Spain, I hope to see you in passing." His dream was to go to Rome and carry the gospel of Jesus Christ there.

Instead, Paul wound up in a Roman prison. Instead of an opportunity to proclaim Christ, Paul became a prisoner of the emperor and eventually was executed for his faith, but he didn't lash out at God. Neither did he just fold his hands and do nothing. He asked himself, "If I can't go to Spain, what can I do?"

As he always does, God gave him his answer. Paul took pen and paper and began to write. Of the 27 books in our New Testament 13 of them are letters written by Paul, and the ones that have been the greatest blessing to our world are the ones he wrote from prison.

Someone has said, "Our disappointments may be God's appointments." I don't know whether God planned Paul's imprisonment or not. What I do know is that God used his imprisonment. Paul knew it, too. He wrote to the Philippians, "I want you to know that what has happened to me has actually advanced the spreading of the gospel."

What God did for Paul, he can do for you and me. To be sure, it requires faith. In spite of prison, Paul still believed that God had a purpose for his life. Because he believed it, he held on until he found it.

An old hymn of the church voices this conviction:

> He leadeth me! O blessed thought!
> Oh words with heavenly comfort fraught!
> Whate'er I do, where'er I be,
> Still 'tis God's hand that leadeth me.

It's an easy matter to sing it. But when we dream the impossible dream of some Spain, wind up in some prison cell, discover there some purpose of God for our life and fulfill it, then, we really believe it.

Sending Back Acknowledgments

John Winkler was in heaven. How, he didn't know, but there he was. An angel was showing him around. It was a beautiful place. All his life he had heard about "pearly gates" and "streets of gold." He remembered singing about "mansions of glory and endless delight." But heaven was far more wonderful than anything he could have imagined.

He followed his guide as they stepped inside a large workroom. "This," the angel said, "Is the Receiving Section." As John looked around, the angel continued, "Here the prayers and petitions are received." It was a busy place with a multitude of angels rushing around, sorting out hundreds of prayers. Some were on voluminous sheets; others were scribbled on scraps from people all over the world.

They moved down to "Packaging and Delivery." This area," explained the angel, "Is where all the things people have asked for are processed and delivered." It was really a busy place. A host of angels were packing, addressing and sending out thousands of blessings.

Finally, they moved out of all the hustle, bustle and noise and on down the corridor. There at the farthest end they stopped at the entrance of a very small station. To his astonishment, John saw a single angel, seated, idly doing nothing. Noting his surprise the guide, noticeably abashed, admitted, "This is the Acknowledgement Room."

"I don't understand," he said, "There is no work going on here." Greatly embarrassed, the shamefaced angel, continued, "As you can see, one angel takes care of everything here and he works only part time. Millions of petitions come in and millions of blessings are sent out, but very few people send back acknowledgments."

"How sad," John heard himself saying, "Maybe they don't understand. How does one go about sending back an acknowledgment?" The angel answered, "Simple, you just whisper, 'Thank you, Lord.' Here comes one now from a darling little two-year-old. Listen!"

> "Thank you, Lord,
> For this, our food;
> For life and love
> And every good. Amen."

Suddenly, John Winkler was awake. It was morning and he realized that he had been dreaming, and yet, it seemed that it was all true.

June 29   **John 10: 10**
Shutting Out the Lord of Life

After a critical event in the life of Jesus, many of his followers drew back and no longer followed him. Jesus said to the twelve, "Do you also wish to go away?" Peter answered for the group, "Lord, to whom shall we go? You have the words of eternal life."

Dr. Hazen Werner once told about a doctor who was called by another doctor in a town some 50 miles away. A young boy was critically ill with an infection that was causing internal hemorrhaging. "I don't know how to treat this," the caller said, "But you do; it is your specialty. Can you come at once?" The doctor assured him, "Of course, I am on my way." He hurried out to his car and headed toward the hospital where the boy was.

On his way out of town he stopped for a traffic light. Suddenly the door of his car was yanked open. A man wearing a gray cap and a brown leather jacket thrust a handgun in his face and shouted, "Get out of the car!"

"I can't do that," the doctor tried to explain, "I'm on my way—" The man with the gun cut him off, "I don't care where you are going. Get out this instant or I will kill you." Heartsick, the doctor got out. The man in the gray cap and brown leather jacket jumped in behind the wheel, gunned the motor and sped away.

Realizing that he needed to find another car, the doctor went to the nearest house and knocked on the door. No answer. He went to another, and another, and another. Finally his knock was rewarded. He explained his situation, was loaned a car and drove to the hospital.

When he arrived the other doctor said, "I am glad you came, but you are too late. The boy died a few minutes ago, but please come in and meet his father. He is almost hysterical with grief."

They went into the waiting room and the doctor met the father—wearing a gray cap and a brown leather jacket. In his rush to get to the hospital the father had shut out of the car and out of their lives the one man who could have made all the difference.

It is a grave danger that we all face. Let us beware; lest in quest for life that has meaning we shut out the One who came that we might have abundant life. Today he speaks to your heart and mine: "I am the Way, and the Truth, and the Life; no one comes to the Father, but by me."

181

Whose Side Are You On?

Jesus asked the question in the Sermon on the Mount, and he asks it of you and me today: "Why do you call me Lord, Lord, and not do what I tell you?"

There is a story told about a very poor and highly emotional congregation down South, years ago, that failed to meet the payments on the building where they met to worship.

Finally, the mortgage was foreclosed, but the congregation refused to vacate the property. The owner hesitated at having the sheriff evict a church congregation, so he resorted to a trick.

One night during their annual summer revival, he drove his pickup to the side of the building and turned his headlights on one of the windows. Then, dressed in a red devil's costume, forked tail, horns and all, he raised the window, climbed up on the sill and stood there brandishing his pitchfork.

There was quite a commotion following as with shrieks of terror the people fled helter skelter from the building. That is, all except one elderly lady who was crippled with arthritis. She couldn't make it, but standing there, she managed to balance herself with her cane. Then she pointed her finger at the devil figure advancing menacingly toward her.

"Now, Mr. Devil," she said, "You stop right there where you are! I have something to say to you. I want you to know that I have been a faithful member of this church for over seventy years. As a young girl, I taught a Sunday school class. Since then, I have taught every class there is to teach. "I have served as a deaconess, as Sunday school superintendent, as a circle chairperson, and as president of the Ladies Aid Society.

"I have never missed a single church service. I have attended prayer meeting every Wednesday night. No one has been as faithful to the church as I have been, but I want you to know that I have been on your side all the time!"

What about you and me? Are our lives totally committed to the Master, or a halfhearted effort with little or no meaning for our lives?

They are perhaps the most important questions we will ever be called on to answer: "Who am I serving? To whom do I really belong?"

Facing Failure Unafraid

Charles F. Kettering was a farmer, school teacher, mechanic, engineer, scientist, inventor and social philosopher. He held more than 300 U.S. patents. He is best known for the all-electric starting ignition and lighting system that replaced crank ignitions for automobiles.

Jerome Beatty once wrote of him, "Charles F. Kettering was never afraid of failure. He always said the only time you must not fail is the last time you try." This willingness to take a chance, to risk failure is a quality we of today seem to be losing. We forfeit the excitement and thrill of living because of our fear of failure.

It begins, I think, when we start to school. We are made to feel that to flunk anything is disaster. By the time we get out into the world we are so afraid of failure we won't try anything that involves risk. How do we learn to deal with this? How do we learn to face failure unafraid?

First, we must realize that failure is a part of life. Not every athlete that enters a race wins. Although they do their best, most of the runners lose. We should always strive to succeed, but failure is a part of life and should be expected.

Second, failure can serve as a stepping stone to bigger and better things. After 700 experiments had been total failures, a young assistant of Thomas A. Edison said to him, "All of our time has been wasted; we have accomplished absolutely nothing!" Edison replied, "Not at all. We now know 700 things that won't work." It is said that on the next attempt he hit upon the principle that made possible the incandescent light bulb.

Finally, let us remember that there is no ultimate failure for the Christian who trusts God. Our Master showed us that. Where could one find a more apparent failure than the Christ as on that Black Friday he hung suspended between heaven and earth, dying on a cross between two thieves?

Today, we know that what seemed defeat was the greatest victory our world has ever known. It can be so for you and me. Expect failure; it is part of life. Use failure as a stepping-stone to success.

Above all, keep your eyes upon Christ. He will lead you through the shadows of failure today and tomorrow and out into the sunlight of victory on the third day.

I Pledge Allegiance

Red Skelton was one of the truly great comedians of all times. One of his best known routines was "The Pledge of Allegiance," in which he explained the pledge word by word. As we look forward to celebrating Independence Day, I would like to share it with you.

"I remember this one teacher. To me he was the greatest teacher, a real sage of my time. He had such wisdom. We were all reciting the Pledge of Allegiance and he walked over. Mr. Lasswell was his name. He said, "I've been listening to you boys and girls recite the Pledge of Allegiance all semester, and it seems as though it is becoming monotonous to you. If I may, may I recite it and try to explain to you the meaning of each word?

"**I**—Me, an individual, a committee of one. **Pledge**—dedicate all my worldly goods to give without self-pity. **Allegiance**—my love and devotion. **To the Flag**—our standard, Old Glory, a symbol of freedom. Wherever she waves there is respect because your loyalty has given her a dignity that shouts freedom is everybody's job.

"**Of the United States of America**—that means we have all come together. Individual communities that have united into 50 great states. Fifty individual communities with pride and dignity and purpose; all divided with imaginary boundaries, yet united to a common purpose and that is love for country.

"**And to the republic**—a state in which sovereign power is invested in representatives chosen by the people to govern, and government is the people and it is from the people to the leaders and not from the leaders to the people.

"**For which it stands. One Nation**—meaning so blessed by God. **Under God, indivisible**—incapable of being divided. **With liberty**— which is freedom and the right of power to live one's own life without threats or fear of some sort of retaliation.
"**And justice**—the principle of equality of dealing with others. **For all** – which means it is as much your country as it is mine.

"Since I was a small boy, two states have been added to our country and two words have been added to the Pledge of Allegiance—**under God**. Wouldn't it be a pity if someone said, 'That's a prayer,' and it would be eliminated from schools, too?"

Pollen

Tomorrow we will celebrate Independence Day, the anniversary of the birth of our nation. What a heritage is ours! There comes to mind phrases thick and fast—"one nation under God," "give me your tired, your poor," "liberty and justice for all."

I think of the giant bell in Philadelphia proclaiming liberty. I think of the statue standing in New York harbor—"Liberty Enlightening the World." Then I think of all the prejudice, suspicion, hatred, and reluctance to share, which I observe and hear on every hand. I think all of us need desperately to remember some things that perhaps we have forgotten.

In 1918, at the close of World War I, Susan Glaspel wrote a short story for *Harper's Magazine* entitled "Pollen." It still speaks a message that we as Americans need to hear.

Ira Mead was a farmer in the Midwest. He was a solitary man who lived with his mother and kept pretty much to himself. The Balch and Dietz families lived on either side of his farm, but he had little to do with them.

Ira's one interest was corn, and he raised the finest in the county. Year after year, it took the blue ribbon at the fair. When people asked him for seed, he would answer, "I reckon it has all been spoken for."

But something puzzled him. For several years, the corn on the side next to the Balches had been inferior, and one day he heard the Dietz boy exclaim how much finer their corn was next to the Mead farm.

Then, late one summer afternoon, Ira Mead stood and witnessed the awful truth—millions of golden particles between him and the sun. The trade winds were carrying pollen from the Balch farm to his farm, and from his farm to the Dietz farm—life, changing life!

That evening after supper, Ira went out to the barn and came back with two sacks of seed corn. In the kitchen, he picked up his cap. "Where in the world are you going?" his mother asked. "Over to the Balches and the Dietzes," Ira answered.

Ira's mother was completely taken back. "Why?" she asked, "What in the world for?" Ira's answer carried deep conviction, "I am taking them seed corn, and I'm going to tell them all I know about raising corn. I know now that I can never have good corn unless they have good corn, too."

The Lifted Lamp

Her name was Carley Leonard, and she had made a long trip back east to visit her grandparents. There had been so many wonderful things to see and do, and so many exciting places to go.

The most memorable of all for Carley was their trip to Liberty Island to see the great Statue of Liberty, a colossus of copper, iron, and steel. She had been impressed by its proper name, *Liberty Enlightening the World* and the observation platform with twenty-five windows that afforded a magnificent view of the harbor and the city.

She was told that it was 151' 1" tall and weighed 450,000 pounds. Carley would never forget that proud woman dressed in flowing robes, her right arm holding aloft the great torch.

It had been a long day, and that evening, after they retired, they heard Carley tossing restlessly on her bed, unable to sleep. Finally, her grandfather walked down the hall, tapped on her door, went in and sat down on the side of her bed. "What is the matter, Carley? You should be asleep."

The little granddaughter answered, "I can't go to sleep, Grandpa. I keep thinking about that lady out in the harbor holding up that lamp all by herself."

Today we celebrate America's birthday. Let us pause amidst the parades, picnics and fireworks and consider that lifted lamp and what it costs to keep the light held high.

Freedom never comes cheap. The fifty-six men who signed the Declaration of Independence did a very brave thing. We of today little realize the courage required for these to "stand up and be counted."

As each in turn took up the pen, he was publicly proclaiming himself a rebel, an enemy of the crown. Benjamin Franklin's statement, "We must all hang together, or we shall all hang separately," was no idle quip. In the days that followed, they were separated from their families; their homes were burned and destroyed; they were hunted down and imprisoned, and many lost their lives.

As we celebrate the fourth, let us give thanks to Almighty God for those men of faith who first lifted up the lamp. Let us dedicate ourselves anew to the task which is ours of helping to hold it high.

July 5   **John 8: 36**
The Source of Our Freedom

Many service clubs open their weekly meetings with the singing of the first stanza of "My Country 'Tis of Thee," also known as "America."

> "My country 'tis of thee,
> Sweet land of liberty,
> Of thee I sing;
> Land where my fathers died,
> Land of the pilgrim's pride,
> From every mountainside
> Let freedom ring!"

But I spoke at one service club recently that changed things a bit. They sang the last stanza.

> "Our fathers' God, to Thee,
> Author of liberty,
> To Thee we sing:
> Long may our land be bright
> With freedom's holy light;
> Protect us by Thy might,
> Great God, our King!"

You will notice that there is a colon after the third line and that the rest of that last stanza is a prayer to Almighty God. He is the source of our liberty, our freedom, our way of life. It is something we ought never to forget.

Soren Kierkegaard told the parable of a spider that lived high up in the rafters of a barn. One day he extruded a filament of silk and by it let himself down to the floor of one of the cribs. There, in one of the corners, he spun a web and set up housekeeping. Flies were plentiful, and as the days passed, he grew prosperous and fat.

One day, as he strolled around, surveying his vast domain, he chanced upon the single thread of silk reaching up into the great unknown. For a while he studied it. "What in the world is that for, I wonder? I cannot see that it serves any purpose at all." So saying, he clipped the thread, and when he did the web collapsed and his house came crashing down in ruin about him.

> "Lord God of Hosts, be with us yet,
> Lest we forget—lest we forget!"

"I Gave Myself"

On December 30, 1903, downtown Chicago was hit with the icy fist of winter. The Iroquois theater could seat 1,724, but for the matinee 1,900 had filled it to "standing room only" to see vaudeville comedian Eddie Foy in "Mr. Bluebeard." That fateful afternoon, there was a blast of flame, and 602 people lost their lives.

When the alarm sounded, two young men in attendance rushed for an exit and got out safely. Amidst the confusion, they got separated. One of the boys went around to a side door and re-entered the building.

He stumbled over a person who had been trampled and was unconscious. Picking him up, he carried him to safety. Then back he went to rescue another and another. On the fourteenth trip he was overcome by the heat and smoke.

Firemen found him on the floor unconscious and rushed him to the emergency room of a hospital. The road to recovery was painful and slow. When some friends came to visit him and expressed sympathy, he said, "Don't feel sorry for me. Some people live for years and never get a chance at life. I had my chance at twenty-three, and I gave myself."

The other boy, once he was safely out of the burning theater and in the street, panicked and fled in fear. Later he went berserk and was never himself again. He spent the rest of his life going through the same routine. He would ask those about him, many of them total strangers, "Do you know who I am?" When they told him they didn't, he would say, "I was at the Iroquois Theater the afternoon it burned, but I saved myself."

In the story of those two boys is to be found two ways of life. We can give ourselves or we can save ourselves. John Oxenham said it in these words:

> To every man there opens
> A high way and a low.
> And every man decides
> The way his soul shall go.

But Jesus said it best. Listen to his words: "Whoever cares for his own safety is lost, but if anyone will let himself be lost for my sake, he will find his true self."

July 7   **Matthew 16:24**
Living In A Lower Key

Looking through the church hymnal for the hymn "Immortal Love, Forever Full," that someone had called to ask me about, I stumbled across something I had never noticed before. At the bottom of the page was this notation: "This tune in a lower key, No. 73." I got to thinking about how prone we are to want to do that to the great music of the Gospel—put it in a lower key to make it easier.

The hymn "Make me a Channel of Blessing" has these words: "Make me a channel of blessing I pray." It is a prayer for us to be used by God to accomplish his work in the world. The work is there—plenty of it, and there is a crying need for workers.

There are hundreds of boys and girls in our nation who are eager to be a part of Scouting, but Scouting calls for volunteers, and they are not to be found. Their parents say, "We would like for our children to be in the program, but we just don't have time to help." We want to put it in a lower key.

Or the hymn "In Christ there is no East or West." No East or West? Really? Out in West Texas one Sunday morning, a Mexican American family came forward during the singing of the invitation hymn to become members of the church. Later that week one of the women of the congregation said to the minister, "I'm glad they joined, but wouldn't it be wonderful if they had a church of their own." One great fellowship of love throughout the whole wide earth? Not quite! We want to put it in a lower key.

"Take My Life and Let It Be" is a great hymn, and we sing it with zest. That is until we come to "Take my silver and my gold, not a mite would I withhold." Then our voices trail off in a whisper. Could we have the tune in a lower key? Please!

The last stanza of that hymn presents us with a fantastic possibility. "Take my love, my God, I pour at Thy feet its treasure store; take myself and I will be ever, only, all for Thee."

Once at an Easter Worship on the *Hallelujah Chorus* the soprano section of the choir sang the descant (the small counterpoint, high notes). It was glorious to hear. What a wonderful world it would be if all of us sang the descant morally and spiritually!

How well do you do on the high notes?

189

A Royal Priesthood

In his first letter, the Apostle Peter informs us that we are "a royal priesthood." He is referring to all members of the church, making no distinction between laity and clergy, but it means even more. We are to be priests to one another.

One day Abraham Lincoln called Gilbert Greene and asked if he would go with him to the home of a woman who was extremely ill. Lincoln had been asked to come to her house and to draw up a will for her. Abraham Lincoln wanted Gilbert Greene to be a witness to the woman's will. They found the woman very ill and near her end. With great gentleness Lincoln completed the document she desired.

After it had been duly signed and notarized, the woman with a wane smile said, "Now I have my affairs of this world satisfactorily in order. Long before this I made preparations for the other life I am about to enter. I do not fear death, Mr. Lincoln; to tell the truth I am glad that my time has come."

Lincoln bent toward the woman and said, "Your faith in Christ is wise and strong; your hope of a future life is blessed. You are to be congratulated in passing through life so usefully and into the life beyond so hopefully."

"Mr. Lincoln," she said, "Won't you read a few verses out of the Bible for me?" Instead of picking up her Bible, Lincoln began reciting the Twenty-third Psalm from memory, emphasizing "Though I walk through the valley of the shadow of death, I will fear no evil, for Thou art with me."

Still without picking up the Bible he quoted, "Let not your hearts be troubled; believe in God, believe also in me. In my Father's house are many mansions . . . ."

As he continued with quotation after quotation from God's word, Gilbert Greene and the neighbors gathered about the bedside, wondered where he had learned so many verses. It was back in the hills of Kentucky where his mother had recited them to him many years before. While he was speaking, a look of peace lighted up the face of the dying woman. Her eyes closed and she passed away. Listen to the words of Peter, "You are a chosen race, a royal priesthood, a holy nation, God's own people, that you may declare the wonderful deeds of him who called you out of darkness into his marvelous light."

Created For The Heights

Once upon a time, a man was out in the woods and came upon a young golden eagle. He caught it, brought it home, and put it in the pen with the chickens. For five years, this king of birds lived in the barnyard, dabbling around in the dirt and muck for its share of the feed.

One day a naturalist was visiting and saw it. He said, "Look, there's an eagle in the pen!" The farmer said, "That's right, but I have trained it to be a chicken. It measures thirty-three inches from the tip of its beak to the tip of its tail and has a wingspread of seven feet, but it's a chicken."

"No, you are wrong," said the naturalist, "It is still an eagle. Just give it a chance to fly." The farmer consented; and the naturalist picked it up in his arms and said, "You are not a chicken; you are an eagle, spread your wings and fly." The eagle looked down at the chickens scratching in the barnyard dirt and jumped to the ground. "See," said the farmer, "It's a chicken," but the naturalist persisted, "No, it is an eagle. We will give it another try tomorrow."

The next day he took it to the top of the house and said, "You do not belong in the barnyard with a bunch of chickens. You are an eagle. Your home is the mountains and the sky. Rise up and fly!", but the giant bird's eyes were on the chickens in the barnyard and down it flew. The naturalist was undaunted. "It is an eagle and has the heart of an eagle. Tomorrow it will fly."

Morning came, and they took the bird to the foot of a mountain whose crags gleamed in the rays of the rising sun. The naturalist said, "You are an eagle, created for the wild-blue yonder."

As though it understood, the great bird cocked a quizzical eye upward, spread its gigantic wings, and with an incredible screech mounted into the sky. It circled once and was then off to the mountain heights where it belonged.

Even so, you and I were created for the heights. We may experience difficulties, setbacks and disappointments. In a moment of weakness, we may even turn and for a while be contented with barnyard muck.

But God, who created us, will not let us forget for long. He keeps speaking to our hearts, reminding us "They who wait for the Lord shall renew their strength; they shall mount up with wings like eagles; they shall run and not be weary; they shall walk and not faint."

Friends Indeed

The city was all astir. Jesus had returned to Capernaum, and the entire town was coming to see and hear him. Well, not everyone. One man was not joining the excited throng. Paralyzed, he couldn't walk.

As the excited voices faded in the distance, he tried to remember. How long had he lain there? As long as he could remember—all of his life, he had been a cripple.

He heard the news and watched as the people hurried by. How he longed to join them! If only he could walk! He shifted his body, closed his eyes, and resigned himself.

Then looking up, he saw four men. These were his friends; they had remembered him! Picking up the pallet on which he lay, they brought him to Jesus.

The house was packed, but they were not to be denied. Their paralyzed friend ended up coming face to face with Jesus by being lowered down through a hole they had cut in the roof.

Faith is the essential, and nothing indicates that this paralytic had **any** faith whatsoever. Instead, we read, "When Jesus saw **their** faith (that of the four friends), he said to the paralytic, "Son, your sins are forgiven. Get up, take your mat, and go home."

In their 1986 song, *Faith of a Few Close Friends,* Steve and Annie Chapman told this story. However, their song goes a step further. It reminds you and me that we can bring someone to Jesus. Our faith can be the key that unlocks the touch of Jesus that heals and changes life. Listen to the closing words of that song:

> Now there are homes filled with husbands
> And children and wives
> Who feel like the man who was paralyzed.
> They have no hope they will ever survive
> But let the miracles begin.
>
> They took that man to Jesus
> He had no faith of his own;
> But when Jesus saw the faith of a few close friends
> He said, "Take up your bed, man
> Take up your bed and go home.

July 11   I John 5: 15
God Answers Prayer

He was a little boy of six. Holding up a ten cent piece, he said, "Look, Daddy, what God gave me!" His dad looked down at him for a moment and replied, "God doesn't give dimes to little boys." Unfazed, the youngster said, "Well, he gave me one. I asked God to give me a dime to buy candy, and kept asking, until walking down the sidewalk, I saw a dime in front of me right where God dropped it." The father was deeply moved by his son's faith and trust.

Growing older, many of us are less inclined to pray because we don't see the immediate answer lying like the little boy's dime on the sidewalk. Somehow we need to be able to recognize the answer for what it is when it comes.

Some years ago a member of my church almost fell to pieces when her husband was diagnosed with pancreatic cancer with no chance for recovery. She asked me to join with her in daily prayer. Day after day I prayed for his recovery. She prayed. Many others prayed, but the poor man died.

Now my concern was for her. I feared what it might do to her faith, but she said, "Preacher, you know I didn't think I could ever bear to lose him, but God gave me the strength to accept what had to be. He answered our prayers in a greater way than I ever dreamed of."

For many years now my favorite prayer has been the prayer of St. Francis of Assisi written at the beginning of the thirteenth century.

> Lord, make me an instrument of your peace.
> Where there is hatred, let me sow love;
> Where there is injury, pardon;
> Where there is doubt, faith;
> Where there is despair, hope;
> Where there is darkness, light;
> Where there is sadness, joy.
>
> O Divine Master, grant that I may not so much seek
> To be consoled as to console;
> To be understood as to understand;
> To be loved as to love.
> For it is in giving that we receive;
> It is in pardoning that we are pardoned;
> And it is in dying that we are born to eternal life. Amen.

Unsearchable Riches

There is a story making the rounds about Robert Hightower of Queens, New York. In April, 1953, he went to the Masters Tournament in Augusta. There his hero, Ben Hogan, won the championship with a 14 under par, 274 score.

Robert met King Saud of Saudi Arabia. They became close friends, and toward the end of the week the king said, "You will have to come to my country and play a round with me." At the time, Robert felt it was a kind gesture but thought no more about it.

A month later, after returning home, Robert received a long distance call inviting him to be the weekend guest of the king. The caller said, "The king's private jet will pick you and your family up at La Guardia Friday at noon."

It was a never-to-be-forgotten experience. The golf was great and there were brunches, dinners and lavish entertainment. At the end of the visit the king said, "I would like to give you something to remember your visit. What can I give you?"

Robert protested, "It's been a wonderful weekend we will never forget; a gift isn't necessary," but the king insisted, "I want to give you something. What would you like?" Finally, Robert said, "O. K., what about a golf club?" The king said, "Fine, a golf club it will be!" On the way home, Robert wondered what a golf club from the oil-rich king would be like? Made of mahogany, inlaid with gold and bearing the king's signature?

It arrived at last, not a package as expected, but a certified letter from Saudi Arabia. Inside, along with a hand written note, there was a deed to the Pine Hills Golf Course in Myrtle Beach. I can't vouch for the accuracy of the story, but it reminds us that kings think in different terms than you and I. And we serve the King of Kings.

Listen to the words of Jesus, "What human father among you, if his son asks him for bread, will give him a stone? If you then, as imperfect as you are, know how to give good gifts to your children, how much more will your Father who is in heaven give good things to those who ask him!"

Our heavenly Father waits to bestow upon his children "unsearchable riches." All we have to do is ask.

Do You Think If God Had A Son—!

The Testing of Abraham is one of the most beautiful stories in all the Bible. It is a story hard for me to understand and comprehend, but as I recall it was also hard for Martin Luther. He said, "The text is too big; I can't preach on it."

With no explanation, you remember, God commands Abraham to do the unthinkable—take his son Isaac to Mount Moriah and offer him as a burnt offering. So Abraham rises early in the morning, takes his son and goes. On the way, Isaac says, "Here is the fire and wood but where is the lamb for a burnt offering?" Abraham, with an ache in his throat, replies, "God will provide the lamb for the burnt offering, my son."

Abraham builds an altar, lays the wood in order, binds Isaac and places him on the wood. But as he draws back the knife, a voice calls from heaven, "Abraham, don't harm the lad, now I know you fear God since you have not withheld your only son from me." Then Abraham sees a ram caught by its horns in a thicket offers it as a burnt offering.

Abraham must have told his wife Sarah about God's command the night before, perhaps as they were preparing to retire for the night. Can you imagine the shock and horror Sarah felt as she listened to his words?

There was no sleep for them that night. I hear Sarah saying, "No! No! It has to be some kind of a tragic mistake! God could never require that. Isaac is all we have. We waited so long for him. And now to give him up? No! We can't."

I can hear Abraham, heartbroken, saying, "Sarah, my dear, I know! I don't understand it either, but it is God's command. I have to obey." But Sarah will have none of it. "No, you don't!" she cries out through her tears, "I don't care if it is God's command. We won't do it!"

Before daylight, Sarah preparing breakfast, is still protesting, pleading, defying. Abraham, preparing for the journey, tries to reason, "I don't like it either, but it is something I have to do!" "No!" Sarah cries, "No! No! Don't do this! It's wrong! God has no right to make such a demand." Then she asks the question: "Do you think if God had a son—"

Abraham stands silent, saying nothing. He knows not what to say. The answer to Sarah's question came some two thousand years later when John wrote in his gospel, "For God so loved the world ..."

A Message Of Hope

Thomas A. Dorsey, often called the Father of Gospel Music, was born in Villa Rica, Georgia in 1899. His father was a Baptist minister, and his mother played the organ and piano wherever her husband preached.

Thomas quit school early and was soon hanging around theaters and dance halls. Musicians there encouraged him to practice at home on his mother's piano. He did, and by the age of 12 was earning money playing at parties and private get-togethers.

He moved to Chicago, and in 1920 was married to Nettie Harper, but the demanding schedule of playing at night, working at other jobs during the day and studying in between, led to a nervous breakdown. He was unable to work for two years. In order to survive, Nettie took a job in a laundry to support them.

His uncle encouraged him to attend the National Baptist Convention. There he was impressed by the singing of W.M. Nix. He soon began composing sacred songs and was hired music director at Chicago's Pilgrim Baptist Church, a position he held for nearly 40 years.

In 1932 they were living on Chicago's South Side, and he and Nettie were expecting their first child. Thomas was scheduled to be the featured soloist for a revival in St. Louis. The second night, as he finished his solo, a Western Union messenger brought the news that Nettie had died along with their new born son.

He managed to get through the funeral service, but when it was over, he withdrew from his family, his friends, and even his beloved music. In despair, he sat one evening at the piano idly running over the keys when suddenly he felt at peace and found himself playing a melody he had not heard or played before. The words for it came into his head—just seemed to fall in place. What has been called "the greatest gospel song of all time" was born. People around the world know it, sing it, and love it because of its profound message of hope and faith.

> Precious Lord, take my hand,
> Lead me on, help me stand,
> I am tired, I am weak, I am worn.
> Through the storm, through the night,
> Lead me on to the light,
> Take my hand, precious Lord,
> Lead me home.

Teachers Affect Eternity

All of us are living lives that touch other lives for good or bad. It is my conviction that most of us do not realize the extent of our influence. H. L. Gee in one of his writings tells about a lonely old man in the church he attends. Old Thomas had outlived all of his friends. When he died, Mr. Gee felt that very likely there would be no one at the funeral. It was a cold and rainy day and as he had surmised there was no one else at the service.

However, when they reached the cemetery there was a soldier waiting at the gate. The soldier came to the graveside for the ceremony, and when it was over, he stepped forward and swept his hand in an impressive salute which might have been given to a king.

Mr. Gee walked away with the soldier. As they walked together, the wind blew open the soldier's trench coat revealing the shoulder badges of a brigadier general. He said, "No doubt you are wondering why I am here. Mr. Thomas was my Sunday school teacher. I was a wild and mischievous boy and gave him lots of trouble. He never knew what he did for me, but I owe everything I am or will be to Old Thomas. I had to come to salute him today."

Just as the soldier said, Old Thomas didn't know the extent of his influence. Probably no teacher ever does. In Frances Patton's book, *Good Morning, Miss Dove*, the heroine looked upon her lifetime of efforts as very meager. But former students like Thomas Baker, the physician, William Holloway, the police officer, Reverend Alexander Randham, the minister, Billie Jean McVay, the homemaker and mother, and hundreds of others knew better. Miss Dove had made all the difference in the world in their lives.

In 1869, Henry M. Stanley was sent to Africa by the New York Herald to look for the missionary, David Livingstone. At the time Henry M. Stanley was not a Christian. In fact, he had given little thought to God. When he returned to America, it was as a follower of Jesus Christ. Speaking of his conversion, he said, "David Livingstone won me to Christ and did so without realizing it." Then he added, "No one could be around David Livingstone very long without being drawn to the Christ whom he serves."

The Apostle Paul, in his letter to the Galatians, gives us this wise counsel: "Let us never grow tired of well doing, for in due season we shall reap, if we do not get discouraged and give up."

He is Able To Keep

Our God is a great God. Writing to Timothy, the Apostle Paul, totally without reservation, declared, "I know whom I have believed, and am persuaded that he is able to keep that which I have committed to him."

The little boy had gone swimming in a lake near his house, eager to cool off from the sweltering heat of the South Florida sun. He quickly pulled off shoes, socks and shirt and plunged into the cool water.

Swimming toward the center of the lake, he didn't see an alligator swimming toward him. The boy's father was gardening in the back yard and saw that his son was on a collision course with the alligator.

Instantly the father ran toward the lake yelling at the top of his lungs. The son heard his father's screams and started swimming back toward the shore, and just as the boy reached the shore, the alligator reached the boy and locked its deadly jaws on the boy's legs.

On the dock, the father grabbed his little boy by the hands and arms just as the alligator snapped down on the boy's legs. An incredible tug of war ensued between the father and the alligator.

The alligator was strong, but the love of the father was stronger. Just as the alligator opened its mouth slightly to take an ever bigger bite on the boy's legs, the father was able to snatch his son away.

It took weeks and weeks in the hospital, but the little boy miraculously survived. Of course, his legs were terribly scarred from the vicious attack of the alligator. On his arms and hands were black and blue bruises and deep penetrating scratches where his father's vice-like grip and fingernails dug into the flesh as he fought to hold on to the son he loved.

The news media all over the world covered the story. One of the reporters who interviewed him after the trauma was over asked if he would show him his scars. The boy gladly pulled up the legs of his pajamas for him to see; and then with obvious pride he said to the reporter, "But I want you to look at my arms and my hands. My arms and hands have scars on them, too, because my daddy wouldn't let go!"

Yes, our God is a great God. He has loved us with an everlasting love. He is, indeed, able to keep that which we have committed to him, and He will never, ever, let us go!

July 17   Romans 12: 2

A Brand New Start

In one of her poems, Louisa Fletcher writes longingly,

> I wish there were some wonderful place
> Called the land of beginning again,
> Where all our mistakes and all our heartaches
> And all of our poor selfish grief
> Could be dropped like a shabby old coat at the door,
> And never put on again.

Who of us has not experienced her feelings?

Once in the days long gone and dead, my very first year in public school, I sat at my desk trying desperately to make those ABCs look the same as the copy at the top of the page, but they just wouldn't come out right. I would write, and then erase, write, and again erase. The letters looked no better. In fact, with all of the black smudges, they looked worse!

Then my teacher walked by. She looked down at my paper, stained, blotted, a big hole almost rubbed through by erasures. Compassionately, reaching down she picked it up. Then she placed a brand new clean white sheet in front of me. "Now," she said, smiling, "Make a new start and copy them as well as I know you can!"

You will understand when I say I have never forgotten Miss Patterson. When I think of her, my heart warms in gratitude. She did more for me than she would ever know. She enabled me to begin again, and there is nothing to compare with an opportunity to make a new start.

God does that for you and me. Amidst all of our failures and mistakes he is constantly saying, "You don't have to stay the way you are. If you want to, really want to, you can make a new start."

Paul, writing to the Romans, said it in these words: "Do not be conformed to this world but be transformed...." You and I, by the grace of God, can be made different. We can be transformed and changed. We can have brand new lives for our old ones.

It begins, I think, with a simple prayer: "Lord Jesus, come into my heart; 'Melt me, Mold me, Fill me, Use me.'" When we pray that prayer, God will have the chance he needs. He will come into our lives, change us, and give us a brand new start.

July 18 Romans 13:2

Shining Lights

In the Sermon on the Mount Jesus said, "You are the light of the world." That is what we are as Christians. We are to be light dispelling the darkness of the world.

But we live in an age concerned with missiles, mobs and millions and while we are busy with the supposedly big things, the individual is crushed in the crowd.

God seeks to use every person in his work. Everyone is important. That is why the Master of Men urged, "Let your light shine before men that they may see your good works and give glory to your Father who is in heaven." When we fail to let God's light shine through our lives, there is darkness where God intended for there to be light.

Paul Quillian once told about a certain sunbeam that was winging its way earthward along with millions of its sunbeam companions. Along the way it decided, "I don't make any difference. I will go where I please. After all, there are so many other rays, how could I possibly be missed?" So where moments before there had been a dazzling white light, now there was an opaque blur.

A doctor had been called to a farmhouse on an emergency. A little boy had severely injured his eye. If his sight was to be saved, an operation had to be performed at once, right there.

The little boy was placed on a table near an open window where the bright sunlight was streaming in and the doctor set to work. With great skill he tied off the arteries, and the muscles and nerves were pushed aside with care.

At last he was ready for the delicate stroke of the scalpel. Suddenly, there was a dark blur. Only for a fraction of a second, but the blade went too deep. The little boy would never see again. The failure of one little sunbeam to shine had cost him the gift of sight.

How easy it is for each of us to underestimate our value. To say, "What can I do? I am only one person. I don't count." Jesus knows better. He knows that every person is a part of God's plan.

The way you go about living your life, the way you face problems, the way you handle trouble, the way you deal with death—all these things influence those about you. Let your light shine!

200

Overcoming Evil With Good

Henry Ward Beecher once said, "There is no faculty of the human soul so persistent and universal as that of hatred." It is indeed an emotion that runs deep in the human heart and finds expression in man in varied ways.

To punish her five-year-old boy for disobeying, his mother shut him up in the clothes closet. He was furious, kicked and screamed at the top of his lungs. After a while the yelling subsided and he became very, very quiet—too quiet.

The mother tiptoed to the door, listened for a moment, and finally called to him, "Johnny, what are you doing in there?" No answer. Slowly she opened the door. There he sat with tearful eyes, his face red and swollen.

Filled with compassion for the little fellow, she asked again, "What are you doing, Johnny?" Johnny blurted out, "I spit on your coat. I spit on your hats. I spit on your shoes, and now I'm just sitting waiting for more spit!"

There is an old legend that tells about a traveler who crossing the desert came to the tent of Abraham seeking food and shelter. The stranger was welcomed, and food was placed before him. During the course of the meal, when it was disclosed that he didn't believe in God, Abraham drove him from his tent.

That night, the Lord appeared to Abraham in a dream and asked, "Where is your guest?" Abraham replied, "He didn't believe in God, so I put him out of my tent."

Then God said, "Go out, look up at the stars, and behold the vast dome of my dwelling. I have never shut anyone out because of their unbelief. Could you not then have given an unworthy guest shelter for a single night?"

Edwin Markham, the American poet, showed us the way. In his poem *Outwitted*, he wrote:

> He drew a circle that shut me out—
> Heretic, rebel, a thing to flout.
> But love and I had the wit to win:
> We drew a circle that took him in.

The Altar Stairs

In his letter to Timothy, the Apostle Paul sounds the supreme note of the Christian faith. Listen to his words: "I know whom I have believed and am persuaded that he is able to keep what I have committed to him."

He was a man strongly disciplined in the school of Christian living, a man highly respected both by the church to which he belonged and the community in which he lived. He said to a group of neighbors and friends gathered to celebrate his birthday, "I have been young and now I am old. Looking back over my life I cannot recall a single day since boyhood when everything went exactly as I would like to have had it go.

"Sometimes it was the heartaches that go with rearing a family. Sometimes it was bereavement, financial anxiety, falsehoods and slander. Yet I cannot recall a single day since my maturity when God's grace was not more than sufficient for my every need." Haven't you and I found it to be so?

Some years ago a certain minister from the Midwest was in Boston attending a church conference. Late one afternoon he made his way to Trinity Church, a church made famous by the preaching of Phillips Brooks.

Entering the sanctuary, he went halfway up the center aisle, entered a pew and sat down in prayerful meditation. He thought himself to be alone, when suddenly he heard someone crying.

In the fading light, he saw some five rows in front of him a woman kneeling in prayer. Her face was buried in her hands, and her slender shoulders shook with sobs.

Then the crying ceased. She arose and came down the aisle. She was so close that the minister could have reached out and touched her. The soft light silhouetted her head and shoulders as she passed. Her head was erect and there was the look of serene courage on her face. Kneeling there in prayer, she had found the altar stairs that reach through the darkness up to God.

This is the heritage of all who bear the name Christian. Amidst all of the problems and perplexities that life presents, they are able to declare, "In all these things we are more than conquerors through him who loved us."

When Grace Descends

Bill Moyers'TV documentary on the hymn "Amazing Grace" shows a scene from London's Wembley Stadium where some 70,000 people gathered to celebrate the end of apartheid in South Africa. Various musical groups donated their time and talent. For the closing, the promoters scheduled the Metropolitan Opera singer, Jessye Norman.

For twelve hours, groups like *Guns and Roses* blasted the crowd through banks of speakers. In the meantime, Jessye Norman is in her dressing room discussing "Amazing Grace" with Bill Moyers.

The words to the hymn were written by John Newton, a slave trader of eighteenth century England. The turning point in Newton's spiritual life was a violent storm that occurred one night while at sea.

It changed John Newton's life. He renounced the slave trade, became a minister and joined William Wilberforce in the fight against slavery. For the rest of his life he never forgot the depth from which grace raised him.

The time came for Jessye Norman to sing. No backup band, no instrumental accompaniment, just Jessye. Standing all alone, Jessye Norman began to sing:

> Amazing grace, how sweet the sound
> That saved a wretch like me!
> I once was lost but now am found—
> Was blind, but now I see.

Then a most remarkable thing happened. Seventy thousand noisy fans suddenly fell silent. By the time she came to the second stanza, "'Twas grace that taught my heart to fear, And grace my heart relieved . . .," she held the crowd enthralled in the palm of her hands. She continued,

> When we've been there ten thousand years
> Bright shining as the sun,
> We've no less days to sing God's praise
> Than when we first begun.

Later, Jessye Norman said she had no idea what power descended on Wembley Stadium that night. I think I know. This world of ours hungers for grace, the unmerited love and forgiveness of God, in ways it doesn't even realize. And when grace descends the world falls silent.

True Greatness

It was Henry Wadsworth Longfellow who said, "Great men stand like solitary towers in the City Of God." Simon Peter was such a man. In all four gospels when the twelve apostles are named, his name is listed first. What was his secret? What made Simon Peter great?

First of all, Peter had the courage to act. One night on the Sea of Galilee, in the midst of a raging storm, the disciples saw a form coming toward their boat. Peter said, "Lord, if it is you, bid me come to you on the water."

It is really amazing what people can do when they have the courage to try. We can be victorious in the face of overwhelming odds when we dare to act. It was so in the case of Simon Peter. Jesus said, "Come," and Peter got out of the boat and walked on the water to Jesus.

On the day of Pentecost, while the crowd mocked and jeered and the other disciples wondered what they should do, Peter stood up and spoke. He didn't have a manuscript or a prepared sermon, but that didn't stop him. He spoke out of his heart for God, and that day 3,000 people decided to follow Jesus and were added to the church.

Secondly, Peter wasn't afraid to fail. That night on the Sea of Galilee Peter saw the giant waves, panicked, and began to sink; but in the midst of failure he looked to the Master of the Sea who reached out and rescued him.

Finally, Peter was always ready to try again. When Jesus predicted that Peter would deny him, Peter answered, "All the others may, but I will never desert you." When they led Jesus away, Peter followed at a distance, right into the courtyard. But a short time later, when a little serving maid asked if he was a friend and follower of Jesus, Peter denied it with oaths, swearing that he didn't even know Jesus.

Here was the secret of Peter's true greatness. He knew he had failed. He didn't try to make excuses or cover up that failure. He went out into the night to repent with bitter tears. After the resurrection the Master gave him a second chance, and this time he did not fail.

Your life can be like that of Simon Peter. Go forth in the knowledge that Christ is with you and act with courage. Don't ever be afraid of failure. When you fall down, get up and begin again. Your life, too, will be great, and you will be a child of the Most High.

The Unchanging Christ

It was a young high school graduate who posed the question. With startling candidness she said, "Don't you think that Jesus is rather out of date?" It was up-to-date ideas and concepts that interested her.

Like many of us she had come to see that new things—blouses, skirts, coats and shoes are better than old ones. The latest model cars, radios and TVs are vastly superior to the older models.

In the book of Hebrews we read, "Jesus Christ is the same yesterday and today and forever." It does sound old and outdated. Should we stake our hope on something like that?

If we are to build our lives wisely and well, they must be laid on a solid foundation. I was in a home once where a large gaping crack ran down the front wall of the living room. The owner explained that the building had shifted. The foundation was not solid.

That can happen in our lives as well. We must make sure that the foundation is secure. There is the chorus of an old hymn that goes like this, "On Christ the solid rock I stand; All other ground is sinking sand." Paul counsels us, "No other foundation can anyone lay than that which is laid, which is Jesus Christ."

A certain man asked sometime ago, "What do you do when your whole world falls apart?" Soon or late life tumbles in for each of us. In such hours we reach out for something secure and dependable. We find it in Jesus Christ who is the same yesterday and today and forever.

But, then, who says Jesus is out of date? We classify something as "an old model" when a newer and better model takes its place. Jesus will be outdated when a newer and better Son of God takes his place.

And what if Christ is old? The sun is old, but there would be no life on earth without it. Love is old, but every day hearts thrill anew at its discovery. Sorrow and death are old, but when they come eyes are filled with glistening tears and hearts are broken. Sin is old, but still it comes into our lives to wreak its havoc and destruction and separate us from the love of God, and for it we need an unchanging Savior.

In fact, all of life, where it is most real, is unchanging, and to meet the challenges of an unchanging life we need an unchanging Master and Guide—Jesus Christ who is the same yesterday and today and forever.

Christ Died For Me

Isaac Shupp of Dayton, Ohio, a long-time Christian, was over eighty years of age when he received his first traffic ticket. While pulling slowly out of a shopping center, he drove directly into the path of an oncoming car and was cited for the ensuing collision.

He was terribly upset—not at the police, but at himself—because he was afraid he had embarrassed God. Feeling certain that he had now earned a criminal record, he went to his minister, the Rev. David Grubbs, to ask for help.

"Oh, Pastor," he said, "I won't ever come back to church. I'm sure my name will be in the newspaper for this terrible thing I have done. I have broken the law!" The minister put his arm on his shoulder and assured him that he had done nothing that couldn't be corrected.

On the day of his court hearing, Rev. Grubbs went with him. They were surprised to learn that the regular judge was not presiding. Soon they came to the Shupp case. The bailiff called his name and Mr. Shupp approached the bench.

"How do you plead?" the judge asked. Mr. Shupp lowered his head in shame, "I plead guilty, your honor." He looked so forlorn standing there, everyone wanted to rush up and comfort him. Every heart was touched. Many were wiping tears from their eyes. The judge paused and then banged the desk with his gavel. "Mr. Shupp, I find you guilty. Your fine will be thirty dollars and court costs."

Then to the surprise of every one present, the judge rose from behind his bench and walked around to the court clerk's desk. "Mr. Shupp, as your judge I must declare you guilty as charged, but as a private citizen I want to pay your fine."

What the judge did for Isaac Shupp, Jesus Christ did for you and me, and every man and woman, boy and girl who ever lived. As a just judge, God has to declare, "I find you guilty as charged," but in his love and mercy he has come around the bench of eternal judgment and has taken upon himself the form of a man. As that man, Jesus, he has died on the cross for our sins. In his letter to the church at Ephesus Paul wrote, "In Him we have redemption," and as the old hymn declares,

> On the cross He sealed my pardon,
> Paid the debt and made me free.

Listen With Your Heart

Carlo Carretto, after a life of intense social involvement with Catholic Action in Italy during the turbulent years following World War II, went to serve in North Africa.

He was resting at midday in the shade of some huge rocks. He reached up, took a blanket and put it under his head. As he did so he became acutely aware of another blanket by his side, unused. The evening before, he had passed through the little village of Irafog. There he had seen Old Kada trembling from the cold. Cold in the desert? Yes. In fact, the Sahara is often called "a cold country where it is very hot in the sun."

At the time he had thought of giving Old Kada one of his blankets, but then decided he needed it for himself. Now the extra blanket was troubling his conscience. Finally he managed to doze off and had a very strange dream. In his dream the giant boulder fell over crushing and pinning him where he couldn't move.

In pain, he opened his eyes and looked around. There was Old Kada, and he was shivering from the cold. The unused blanket was lying there beside him—unused. He wanted desperately to give it to the poor man, but the huge boulder wouldn't allow him to move.

In those few moments he came to understand, in a small measure, what hell is like—"No longer to have the possibility of doing what before one could and should have done."

Carlo Carretto's story is also a parable, don't you agree? A parable of the possibilities that are offered to each of us, not only to listen with our ears, but to listen with our hearts, our souls, and our minds and then to act.

For the followers of Jesus Christ:

> "A bell's not a bell
> Till you ring it;
> A song's not a song
> Till you sing it.
> And love in your heart
> Is not put there to stay;
> Love is not love
> Till you give it away."

When We Hit A Slump

Frank Glieber was the sports director of KRLD radio in Dallas, Texas. I once heard him interview a baseball player who was in a slump; a batter who had gone to the plate thirty times and not a single hit.

Batting slumps happen for no apparent reason, and it is something all batters fear. One of the worst slumps in baseball history happened in the career of Rogers Hornsby, one of the greatest right-hand batters the game has ever known. He led the National League in batting seven times. Three times his batting average was over .400. He was a great player, but once he went for weeks without so much as a single.

It happens in life, too. In the book of Psalms are found these words: "My feet had almost stumbled, my steps had well nigh slipped." The Psalmist was in a batting slump.

It happens to you and me. Sometimes we are hitting well, then all at once a dry spell comes, and we couldn't buy a place on first base. How do we deal with this?

First of all, remember that life fluctuates. All of us have our ups and downs, good days and bad days. Think about Elijah in the Old Testament? Things were going great on Mount Carmel in his contest with the prophets of Baal. Then Elijah went into a slump, ran away from life, and wanted to die, but he rebounded. How did he manage it?

A good night's sleep and a nourishing meal worked wonders. Often it is simply exhaustion. We don't realize how tired and hungry we are. Food and rest and we bounce right back, ready to take on the world.

Above all, Elijah renewed his relationship with God. He found that he was trying to do it all by himself. You remember, there was the earthquake, wind and fire, and then a still small voice that gave Elijah a new lease on life. It is forever true, "Those who wait upon the Lord shall renew their strength."

God comforted, reassured, and strengthened Elijah, but he did much more—God challenged him, saying in effect, "Now, get up and get going. We have a lot to do!"

This same great God is available to you and me when we hit a slump. He waits to speak to our hearts, put us back on our feet, and bring us back to our God-given tasks.

Hidden In Clay

The Gospel According to Matthew asks, "What will it profit a man, if he gains the whole world and forfeits his life?" Envision it: Place the world in one side of a balance scale, place one human being in the other side. It is no contest. That one individual tips the scale. In the sight of God, one single person is worth more than all the world.

There was a certain man who decided to explore a cave near the seashore. Deep inside he came across a canvas bag filled with dozens and dozens of clay balls. It was as if someone had rolled them perfectly round and let them harden in the sun. They didn't weigh very much, and they didn't look like much, but they were intriguing, so he carried the bag out with him.

Strolling along the beach, he carelessly took out one of the balls and threw it out into the ocean as far as he could throw it. It was fun and so he threw another, and another, and another, thinking little about it. Taking out still another, he accidentally dropped it. It fell on a rock and cracked open. To the man's amazement, inside was a beautiful, precious stone!

Excitedly, he started breaking open the others. Each one contained a similar treasure. There were pearls, rubies, emeralds and diamonds. He had in his possession a king's ransom. Then the awful truth hit home. Walking the beach, he had taken dozens and dozens of clay balls with their hidden treasure and one by one thrown them away!

It is like that with people, too. We look at someone (ourselves perhaps?), and we see the external clay vessel. It doesn't look like much from the outside. It isn't always beautiful or sparkling, and so we discount it. We see it as less important than one that is more beautiful or stylish or well known or wealthy. We haven't taken time to discover the treasure that is hidden within.

God's Word states it plainly—there is a treasure in each and every one. If we take the time to get to know that person, if we ask God to show us that person the way He sees them, then the clay begins to peel away, and the brilliance begins to shine forth.

It is tragic to come to the end of the way and find that we have wasted a potential-filled life, and it is equally tragic to find that a fortune in friendships have been thrown away simply because the precious stones were hidden in clay.

The Prodigal

A lonely young man in his early twenties sat next to the window of the Greyhound Bus staring out at the landscape rushing by. After a while, the elderly man seated next to him sensed his anxiety. Clearing his throat, he said to him, "It's very beautiful out this time of year isn't it?"

Jolted out of his reverie, the young man responded, "Yes, Sir. Yes, it surely is." He turned back toward the window. Again, the elderly man waited. Suddenly the young man blurted out, "Sir, I'm going home. I've been away for years. Now I am going home, and I'm scared!" Then, as the bus sped over the long miles, the young man shared the sordid details of his life.

"Years ago," he said, "I tired of my home and family. I forged my father's signature to a check, stealing all of his life's savings, and ran away. I don't know how I avoided being caught. I have always felt sure that my dad, knowing all about what I had done, never reported it to the authorities."

He paused, swallowed hard, wiped tears from his eyes, and then continued, "Two days ago in desperation I wrote a letter to my family." Fumbling in his pocket he took out a much-worn sheet, "This is a copy of my letter." Amazed at the young man's trust, the man took it and read, "Mom and Dad, I had to write to you. I didn't know what else to do. I wish you could know my heart and how I feel. What can I say about my past, the terrible crime I committed, the shame and disgrace I brought upon you.

"I have no place to go. I just wander from place to place. Day after tomorrow I will be on a bus passing through our town. How I would like to come home and stay the rest of my life.

"I remember the bus passes in front of our house. If you can let me come home, tie a white ribbon to the old oak in our front yard. If it is there, I will get off. If not, I will go on and not bother you again."

The newfound friend could tell he was growing more and more anxious, and he could easily tell why. "My son," he said, "Why don't you sit back, close your eyes and let me look for you?"

There it was—no doubt about it. He grabbed the young man, gripping his shoulder. "Look! You can look now! There is the old oak, and a white ribbon is tied to every branch!"

Finding Heaven On Earth

King Solomon had come to the end of his life's journey. At the very beginning, you remember, he had requested that God give him wisdom to enable him to rule wisely. Now it seems the final installment of that gift has been made.

Tears well up in the eyes of the world's richest, wisest, and most powerful man as he looks down on his journal, *Ecclesiastes.* In it he had searched and tried to answer the question, "How do we find happiness—heaven on earth—in this life?" At the bottom, with a hand trembling with age and deep emotion, he scribbles, "FEAR GOD."

Then just below those words, this mighty monarch scrawls, "KEEP HIS COMMANDMENTS." Find out what God wants you to do, and do it regardless of the cost. "Yes," Solomon whispers to himself, "It is the only way; the rest is vanity of vanities, meaningless, empty wandering."

Life is very much like a trip to the mall on Christmas Eve. There is color and music and mingled fragrance everywhere, all sensuous, all seductive, all competing for our attention—all the vanities and pursuits that come up empty. Solomon had tried every one of them.

Years ago Dwight L. Moody was holding an evangelistic meeting in Massachusetts. Daniel B. Towner was leading the singing. A young man giving his testimony of following Christ concluded with these words: "I am not quite sure—but I'm going to trust, and I'm going to obey."

Mr. Towner was deeply touched by the young man's words and jotted them down for future reference. Later he sent them to the Reverend J. H. Sammis, a Presbyterian minister, who took them and composed the wonderful hymn, "Trust and Obey."

> When we walk with the Lord,
> In the light of his word
> What a glory He sheds on our way!
> While we do his good will,
> He abides with us still,
> And with all who will trust and obey.
> Trust and obey
> For there's no other way
> To be happy in Jesus,
> But to trust and obey.

Parenthood

Once when speaking of children, Jesus said, "To such belongs the kingdom of God." Indeed, it does! For a middle income family to rear a child from birth to 18 the cost is $160,140, but it really isn't that bad once you break it down. It comes to $8,896.66 a year, $741.33 per month, $171.08 per week, a mere $24.24 a day.

You might think the best financial advice would be: "If you plan to be 'rich,' don't have children!" Actually, just the opposite is true. Just think what you get for your money. For a mere $160,140 you get: Naming rights, first, middle and last, glimpses of God every day, giggles under the covers every night, more love than your heart can hold, butterfly kisses and Velcro hugs, endless wonder over rocks, ants, clouds, and warm cookies, a hand to hold (usually covered with jelly or chocolate), a partner for blowing bubbles and flying kites, someone to laugh yourself silly with, no matter what the boss said or how your stocks performed that day.

For just $160,140, you never have to grow up. You get to finger-paint, carve pumpkins, play hide-and-seek, catch lightning bugs, and never stop believing in Santa Claus.

For a mere $160,140, there is no greater bang for your buck. You get to be a hero just for: retrieving a Frisbee off the garage roof, taking the training wheels off a bike, removing a splinter, filling a wading pool, coaxing a wad of gum out of bangs, and coaching a baseball team that never wins but always gets treated to ice cream regardless. You get a front row seat to witness the first step, to hear the first "Da Da," and "Peep Eye!" You get to be there for the first bra, the first date, and the first time behind the steering wheel.

Just think! For a measly $160,140 you get to be immortal. You get another branch added to your family tree, and if you're lucky, a long list of limbs in your obituary called grandchildren, great grandchildren, and who knows, maybe great, great grandchildren.

In the eyes of a child, you rank right up there next to God. You have all the power to heal a boo-boo, scare away the monsters under the bed, patch a broken heart, police a slumber party, ground them forever and love them without limits.

Then, one day, somewhere out yonder they, like you, will love without counting the cost. That is quite a deal for the price! Don't you agree?

Beyond The Sunset

"I am the resurrection and the life; he who believes in me, though he die, yet shall he live, and whoever lives and believes in me shall never die." These are the words of Christ, and deep in the hearts of his followers, there is the certainty that it is so. Somehow we seem to know that "If the earthly tent we live in is destroyed, we have a building from God, a house not made with hands, eternal in the heavens."

Shortly before his death, Robert Burdette wrote a personal letter to the editor of an eastern paper. In it he said, "I watch the sunset as I look out over the rim of the blue Pacific. There is no mystery beyond the horizon line, because I know what is over there.

"I have journeyed in those lands. Over there where the sun is sinking is Japan. That star is rising over China. In that direction lie the Philippines. I know all that.

"There is another land beyond the sunset, this land of immortality, this fair and blessed country of the soul—why this heaven of ours is the one thing in the world which I know with absolute, unshaken, unchangeable certainty. This I know with a knowledge that is never shadowed by a passing cloud of doubt. I may not always be certain about this world; my geographical locations may sometimes become confused, but the other world—that I know, and as the afternoon sun sinks lower, faith shines more clearly still.

"My work is about ended, I think. The best of it I have done poorly. Any of it I might have done better, but I have done it, and in a fairer land, with finer material, and a better working light, I will do better work."

It was Richard Baxter who wrote:

If life be long, I will be glad
That I may long obey;
If short, yet why should I be sad
To soar to endless day?

Come Lord, when grace has made me meet
Thy blessed face to see;
For if thy world on earth is sweet,
What will thy glory be?

A Father's Example

The Book of Proverbs teaches us: "Train up a child in the way he should go, and when he is old he will not depart from it." What does the writer of Proverbs mean by training? It is teaching, yes; but it is much more. It was Ralph W. Emerson who said, "What you are stands over you and shouts so loudly, I cannot hear what you say."

Teaching in words is important, but teaching in deeds is more so. The saying is true, "Until a boy is fourteen, he does what his father says; after that, he does what his father does."

Clay Doss is the vice president of the Nash-Kelvinator Corporation. He was shopping with his young son one day in downtown Detroit. Because of an inefficient salesgirl the purchase which should have taken only five minutes took over thirty.

When they finally got home, they discovered that she had given them twice as many items as they had bought. Clay, Jr. thought it served her right, but his dad said, "No, Clay, it wouldn't be honest. One of us will have to take the extra items back."

It was Clay, Jr. who made the trip back down town on the bus. When he gave her the items and explained what had happened, the salesgirl took them without as much as one word of appreciation.

Clay, Jr. came home boiling with anger and said, "You were wrong, Dad. The saleslady was very rude. She took the returned items without a word. She didn't even say thank you."

"I know how you feel, Son," his father replied, "But you did what was honest, and being honest is never a mistake. Never!"

Clay Doss forgot all about the incident. It was several days later that his wife related how Clay, Jr. had recounted the entire episode to her. She told how, when he had finished the story, he had said, "You know, Mom, I bet I have the most honest dad in the whole wide world!"

Clay Doss, talking about it later to a fellow worker, said to him, "I would rather have my son say that about me than to have all the money in the world."

"Rear up a child in the way he should go," but remember this: What you say is important, but what you do is the thing that matters most.

God Sees, God Knows, God Cares

Charles M. Schultz, the cartoonist who created the comic strip *Peanuts*, was an outstanding Christian. He was frank to admit that he had a message, and all kinds of people over the years wrote to him, thanking him for preaching in his own way through the comics.

In one of the Peanuts strips, Linus is busy figuring. He comes up to Lucy and says, "Do you know that there are 3,419,420,000 people in the world?" Lucy replies, "Well, those figures are not exactly right."

"I was lying awake the other night thinking about this very thing, and there are more than that. There's Bill, and Henry, and Sally . . . ." Then for three panels she goes on naming names. In the last panel Linus says, "She is the only person I know who can name every person in the world."

Well, maybe Lucy can't, but God can. He sees, he knows, he cares for each and every one of us. That is why it is so meaningful when he promises, "I will never leave you nor forsake you." God never lets us down.

Early one winter morning, a man came into the study of Dr. Ralph W. Sockman, Minister of Christ Church in New York, decidedly shaken. Two men had come to his home earlier that day and at gun point had driven him outside the city. There they threatened his life unless he agreed not to testify against a gambling ring.

He thought about his wife and children and his responsibility to them. Then he thought about his obligation to his community and to God. "I cannot agree to anything like that," he said, "You had better go ahead with what you plan to do."

Then they changed their minds, put him back in car, drove back to the city, and let him out on Madison Avenue. He felt that he needed to tell someone, so he had come to his minister, Dr. Sockman.

"How were you able to do it, to be true to your convictions?" Dr. Sockman asked. The man replied, "I don't know. I guess I just couldn't let God down." Dr. Sockman smiled at him, "And that is just half of it," he said, "God couldn't let you down, either."

It is something we can all count on. God is dependable. He sees, he knows, he cares; and he will never, never let us down.

How Much Land Does A Man Need?

In his short story, *How Much Land Does A Man Need?* Leo Tolstoy told the story of Pakhom, a Russian peasant whose one consuming passion was acquiring land. He felt sure that if he had just a little more land, his life would be complete, so when the Chief of the Baskirs offered to sell for 1,000 rubles all the land Pakhom could walk around in a day, his heart was filled with joy.

The next morning at sunrise he started. The Chief of the Baskirs placed his fur cap on the ground. "Start and return here," he said, "All the land you walk around shall be yours, but if you fail to return to the starting point by sunset, you forfeit both your money and the land."

Pakhom placed his 1,000 rubles on the cap and started toward the rising sun. He traveled eastward for three miles and then three miles more. He looked back toward the starting place. The hillock was scarcely visible, and the people looked like ants. It was time to turn north. He took a drink of water and hurried on.

It was high noon. Pakhom was hungry and was getting tired. He stopped for a bite to eat, but dared not rest for fear of falling asleep. Several times he thought about turning westward, but the land looked so rich and fertile he decided to take in just a little bit more.

At last he turned toward the west. He glanced up at the sun. It was almost halfway to the horizon. "I must hurry back to the starting place," Pakhom said to himself, "My land will be lopsided, but I can't take chances. Anyway, I have lots of land."

He began to run. His lungs were burning and his clothing, saturated with perspiration, clung to his body. The sun touched the distant horizon. Pakhom gathered his remaining strength and ran toward the people waiting at the finish line. They were waving their arms, shouting to him to hurry, as the sun began to disappear.

Suddenly, Pakhom felt his legs give way. Uttering a cry, he fell forward and touched his cap. He heard the whir of voices saying, "Pakhom has gained much land!" They gathered around and tried to raise him up, but something was wrong. Blood was flowing from his mouth. Pakhom was dead!

There in the twilight, they dug his grave. A little plot three feet wide and six feet long was all the land Pakhom needed.

Who was that masked man?

"A fiery horse with the speed of light, a cloud of dust, and a hearty, 'Heigh-ho, Silver!'" It was the Lone Ranger. With his faithful companion, Tonto, the daring and resourceful masked rider of the plains led the fight for law and order in the early western United States.

As children, we thrilled at the invitation: "Return with us, now, to those thrilling days of yesteryear. From out of the past comes the thundering hoof beats of the great horse, Silver. The Lone Ranger rides again!"

Every episode followed the same line. There was a crisis, usually a wrong needing righting. The Lone Ranger came upon the scene, set everything right, and left as mysteriously as he came, and always near the close, the question was asked, "Who was that masked man?"

Our world has been blessed throughout history by anonymous givers. Who do you suppose invented the wheel, lighted the first fire, or discovered the lever? What was the name of the little boy who shared his lunch in the feeding of the 5,000? Who furnished the colt for Jesus' triumphal entry into Jerusalem? Who was the householder who provided the room for the Last Supper?

All are anonymous. On numerous occasions, when Jesus did a service for someone, he would ask the recipient as a special favor not to tell anyone about it.

In the Sermon on the Mount, Jesus talked at length about this manner of giving and living. It seems that it was clear to him that there is a strange relationship between voluntary, secret giving, or the rendering of a good deed with no expectation of reward, and significant and meaningful results that accrue from it in the life of the giver.

Have you tried it? I can assure you, as can hundreds of others, it works. Take Jesus at his word, and let your deeds be done in secret. Your Father will see in secret and will reward you.

John Oxenham was right when he wrote:

> There's a destiny that makes us brothers,
> None goes his way alone;
> All that we send into the lives of others
> Comes back into our own.

Look Up and Laugh and Love and Lift

Some years ago there was a story in *Guideposts* in which Mary Martin told about a hymn that helped her make the most of her life—"I Would Be True." Perhaps you recall the closing words of the second stanza—"I would look up, and laugh, and love, and lift."

When we look up to God, life takes on new meaning. A certain man was busy shaving one morning, when his electric shaver suddenly went dead. "Burned out, I guess," he mumbled to himself, but it wasn't. It had come unplugged.

John's gospel says, "To as many as received him, to them he gave power." When we look up in faith, we find the power we need for living life at its highest and best.

Reader's Digest has a section called *Laughter, the Best Medicine.* What a tonic laughter is. When we laugh, tensions are broken, and we are able to cope with life's problems far more effectively.

A writer of inspirational books says, "Each morning I look in my bathroom mirror and realize what a keen sense of humor God must have, and it reminds me to laugh and to smile."

Jesus said once, "A new commandment I give unto you, that you love one another." Love is the supreme mark of the Christian. In fact, Jesus declared that this was the way people would know that we are his disciples.

Let me share with you the most inspiring and challenging definition of love I have ever heard: "Love is the desire to give oneself in affirming the well-being of another.", and that is, indeed, what makes the world go 'round!

Finally, lift. Your own burdens of life, to be sure; but more, I think, the heavy loads of others. That is why we are here, and it is as we lift our brother's load that we find our own made light.

Christ pointed the way. His was the "upward look." He taught us to pray, "Our Father, who art in heaven," and promised us power from on high. His life was filled with laughter and joy. "Be of good cheer," he said to the Twelve on the eve of his crucifixion, and no one ever loved as Jesus loved. He died for you and me, and "greater love has no one than this."

Children Of The King

Once upon a time, there was a king who had two sons. He loved both of them very much and looked upon them with great pride as they grew from infants to fine looking boys.

One day bandits kidnapped the younger son and carried him far away to the mountains. Then they sent a note to the king demanding a large ransom for the son's return. Fearing for the life of his son, the king met the demands of the outlaws and paid them a large amount of money.

When the captors received the money, they were afraid to return the king's son for fear they would be caught and punished, so they took him to a distant country where they sold him as a slave.

As he grew to manhood, the younger son forgot about his home and family. All he remembered was his life as a scullery boy in the great castle where he was held captive.

His life as a slave was unbearable. He worked hard from morning to night but was constantly beaten for not doing more and for anything he happened to forget.

When the older brother was grown, he saw the sorrow in the eyes of his father. He learned the fate of his younger brother and resolved somehow to find him. For many years, he traveled over land and sea searching.

Then one day he found the castle where his brother was held captive. Carefully, he planned his strategy. Under cover of darkness, he stormed the castle walls, defeated the defending guards, and rescued his brother.

However, in the ensuing battle to escape, the older brother was struck by an arrow and mortally wounded. As he was dying, he told his younger brother, "I came from my father and your father to rescue you. You are not a slave. You are a son of the king."

Even so, Christ is our older brother. He left his home in heaven and came farther to be a missionary to you and me than anyone else has ever gone. As the Savior of the world, he suffered and died on Calvary's cross to rescue you and me. He came to tell us, as Paul wrote in his letter to the Romans, that we are no longer slaves to sin; we are Children of the King.

In Time Of Trial

The year was 1988. The LA Dodgers were playing the Oakland A's in the World Series. Kirk Gibson of the Dodgers' had played so intensely in the pennant race he had seriously injured both legs. Now, sidelined in the clubhouse, he envisioned himself winning the game. One at bat, that would be all he would be able to contribute.

At the bottom of the ninth inning Oakland led 4-3, and Kirk heard the announcer saying, "Batting for the Dodgers will be Scosby, Hamilton, Griffin, followed by the pitcher." The pitcher! He was not a good hitter. Kirk called the manager, Tommy Lasorda. "Tommy, put me in to bat for the pitcher." Lasorda asked, "Kirk, are you sure you are able?" "I'm OK," Kirk replied, "Put me in."

When Kirk stepped out on the field the crowd went wild. No longer did he feel the pain. Limping up to the plate, he took his stance. Then, looking at Dennis Eckersley, the relief pitcher, who had struck out the first two batters and walked the third, he said under his breath, "You have no idea what's coming. The Dodgers are going to win this game, and I'm the guy who is going to do it for them."

He took the first pitch. "Strike one!" The second pitch whizzed by. "Strike two!" Now there were two outs and two strikes. One more strike and the game would be over, but the tying run was on first, and his would win the game for the Dodgers.

The next three pitches went for balls. The count was 3-2. The scout had told them if Eskersley got a batter to three balls and two strikes he would throw a pitch called a backdoor slider. Stepping out of the batter's box, Kirk prepared himself. This was his last chance. It was now or never. Sure enough, the next pitch was a backdoor slider, and Kirk connected for a home run.

Kirk Gibson, hobbling around the bases, his arms in the air, has been played on sports highlights over and over. He said later, "In the time of adversity, if you have faith, you have someplace to turn and somebody to help you, and in the process you will become a better person. Then you are prepared to help others in their time of need. That is what it is all about."

The A's never recovered, and the Dodgers went on to win the Series. It brings to mind a favorite saying in the world of sports: "A quitter never wins; a winner never quits."

On Eagle Wings

The poet has written, "Oh, that a man might arise in me that the man I am might cease to be!" Who among us has not felt that need? But what can we do when things go awry, and we long somehow to be made new?

Long ago Jeremiah asked, "Can a leopard change its spots?" Where do we turn when our purpose and direction in life goes adrift, when all meaning is lost and hope is gone?

In a remote Swiss village years ago there stood a wonderful church, known throughout the region as the Mountain Village Cathedral. Its Gothic design impelled faith, and its tall towers seemed to soar toward heaven. Inside, along the nave, marble pillars and majestic arches alternated in steady rhythm pointing toward the great altar.

The most impressive thing was the organ. People came from far and near to see and hear it, but there was a problem. As time passed things had gone wrong, and at last the great organ stood silent. No one had heard its music for years. Hundreds of musicians and experts were brought in, but their efforts were in vain. They could do nothing.

Then one day an old man appeared at the door of the church and asked the sexton if he might look at the organ and see if he could help. The sexton was hesitant but finally agreed. For two whole days the old man worked in almost total silence. The sexton began to wonder if he had not been wrong in granting permission, but on the third day at high noon there pealed forth from the tower beautiful music.

The entire village rushed to the church. "How did you do it?" they asked, "No one has been able to help. What did you do?" The old man replied, "It was an inside job. It was I who built this organ years ago, and now I have restored it." It is a picture of God himself—God in Jesus Christ who created the universe and who created you and me. Having created us he knows all about us and is able to restore and give meaning to our broken lives. Today, if we would have it so, he can get us back on track, steer our lives to a great cause and give us everlasting life.

> "Whoso draws near to God one step
> through doubtings dim,
> God will advance a mile
> In blazing light to him."

When We Ask In Jesus' Name

It was an amazing promise. Jesus said, "If you ask anything in my name, I will do it,", and that is the way we pray, isn't it? We close our prayers with the words "In Jesus' name."

As children we thought it meant all we had to do was to say, "In Jesus' name," and we could get anything and everything we asked for. Is that what "In Jesus' name" is all about?

The word "name" as used in the Bible is something you almost have to be a Hebrew to understand. A name was more than what a person was called. A name was what a person was.

For example the name "Jacob" meant "Twister." Then at Jabok he was changed, and his name was changed to "Israel," "Prince with God." His name "Simon" meant "Shifting Sand"; Jesus changed his name to "Peter" which meant "Rock." You see a name defined a person's character.

So praying "In Jesus' name" isn't some kind of magic we attach at the end of our prayers to ensure we get what we want. Rather, it is aligning our lives and our prayers with the character and will of the Master.

When we pray, our thinking is very important. In Richard Llewellyn's "How Green Was My Valley," Mr. Gruffydd, the minister, says to the young Huw, "Prayer is only another name for clean direct thinking."

In Shakespeare's "Hamlet," the king goes into the church to pray, but after a while he gives up. He feels his prayers are getting no higher than the ceiling. He walks out, but then stops to analyze the reason for his failure. He says, "My words fly up, my thoughts remain below; words without thoughts never to heaven go."

The Bible says the same thing: "Let the words of my mouth and the meditations of my heart be acceptable in thy sight, O Lord, my rock and my redeemer."

"In Jesus' name" is far more than magic. It is a pledge that we have carefully thought through what we are praying and have found it totally in keeping with the character and spirit of Jesus Christ.

You can believe it; it's true. Jesus meant exactly what he said. Listen again to his promise: "If you ask anything in my name, I will do it."

The Harbor Lamp

On Liberty Island in New York Harbor stands the Statue of Liberty, a colossus of copper, iron, and steel. Its proper name is "Liberty Enlightening the World."

It was created by Frederic Bartholdi, a noted French sculptor, and given to the United States by the people of France in 1884 as a symbol of friendship and of the liberty that citizens enjoy under a free form of government.

The largest statue that had ever been made, it stands 151 feet 1 inch high and weighs 450,000 pounds. It is the figure of a proud woman dressed in flowing robes. Her right arm holds aloft a great torch. In her left arm, she carries a tablet inscribed with the words "July 4, 1776," the date of the Declaration of Independence. A crown with huge spikes, like the rays of the sun, rests on her head. It has an observation platform with twenty-five windows that affords a magnificent view of the harbor and the city.

At the foot of the monument is something all of us are likely to fail to notice. It is a broken shackle, symbolizing the overthrow of tyranny. At night the giant torch gleams with powerful incandescent and mercury vapor lights as a symbol of liberty shedding light upon the world.

Standing in the middle of the harbor, the statue faces out to the sea so as to meet the view of passengers on incoming ships. It has become a symbol of the United States and of freedom.

Each year on July 4 we celebrate the birth of our nation. The Statue of Liberty stands as a constant reminder that we the people are ever dedicated to securing "liberty and justice for all."

That spirit is well expressed in the words of a poem written by Emma Lazarus and inscribed on a tablet in the pedestal. It reads:

> Give me your tired, your poor,
> Your huddled masses yearning
> to breathe free.
> The wretched refuse of your
> teeming shore.
> Send these, the homeless,
> tempest-tossed to me,
> I lift my lamp beside the golden door.

Never Too Late!

He was a judge known for his wisdom and understanding. He tried to help everyone he possibly could. The nineteen year old standing before him had been in trouble with the law a number of times before.

Looking at him, the judge recalled his own boyhood. He knew quite well all that can happen to get a fellow into trouble. He realized, too, that in life, as in a race, sometimes we can get off on the wrong foot.

"John," he said, "All of us have but one life to live. You haven't been doing very well with living yours. We all make mistakes, but, now, why don't you turn over a new leaf. Start over and make a man of yourself?"

John was silent for a moment. Then he replied, "Yes, Sir, I know. I am sorry for what I have done. I wish I could make a new start, but it is too late."

"No, John," the judge said, "It is never too late to begin. Then he shared with him this story:

"Some four hundred years ago, there lived in the city of Florence, Italy, a sculptor by the name of D'Antonio. One day he took a great block of marble and began work on a piece of sculpture, but the marble had a flaw. D'Antonio was not as careful as he should have been, and the piece of marble was ruined. He threw it on the trash heap behind his shop, and it was forgotten.

"Forty years later, in 1501, a young man named Michaelangelo came across the castoff piece of marble with its strange shape, weatherworn and covered with dust. After studying it carefully, he asked if he might have it, and from that old block of marble, ruined by an irreparable flaw and thrown aside, Michaelangelo carved the famous statue of David."

"When things go wrong, as they sometimes will, When the road you're trudging seems all uphill, When the funds are low, and the debts are high, And you want to smile, but you have to sigh, When care is pressing you down a bit, Rest if you must—but don't you quit!"

Remember: In the Academy of Fine Arts in the city of Florence, Italy, there stands an 18-foot statue, "The Boy David," that Michaelangelo carved out of an old dusty block of marble that had been thrown away as useless.

I Surrender All

F. B. Meyer was a young man whose life was empty and meaningless. He had no goal. He had no idea what he wanted to do or be. All of that changed through the influence of C. T. Studd, one of "The Cambridge Seven." F. B. Meyer saw in this man's life dedication, intensity, integrity and knew that he wanted what C. T. Studd had.

One day he said abruptly, "Mr. Studd, how can I be like you?" C. T. Studd smiled, "Well, young man, have you given your heart to Christ?" F. B. Meyer's answer has become a classic. He said, "Yes, Sir, in a general sort of way." C. T. Studd began to laugh, "Well, until you give your heart to Christ in a particular sort of way, he is not your Lord."

F. B. Meyer was stunned. They talked a little longer, and then he left, but that night he made the decision to give his heart to Christ in a particular sort of way. On his knees beside his bed, he visualized an iron ring on which he put a key to every relationship in his life, every business matter, every project, every concern. However, one key he decided to hold back, a key to a very small closet he didn't want Christ to see.

Then holding up the ring with all the other keys, he offered them to Christ, asking him to take possession of his heart. As Christ reached for the ring, he said, "My son, is this all?" F. B. Meyer answered, "Well, all except one. It's to a little bitty closet that isn't important, but here are all the other keys."

Sadly Christ shook his head. "If I am not Lord of all, I am not Lord at all." F. B. Meyer began to tremble. Knowing he couldn't let Christ go, he cried out, "My Lord, I'm not willing to give you all the keys, but I am willing to be made willing!"

He remembered it so well. "Jesus came back, took the ring of keys and then took the little key I had tried to hold back, and the first place he went was into that little closet that I didn't want him to see! In just a week, he cleaned it all away, and I found that what he took away was what had been eating me alive, what in time would have killed me. He gave me instead himself and filled what had been a source of death with life."

F. B. Meyer went on to become an incredible, mighty man of God, one of the truly great Christian leaders of Nineteenth Century England and the world.

Johnny Ring

Up in the Berkshire Hills of Massachusetts, there is a windswept grave, the final resting place of Johnny Ring. You never heard of Johnny Ring? Not surprising, few people have, but Johnny Ring was responsible for Russell Conwell whose lecture, "Acres of Diamonds," was delivered over 5,000 times and inspired and influenced countless individuals.

Russell Conwell was a student in his first year at Yale when the Civil War broke out. He enlisted, and the men insisted that he be their captain. He was only nineteen years old, but they appealed to the governor who gave permission for this young boy to be commissioned.

The men under his command loved and respected him so much they gave of their scant means and bought him a sword. Russell Conwell was deeply touched by their action and prized his sword very highly.

Johnny Ring was also from the Berkshires. He was too small to enlist but was deeply devoted to Captain Conwell and went along as his servant. The captain didn't need a servant nor did he want one, but it was the only way Johnny Ring could be a part of the unit, so he agreed.

On the fateful day that the Confederates stormed their position, Russell Conwell and his men retreated across the river and once across set fire to the wooden bridge. The blazing barrier stopped the Southern forces, but unknown to anyone, Johnny Ring had dashed back to get the captain's sword that had been left behind.

He reached the burning bridge and started across. Both sides watched as he dashed across. By the time he reached the other side, his clothes were ablaze. Losing consciousness, he toppled to the ground.

As he stood over the body of Johnny Ring, Russell Conwell realized that this young boy had died out of love and devotion to him. There that day he made a solemn vow that from that day on he would live not only his own life but also the life of Johnny Ring.

He kept his vow. He worked eight hours a day for himself and eight for Johnny Ring. Years later he said, "It was because of Johnny Ring, who gave his life for me, that I became a Christian."

Someone has said, "Inasmuch as anyone pushes you nearer to God, he is your friend,", and it was the Man from Nazareth who said, "Greater love has no one than this, that a man lay down his life for his friends."

August 14 Psalms 37:39

The Source of America's Greatness

In one of his books, Roger W. Babson tells of taking a trip to South America where he was a guest in the home of the president of Argentina.

One evening after dinner they moved out on the sun deck, which overlooked the Pilcomayo River. As they were talking, the leader of the Argentine Republic asked a question. "Mr. Babson, why is your continent of North America so much further advanced than our continent of South America?"

Then he proceeded to talk about the abounding natural resources of his native land. He said, "Mr. Babson, did you know that in the forests of South America there are 286 kinds of trees which are not listed in any book of botany."

He went on to describe the great South American ranches with their fields of grain and large unbroken tracts of pastureland. He dwelt at length on their great reserves of ore—iron, coal, copper, zinc, silver and gold. He pointed out that with their great rivers the potential waterpower exceeded that of the Niagara.

"Why is it," he continued, "That with all these advantages, South America is so far behind North America? I have been giving this matter a great deal of serious thought lately, and I think I know the answer.

"When the Spaniards came to our country, they came to conquer and to plunder. They came to South America in search of gold. When the Pilgrims came to your country they came seeking a place where they could worship and live in freedom. They came to North America in search of God."

On our coins are to be found these words: "In God we trust." This is the source of our greatness as a nation. Let us unite our hearts in the prayer of Samuel F. Smith:

> Our fathers' God, to Thee,
> Author of liberty,
> To Thee, we sing:
> Long may our land be bright
> With freedom's holy light:
> Protect us by Thy might,
> Great God, our King!

The Trail Of A Gift

I want to share a true story from an article written years ago for the *Atlantic Monthly* by James Norman Hall. After World War I, he went to the island of Tahiti to get away, to rest and to think. At the time he was an unknown and faced the problem of making a living until he could sell some of his writings.

After paying the rent on a one-room shack, he had only five dollars left for food. Among his things he ran across a package of vegetable seed. Not knowing the climate, instead of planting them, he gave them to Hop Sing, a Chinese neighbor who lived next door.

A few days later, Hop Sing came over bringing a "littly plesent," three melons, a hen, and a dozen eggs in the process of being hatched. That afternoon, walking to town, he met a relative of Hop Sing who had heard of Mr. Hall's kindness who gave him a box of chocolates.

When his landlord came by the next day with his children, they got the chocolates. The landlord was so pleased that afterwards he kept his tenant supplied with fruits and vegetables from his garden. In fact, the supply was so bountiful, the five dollars never had to be spent.

Then one day a five hundred dollar check arrived—an advance on some short stories he had sent to a publisher in America. James Norman Hall decided to leave Tahiti. As a farewell gift Hop Sing gave him a dozen ears of Golden Bantam sweet corn grown from the package of seed he had received months before.

On the first night out, the cook prepared the roasting ears for supper. A silent, gloomy Englishman ate three of them. Later, on deck, he explained that he suffered from indigestion and that sweet corn was one of the few things he could eat. As it turned out, he was an editor and bought four of his stories.

It was this article, "The Trail of a Gift," which brought James Norman Hall to the attention of the reading public. Later, in collaboration with Charles Nordhoff, he wrote, *Mutiny on the Bounty*, a best seller that was made into a motion picture, and it all began with a gift—a package of seed corn given in friendship to a neighbor next door.

It was the Man from Galilee who said, "Give, and it will be given to you, good measure, pressed down, shaken together and running over." It is a great truth. Why don't you give it a try?

August 16   **Luke 9: 62**

Excuses! Excuses!

All of his life he had been a cripple. For thirty-eight long years, he sat beside the pool of Bethesda. It was believed that at certain seasons, an angel went down into the pool and stirred the water. Whenever that happened, the first person stepping into the water would be healed.

Passing by, Jesus saw the cripple, and having compassion on him, asked, "Do you want to be healed?" Sadly he replied, "Yes, but I have no one to help me into the water."

This cripple had become very adept at saying, "I would like to, but I can't because—". Our world is filled with people like that. On any given day you can hear them making excuses.

When some young man says, "I didn't get to go to college, and you can't do anything without an education," my heart goes out to him.

Then I think of Abraham Lincoln who was denied a formal education but rose to the office of president of the United States. An education is important, but it isn't everything.

Another person explains, "I don't have good health, and it has prevented me from doing anything with my life," but then I think of Beethoven writing music he was never able to hear. I picture John Milton writing poetry although he was blind. I remember Louis Pasteur, paralyzed, upon whose research modern medicine rests.

Still another says, "Everything seems to turn out bad for me. I'm just unlucky," but hard luck and trouble can make us strong if we have the courage to hold on. It was Jim Corbett, the heavy weight champion, who said, "It's awfully hard to beat a man who will fight another round."

There is a story told about a certain Arab sheik who was asked by a neighbor for the loan of a rope. "I can't lend it to you," he said, "I need it to tie up my milk." Baffled, the neighbor exclaimed, "You can't tie up milk with a rope!" The sheik answered, "My friend, when you don't want to do something, one excuse is just as good as another."

It is so true in your life and mine. If we are looking for excuses to justify failure, they are easy to find, but no amount of alibis can take the place of action. This was the lesson learned by the cripple of Bethesda. Jesus ignored his excuses, pushed them all aside and said to him, "Rise, take up your pallet, and walk," and he did!

229

Warriors of the Broken Sword

Edward Rowland Sill, in his poem "Opportunity," tells of a cowardly soldier who stood at the edge of a battlefield where two armies were engaged in a life and death struggle. The prince leading the fight had fought with courage and daring, but the odds were simply too great.

As he watched, the craven muttered, "If I had a decent sword, that blue blade the king's son bears, I would be in the thick of the fight, but this blunt thing—." Snapping and flinging it away, he left the field.

Then came the king's son, wounded, sore bestead, weaponless, and saw the broken sword hilt buried in the sand. Suddenly everything changed. Reaching down, he took up the broken sword, and with battle shout, cut the enemy down and won a great cause that heroic day.

So it is in the battle of life. Over and over, we witness great battles being fought and victories won against overwhelming odds by warriors with broken swords.

Across the stages of our minds, many such heroes march. We remember William Wilberforce, always in ill health, single-handed, putting an end to the British slave trade; Beethoven, composing great symphonies deaf, unable to hear them; John Milton, writing magnificent poetry in the midst of blindness; John Bunyan, locked in prison for preaching without a license, writing the immortal *Pilgrim's Progress*.

Something stirs within us when we see lives like that—warriors of the broken sword, undaunted, determined, high spirited, and unafraid, fighting on.

It is then, I think, that we look anew at our own swords, shining with good fortune, good health, and ample happiness and with newfound courage voice our prayer:

"Out of the shame of my coward heart,
Out of my night of defeat,
Lift me, O God, to the battle again,
Cover my bitter retreat.

By the wonder of Heaven's forgiveness,
By the lovely lure of Thy light,
By the spirit of victory eternal,
God, fling me again to the fight!"

Seeing the Invisible

In the Old Testament there is recorded the story of how the king of Syria, warring against Israel, found it necessary to capture the prophet Elisha. Dispatched spies discovered that the prophet was staying in Dothan, and the king sent an army by night that surrounded the village.

The next morning, going out early, Elisha's servant found the city surrounded by the enemy. Rushing back he cried, "Alas, Master, what shall we do?" Calming him, Elisha said, "Don't be afraid, for those who are with us are more than those who are with them."

Then Elisha prayed a rather strange prayer: "Lord, open the young man's eyes that he may see." The Lord opened his servant's eyes and he saw. "And behold, the mountains were full of horses and chariots of fire round about Elisha."

This story speaks a great lesson. Physical sight is important, but the ability to see the unseen is more important. Today as never before, we need to be able to see spiritual reality, the power of God in the world around us, to know with the poet that "Beyond the dim unknown, stands God within the shadows, keeping watch above His own."

When the English poet, John Milton lost his sight, he wrote to a friend, "I do not complain of my absence of sight. In the night surrounding me, the light of God's presence shines with even more brilliant luster." That was Paul's secret, too. Because God had opened his eyes, he knew, "that in everything God works for good with those who love him."

Such God-given sight enables us to see others in a far different way. In his book *Les Miserables*, Victor Hugo says of the escaped convict, Jean Valjean, "It would be difficult to meet a man of more wretched appearance." So sinister were his looks, no one in the village would give him shelter for the night.

Finally, the bishop takes him in and Jean Valjean rewards his kindness by stealing his silverware, but when the police bring him back, the Bishop is able to see in him more than a thief. He says to him, "My brother, you no longer belong to evil but to good. Use the silver to become an honest man." That night, for the first time in years, Jean Valjean broke down and cried. He was a changed man.

God, who gave us sight, can do that for you and me if we would have it so. Lord, open my eyes that I may see!

August 19   **Mark 5: 25-29**
Standing On The Promises

They are the words of Jesus spoken when the disciples asked why they couldn't heal an epileptic boy. He said, "Because of your little faith." Then he said, "If you have faith as a grain of mustard seed, you will say to this mountain, 'move from here to there,' and it will move; and nothing will be impossible to you."

It is an amazing statement; do we believe it? Really believe it? Most of us wouldn't question it. We give lip service and accept it as true, but do we ever act on it? Jesus was placing a tremendous power at our disposal. Using picturesque language he was saying, "If you have just a little faith, you can do impossible things."

Jesus was on his way to heal the little daughter of Jairus. Waiting on the roadside was a woman who had had a hemorrhage of blood for twelve years. When she heard that Jesus was coming, she said to herself, "If I could so much as touch his clothes, I know I would be healed."

So it was that as Jesus passed by, she reached out a trembling hand and ever so lightly touched his garment. Power surged through her and she knew that she had been made well. Sensing what had happened, Jesus stopped and asked, "Who touched me?" The disciples answered, "The crowd is thronging you on every side. How can you ask such a question?"

Then Jesus said something that they never forgot. "I know," he said, "But this person touched me!" His words speak a vital message to every heart and life. There is all the difference in the world in "thronging" Jesus and reaching out in faith and "touching" him. In our Bible reading, our prayer life, small groups, Sunday worship, our thoughts throng Jesus but how seldom do we really reach out and touch.

Are there mountains in your life with which you would like to deal? Listen again to Jesus: "If you have faith as a grain of mustard seed, you will say to this mountain, 'Move from here to there,' and it will move; and nothing will be impossible to you."

His love has no limit;
His grace has no measure;
His power has no boundary
Known unto men.
For out of his infinite riches in Jesus,
He giveth, and giveth, and giveth again!

232

Laying A-Hold on the Greatness of God

It happened in church. The family was there for Morning Worship, a mother, father, and their little boy of five. The minister finished the pastoral prayer, and holding hands, the congregation began the Lord's Prayer in unison. The mother overheard Jimmy praying, "Our Father who art in heaven, how do you know my name?"

The young man may not have had the Lord's Prayer down just right, but he was asking a good theological question. Scientists tell us that our earth is over four billion years old. It is only one of several planets that revolve around our sun. The sun itself is a star of only average size among a hundred billion stars in our galaxy that we call the Milky Way, and there are as many galaxies in our universe as there are stars in our galaxy. The eighth Psalm speaks for all of us when it exclaims, "When I look at thy heavens, what is man that you are mindful of him?"

Dr. James Gordon Gilkey when asked by one of his students, "Do you think God knows my name?" replied, "Yes, God knows your name. Not only that, he knows all about you—your abilities, your problems, your heartaches, your joys."

God gives personal attention to each of us. His mind is of measureless power. Have you ever noticed that when you toss a pebble in the ocean, it is no problem for the ocean to completely surround it? And it can just as easily encompass as many pebbles as are thrown into its waters. In the same way, it is no problem for God to give his undivided attention to you and me and millions of others at the same time.

Once just before a concert by the NBC Symphony, the bassoon player came to Arturo Toscanini for help. His instrument had been damaged and couldn't sound E-flat. The great conductor put his head in his hands for a few moments and then looking up said, "It's all right, the note of E- flat doesn't appear in your music today."

If a man like Toscanini can know all the notes in a symphony, then surely the Great Conductor knows the symphony that is our universe. He knows it from the tiniest atom to the most gigantic star, and he also knows intensively each and every one of his children who are its notes.

Jimmy, I don't know how, but God does know your name. He knows the name of each and every one of us, and if we trust him, he will sustain and keep us all the days of our lives and lead us at last into the realms of everlasting day.

They Signed For Us

It was July 4, 1776. In the city of Philadelphia, the Second Continental Congress had formally declared the American colonies independent of Great Britain. But now, looking at the wording describing King George VI as: "...a tyrant, unfit to be the ruler of a free people," they were having second thoughts.

"Have we gone too far?" they wondered. There was little doubt that if they signed the Declaration they would be branded as rebels and enemies of the crown—and every one of them knew it! The discussion went back and forth. Tempers flared. A few ardent patriots argued against any compromise. However, it was evident that they were not ready to approve the Declaration as it was written.

The cause seemed lost. Then a tall, dignified man arose. "The chair recognizes Dr. John Witherspoon, delegate from New Jersey," announced the presiding officer, John Hancock. A hush fell over the assembly. All eyes focused on the speaker.

"There is a tide in the affairs of men," John Witherspoon said, speaking slowly and emphasizing every word, "It is before us now. To hesitate is to consent to our own slavery. That noble instrument on your table, which insures immortality to its author, should be subscribed this very morning by every pen in this house. He who will not respond to its accents and strain every nerve to carry into effect its provisions is unworthy the name of free man."

He paused, his eyes fixed on the tense faces before him. "For my own part," he continued, "My reputation is staked, my property, such as I have, is pledged on the issues of this contest. I do not have too many years left to live, but I would infinitely rather die at the hand of the executioner than desert at this crisis the sacred cause of my country."

For a while there was silence. One could have heard a pin drop. Then the delegates leaped to their feet, calling for action. The Declaration of Independence was signed by every one of the delegates, and liberty was preserved.

With grateful hearts, let us give thanks to Almighty God whose "love divine has led us in the past." Then in support of the Declaration of Independence, along with the fifty-six who signed for us, let us "mutually pledge to each other our lives, our fortunes, and our sacred honor."

Acts 2: 21

God's Way Works!

On April 18, 1942, sixteen American B 25s, led by the famed Jimmy Doolittle, roared over Japan at treetop level taking the Japanese air defense by surprise.

In plane number 16, eager to repay the enemy for the thousands of Americans they killed at Pearl Harbor, was a young bombardier, Jacob DeShazer, whose target was an oil refinery south of Tokyo. He planted three incendiary bombs squarely on the tanks. They burst into flames, and the cheering crew headed for China.

On the mainland, thick fog had moved in. Flying blind for hours, out of fuel, they jumped. Captured by the Japanese who were enraged over the Doolittle raid, they faced savage revenge. Starved and beaten, they soon began to hate the Japanese with a consuming rage.

Found guilty by a military court, three were executed by a firing squad. Jacob DeShazer and four others received life imprisonment. Confined to five-foot stone cells, life became unbearable.

One day a guard thrust a book into his hands. It was a Bible. In the dim light of the cell, he began reading, The Old Testament and then the New. He read of Jesus who fulfilled all of the prophesies. Joy filled his heart. He prayed and rose from his knees a committed Christian.

Soon he knew he had to forgive his brutal captors as God had forgiven him. The words of Christ spoke to his soul, "Love your enemies and pray for those who persecute you."

The next day when he said good morning in Japanese, the guard stared in amazement. He continued to be friendly, and out of the blue, the guard gave him some fruit and candy. Jacob DeShazer's heart sang. God's way worked! He had made a friend out of an enemy.

At last, rescued by American paratroopers, Jacob DeShazer returned to America, studied to become a missionary and returned to Japan. There he spoke to thousands, simply telling about his own conversion. Hundreds of people responded to his call for love and forgiveness and received Christ as their Lord and Savior.

One of Jacob DeShazer's converts was Mitsuo Fuchida who testified that had he known Jesus Christ as Lord and Savior, he would never have participated in, much less led, the attack on Pearl Harbor.

August 23   **Romans 14:12**

"Please, God, I Am Only 17"

It was growing dark. My neighbor and I had been visiting in the front yard. Suddenly, a car came out of nowhere and came blazing down the street. The young driver burned rubber as he took the curve and disappeared around the corner. Just a few moments before, two children had crossed that street on their way home. It could have been tragic.

Sometime later, I found the following article that I had saved. It is said that Coach "Bear" Bryant used to read it to every freshman class on opening day of classes. I took it to our youth director to share with the young people of our church, and I want to share it with you.

"When I first got here I felt very much alone. I was overwhelmed with grief, and I expected to find sympathy. I saw only thousands of others whose bodies were as mangled as mine. I was given a number and placed in a category: "Traffic Fatalities."

"The day I died was an ordinary school day. I wheedled the car out of Mom. 'Special favor,' I pleaded, 'All the kids drive.' The accident? I was goofing off—going too fast, taking chances. The last thing I remember was passing a car I thought was going too slow. I heard a crash as glass and steel flew everywhere. I heard myself scream.

"Suddenly I awakened. A police officer and a doctor were standing over me. My body was mangled, and I was saturated with blood. Jagged glass was sticking out all over. I couldn't feel a thing. Hey, don't pull that sheet over my head. I can't be dead. I'm only 17.

"Later, placed in a drawer, my folks came to identify me. Why did they have to see me like this? They were weeping so hard. Dad told the man in charge, 'Yes, he is our son.'

"The funeral was weird. I saw all my relatives and friends walk toward the casket. They looked at me with the saddest eyes I've ever seen. Some of my buddies were crying. Some of the girls touched my hand and sobbed as they passed by. Please—somebody—wake me up! I can't bear to see my Mom, my Dad, all my friends in such pain.

"Please don't bury me! I have a lot of living to do! I want to laugh and run and sing and dance. Please, God, I promise if you give me one more chance, I'll be the most careful driver in the whole world. All I want is one more chance. Please, God, I'm only 17."

Closed Doors

In the city of Enterprise, Alabama is one of the most amazing statues in all North America. It is a large statue of a boll weevil. A boll weevil! Why would anyone erect a statue to a boll weevil?

Back in the eighteen hundreds, the number one crop of Enterprise, Alabama, indeed of most of the Deep South, was cotton. Cotton was king, and every industry was related to cotton in one way or another.

Then one year the boll weevils moved in and totally wiped out the crops. The destruction was catastrophic. The farmers faced starvation. They didn't even have seed for another year, and the merchants, bankers— every industry in the town faced bankruptcy and ruin.

The town was being blown away, and no one knew what to do. A special prayer service was held seeking God's help, asking God to show them what they should do. Then they started looking around for some kind of solution, and they discovered peanuts.

They had always known about peanuts but never had anyone considered farming peanuts. They studied the possibility, decided that it was a good one, and started farming peanuts. An amazing thing happened. Within six years the farmers of Enterprise, Alabama, and all the businesses that depended on the farmers were making five times as much from peanuts as they had made from cotton.

It was out of that experience that they decided to build a statue to the boll weevil. From that day to this, that statue has served as a permanent reminder. It says to every person in Enterprise, Alabama, indeed to people everywhere, that just because a door closes, it doesn't mean that life is over.

Soon or late all of us come to closed doors, and the great truth is that no matter what door closes on you, as long as you live in Jesus Christ you have life eternal and have it abundantly. For the same God who did good works, by and for and through you in the past, is still with you in the present and will be with you in the future.

God who gave you that which you lose, as incredibly wonderful as it may have been, is still with you and will give great gifts for the future. Even when the day comes for the door of death itself to be slammed in your face, God is still there. His grace is still good, and his plans for you stretch into eternity.

This Above All

In William Shakespeare's play *Hamlet*, Polonius gives this advice to his son Laertes, "This above all: to thine own self be true, and it must follow, as the night the day, Thou canst not then be false to any man."

This is what real living is all about. God has given each of us one life to live. That life is God's gift to us; what we do with it is our gift to God. If life is to be lived successfully, we must take charge and be responsible for our thoughts, our words, our actions, and God's word tells us how.

In the book of Proverbs are found these words: "Keep your heart with all vigilance, for from it flows the springs of life." It's true—we become what we think about, so stand constant guard against envy and jealousy, prejudice and hatred, fear and doubt.

Margaret Mitchell was right when she had a character in *Gone With The Wind* say, "Nothing from the outside can lick any of us, but what the whole world can't do, our own hearts can." Keep your heart!

In the book of Psalms is this counsel: "Keep your tongue from evil." As children when we said something that hurt someone's feelings and for which we were sorry, we would say, "I take it back." But the bitter truth is we can never recall words once they have passed from our lips. For good or bad, they are gone forever. Keep your tongue!

Paul, in his letter to the young man Timothy, gave him this charge: "Keep yourself pure." Sometimes our thoughts get out from under our control, but we can with God's help keep in command of our actions. As someone has pointed out, "We can't keep birds from flying over our heads, but we can keep them from building nests in our hair." Keep yourself pure!

Responsible living. To your own self be true. Keep your heart, keep your tongue, and keep yourself pure. God has shown us what to do. It is up to us to act.

In the words of John Drinkwater:

> "Knowledge we ask not—
> Knowledge Thou hast lent
> But, Lord, the will—there lies our bitter need.
> Give us to build above the deep intent
> The deed, the deed."

The Faithfulness of a Father

In 1989, there was a devastating earthquake in Armenia that made headlines worldwide. Over 30,000 people were killed and thousands were injured. One father raced to his son's school and found that it had been leveled. There was only a mountain of stones where the school had once stood.

The father stood confused for a while as to what to do. Then he remembered a promise he had made his son even before he was big enough to understand: "Son, no matter what, I'll always be there for you."

Rushing to the back corner where his son's classroom had been, he started digging with his bare hands. Other parents arrived and were shocked by what he was doing. "Don't do this to yourself," they said, "There is no hope." Glancing up, the father asked, "Will you help me?" They looked at him with pity. One by one, they sadly drifted away.

A policeman watched for a moment. Then he said, "My friend, I know you are upset, but if you keep digging, the rubble is going to cave in, and you will be trapped, too." The father, asked, "Will you help me?" The officer paused for a moment, shook his head and walked on.

The fire chief came over and said to him, "Sir, you are risking your life. Let the professionals do what they are trained to do. Go home." Not so much as looking up, the father said to him, "Will you help me?" The fire chief moved on to work somewhere else. The father kept digging.

Eight hours passed, then twelve and then twenty-four—an entire day. Left alone, the father kept digging, his hands swollen and bleeding. The clock said thirty-six hours had passed when he heard faint voices down inside. He cried out, "Who's there? Armon? Armon?" Then he heard the most wonderful words he had ever heard in his life, "Dad! Is that you?"

Suddenly, hope and assurance filled the air. Villagers came running and began pulling the stones off. All 14 of the children came out safe and sound, and as they did, the father hugged each one.

Over and over the son kept saying, "Dad, you promised, and I knew you'd come. I kept telling the other kids, 'If my Dad is alive after the earthquake, he will come and save me and when he does, he will save all of you, too.'"

Growing Older or Growing Up

She was very exceptional, the kind of person you never forgot. In a brief period of time she managed to change the lives of many people around her, but I want you to hear about her from a young man who knew her best:

"The very first day of class our professor challenged us to get to know someone we didn't already know. As I looked around, a hand touched my shoulder.

"A little old lady was beaming a smile, 'Hi handsome. My name is Rose. I'm eighty-seven years old. May I give you a hug?' I laughed enthusiastically, 'Of course you may!'

"Why are you in college at such a young, innocent age?' I asked. She replied, 'I'm here to meet a rich husband, get married, and have a couple of kids.' 'No, seriously?' I asked. Then she said, 'I always dreamed of having a college education, and now I'm getting one!'

"Over the years, Rose became a campus icon, making friends wherever she went. All the students loved her. She used to say, 'We don't stop playing because we grow old; we grow old because we stop playing.' She said, 'To stay young, you have to laugh, and see humor every day, and you've got to have a dream. When you lose your dream, you die.'

"She had a wonderful philosophy of life. She said to a group of us one day, 'Life is all about giving, not getting. We make a living by what we get; we make a life by what we give.'

"She couldn't care less about her age. She said once, 'When people ask me how old I am, I tell them right off. If I don't they guess, and they always guess me to be a lot older than I am!'

"'Just remember,' she counseled, 'There's a lot of difference between growing older and growing up. Anybody can grow older. That doesn't take any talent or ability. The idea is to grow up by always finding opportunity in change.' She said, 'You know, I don't have any regrets for what I did, but I am haunted by lots and lots of things I didn't do.'

"Rose finished college. She earned the degree she dreamed of. One week after graduation, she died peacefully in her sleep. Thousands of students attended her funeral in tribute to the wonderful woman who taught by example that it's never too late to be all you can possibly be."

Love Is Something You Do

"Mommy, what does love look like?" The question came from a little child. It was asked innocently, but as seriously as any adult could have asked it. How would you have answered it? If you were asked what love looks like, what would you say?

Augustine the Great, one of the Fathers of the Church who lived during the fourth century, once described love. He said four things about it, painting an unforgettable word picture.

1. "Love has eyes to see." It has been said that love is blind. In a way, perhaps, but it is only a particle of the whole truth. At the height of the Great Depression, a certain woman said, "I don't think times are so hard."

In the tenement next door, there were men and women out of work, families out of food, and babies with empty bottles. There was dire need all around. She just couldn't see, then love opened her eyes.

2. "Love has ears to hear." Isn't it strange? A mother, keeping watch beside the crib of her baby who is ill, toward daybreak drifts off to sleep. The clock in the hall strikes six, but she sleeps on. The morning newspaper, thrown by the paperboy, lands on the porch, not a move. A heavy truck lumbers by, peaceful slumber. Then the baby stirs, ever so lightly, and the mother is wide-awake. Love listens—and hears.

3. "Love has feet to hasten." God is love, and he sent his Son into the world that we might know what love is like. The Bible has a lot to say about Jesus, about his teachings, about his miracles; but I think the words of Peter describe him best: "Jesus went about doing good." Love has feet, and they hurry to bring aid.

4. "Love has hands to help." Recently I watched and listened as a little girl of five, her eyes filled with love, looked up at her mother and asked, "May I help set the table?" You see, this is love's prerogative.

Luke begins the Book of Acts with the phrase "All that Jesus began to do and teach ...." Jesus was a great teacher. People remembered his words.

But what people remembered mostly was what he did. This above all, love is something you do.

The Power of the Gospel

On a Sunday evening in May of 1947, a man by the name of Felix Ayala sat in a little church in Puerto Rico and heard the minister say, "The gospel of Christ is the power of God unto salvation to everyone who believes."

He wondered if such good news could be true. He decided it was worth trying at least. When the invitation was given, he went forward and made his commitment to Christ.

Felix Ayala had a terrible reputation. The people in church that evening believed he was under the influence of alcohol. They couldn't remember a single week that he hadn't been arrested for drunkenness, stealing, or disturbing the peace. They all felt certain that he would never change, but Felix Ayala was sincere.

It was a real battle giving up his drinking and "going straight," but with the help of the men of the church, he did it. The entire village began to notice the difference. He was becoming a new person.

Then, trouble from the past reared its' ugly head. In 1943 there had been a murder. Felix Ayala was a suspect. "Three of us were drinking, and there was a fight," he told the judge, "I could have done it, and I want to plead guilty," and so, he was sent to prison for murder.

The years passed, and one day at the request of his friends the missionary asked the governor to consider parole. The governor reviewed the record. Every week some kind of charge—drunkenness, theft, assault, destruction of property—no favor could be shown to a criminal like that!

Then the governor came to May 1947. Could it be true, a week when Ayala didn't go to jail? The governor was amazed. There was nothing against Felix Ayala after May, 1947.

He called in John Vincent, the missionary to the village. "Do you know what happened in May, 1947?" The answer: "Sir, Felix Ayala became a Christian." The police record proved it. Felix Ayala's life had been changed by the power of the gospel. Today, he is back with his family, working in the little church where it all took place. It's true. The gospel is the power of God unto salvation. It can be so for anyone and everyone who believes!

August 30   **Romans 1:16**
Transformed Lives

In his letter to the Romans, Paul offers this challenge:"Do not be conformed to this world but be transformed by the renewal of your mind."

Deep within every person, there is a longing to be better. Jesus knew this, and he found it in the most unpromising places. The woman at the well had had five husbands and was living with a man who was not her husband, yet when Jesus offered her "living water," she wanted it.

Matthew, the tax collector, heard Christ call, "Come, follow me." He rose up and followed. Bartimaeus, the blind beggar, heard Jesus passing by and cried out, then, sight restored, he followed Christ to Calvary. The same hunger is in your life and mine. The trouble is we try to satisfy that hunger by trying to make ourselves good, and we can't.

In a church camp that I directed one summer, there was a young boy who was giving all kinds of trouble. He was breaking all the rules, and it looked like we might have to send him home.

I called him in for a conference. We talked about the camp, how he was enjoying it, and, finally, about his conduct as a camper. His head dropped in embarrassment. "Mr. Nichols, I'm sorry I am such a problem." He said, "I try to be a good—I really do, but for some reason I keep doing the wrong things!" Isn't that our problem, too?

Paul faced this dilemma. He wrote, "The good I want to do, I don't do, and the bad that I don't want to do is the very thing I do! Miserable man that I am, who will deliver me from this bondage of death?" He found the answer. Listen: "Thanks be to God who gives us the victory through Jesus Christ . . . ." Everything changed when he discovered that with Christ's help, he could achieve what he could never achieve alone.

Early one morning I glanced out my study window and noticed leaves falling from a small oak tree and suddenly realized that those dark brown leaves had been on that little tree all winter. They had clung tenaciously to the branches in spite of wind and rain, ice and snow. Why were they falling now? I went out to investigate.

The answer wasn't hard to find—tiny, green buds! New life rising up within! This is the secret for us, too. Christ living within, forces old sins to fall away like autumn leaves when spring arrives.

The Magic of Believing

Jim Brown is an all-time great of football. He was a fullback for the Cleveland Browns from 1957 to 1965. He holds the record for career rushing—12,312 yards. Twice he was chosen as the NFL player of the year, 1958 and 1963.

In 1965, playing against the New York Giants, Jim Brown gained nearly 200 yards rushing. That is as many as some backs gain in an entire season. Jim Brown was great in every game he played, but that afternoon, he was simply superb.

After the game, one of his friends asked, "Jim, how in the world did you do it?" Jim hesitated for a moment, then he said, "You wouldn't believe it if I told you."

His friend urged, "Go ahead and try me."

After another pause, Jim Brown replied, "Well, I will tell you. I have been playing that game all week long. Everywhere I have been—in my room, driving my car, eating my meals, lying in bed—I have played that game. Every thought was on that game. I played it over and over.

"I have seen myself taking the ball, breaking over tackles, sweeping the end, eluding linebackers. I have pictured myself taking passes and running over, around, and through every opposing player on the field.

"Finally, when game time arrived, it was nothing new. I just did what I had been doing all week."

Jim Brown was using "the magic of believing." He used it to play an outstanding game and win a victory. I have seen this power at work many, many times.

You have seen it, too. "The magic of believing" enables a football team to crush an opponent of far greater ability. It enables a person of average ability to far surpass another possessing twice the talent. "The magic of believing" causes patients in hospitals to live, while others, not nearly as ill, die.

William James, the great psychologist, once wrote, "Belief is the thing that assures success," and the Man from Nazareth gave it a central place time and again: "If you can! All things are possible to him who believes."

September 1   **Revelation 21:2**
                    Builders on the Sands of Time

Dawson Bryan tells how on a summer afternoon a little boy played on the
seashore close to his home. He was building a city in the sand. He laid out
streets lined with houses, added stores and banks, churches and schools,
playgrounds and parks.

With a boy's fancy, he built a wall around it and beyond, roads and bridges,
meadows, orchards, and fields of grain. Throughout the long afternoon,
he built the city of his dreams.

So intent was he with the undertaking, he lost track of time. All at once
the afternoon was gone, the sun was going down, and dark clouds were
gathering.

Busy building his city, he had not noticed that the tide was coming in. The
white-capped waves mounted higher and higher. Suddenly, one wave,
bigger than the others, came rolling in at his feet.

Then another, even larger, and city and farms, houses and land, were
swept away. In terror, the little boy ran back against the cliff. All alone, he
looked out at the dark, rolling tide in fear.

But above him, on the cliff, was his older brother. He had watched it all.
He went back in memory to his own boyhood, when he, too, had been
a builder on the sand. He had seen the big waves come rolling in, as
eventually they always do. He had seen everything swept away.

He had seen the look of fear on the face of his younger brother. Leaning
over the edge, he called. Reaching down, he caught him by the hand and
lifted him to safety. Then, placing his arm about him, they turned away
from the tide and foam and started home. There, a light burned brightly
in the window, and love awaited their coming.

Like that little boy, you and I spend our days upon the sands of time. We
too are builders, and so intent we become, we fail to note life's setting sun,
the dark clouds, and rising wind. Before we know it, the tide rushes in, all
of our earthly possessions are swept away, and we are left terrified and
alone.

But above is our Elder Brother who has seen it all. His hand reaches down
for our hand, and we are lifted up. Then arm in arm, we turn away from this
bourne of time and place and toward the house of many mansions. There
our Father waits.

245

This Old House

John Quincy Adams, well past 80 years of age, was tottering down the street one day when he was stopped by a friend. "And how is John Quincy Adams today?" he asked.

The former president of our nation replied, "John Quincy Adams is quite well, thank you. Of course, the house in which he lives at present is becoming rather dilapidated. In fact, it is teetering on its foundation.

"Time and seasons have nearly destroyed it. The roof is pretty well worn. Its walls are shattered, and it trembles with the wind. The old tenement is becoming uninhabitable, and I think John Quincy Adams will have to move out soon, but he himself is quite well, Sir, quite well."

John Quincy Adams knew, as every follower of Christ ought to know "that if the earthly tent in which we live in is destroyed, we have a building from God, a house not made with hands, a home eternal in the heavens."

It was a great shock to Dr. A. T. Pierson when he received news of the death of his close friend, the Rev. Dr. A. J. Gordon. The family requested that he conduct the memorial service.

That evening, thinking about his friend and unable to sleep, Dr. Pierson picked up his Greek New Testament to see what it said about death. He made a great personal discovery. He found that after the resurrection of Christ, the word "death" is never again used to denote the close of a Christian's life.

The Apostles spoke of being "at home with the Lord." They mentioned having "fallen asleep." They talked about "departing to be with Christ," and of being "forever with the Lord," but never again did they speak of death.

Once in the days long gone and dead a little boy of some five years of age, having played all afternoon, was so tired and sleepy he could scarcely hold his eyes open, but he still didn't want to go to sleep.

Finally, his mother took him in her arms and sat down to rock him. Not realizing how sleepy he was, he protested loud and long, but gradually his strivings ceased. His tearful eyes closed, and soon he was peacefully asleep, to awake at dawn and find all things made new. I think the close of our earthly life must be like that.

Silence In Heaven

Shortly after World War II, Roland Hayes, the great American tenor, was to sing a concert in Beethoven Hall in Berlin. Being a non-Aryan Black, he was hissed and booed. Anger welled up, but he stood in silence remembering the words of an African American spiritual describing Jesus—"He never said a mumbling word." His silent humility touched the hearts of the crowd. He began to sing, and following his first number the applause was deafening.

So many times Jesus kept silent, on trial before Herod, and again in the presence of Pontius Pilate, but of all the incidences recorded in the New Testament where Jesus kept silent, none is quite as impressive as his silence before the woman taken in adultery.

The Pharisees dragged and shoved her into the presence of Jesus. She had been caught. The Law said she was to be stoned; what did Jesus say? Jesus was embarrassed for her and wouldn't even look up. He knelt down and wrote with his finger in the sand. The Pharisees persisted. Finally, Jesus looked up and said, "Let him who is without sin cast the first stone." Then, once more, he bent down and wrote on the ground.

One by one, stricken with guilty consciences, the Pharisees slipped away. Lifting his eyes and looking into hers, Jesus asked, "Where are your accusers?" She answered softly, "No one has accused me, Lord." Then Jesus spoke again, and the words on his lips were words of mercy, love, and life—"Neither do I condemn you; go, and do not sin again."

Ian Burnett, commenting on the story in his book, *Lord of All Life*, says, "Someday you and I must appear before the judgment seat of Christ, and if he shall speak, who will stand? But I know my Savior well. I know that where sin abounds, grace abounds much more. I know that love will seal his lips, and that we who have deserved death shall find life. For when our sins parade before him in their hideous liveries and accuse us, then he who died for us will hold his peace.

"There will be silence in heaven. Even the angels will cease their singing and hold their breath to hear his word, and that word will be life and immortality for you and me.

"For the silence will at last be broken, and out of his lips shall come salvation. We shall hear him say, 'Neither do I condemn you. Go. Go into eternity and sin no more.'"

Lest We Forget!

In the year 1897, Great Britain celebrated Queen Victoria's Diamond Jubilee. Amidst the pomp and pageantry, Rudyard Kipling, England's great poet, wrote "Recessional" in observance of the great event. The poem is a very sobering prayer, and each stanza closes with this awesome petition: *Lord God of Hosts, be with us yet, Lest we forget—Lest we forget!*

This might well be America's prayer as we ask again, "What makes America great, and what is the source of her greatness?"

In 1835, Alexis de Tocqueville of France came to the United States to study our democracy. After extensive investigation, he said, "I looked for the greatness of America in her fields and forests, her factories and farms. I looked for it in her schools and institutions of learning, her Congress and Constitution, but it was not until I went to America's churches that I discovered the genius that makes America great. America is great, because she is good, and if she ever ceases to be good, she will cease to be great."

Soren Kierkegaard, the great Danish theologian, tells the parable of the spider that lived high up in the rafters of a barn. One day he let himself down, by a single filament of web, to the floor of one of the cribs.

There, in one of the corners, he spun a web and set up housekeeping. Flies were plentiful, and as the days passed, he grew prosperous and fat. Where he came from was totally forgotten.

One day, as he strolled around surveying his vast domain, he chanced upon the single thread reaching up into the great unknown. For a while he studied it. "What in the world is that for, I wonder? I cannot see that it serves any purpose at all." So saying, he clipped the thread, and when he did his web collapsed and tumbled in ruin about him.

The hymn, "My Country, 'Tis of Thee," closes with this stanza: *Our Fathers' God, to Thee, Author of liberty, To Thee we sing: Long may our land be bright with freedom's holy light; Protect us by Thy might, Great God, our King!* This is the source of America's greatness, and any other theory we may come up with isn't worth the scotch tape that it takes to hold it together!

"Lord God of Hosts, be with us yet,
Lest we forget—Lest we forget!"

When Did You See Jesus Last?

When was the last time that you saw Jesus? In the Gospel of Luke, there is recorded the account of how a tax collector by the name of Zacchaeus climbed up in a sycamore tree so he could see Jesus who "was to pass that way."

Over and over it happens in your life and mine. Jesus passes our way. If we have eyes to see, we may behold him. When was the last time you saw Jesus?

The last time you looked into the face of a little child you saw Jesus. Jesus said of children, "Of such is the kingdom of heaven." Beholding their little faces, you looked into the face of Christ.

The last time a tired and hungry man looked to you for help, Jesus stood before you. As you gave him food to eat, clothes to wear, or a cold drink of water, it was Jesus to whom you gave.

The last time you saw a stranger standing all alone, self-conscious and ill-at-ease, you saw Jesus. When you smiled, spoke a word of kindness making that person feel relaxed and at ease, you were ministering to the Master.

The last time you entered a sick room and looked down on one in pain, you looked into the eyes of Jesus. Your words of comfort and concern were spoken to him.

As you held a trembling hand, as you touched a fevered brow, you were holding the hand and touching the brow of Jesus. It was Christ who was suffering there.

Strange, isn't it? But that is what Jesus always does. He hides himself in the face of a child, in the form of a beggar, tired and worn, in the life of a stranger, lost and alone, in a mind and body wracked with pain.

Jesus once told how at the last judgment, the King shall say, "Come, inherit the kingdom prepared for you . . . for I was hungry and you fed me. I was a stranger and you welcomed me. I was sick and you visited me. For as you did it unto the least of these my brothers, you did it to me."

Today he will walk among us, but only those with eyes shall see. What about you, when did you see Jesus last?

September 6

How Do You Say It?

I was visiting in the home of a young couple when their little boy of eight came into the living room. He held a book in his left hand, and the index finger of his right was pressed tightly under a word. Holding it for his mother to see, he asked, "Mommy, how do you say it?"

Webster's Third New International Dictionary contains 450,000 words, and some of them are pretty hard to pronounce. But our problem is not with words like "pneumonoultramicroscopicsilicovolcanokoniosis," antidisestablishmentarianism," or "floccipaucinihilipilification," but with the simple little words that we use every day.

The word "God" has only three letters and yet, what trouble it gives us. Perhaps the biggest problem is that many of us never pronounce it at all. Created and sustained by God, we go our ways ignoring him completely. Some pronounce it only as a profane oath and others as though he were a million miles away. Jesus taught us how to say it. He pronounced it "Father."

Another word that gives us trouble is the two letter word, "we." Why do we persist in pronouncing it "I"—too often and too loudly, or "they"? Bob Zupkee, football coach at Illinois, said to his team one Saturday, after lack of team play had cost them a crucial game, "All of you played your positions well. Where we failed was between the positions, where the other team went through for gains and touchdowns."

Christ prayed that his church might be one. Our refusal to say "we" has split it into hundreds of sects. Oh, we all play our positions fairly well at least. It is the between the positions that is tragic.

One afternoon on a wheat farm in Kansas, a little girl of three wandered off into the waving grain and was lost. The neighbors came in and long into the cold night, they searched.

Then one of the men had an idea. They would all join hands and spread out until they covered the entire side of the field and walk across. Half way across, they found her, but they were too late. Hunger, thirst, and exposure had taken her life.

Holding the lifeless little form in her arms, the heartbroken mother could only repeat the soul-searching question, "Why didn't you join hands sooner?" Be careful with your pronunciation, especially the little words. They are the hardest to say.

Beggars At The Gate

It happened at the gate of the Temple. Before the gate called Beautiful lay a crippled beggar. It was now past noon, and he had been lying there since early morning. As he thought of his life, his heart was warmed by the thought of his friends and how much they meant to him. They were poor themselves or else they would care for him out of their own means, but they did do something for him. Early each morning before going to work, they came by his little room, picked him up on his pallet and carried him down to the gate of the temple where he could beg his living from the passersby.

As he continued to think, his mood changed. Bitterness and anger swept over him. "It is not enough!" he said, "It simply isn't enough!" His friends meant well. He would starve to death without their help, but the fact was that after they had done all they could, he was still a cripple!

Suddenly his thinking was interrupted. Two men were coming toward him. As was his custom, he called out to them for alms and looked up expecting to receive something in his tin cup. You can imagine his disappointment when one of them said, "I have no silver or gold."

He was ready to turn away with a curse on his lips, but there was something different about these men. They were still standing over him, and looking up he heard one of them say, "But I will give you what I have. In the name of Jesus of Nazareth rise up and walk!"

Then he reached down, took him by the hand, and lifted him to his feet. For the very first time in all his life the beggar stood up and walked. With his heart running over with joy, he entered with them into the Temple, walking, leaping and praising God. You would have done the same had you been in his place. Peter and John had done something far greater than improve his living conditions—they had changed the man himself.

This is the real cure for all who are crippled. In the name of Jesus Christ lame men walk, gamblers become workers, drunkards become sober, sinners become righteous men. It is the gift of God through his Son and is offered to all who will receive it.

Remember, in your own strength you are but a cripple begging before the gate of the temple of life, but in the name of Jesus Christ of Nazareth you can rise up and walk!

The Flowers of the Canyon

In his classic novel, *The Sky Pilot*, Ralph Conner tells the story of Gwen, a wild willful young girl who one day met with an accident that left her a cripple for life. In the midst of her bitterness, the Sky Pilot, a missionary among the hills, came. They talked. Gwen poured out in deep, passionate sobs her resentments and fears.

In reply, the Sky Pilot told her the parable of the canyon. "In the beginning," he said, "there was no canyon at all, only open prairie. One day the Master of the Prairie asked, 'Where are your flowers?' The Prairie answered, 'I have no seed.'

"Birds were sent to scatter seed, and soon sunflowers, crocuses, and lilies were everywhere, but there were none of the flowers the Master loved best. 'Oh, Master,' cried the Prairie, in answer to his questionings, 'The fierce wind and hot sun cause them to wilt and die.'

"Then the Master spoke to the Lightning, and with a blow the Lightning cleft the Prairie asunder. For days, the Prairie groaned in agony, but the river poured its water through the cleft, carried down mold, and once more the birds brought seed.

"Time passed and the Master came again, this time to find the rough rocks decked with moss and every nook hung with columbine, and under the trees were violets, ferns, and all kinds of flowering shrubs."

The Sky Pilot took out his New Testament and read, "The fruits—I'll read flowers—of the spirit are love, joy, peace, patience, kindness, goodness, faithfulness, gentleness, self-control, and some of these grow only in the canyon."

"Which are the canyon flowers?" Gwen asked softly. "Gentleness, patience, self-control; and though the others, love, joy, peace, bloom in the open, never so rich and sweet as in the canyon."

For a long time, Gwen lay quite still. Then, with trembling lips, she said, "There are no flowers in my canyon, only jagged rocks!" The Sky Pilot replied, "Someday there will be, Gwen. The Master will find them, and we shall see them, too."

Suffering can do that for anyone who will reach out amid the pain and, in faith, take hold of the hand of God. Remember that when you come to the canyon of your life!

I Corinthians 15: 54
                              Not Taps But Reveille

For many years I have been a great admirer of Sir Winston Churchill. More than any other person he saved England and the free world from Nazi Germany.

Many of us remember his stirring words of challenge when he said to the people of Great Britain, "I have nothing to offer but blood, sweat and tears."

We watched as one after another the nations of Europe fell before the Nazi onslaught—Poland, Denmark, Norway, Belgium, and the Netherlands. Then the Nazi army marched into France. The French surrendered and Great Britain stood alone.

The next day in a speech before Commons, Churchill declared that though all Europe might fall, ". . . we shall not falter or fail. We shall go on to the end . . . we shall fight on the seas and oceans . . . we shall fight on the beaches . . . we shall fight in the fields and in the streets, we shall fight in the hills and we shall never surrender."

In 1940, at the age of 66, he became the Prime Minister. Later he wrote, "I felt as if I were walking with destiny and that my past life was but a preparation for this hour."

Sir Winston Churchill died in 1965 at the age of 91. Before his death he planned his own funeral service. It was held in St. Paul's Cathedral in London. He selected the great hymns of the church and used the eloquent Anglican liturgy.

After the benediction had been pronounced, as Churchill had given direction, a bugler positioned high in the dome of the cathedral played *Taps.*

When the last note died away, there came a dramatic turn. As Churchill had instructed, another bugler, placed on the other side of the great dome sounded *Reveille.*

It was Sir Winston Churchill's testimony to the entire world, a statement of his Christian faith. The end of life, the end of history, will not be *Taps,* but *Reveille.*

Cage Rattlers for Christ

We have been reminded in God's Word that "None of us lives to himself, and none of us dies to himself." My life and I am sure your life as well, has been touched, blessed, challenged, and changed by an innumerable host of people.

My mother, my father, my teacher in the first grade, my coach and math teacher in high school, my roommate in college, my mentor, an aunt, the girl to whom I am married, an almost endless parade of persons to whom I am deeply indebted for all I am or ever hope to be.

That, I think, is what life is all about—people helping people to become all that God dreams of them becoming.

Bruce Larson tells a wonderful story about a certain little boy who many years ago went to the county fair. There he encountered a man with a cage filled with wild birds.

He stood watching for a while, as the man sold them. Finally, he asked, "Mister, what are you going to do with those you don't sell?" The man said, "Kill them, I guess. They aren't worth anything."

"Could I buy them?" the boy asked, "I will give you all the money I have." The wild-bird catcher looked at him suspiciously, "Yeah, just how much money are we talking about?"

The youngster began emptying his pockets of all the pennies, nickels and dimes he had saved in his brief lifetime. The wild-bird catcher was dumbfounded. It was enough!

That night he took the cage of birds home. His heart was filled with excitement and joy. He couldn't wait for what he had planned to do, but when he opened the door of the cage to set the birds free, they wouldn't leave. They had grown accustomed to their life in prison.

In desperation he began to rattle and beat on the cage. He continued until every single bird had flown out, up and away into its true home under the wide blue sky.

God paid a great price—the gift of his Son, to open the cage door and set us free, and because he has done so much for us, let us become Fellow Cage Rattlers, willing to settle for nothing less than the freedom and flight of all God's children.

September 11   Luke 18: 1
Taking Time To Pray

The couple was driving on the turnpike in upstate New York when they noticed up ahead a well-dressed man standing alongside a shiny new Cadillac looking rather disgusted. They pulled off the road behind him. "What's the trouble?" the husband asked, "Can we help?" "I have run out of gas," the man answered. Looking at his watch, he said, "Of all times for this to happen. I'm already late for my meeting."

The couple had a gallon can of gas in their trunk. As he emptied it into the empty tank, the husband said, "There's a service area five miles ahead. You can fill up there." The man thanked them, got in his car, and sped away.

The couple put the can back in the trunk and continued down the turnpike. Twelve miles later they spotted a man standing beside a Cadillac. It was the same man, the same car, and the same predicament! Feeling that he couldn't afford to take the time to stop for gas, he had passed up the service station! You wonder what in the world the man was thinking. If you want a car to run, you have to take time to fill up with gasoline.

Sometimes we Christians act just as foolishly as that man did. We must have power if we are to live life at its highest and best. We know that our source is prayer, but we are so busy we feel that we just don't have time to stop for this resource which God makes available to us. Someone has said that Jesus prayed for the very reason we don't pray. We are so busy, we cannot stop to pray. Jesus was so busy he had to stop and pray.

Prayer is a vital necessity for the Christian. We read everything we can find on prayer. We talk about prayer. We do everything except pray.

One day the disciples, coming upon Jesus in prayer, asked him to teach them to pray. As far as we know, that is the only thing they ever asked him to teach them. They didn't ask him to teach them how to heal, or teach, or evangelize. They seemed to know that if they learned to pray, the power of God would be available to do whatever they needed to do. That power is available to you and me, if we will but ask.

> O Thou, by whom we come to God,
> The Life, the Truth, the Way;
> The path of prayer thyself hast trod,
> Lord, teach us how to pray.

255

Cast Off As Worthless

When Madame Curie discovered radium in 1902 it introduced the new fact called radioactivity, changed the thinking of the scientific world about matter and led to the understanding of the atom.

When she began her search, she discovered it was most likely to be found in uranium ore or pitchblende. She didn't have the money to buy this high priced ore and was just about ready to give up.

Then she remembered that after pitchblende had been used in making glass, most of the ore was discarded. It was a worthless ash heap, but for her purpose it would work as well as ore fresh from the mine.

Tons of ashes were hauled to the old shack of a building where she was working. Weeks lengthened into months and months into years as she boiled down tons and tons of the castoff ore. What she was interested in was the residue left after hours of boiling.

The old building was hot in the summer and bitter cold in the winter, but finally, the boiling had been done. She was ready for the final test. All the bits of grounds that had been gathered were placed in a crucible for the final boiling down.

Breathlessly, she waited. The work of a lifetime hung in the balance. As she stood watching, it slowly boiled away. Nothing was left. All of her work was for nothing. Failure!

That night, Marie Curie, with a heavy heart, walked around in far away thought. She gazed over at the empty crucible. Suddenly her heart leaped within her. Through the darkness from the residue around the edge of the crucible there came a glow of light. It was what our modern world knows today as radium. Radium is used in the treatment of cancer, and strange as it seems, it was found in an ash heap.

Even so, God saw men and women, cast off and worthless in the eyes of the world, but God looked deeper and saw something of infinite value. He sent his Son that whoever believes in him should not perish but have eternal life.

God calls you and me to find those who are discouraged, alone and lost, and tell them of God's love. Whether they live in a motel or a mansion, an apartment or a palace, God wants them to know his love and share his gift of life abundant and everlasting.

September 13

Philippians 3:7

Unanswered Prayer

The great hymn, "Spirit of God, Descend upon My Heart," has these words: "Teach me the patience of unanswered prayer." Who among us has not felt this need?

In his little book, *The Meaning of Prayer*, Harry Emerson Fosdick told what he had learned from studying the prayer life of the renowned missionary, Adoniram Judson.

Toward the end of his life, Judson said, "I never prayed sincerely and earnestly for anything but it came; at some time—no matter at how distant a day—somehow, in some shape—probably the last I should have devised—it came.

Knowing so well Judson's life and work, Dr. Fosdick read his words with amazement. Judson had prayed to be sent to India. He was sent to Burma.

While he was away on mission business, his wife, Ann, contracted Indian fever. Judson prayed that her life might be spared. Both Ann and his little daughter were buried in Rangoon.

When war broke out between the British and Burmese, Judson was arrested as an "enemy alien." He prayed to God for his release, but for eleven months, he lay chained in the death prison at Ava.

His cell was never washed or even swept. The temperature stayed at 100 degrees day and night. The heavy chains, which prevented him from fighting off the swarming mosquitoes, made scars on his wrists he would to carry the rest of his life.

Judson's record goes on listing petition after petition without an affirmative answer. Finally, it dawned on Dr. Fosdick what Judson meant.

Judson's petitions had been denied, but God had always answered Judson. God had been there, guiding, and keeping. In spite of persecution and opposition, Judson's dreams and goals were realized.

It can be so for you and me. Listen to this message from God's Word: "Have no anxiety about anything, but in everything by prayer and supplication with thanksgiving let your requests be made known to God, and God will supply your every need."

Go Home To Your Friends!

In the gospel of Mark, there is recorded the story of how Jesus and the disciples crossed over the Sea of Galilee and came to the country of Gadera. There they met a man out of the tombs, a demoniac. Jesus healed him, you remember, by casting out the demons.

The man felt so indebted that when they went down to the boat and were leaving, he begged to go with him, but Jesus said to him, "Go home to your friends and tell them what the Lord has done for you."

Not all of us are called overseas as missionaries, but the Master does make this request of each of us: "If my coming into your life has made a difference, if it is helping you live a richer, more meaningful life, won't you tell others?"

Years ago in the city of Boston, a man walked up and down in front of a shoe store until he got up courage enough to go in. He had one purpose—to talk with one of the clerks, a member of his Sunday school class, about Jesus.

The young man had just completed a sale and was wrapping up the purchase. He smiled as he called out a cheerful greeting. When the customer had gone, the teacher laid his hand on the young man's shoulder. "Dwight," he said, "I have come to talk with you about accepting Christ. He means everything to me, and I want you to know him as your Lord and Savior."

As he talked about it later, the Sunday school teacher, a man by the name of Kimball, said, "It was a very weak and stumbling endeavor, but the young shoe clerk didn't think so. He made a public confession of Christ and went on to become one of the greatest missionaries our world has ever known."

Years later, telling about the experience and the man who won him to Christ, Dwight L. Moody said, "After all these years, I can still hear Mr. Kimball's voice and feel his hand on my shoulder."

You and I must ask ourselves the question, "How much does Jesus Christ mean to me? Has his coming into my life made a difference?"

Down the long curves of the centuries come his words, speaking to our hearts: "Go home to your friends and tell them what the Lord has done for you."

Yes, In Everything!

Paul in his letter to the Christians at Rome wrote these words: "We know that in everything God works for good with those who love him, who are called according to his purpose."

"Everything?" we want to ask, "Are you sure about that? It is easy to see God at work in some situations, but in others it is virtually impossible," but the man who wrote those words had no doubts at all. "Yes," he would say, "Everything!"

I think at times we are too impulsive. We make snap judgments. Lin Yutang tells about an old man and his only son. They made a bare living cultivating a tiny plot of ground with the help of an old broken-down horse.

One night the horse broke out of the lot and ran off. The old man's neighbor came by and expressed his sympathy at their loss, but the old man asked, "How do you know it was bad luck?"

The next night the horse came home with nine wild horses. When the neighbor heard about it he came by and congratulated them on their good luck, but the old man asked, "How do you know it was good luck?"

A few days later, while trying to break the wild horses, the son suffered a broken leg. Again the neighbor came by to express regret at their bad luck. Again the old man said, "How do you know it was bad luck?"

That same week a Chinese war lord came to the village recruiting young men for his army. Because of his broken leg the son was passed over. The story ends here with the neighbor offering congratulations and the old man saying, "How do you know it was good luck?"

Looking back in history it seemed a bad day when Joseph's brothers sold him into slavery, but God was at work in Egypt no less than in Canaan. In time Joseph rose to a position of leadership and was able to save all Israel from starvation.

It seemed a bad day for the missionary Adoniram Judson when the doors closed on his dream of going to India, but God had other plans for him and was working for good. Judson went to Burma instead. There he did such outstanding work that today to think of Judson is to think of Burma, and to think of Burma is to think of Judson.

Angel Unaware

In one of his short stories H. G. Wells tells about an English vicar whose hobby was bird watching. Out on the moor one evening he happened upon a man with great wings. The mysterious stranger explained that he was an angel who had strayed from heaven to earth.

Reluctantly, the vicar took him home. Soon the village was in turmoil. No one seemed to know quite how to deal with the divine messenger. But the heavenly visitor took his leave, and none too soon. Wells said, "There is no room for angels in the hearts and lives of this world."

Have you seen any angels lately? They don't seem to fit into our twenty first century very well. Perhaps it is because we picture them with haloes, white robes and gossamer wings. The word angel comes from the Greek; it means messenger. The dictionary gives this definition: "a messenger, especially of God."

Angels come to us amidst the happenings of everyday life. Gideon was threshing grain when the angel of the Lord appeared to him. The shepherds were keeping watch over their flocks by night when an angel appeared to them the night that Christ was born. Brother Lawrence was washing pots and pans in a monastery kitchen. It is generally so. God's angelic hosts meet us amidst our routine lives.

Angels usually appear when we need them most. An angel of the Lord warned Joseph that Herod was searching for the baby Jesus to kill him. An angel appeared in the jail cell and delivered Peter on the night before he was scheduled to be executed.

Angels come to meet the need of the moment. During my first year in college, I was facing financial problems that would force me to drop out of school. On my way to class one morning, Otto Neilson, the dean of men who knew the problem I was facing called from his office window, "Keep your chin up!" For me he was an angel sent from God.

Roy Rogers and Dale Evans' baby girl was born hopelessly mentally disabled. Out of that home of broken hearts came a book that has blessed the lives of countless thousands of parents facing similar situations. The title of the book: *Angel Unaware.*

Angels? They are all around us, secret agents of the Most High. They meet us all along the road of life. They usually come in forms we never recognize but always at the time and place they are needed most.

If A Man Dies

Job asked the question that haunts the minds of mankind: "If a man dies, shall he live again?" Christ gives us the ringing assurance: "I am the resurrection and the life; he who believes in me, though he die, yet shall he live, and whoever lives and believes in me shall never die."

The late Cecil B. de Mille, motion picture producer and director, tells of a first-hand experience that illustrates our Easter hope. One warm spring afternoon, he was out on the lake in his boat. Anchored close to the shore, he was reading when a large black beetle crawled out of the water and up the side of the boat.

For a little while, Mr. de Mille watched the creature blinking at him. Then, for the first time, he noticed scores of the beetle's relatives. Some were in the form of eggs, others in the form of grubs, crawling about on the muddy bottom of the lake.

Suddenly the big ugly beetle on the upper edge of his boat appeared to be dying. Then a strange and wonderful thing happened. The shell split down the back, and out of it emerged a most beautiful and brilliant shape.

The new life sat there with the warm sunlight shining down on it. Slowly four iridescent wings unfolded from which flashed all the colors of the rainbow. It had all happened right there before his eyes. The ugly beetle had undergone complete metamorphosis and had been transformed into a glamorous dragonfly.

Spreading its wings, the dragonfly rose into the air, wheeling and soaring over the sunlit water. Far below, clinging to the gun-whale of the boat, was the empty shell of a body that once had housed its life.

He looked down again at the eggs and the creatures moving slowly around in the muck and mire. He mused to himself, "I wonder if they are aware of the glorious creature gliding overhead which so short a time ago was one of them?"

It dawned upon him that he had witnessed one of God's miracles, and if God could work such a wonder with a grub from the bottom of the lake, what wonders undreamed of were in store for man?

Paul expressed it in these words: "This mortal nature must put on immortality." This is our living hope.

September 18

Of Faith and Friends

Ecclesiastes 4: 9-10

All America cheered when Tiger Woods won the U. S. Open on the 91st hole of the playoff. It was, in Tiger Woods own words, "probably the best ever." His come-from-behind win was highly reminiscent of another one of America's greatest golfers of the 1950's, Ben Hogan. His story, like that of Tiger Woods, is one of inspiration and challenge.

Ben Hogan started working as a caddy at the age of 12 and at 13 decided to try the game himself. Not having a natural swing, he had to work long and hard at the game.

He developed a system of playing called "Muscle Memory." The theory: "If you practice a swing long enough it becomes second nature, and you can do it automatically." It worked. In May of 1948 he won the PGA Championship and three weeks later won the U. S. Open.

Then tragedy struck. On the morning of February 2, 1949, a Greyhound Bus crossed a center divider and crashed into Hogan's car. He was rushed to the hospital with a crushed pelvis, a broken leg and ankle and a shattered shoulder. The doctors said he might live, but in all likelihood he would never walk again.

A year later Ben Hogan amazed the world by entering the Los Angeles Open where he tied for the championship. He lost the playoff, but no one seemed to notice that little detail. All the sports world could talk about was "Hogan's Victory."

The 1950 U. S. Open marked Ben Hogan's comeback. On the 72nd hole (and 36th of the day), in extreme pain and facing a shot of over 200 yards into the wind, Hogan needed a par to force a playoff. He used a 1-iron to hit a superb shot which landed on the distant green well within two-putt range and made his par. The next day he defeated Lloyd Mangrum and George Fazio in an 18-hole playoff to win the championship.

In 1951 he won his first Masters and the U. S. Open, and in 1953, his greatest year, he won his second Masters, his fourth U. S. Open and the British Open. What was the secret of his success? Ben Hogan said it began in a Fort Worth hospital room with thousands of encouraging letters saying, "You can make it, Ben, we will be praying for you." All of the prayers on his behalf, friends who believed in him, and their faith in God helped him believe in himself and to have faith.

September 19   I John 3: 11
Wanted: Telephone Repairmen

Eugene Brice, a ministerial friend of mine, tells of visiting a little old lady in a nursing home one afternoon. She had been a resident there for only three months or so and wasn't too happy about being there. She had led a very active life, had participated vigorously in the program of her church and in civic affairs. She was a very outgoing person and had a great host of friends.

She was lying on the bed when he entered her room, curled around a telephone that was on the bed beside her. The residents in this center could have a private phone installed that would have the same number as the phone at home. This is what she had done.

Now the phone was on her bed, and she was holding on to it. There was a deeply concerned look on her face, and after a brief conversation, the minister learned why. "My phone is broken," she explained. "Even after I paid them the service charge for installation, it still won't work."

Looking at the phone cradled in her hands, he asked, "What seems to be the trouble?" "It just doesn't work right," she said, "I can call out, but people can't call in. It won't ring for me." "Perhaps you ought to call the repair service," he said. "Oh, I already have," she said. "The man said he would be out this afternoon." They had an enjoyable visit. She reminisced about her work in the church across the years, talked about her children, her grandchildren, and friends. Finally, they had prayer together, and he took his leave.

As he came out into the hall, he met the repairman. "Are you some of her family?" he asked. "No, I am her pastor." "Great," he said. "I need to talk with you." "She told me you were coming to fix her phone."

He shook his head, "No, I'm afraid only you can do that. This is the fourth time she has called. There is nothing wrong with the phone. The trouble is nobody calls her. I don't have the heart to tell her what's wrong, so I pretend to work on it and tell her it's OK."

They stood in silence for a moment, then the repairman said, "Preacher, see if you can get someone to call her up." He went into her room, and my friend went on his way.

There are a lot of broken phones in our world—some of them right where you live. You can almost see the big ad, can't you? An ad that reads: WANTED: REPAIRMEN TO FIX PHONES SO THEY WILL RING.

Psalms 92: 1
Giving Thanks In All Circumstances

In her book, *The Hiding Place*, Corrie ten Boom told how she and her sister, Betsie, as prisoners of the Nazis were brought to Ravenbrook, the notorious women's extermination camp. The living conditions were horrifying; just to read about them leaves one sick deep down inside.

When they discovered that the big room in which they were jammed was swarming alive with fleas, Corrie felt it was more than she could stand. "Betsie," she cried, "how can we possibly live in such a place?"

"Show us, show us how." It was said so matter of factly, it took Corrie a second to realize that Betsie was praying. "Corrie!" she said excitedly, "He has given us the answer! Before we asked, just as he always does! Where was it in the Bible this morning? Read it again!" Cautiously, Corrie took out the Bible from which she read to the women each day and found the passage in I Thessalonians: "Comfort the frightened, help the weak, be patient with everyone." It seemed written expressly to Ravenbrook. She read on, "Rejoice always, pray constantly, continue to give thanks in all circumstances; for this is the will of God in Christ Jesus."

"That's it, Corrie. That's what we can do. We can start right now to thank God for everything about this new barracks!" Corrie stared at her, "Such as?"

"Such as being assigned here together." Corrie agreed. "Such as what you are holding in your hands." Corrie gripped the Bible as she thought of all the women who would meet the Lord in those pages.

"For the very crowding. Packed so close, many more will hear." She waited. "Oh, all right. 'Thank you for the suffocating crowds,' Corrie said. Betsie went serenely on, "Thank you for the fleas and for—"

"The fleas? No Way!" Corrie exploded. Betsie insisted, "It says 'Give thanks in all circumstances.' It doesn't say 'in pleasant circumstances.' Fleas are a part of this place." So they gave thanks for the fleas.

One evening Corrie returned to the barracks to find Betsie waiting, her eyes twinkling. "You know we have never understood why we had such freedom in the big room," she said, "Well, I have found out. We had trouble with our work this afternoon and asked the supervisor to come and settle it, but neither of the guards would step through the door. They said, 'That place is crawling with fleas!'"

Between Gibeah and Michmash

Israel, under the leadership of King Saul, was at war with the Philistines. Two thousand Israelites under the king's command cut off the Philistine garrison at Geva from the rear, then in a frontal assault wiped it out.

The Philistines reacted swiftly. They sent a strong army back into the hills and occupied Michmash. The Israelites fled, and Saul was left in a desperate situation with only a remnant of six hundred men.

A personal exploit by Jonathan, Saul's son, saved the day. Taking only his young armor bearer with him, he charged up the hill against the Philistines. Halfway through the pass, between Gibeah and Michmash, they paused for a moment in indecision.

Jonathan spoke saying, "It may be that God will do something for us." Then with battle shout, the two foxhole comrades stormed the enemy stronghold. Thinking they were surrounded, the enemy fled in disarray, and the Israelites won a great victory.

How often in life, we find ourselves between our own Gibeah and Michmash. At that critical point, we do one of two things—we fail and fall back, or we go forward to victory. In such an hour, we need to be armed. There are five things we can do, five steps that can spell the difference between victory and defeat.

1. Establish a goal—that first of all. Know where you are going.

2. Believe you can reach your goal—that God is helping you. Keep ever in mind the words of Jesus: "If you can believe, all things are possible to him who believes."

3. Keep a positive attitude and outlook. If you think failure, in all likelihood, you will fail. It is in thinking success that we succeed.

4. Don't forget to pray. It is eternally true—"More things are wrought by prayer than this world dreams of."

5. Finally, act. John Drinkwater put his finger on what is perhaps the most critical factor any of us face when he wrote:

The will—there lies our bitter need.
Give us to build above the deep intent the deed, the deed.

Back To Bethel

The sun had gone down and darkness was falling. A lone traveler, tired and weary, stopped and looked around. Then, exhausted from his long day's travel, he took a stone for a pillow and lay down to sleep.

The traveler was Jacob. Urged on by his cunning mother, he had cheated his brother, deceived his father and had stolen the birthright and blessing. Then, with an angry Esau planning to kill him, his mother persuaded him to flee for his life, to go north of Beersheba to Haran the home of his uncle, her brother. She was to pay dearly for her part in the evil deed. She never saw her son again.

You know the story of course. In Haran he met the beautiful Rachel, and they fell deeply in love. After working seven long years for her hand in marriage, her homely older sister, Leah, was pawned off on him. This meant seven more years of labor for the one he truly loved.

In time his name was changed to Israel, and he became the father of a great nation, but it all began there at Bethel. That night under the stars Jacob had a never-to-be-forgotten experience—he found God. Rather, God found him, and his life was changed forever.

He awoke exclaiming, "Surely the Lord is in this place, and I did not know it!" So strange, he would never have thought of meeting God at a time and place like this. He was taken completely by surprise, but then God is never where we expect him to be.

We expect him to come in the high and the mighty; he comes to us in the lowly. We expect him to come with a thundering voice of judgment; he looks down in heartbroken silence. We watch for him in high moments of worship; he draws near in the deep needs of people all around us.

We expect him to be made manifest while we are kneeling in prayer; he comes as we rise to confront a challenge or right a wrong. We dream of his drawing near as daylight dies and the shades of night come on; instead, he comes at the dawn of each new day with its manifold opportunities.

Look again carefully at your life and all the things that pertain to it. You will discover with the Apostle Paul that "he is not far from each one of us, for 'In him we live and move and have our being.'" God ever waits to meet us at our Bethel.

September 23

Proverbs 3: 6

God's Marching Orders

His real name is Ralston Young, but to hundreds and hundreds of people he is known as Red Cap 42. He is a porter at Grand Central Station in New York City.

It is the firm conviction of Ralston Young that God has a definite purpose for every one of us if we are willing to listen and obey. One day as he thought about his life, he realized that about all he was interested in was the size of the tips he received.

It was then that he decided that from that day on, he would live his Christian faith every minute. This meant getting rid of his selfishness and loving others as Christ loved them. He began each day with a prayer, requesting "God's Marching Orders." It was a quite simple prayer: "Lord, help me carry the love of Christ to all who need it as I carry their luggage."

His special interest was concern for those in trouble. One day carrying the luggage of a tiny silver-haired woman in a wheelchair, he saw that she was in great pain. He closed his eyes and seemed to be listening. Then he said, "Lady, that surely is a pretty hat you're wearing, and your dress, too—prettiest one I've seen all day."

In spite of her pain, the woman managed a smile, "Whatever made you say such a nice thing to me," she asked. "I just asked the Lord what to say to you to help," he said, "and he told me to look at your hat, but the dress— that was my own idea."

As he pushed her wheelchair along, she began to talk with him about her constant pain. He said, "I know exactly what you are talking about. I had to lose an eye, and for years it burned like a hot iron." She asked, "How were you able to endure it?" He answered, "Just by praying. Of course prayer didn't take away the pain, but it gave me strength to bear the pain."

Long afterwards, a woman came to see him. "Shortly before her death, my mother asked me to find you and tell you that what you told her about learning to endure pain made all the difference in the world."

God's Word tells us, "In love, serve one another." Ralston Young, Red Cap 42, receives his marching orders from God each morning as he kneels in prayer, and such opportunities for ministry are open to you and me. If we really want to help, all we have to do is ask.

Deuteronomy 31:6
One Man Plus God

The Bible story of David and Goliath is one we have all heard since childhood. It is the superb account of how the young David, armed with a slingshot, conquered Goliath, girded with a sword. In doing so, David won a great victory for the nation of Israel.

The story is a constant reminder to us of the giants of war, poverty, and disease against which we are called to do battle in our own day. God is ever on the alert for individuals with the fortitude and courage required to do battle.

The qualities that made up the character of David and made him victorious are the qualities that are required in the character of warriors in any age.

First of all, it was David's dependability, his faithfulness to small responsibilities, which prepared him for greater ones. Facing lions and bears that came against and threatened the flock, prepared him for the task of facing the giant Philistine, Goliath.

Secondly, David was willing to act today. He did not waste his valuable time making excuses about what happened or didn't happen yesterday or bragging about all the things he could and would do tomorrow. He was prepared to act now. He stood ever ready to do things today.

Finally, David went forth to battle with faith in God. That is the only way to slay a giant and this David knew. He was keenly aware of the fact that he was only a shepherd boy. In his own strength, he could do nothing, but with the living God beside him, there was nothing he could not do. One man plus God is always a majority.

Jane Addams was a great American humanitarian who spent her life clearing up the slums of Chicago. The story of her life is a story of courage and daring. In 1889, she founded Hull House to help needy families and to combat juvenile delinquency.

A lifelong advocate of international peace, in 1931 she was awarded the Nobel Peace Prize. On the desk of Jane Addam's office was a framed motto which was the guiding light of her life. The motto read:

> When, if not now?
> Who, if not you?

Psalms 27:11

God Who Guided Lincoln

Abraham Lincoln guided our nation through the Civil War and is considered by many historians to have been one of the greatest men America has ever produced.

Born in a log cabin on a farm in Kentucky, his boyhood was spent in a home without windows or doors, with one whole side open to the sun, wind, and rain. One year in public school was all the formal education he ever received.

He went into business. The business failed because of a worthless partner, and he spent the next seventeen years paying off bad debts. This closed his career as a businessman.

He went as a volunteer to the Black Hawk War. He was so awkward and so faltering with his command as a company commander that he finally eased out of the service. This was the end of his military career.

He fell in love with a beautiful girl by the name of Ann Rutledge. They were engaged to be married when she took ill and died.

Entering politics, he was defeated in his first campaign for the legislature. Then, he was defeated in his first attempt to be nominated to Congress. Next, he tried to get an appointment as Commissioner of the United States Land Office. He failed.

In the election of 1854, he ran for the United States Senate and was defeated. In 1856, he became a candidate for the Vice Presidency. Again, he was defeated. In 1858, he ran for the United States Senate. His opponent was Stephen Douglas. Again, he went down in defeat.

One failure after another, defeat after defeat! And yet, in 1861, Abraham Lincoln was elected to the highest office in our land. He was chosen as the sixteenth President of the United States.

Concerning this strange succession of frustrations and failures, Abraham Lincoln said, ". . . I have been controlled by some power other than my own will."

Amidst the disappointments, defeats, and failures of your life, remember Abraham Lincoln. Never give up, never lose hope, and keep your faith. God who guided Lincoln is the One who is guiding you!

Carry On!

The quality of perseverance is not easily acquired, but it is the key to success and greatness. A. J. Cronin, author of such best sellers as *The Keys of the Kingdom*, and *Hatter's Castle*, was a medical doctor in London at the age of thirty-three when he developed a gastric ulcer and was sent to the country for a six-month rest and put on a milk diet.

Up until that time, he had been quite active but had never stuck to anything very long. He had thought about dermatology, oral surgery, and even pediatrics, only to discard all of them.

One week on the farm just about drove him crazy. For years he had toyed with the idea of writing. This was the opportunity he needed. The next morning found him at an upstairs desk ready to begin. Slowly it dawned on him that he had never written anything in his life. Three hours later, when he was called to lunch, the page was still blank.

The next three months were a nightmare. True, he had a theme and even a title, but beyond that—nothing! Then reading over what he had written, he was appalled. Such nonsense! He gathered it up, carried it outside, and dumped it into the trash.

Quite satisfied with his decisive act, he went for a walk in the drizzling rain and came upon old Angus, a neighboring farmer, who was patiently and laboriously digging a ditch, making a pasture. He had told Angus about the novel, and now he confided as to what he had done.

Angus continued digging. Finally he said, "Perhaps you're right, Doctor, and I am the one who's wrong. I keep digging here to make a pasture. I can't help it. I know if I dig long enough and hard enough a pasture can be made."

Dr. Cronin went home hating himself. Ashamed, he went to the trash can and dug out the soggy bundle. In three months *Hatter's Castle* was finished. It was accepted for publication, dramatized, serialized, and translated into nineteen languages. Later, it was bought by Hollywood, and made into a movie.

It altered the life of A. J. Cronin completely—and all because of a timely lesson by an old farmer on the grace of perseverance. Listen to this promise in the book of Revelation: "Be faithful unto death, and I will give you the crown of life."

The Catcher in the Rye

Writing to the church at Rome, Paul said, "Let love be genuine." But who can tell when it is? Motives are difficult to discern. The Bible tells us, "The heart is deceitful above all things."

In J. D. Salinger's book, *The Catcher In The Rye*, Holden, the little 16-year-old who tells the story, shares his dreams with his little sister Phoebe.

Phoebe asks Holden if he would like to be a scientist, or a lawyer or something. Holden says he couldn't be a scientist, that he is no good in science.

He continues, "Lawyers are all right, I guess—if they go around saving innocent guys' lives, but they don't. All they do is make a lot of dough, and play golf, and buy cars, and look like hotshots.

"And even if you did go around saving guys' lives and all, how would you know whether you did it because you wanted to save guys' lives or because you really wanted to be a terrific lawyer with everybody slapping you on the back and congratulating you in court when the trial was over? How would you know you weren't being a phony?"

Then Holden added, "You know what I'd really like to be? You know that song 'If a body catch a body coming through the Rye?' I'd like—"

"It's 'If a body meet a body coming through the Rye,'!" Phoebe corrected him.

She was right, of course, but Holden didn't know it then. He went on, "I thought it was 'If a body catch a body,' anyway, I keep picturing all these little kids playing in this big field of rye—thousands of little kids, and nobody around—nobody big, I mean—except me. And I'm standing on the edge of some crazy cliff.

"What I have to do, I have to catch everybody if they start to go over the cliff. I mean, if they're running and they don't watch where they are going, I have to come out from somewhere and catch them. That's all I'd do all day. I'd just be the catcher in the Rye. I know it's crazy, but that's what I'd really like to be."

But is it really so crazy? It was the Man from Galilee who said, "Greater love has no man than this, that a man lay down his life for his friends."

Understanding and Love

One day a lawyer asked Jesus, "Which is the great commandment in the law?" At that time there were 3,600 commandments in the Jewish law. How was Jesus to answer? Would it be an answer for the moment or would it be an answer for all time? Jesus said, "You shall love . . . ."

Dr. Karl Menninger in his book *Whatever Became of Sin* declares that Jesus' answer is the message of the minister, the counselor, the psychoanalyst—everyone who is in the caring business. One day, walking through his sanitarium in Topeka, Kansas, looking at the men and women whose problems had driven them to retreat from the world, he asked himself, "Why are they here?"

The Menninger Center had operated on the theory that the patients didn't understand themselves and strived to give them insight. Now Dr. Menninger had a new idea: What if they were there because they had never loved or been loved?

He gathered his entire staff together and said to them, "We are going to organize the whole sanitarium on a new basis. We have been giving understanding; perhaps what is needed is love. From now on, from the chief psychiatrist down to the gardener, all of our contacts are going to be contacts of love."

After six months they made an evaluation to see how the new system was working. It was discovered that the average period of hospitalization had been cut in half. The official finding was that the mind breaks down when love breaks down.

Some years ago when New York's Bellevue Hospital discovered they were losing 32 percent of the children less than one year of age, the doctors were dumbfounded. They were giving scientific treatments, scientific feedings, sterile surroundings, and yet, the children were dying.

Then at someone's suggestion, they sent out a call for love volunteers. Hundreds of women responded, and the death rate began to plunge. Today the superintendent says, "We could no more do without these love volunteers than we could do without penicillin."

John put it in these words: "We know we have passed out of death into life, because we love." And it was Paul who declared, "Love never fails."

Seeking the Lost

It happened on a farm up in Kansas. One morning a mother, busy with her house cleaning, all at once realized that her little four-year-old daughter was no longer in the room. She looked through the house, no daughter. She went out and looked in the front and in the back. The little girl was nowhere to be seen.

Finally she faced the terrible truth—her daughter had wandered out into the wheat field. Acres and acres, and out there somewhere was her little girl. She called her husband and, with the hired hands, they searched until almost noon. No luck!

There had to be a better way. The father got in the pickup, drove into town three miles away and there told what had happened. School was dismissed. The stores, banks, and offices were closed. The entire town went out and joined in the search.

Around four o'clock in the afternoon, the child was found. She was terribly dehydrated. Her eyes were red and her face swollen from crying, but she was safe. The Associated Press carried a picture and the story of the rescue.

I wonder what would happen if we had that kind of concern for those who have wandered away from God; if, joining hands, we went seeking those who have wandered astray.

Jesus said that he came to seek and save those who are lost and added, "As the Father has sent me, even so I send you." Jesus never commanded us to attend church. Can you think of an instance? I can't. But he did command us to go out into highways and hedges looking for the lost.

For followers of Jesus Christ, the field is the world—from the Atlantic to the Pacific, from the Alleghenies to the Rockies, from Canada to Mexico, from the Great Lakes to the Gulf, from Portland, Oregon to Portland, Maine, and it is not only for America.

The field extends from Australia to Africa, from Jamaica to Japan, from Rhodesia to Russia, from Ireland to India. Jesus calls us to go with the good news of salvation. The good news is for the whole world, but if it is to begin, it must first begin with your family and mine, with our neighbors— the neighbors next door and the neighbors down the street. Are you ready to go?

Two Seas
One of our hymns asks, "Is your life a channel of blessing; is the love of
God flowing through you?" God sends blessings. As long as we send
them on, God can send more, but if for some reason we decide to hoard
and keep what we receive, our lives become stagnant pools unable to
receive.

Years ago in *McCall's Magazine*, Bruce Barton told this modern day parable:

"There are two seas in Palestine. One is fresh, and fish are in it. Splashes
of green adorn its banks. Trees spread their branches over it and stretch
out their thirsty roots to sip of its healing waters.

Along its shores the children play as children played when He was there.
He loved it. He could look across its silver surface when He spoke His
parables. On a rolling plain not far away, He fed five thousand people.

"The river Jordan makes this sea with sparkling water from the hills. So it
laughs in the sunshine. Men build their houses near to it, and birds their
nests; and every kind of life is happier because it is there.

"The river Jordan flows on south into another sea. There are no fish, no
fluttering of leaves, no song of birds, no children's laughter. Travelers
choose another route, unless on urgent business. The air hangs heavy
above its water, and neither man nor beast nor fowl will drink.

"What makes this mighty difference in these neighbor seas? Not the river
Jordan. It empties the same good water into both. Not the soil in which
they lie; not the country round about.

"This is the difference. The Sea of Galilee receives but does not keep the
Jordan. For every drop that flows into it, another drop flows out. Giving and
receiving go on in equal measure. The other sea is shrewder, hoarding its
income jealously. It will not be tempted into any generous impulse. Every
drop it gets it keeps.

"The Sea of Galilee gives and lives. The other sea gives nothing. It is
named the 'Dead Sea.' There are two seas in Palestine. There are two
kinds of people in the world."

Jesus gave us this counsel, "Give, and it will be given to you; good measure,
pressed down, shaken together, and running over!"

Treasure in Heaven

It was Jesus who said, "A man's life does not consist in the abundance of his possessions." So saying, he then gave this advice: "Seek first his kingdom and his righteousness, and all these things shall be yours as well."

The couple ran a tire shop in De Queen, Arkansas where they were lovingly known as Pop and Mom Wolfe. Having no children they decided to adopt a child. It was a very unique adoption. They wrote to a church college and asked if they had a student preparing for the mission field who needed financial assistance. The school sent them the name of Verla Elliott, and they wrote back saying they would pay her tuition until she graduated.

God moves in mysterious ways. On the day the letter arrived Verla Elliott had decided to quit school. Her resources were gone, and her parents were unable to help. She was packing her things when the news came: You don't have to leave school. You have been "adopted" by a family who will pay for your education.

Verla Elliott finished college and was sent by her mission board to China. There she served for a year and a half under the national government and two years more after the Communist takeover. She was arrested as a spy for the United States, but in 1951 was released and returned to America.

Shortly afterwards she was invited to speak in one of the southern churches. It wasn't far from De Queen and she decided to pay a surprise visit to her benefactors whom she had never seen.

At the bus station she asked for directions. Just around the corner she saw the sign "The Wolfe Tire Shop." She had expected a large establishment. The Wolfes must be well-to-do. Since her graduation they had adopted two more students to help through college. They had also made a large contribution toward the university's new Bible seminary building.

She couldn't believe what she saw. The Wolfe Tire Shop was a small building of corrugated iron. For sixteen years Pop and Mom Wolfe had lived in a little three-room apartment over the shop, while from the business came three college graduates and support for a Bible seminary.

Some Things Are Not For Sale

Some years ago there was a popular song that declared, "The best things in life are free." It's true. Life's real worth-whiles are as free as the air we breathe. They can neither be bought nor sold; they are free.

For some strange reason, we keep looking for the market where life is sold. "I would like to buy a home." "Sorry, we have houses for sale; homes are free."

"Could I buy some rain?" "No, I'm sorry. You can buy water; rain is free." "I want to buy a friend." "Sorry, I can sell you a companion for the night; friends are free." "I need to buy some additional time." "I am terribly sorry. I can sell you a clock; time is free."

Some things you simply cannot buy. They are not for sale. Parents cannot buy the love of their children. Shower them with toys when they are toddlers. Give them bicycles when they start to kindergarten. Send them an unending supply of money in college. Then wonder why they fail to care.

One father said to his son who had gotten into trouble with the law, "How could you do it? I have given you everything in the world!" The boy replied wistfully, "Dad, you gave me everything except what I wanted and needed most—yourself."

Years ago, the prophet Amos saw Israel trying to buy God's love. They had forgotten the God who loved them and reverted to trying to earn God's favor by sacrificing their crops, their cattle, even their children.

Amos thundered God's message: "I hate and despise your feast days. I will not accept your burnt offerings." He called on them to return to the things God desired of them: "Let justice roll down like waters, and righteousness like a mighty stream."

We still haven't learned the lesson Amos tried so desperately to teach. We go on trying to buy God's love—promising to reform, to be better, to attend church, and on and on. We just won't accept the fact that God's love is not for sale.

God is not a salesman who sells. He is the Lord who gives, who loves us already. He waits for us to respond to that love, by loving God with all our hearts and our neighbor as ourselves. It's really true. The best things in life are free!

October 3   **II Timothy 1:6**

One Life to Live

Years ago in the city of Dallas, Texas a coach was sending his football squad through a hard scrimmage in preparation for their game that weekend. On the practice field that afternoon was a bit of a boy watching all that went on with keen interest, and consequently, getting in the way.

Following a close shave, in which he was almost run over by a big tackle, the coach shouted, "Hey! Get out of here, before you get killed!"

Then, touched by the wistful look on the little face, the great coach picked up an old, worn out football. "Here, take this," he said, "Take it and learn to pass." The little boy's eyes lit up. He took the ball, and with heart running over, left the field.

The years passed, and one Saturday afternoon, Coach Mattie Bell and his boys from SMU took the field for their most crucial game of the year. That afternoon, the mighty Mustangs went down in defeat. Defeat at the hands of a TCU eleven quarterbacked by a little giant by the name of Davy O'Brian, who years before had been given a worn out football and been challenged by that losing coach to do the best he could with what he had.

You know, 153 pounds isn't much to work with when it comes to varsity football, but Davy O'Brian took it and used what God gave him to win the Heisman Trophy, a place on the nation's number one team, and later to be inducted into Football's Hall of Fame.

> Got any rivers they say are uncrossable;
> Got any mountains you can't tunnel through?
> We specialize in the wholly impossible,
> Doing what nobody else can do.

That is what we mean. Believing, scorning the obstacles, refusing to give up, no matter what the odds may be.

It is so easy, I think, to decry the talents God has given us, to brag about all we would do had we been given more, when all the while, there are thousands who would give anything for the life and opportunities which are ours.

You have one life to live. What are you doing with it?

October 4

Matthew 5:48

Christ Believes In You

Last week the New York Yankees completed their season of miracle comebacks with a record-setting World Series victory. Spotting the Los Angeles Dodgers with a two game lead, the incredible Yankees swept four straight games for the championship—the first team to ever do that.

It was the tenth time the Yankees and Dodgers had met in the World Series and there have been some thrillers, but probably the most exciting was played in 1952.

Carl Erskine was pitching for the Dodgers, and they were leading three games to two. Erskine gave up a walk. He gave it little thought because the Dodgers were ahead 5 to 2.

He walked another batter, putting two men on. Johnny Mize was next up for the Yankees. On the very first pitch Mize belted the ball into the bleachers for a home run.

Carl Erskine's heart sank as he realized what had happened. The score was tied 5 to 5, changing the whole picture. He had let his teammates down—he had failed.

The Dodgers' manager, Chuck Dressen, walked out to the mound. Putting his hand on his shoulder, he asked, "Carl, how do you feel?" Erskine replied, "I'm OK, I feel fine," but Dressen knew better. He could see what was going on inside his pitcher. He gripped Erskine's shoulder and said, "You're my man, Carl. You can do it!", and he walked off the field.

What happened next was unbelievable. Carl Erskine retired the next 19 batters! Talking about it later, Carl Erskine said, "What else could I do? I had failed, but he believed in me in spite of my failure and gave me another chance."

This is the kind of faith Christ had in Peter, you remember. Peter denied him with oaths, but Christ continued believing in him, and at last he lived up to Christ's highest expectations. Even so Christ believes in you and me. He dares even to say, "Be perfect, as your heavenly Father is perfect." Amazing faith!

Because Christ believes in us, we ought to believe in one another. The power and potential for transforming lives and changing the world are in these words of affirmation: "I believe in you!"

278

Our Best Or The Rest?

On a rainy Sunday afternoon, two children stood with faces pressed against the windowpane hoping that the rain would stop, but it kept coming down, and finally they gave up and turned away.

For a while they played with the little black and white kitten. Then they tried a jigsaw puzzle. Nothing really interested them. It was turning into a dull and boring afternoon.

Then the little girl had an idea, "I know what we can do. Let's act out the Bible story Mrs. Hunter read to us in Sunday school. You can be Mr. Noah, and I will be your wife."

With enthusiasm they found a box for the ark and began filling it with their animals. The bathtub was the perfect place for the flood. They threw the wall switch, and the sun went out. They turned on the shower, and the rains came down. With the plug in place, the waters rose higher and higher until at last the "ark" was afloat.

When it had rained for what they estimated to be forty days and nights, they turned off the shower and the rains ceased. Next, they pulled the plug and gradually the waters receded down the drain. Again, the wall switch was thrown, and the sun shone once more. They were quite pleased. It had been a wonderful flood, but there had been a concluding part. Noah and his wife had built an altar and made a sacrifice. They needed an altar, and they knew the perfect spot for a burnt offering—the fireplace.

The little girl quickly picked out one of her brother's toys. "This one," she said, "will be just right." "No!" her brother cried, "Not that one!" He reached in the ark and chose one of his sister's toys, "Let's give this one to God," but it was one of her favorites. The problem seemed insurmountable.

Then the little boy thought of something. Dashing up to the attic, he returned with a badly soiled lamb that was torn and most of the stuffing gone. "Here," he said, "Let's give this to God. Nobody wants it." His sister, greatly relieved, agreed, and they offered up the little lamb as a sacrifice to God.

It never really happened. It is only a story told by an anonymous writer to teach a lesson in Christian Stewardship—yours and mine.

Star Trek

When the first Russian cosmonauts returned from their trip into outer space, they were asked if they saw God out there. When the answer was no, many atheists felt that this confirmed their belief that there is no God, but outer space is far, far greater than this.

If we could take an imaginary trip into space, we might realize the vastness of our universe. For years we talked about "breaking the sound barrier"—traveling just over 1,100 feet per second, but if we are to get anywhere in outer space, we must travel much faster than that.

Light travels at the rate of 186,000 miles per second. This is over eleven million miles a minute. Traveling at the speed of light, we could cover the distance to the sun, ninety-three million miles, in eight minutes. From there, we would begin our trip to the nearest star, Alpha Centauri. Traveling eleven million miles a minute, we could reach Alpha Centauri in four years. Then we would begin a trek across our galaxy, the Milky Way.

Often we think of space travel as involving the danger of collision with stars and meteors, but scientists tell us that outer space is practically empty. There are three billion stars in our galaxy. If our sun were the size of the dot over this "i," the nearest star would be a similar dot ten miles away, and other stars would be microscopic to dime-size dots hundreds and thousands of miles apart.

Traveling at the rate of eleven million miles a minute, the trip to the outer edge of our galaxy would take one hundred thousand years, and when we finally reached it, our trip would be just beginning.

We are off again toward the next galaxy. Traveling eleven million miles a minute, we face a journey that would take four million years. In 1961, *Time* magazine reported that with the two hundred-inch Palomar telescope astronomers could see over seventy-five million such galaxies, and at eleven million miles a minute, the farthest known galaxy is over six billion years away from earth.

Today, with the radio telescope, we can reach a distance of twenty-five billion years of travel away, and there is space and more space out beyond this. Such vastness is beyond man's ability to comprehend. How then can we possibly begin to comprehend the infinite and eternal God who created and sustains it? He has truly set our feet in a broad place!

The Measure You Give

Someone has said, "Giving is living." Listen to these words of Jesus: "Give, and it will be given unto you; good measure, pressed down, shaken together, running over will be put in your lap. For the measure you give will be the measure you get back."

A shiny black automobile sped down the highway just outside of Fort Worth. A doctor was making a hurried trip into the city. Off on the side of the road, under a hot summer sun, two women struggled to change a flat tire.

The doctor was in a terrible hurry, but the plight of the two women touched his heart. He pulled to a screeching halt, turned around and went back to render help.

As he took off the flat tire and replaced it with the spare from the luggage compartment, they talked. Finally, the job was finished, and the women thanked him for his kindness.

He watched as their car pulled away, gathered speed and was gone. With a warm feeling in his heart, the doctor returned to his own car and went on his way.

The doctor was busy during the weeks that followed, and the incident of the flat tire was forgotten. Then, returning home late one afternoon, he found a delivery truck at the door unloading a large color television set.

"I'm sorry," he said to the driver, "I'm afraid you have the wrong address. We didn't order a television." The deliveryman handed him an envelope, "Read this," he said. In the envelope was this note: "Thank you for helping my mother and sister change a tire." It was signed, Nat King Cole!

A few months later, newspaper headlines told of the death of Nat King Cole, and the entire world mourned his passing.

No man stands as tall as when he stoops to help and serve. Edwin Markham, with keen insight, pointed the implications out for all of us:

> There's a destiny that makes us brothers,
> None goes his way alone;
> All that we send into the life of others,
> Comes back into our own!

Whiter Than Snow

It was a grand summer morning! I had stepped out our back door and was surveying the scene. My next door neighbor came out in his yard to check on a litter of week-old puppies. "Hi there," I called. "Hello," came his response, "Isn't it a beautiful day?"

Indeed, it was. You probably remember that day—August 23. There had been a big rainstorm the night before, with high winds, lightening, and thunder. I had come home at nine o'clock just as the huge drops of rain began to splatter on the driveway. I was barely inside the house when it started coming down in torrents. I stood and watched through our large picture window as the falling rain drenched the grass, flowers, and trees.

I thought of a poem by William L. Stidger and quoted the words aloud:

> I saw God wash the world last night
> With his sweet showers on high,
> And when the morning came, I saw
> Him hang it out to dry.

Now, it was morning, and what a bright new day it was! The dust that had covered each blade of grass, each bright green leaf, had all been washed away. The white rose was a cleaner white. The red rose was a brighter red. There was no doubt about it; the world really had been "hung out to dry."

I recalled the night before. The lightning flashes, the rolling thunder, and the wild wind lashing the rain against the window until all sight was obliterated, was quite frightening. Now, just look. It was a totally different world.

I stood fully immersed for another moment, reluctant to go in. The morning breeze stirred the branches of the big oak, sending thousands of mist-like raindrops avalanching down.

Then I recalled the closing stanza of Bill Stidger's poem—a prayer, really. I made it my prayer, too.

> I saw God wash the world last night,
> Ah, would He had washed me
> As clean of all my dust and dirt
> As that old white birch tree.

You Can Plant a Standard

Some time ago, I ran across a little poem crammed with inspiration and challenge. It reads:

> You cannot choose your battlefield,
> God does that for you;
> But you can plant a standard,
> Where a standard never flew.

The pages of history fairly bristle with the names of men who have done just that. The Old Testament tells the story of Joseph who found himself on a grim battlefield that you may be sure he did not choose. He was sold into slavery by his jealous brothers, carried down into Egypt, falsely accused of attempted rape by Potiphar's wife and imprisoned. How easy it would have been to have given in to despair and given up the fight, but instead, he planted a standard and made of it a means of saving the nation and his family from starvation

Robert Louis Stevenson never picked his battlefield. In 1893, he wrote to his friend, George Meredith: "For fourteen years I have not had a single day of real health." He awakened sick and went to bed weary, but he fought on. His battlefield was an inglorious one of a sick bed and a medicine bottle. Yet out of it came *Treasure Island*, and *A Child's Garden of Verses* which for generations have continued to make glad the heart of childhood. In the face of overwhelming odds, he planted a standard where a standard never flew

William Wilberforce, the English reformer, was such a soldier. He was a very small man and never had good health. Once, James Boswell went to hear him speak in parliament and later wrote, "I saw a mere shrimp take the floor, but as I listened he grew and grew until the shrimp became a whale."

For twenty years, on his doctor's orders, William Wilberforce took opium to hold body and soul together and had the courage never to increase the dosage. He did more than any other person to put an end to the British slave trade. Three days before his death, he received the news that his bill abolishing slavery had passed. William Wilberforce planted a standard where a standard never flew. It can be so for you, too, with a heart that dares the fight and a will that refuses to accept defeat, and never despising your battlefield because God put you there, may you plant a standard where a standard never flew!

Play Ball!

Baseball fans all over the world are eagerly awaiting the call, "Play ball!" and the first pitch of the World Series. Who could fail to be caught up in all the anticipation, excitement, craziness and tension; pressure escalating into moments of stupidity and shouting, and benches clearing for a fight that marks the playoffs?

Every fall when the Series rolls around, I remember Ben Woodfork. Ben was the custodian at First Christian Church in Temple from 1963 until he retired in 1980. He and his wife Lovie were dedicated Christians and church workers. Ben worked hard to keep our church looking like the house of God and was admired and respected by all who knew him.

Ben loved baseball. He was a talented pitcher and could have made the major leagues if Jackie Robinson had come along twenty years earlier. More than anyone I have ever known, he looked forward to the World Series. He always said, "I don't care who wins as long as it goes for seven full games." He watched the games on TV and enjoyed every minute of every inning.

In memory of Ben Woodfork and for baseball fans all over the world who enjoy the playoffs and the Series, here is "The Baseball Prayer," written by some unknown author who knew and loved the great American game:

"Almighty Father, you who are called the "Mighty Umpire" in this game of life, we are not sure what uniforms we should wear. While we may be Angels in spirit, in reality we are Giants in pride, Dodgers of responsibility, and Tigers in ambition.

"When it comes to faith, we find ourselves in the minor leagues. When it comes to good works, we strike out; when it comes to knowledge of your Word, we are not even sure of the ground rules.

"Therefore, we are thankful for your mercy when we find ourselves in foul territory; for your forgiveness when we commit one error after another; for your uplifting spirit when we find ourselves in pitfalls of a slump.

"Dear God, may our game plan be your will, and our response a sellout crowd with standing room only. And when our number is retired here on earth, may we rejoice to hear you call out, "SAFE," in his name who gives final victory to all who believe! Amen."

Much Obliged, Lord

In the words of Psalms 92, "It is good to give thanks to the Lord." But for the Christian this is not enough. We feel a compulsion to go beyond it. I commend for your consideration a hymn, the refrain of which closes with these words: "Make me a blessing, O Savior, I pray, Make me a blessing to someone today."

In one of his books, Fulton Oursler tells about his old nurse Anna. She was present at his birth. She had also attended the birth of his mother. She was born a slave on the Eastern Shore of Maryland.

Her name was Anna Maria Cecily Sophia Virginia Avalon Thessalonians. It was she who taught him his greatest lesson of the thankful heart.

She ate at the kitchen table of their house. She would fold her hardened brown hands, close her eyes, and pray, "Much obliged, Lord, for my vittles."

Fulton Oursler asked, "Anna, what's vittles?" "It's what I've got to eat and drink, that's vittles." "But you would get your vittles whether you thanked the Lord or not." "Sure, but it makes everything taste better to be thankful."

After the meal, she thanked the Lord again and said, "You know, it's a funny thing about being thankful for things. So many of them you pass right by unless you look for them.

Take this morning, when I woke up I couldn't think of anything to thank him for, and then I started looking. From the kitchen came the most delicious smell in the world. I whispered, "Much obliged, Lord, for the fragrant smell of coffee."

Years later, Fulton Oursler went through a bitter period of discouragement and failure. It was the memory of Anna's spirit of thanksgiving that gave him a handle to hold on to, pulled him up, and gave him a new start.

Then he was called home to the bedside of the dying Anna. He wondered how she felt about things now. What would she have to be thankful for amidst her pain? She looked up at him and smiled, and the last words she spoke were these: "Much obliged, Lord, for such fine friends."

October 12   II Kings 6: 17

How Well Do You See?

On a hunting expedition, the Emperor Hadrian accidentally shot one of his servants and put out his eyes. Conscience stricken, the Roman ruler called the servant. "What can I do to make amends?" he asked. The blinded servant could only repeat over and over, "Give me back my sight! I want to see!"

Even more pathetic than those who cannot see are those who will not see. The Bible refers to them when it says, "Having eyes, they see not." What about you and me, how well do we see?

Are we able to see God at work in his world? While in Paris, Benjamin Franklin was taunted by an agnostic about his belief in God. Franklin asked, "If there is no God, who created the universe?" The man's only answer: "It just happened."

That evening, the ingenious Franklin constructed a small planetarium. The next morning the agnostic found it and was delighted. "Who made it?" he asked. Franklin replied, "No one made it. It just happened." "Oh, come on," the Frenchman persisted, "Who made it?" Franklin said, "Strange, isn't it. You insist this toy had to have a maker. Yesterday, when we talked about the real thing, you said it just happened."

Are we able to see the potential in our lives? Years ago, when thousands were being killed by shattered glass in automobiles, Henry Ford was determined to do something about it. He gave the orders, "Engage engineers and keep them at work until they produce glass that is shatterproof." Then he added, "And hire young men—old men know too many reasons why it can't be done!" Are we able to see our God-given potential and believe we can do what God has created and called us to do?

Finally, are we able to see the people about us? Do we really care about persons? That is a must if we are to follow in the footsteps of our Master. How often we read of Jesus, "He looked upon them with compassion." Jesus was able to see others. Are we able to see? More to the point, do we want to see?

Once, just outside of the city of Jericho, a blind beggar called out to Jesus for help. Jesus stopped and asked him, "What do you want me to do for you?" That is the question you and I must answer. Waiting before us is a land of light!

This Little Light of Mine

Every Sunday during the children's sermon, our boys and girls sing the chorus, "This little light of mine, I'm gonna let it shine." Last Sunday, as the congregation applauded, I thought, "That little song is good theology. That is exactly what followers of Christ are called to do."

I remember an Associated Press news story of some years ago. Twenty-two planes from North Island Naval Air Station were participating in Naval Day maneuvers when fog swept in. Eight of the planes raced to landing fields, but 14 were trapped aloft in misty obscurity.

Twelve pilots dived blindly through the opaque whiteness. Four planes crashed, one bursting into flames, but the men were all unharmed. By eight o'clock that evening, two hours after the fog moved in, two planes were still stranded aloft. The drone of their engines made it unmistakably clear that they were up there somewhere.

Then there went out over the radio a message: "All owners of automobiles go immediately to the old Camp Kearney Airport outside San Diego. Two fliers are lost in the fog. Your going may save their lives."

Soon the roads leading to the abandoned airfield were bumper to bumper with cars making their way slowly through the fog, each barely able to see the car directly ahead.

As the cars arrived, they were lined up around the field in a great circle facing inward. Over twenty-five hundred cars completely surrounded the landing area. The order sounded: "All lights on!"

The lights of one car made no impression whatsoever, but the lights of 2,500 lighted up the field so brightly that a transport pilot was able to go up and guide the two aviators down to safety.

Our lives are like that. Separately, neither your light nor mine count for much. But, if all of us would focus the tiny beams we have been given upon the fog banks of sin and distress, it would be so bright that Christ, the Master Pilot, could go aloft and guide every lost soul of our world to safety.

In his prayer, St. Francis of Assisi prayed that he might bring "Light, where there is darkness," and in the Sermon on the Mount, our Master said, "Let your light shine."

October 14 Isaiah 45: 15

When God Hides Himself

It was the prophet Isaiah who wrote, "Truly, you are a God who hides yourself." Could this be true? We are taught that God is a God who seeks to reveal himself to us through nature, through the Bible, and through his Son, Jesus Christ. Does he also hide himself?

Fletcher Sears was the purchasing agent for the Detroit and Cleveland Navigation Company for fifty years. He had three interests: his church, his home and his business. He was an outstanding churchman and taught a men's Sunday school class.

After a long life free from any kind of illness, Fletcher Sears was stricken with a painful ailment. He had to undergo surgery and was hospitalized for months. While he was hospitalized, his wife fell and broke her hip. She was to spend the rest of her life in another hospital. Dark clouds of discouragement and gloom hung over their lives.

One day his minister, Dr. Edgar DeWitt Jones, called on him in the hospital. When asked how he was, he replied, "Dr. Jones, I have lost God. In my suffering, I have lost him. I know I am saved because I have done everything the Lord has commanded, but amid all the pain, I have lost him."

There was a long silence as their handclasp tightened. Then the minister spoke softly, "My friend, you are in grand company." The words took the sick man totally by surprise. Hardly believing what he had heard, he asked, "What do you mean?"

Dr. Jones answered, "I am talking about Job. You remember, in the midst of his suffering and loss, he lost God for a while. He found himself saying, 'Oh, that I knew where I might find him.'

"Then there was Jeremiah. He, too, once cried out that he had lost God. Even Christ, in one terrible moment on the cross, lost God and cried out, 'Why have you forsaken me?' Yes, my friend, you are in grand company."

I don't know why, I cannot explain it, but I know it's true. God does, indeed, hide himself. He spares none of his children, no matter how faithful, but he will never forsake us, I know that, too. When the dark storm clouds gather in your life and you find yourself feeling alone, remember you are in a grand company of people who lost God for a moment but held on.

Left-handed Warriors

The Book of Judges tells of a band of soldiers, all of whom were left-handed. "Each one could sling a stone at a hair and not miss." Originally, they fought with sword and shield. The shield was carried on the left arm for protection. The right arm held the sword.

These soldiers had been wounded on their fighting arms. No longer able to hold the sword and fight with their right arms, they learned to use the sling shot with their left.

In time, they became the finest outfit in the whole army. They became expert marksmen who were deadly even at long range. Long before the enemies were near enough to use sword and spear, they were brought down with well-aimed stones at their foreheads or temple.

These refused to quit. When they were blocked off in one direction, they looked around and started in another. How different they were in comparison to you and me. So often, when we come face to face with stubborn obstacles, we give up and quit.

The greatest conquests our world has known have been won by handicapped soldiers who when deprived of using swords, took up slingshots and pressed on to victory.

The pages of history are filled with the names of such heroes. Paul, locked in a dungeon cell, his missionary work at an end, didn't let such an obstacle stop him. Instead, he took up a pen and wrote. His letters have blessed our world beyond measure. Beethoven composed in spite of deafness, Milton wrote poetry though blind, and we could go on and on.

Of course, it isn't easy for a man who is right handed to learn to use his left. It takes hours and hours of agonizing practice. It takes days and weeks and months and years of work. It calls for courage of the highest kind.

Left handed warriors! These are the lives that make a difference. They take up slingshots, and shout above the tumult:

> It matters not how straight the gate
> How charged with punishment the scroll:
> I am the master of my fate,
> I am the captain of my soul.

Becoming What You Want to Be?

In Leonard da Vinci's painting, "The Last Supper," two figures stand out in deep contrast. One is the central figure of Christ; the other is Judas Iscariot who betrayed him.

There is an old legend connected with the painting. It is said that the artist searched far and wide for a model to portray the Lord. He wanted a young man of sterling character to show forth the purity, strength, and courage of the Christ.

One day in the cathedral, a chorister caught his attention. The young man's name was Pietro Bandinelli. He was clean-cut and possessed a noble face. He was just the person for whom da Vinci had been searching, and so Pietro Bandinelli posed as the model for the Master.

The years passed. One by one, all the apostles were painted by the artist. That is, all except one—Judas the Traitor, the disciple who sold his Master for thirty pieces of silver.

Everywhere he went, da Vinci looked for some debased character suitable for the part. Then one afternoon on the back streets of Milan, he came face to face with the man for whom he had been seeking.

He was a dirty beggar dressed in rags. He had the most villainous look the artist had ever seen.

The beggar agreed to sit as a model for Judas. When the work was completed, da Vinci paid the man and waited for him to leave the studio. The man waited. When at last da Vinci glanced up, his model said, "You don't remember me at all, do you?"

Scrutinizing the model's face without the faintest recollection, da Vinci asked, "Should I remember you?" The beggar said, "My name is Pietro Bandinelli. Years ago as a young man, I sat for you as the model for the Christ!"

Then da Vinci heard his story. Soon after posing for the painting of the face of Christ, Pietro Bandinelli had left and gone to Rome. There he fell among evil companions who led him into a life of crime and debasing sin.

None of us remains the same. Day by day, we are becoming better or worse. Are you becoming what you want to be?

Just a Closer Walk with Thee

The refrain of *Just A Closer Walk With Thee* is really a prayer: "Just a closer walk with Thee, Grant it, Jesus is my plea, Daily, walking close to Thee, Let it be, dear Lord, let it be."

Dr. Edward Elson, minister of the National Presbyterian Church in Washington D. C., tells about visiting St. Louis Cathedral in New Orleans, a church known worldwide for its art. Many of you have been in that famous church. Standing before one of the murals, Dr. Elson felt a tug at his sleeve. Looking down he saw a little bit of a woman. She was wearing a plain print dress and had a pair of cheap sandals on her feet. "Sir," she said, "Do you know the name of the saint I should pray to for the healing of my eyes?"

Bit by bit, he learned her story. She worked in a factory for fifty cents a day. When cataracts formed on her eyes, and she could no longer see to work, she was sent to the charity hospital. The ward was crowded, and she had to sleep on the floor, but the surgery was successful and soon she returned to work. "But something is wrong," she said, "The shadows are coming back. Please, Sir, tell me the name of the saint I should pray to for healing."

Dr. Elson was deeply moved. "I don't know the name of the saint," he said, "But if you will pray to God through Christ, he will touch you and give you peace."

So it was that the two of them knelt at the altar, she a Roman Catholic and he a Presbyterian minister. There at the foot of the cross, they prayed together, asking Jesus, the Great Physician, to touch and heal her.

Later, Dr. Elson wrote in his diary: "We knelt down together for prayer. Then it happened. As we prayed, Christ came as he always comes. With holy joy, a serene peace and radiant countenance, she rose and made her way out of the cathedral.

"I had gone there to admire art. I came away with the living Christ in my heart. I had seen human suffering and felt the adequacy of Christ to meet it. I walked with him as never before."

It is always true, I think. As we take the story of his redeeming love to others and minister to their needs, he draws near and walks with us as never before.

Will A Man Rob God?

A forlorn beggar sat beside the hot, dusty road, waiting for someone charitably inclined. He was in desperate straits. He hadn't eaten in days. Unless help was forthcoming soon, his very life stood in jeopardy. Just then he saw a man coming toward him. He was a wealthy nobleman; he could tell at a glance. Holding out his dirty hand, the beggar asked for alms.

The traveler stopped. His heart went out to this stranger in need, and he wanted to help. Reaching beneath the folds of his tunic, he took out a leather money pouch and poured the contents into his hand. Ten bright jewels sparkled in the sunlight. He picked out the largest and placed it in the hand of the beggar, then another, and another, and another.

The beggar watched in utter amazement as this continued until nine jewels had been placed in his hand. A single blue sapphire was all that remained in the possession of his benefactor. As the traveler turned to go, the joy that comes from giving oneself with his gifts lighted his face. His voice sounded in loving benediction, "May the Lord bless you and keep you, my son."

The beggar sat spellbound. He held in his hand wealth worth a king's ransom. Then he remembered. In his surprise, he had not even thanked the one who had helped him. His eyes filled with tears.

He looked down at the jewels in his hand, then up at the retreating figure of his benefactor. Suddenly his face clouded. His every feature spoke of insatiable greed.

Stealthily he arose, picked up his heavy walking stick, and started in hot pursuit of the one who had befriended him. Overtaking the stranger, he clubbed him over the head and watched without feeling as he fell unconscious to the ground.

His grimy hand found what he sought, and grasping fingers closed around the blue sapphire. He took one last unfeeling look at the form lying at his feet, tossed the empty pouch aside, and went on his way.

Centuries ago the prophet Malachi asked, "Will a man rob God?" That is still life's searching question. He has given us all we hold in trust, and we are reminded that "the tithe is the Lord's." Could it possibly be that our ingratitude is so great that we would rob God and take the tenth also?

October 19   **II Corinthians 3:11**
                    Architects of Fate

During World War II, a plane with two American pilots aboard was forced down on an island in the Pacific. For days, they wandered through the jungles. Then they came to a village with neat, clean buildings. Natives took them to the chief. Imagine their surprise when they were greeted in English and welcomed as "fellow Christians."

The pilots learned that fifty years before, missionaries had come and, in time, had transformed the cannibal tribe into a Christian community.

The next day, they were taken on a tour of the island. The first place they visited was their church. Telling the story later, they said, "At the top of the hill, we found the most beautiful chapel we had ever seen. It was of Gothic design, and the interior was finished in mahogany. When we inquired, "Who built it?" the old chief said proudly, "We did! The missionaries gave directions and helped, but we did the work."

Then they were taken around behind the church and shown another building—a crude jumble of sticks and stones held together with dried mud. The guide said, "That was our first church."

The young flyers couldn't get over the sharp contrast and remarked about the difference. Then the old chief said something they would never forget: "You see, as we became better Christians, we became better builders."

Called to build a better world, isn't it time for us to become better builders? Paul warns, "... let the builder be careful how he builds!"

> "Isn't it strange
> That princes and kings,
> And clowns that caper
> In sawdust rings,
> And common people like you and me
> Are builders for eternity?
>
> Each is given a bag of tools,
> A shapeless mass
> And a book of rules;
> And each must make,
> Ere his life is flown,
> A stumbling block
> Or a stepping stone."

293

October 20

Matthew 25:21

Second Stringer

His name was James Hampton, but from the day he arrived at TCU as a walk-on to play for the Horned Frogs, he was known to everyone as "Arkansas." During four years of college, he never made the first team.

The highlight of his football career was the homecoming game his senior year, when with other seniors, he started the game. He was pulled after the first three plays, but he started and TCU won their final game.

It is not easy to play second string for four years, watching newer players go ahead of you, but "Arkansas" managed it. He was on the sideline every Saturday, ready to go in anytime he was needed. He gave little thought to being a second stringer. With "Arkansas," being a substitute didn't matter. The main thing was winning the game.

"Arkansas" has always reminded me of Andrew, one of the twelve apostles. Andrew grew up in Capernaum with his brother, Simon Peter, and two neighboring brothers, James and John. In time, the four of them went into the fishing business together. One day they all went down to the Jordan River, near Jericho, to hear the preaching of John the Baptist. While there, Andrew met Jesus. He went and found his brother, Simon Peter and brought him to Jesus.

The four became followers of the Master. Over and over in the gospel record we read: "Jesus took with him Peter, James, and John." They were the starters on the first team. For some reason, Andrew never made it. Throughout his career, he played as a second stringer.

Without a trace of bitterness or envy, he played his role like a man. The team was what mattered. On the day of Pentecost Simon Peter preached and three thousand persons were added to the church. It was Andrew who made it possible.

Andrew was always bringing someone to Jesus. First, his brother, Simon Peter, then the lad with the loaves and fishes, then the Greeks, and eventually, through his brother, three thousand converts.

Andrew—always in the background—went unnoticed and unsung. But I like to think that in the Trophy Case of Eternity there is a bronze plaque on which is inscribed these words: "In tribute to Andrew. He never made the first team, but he played the game with fortitude and courage, and because of him we won!"

294

Show Me Your Hands!

He was great judge of character. He used to say, "I go by people's hands. I can tell more about a person by his hands than anything." It may be that our hands say more about us than we realize.

Years ago in the city of London, a minister, calling on the dwellers in an apartment close to his church, met a little girl of fourteen. Her mother had died when she was eleven, and she had become the housekeeper for her father and the other children—three brothers and a baby sister. She was the only mother they knew.

The hours were long and the work was hard. She worked from early in the morning until late at night. Over the months and years, she literally worked herself to death. Her face was pale and drawn, her body thin and frail. The doctor, who was finally called in, diagnosed it as tuberculosis in the last stages.

Critically ill in the hospital, the minister who had become her friend called on her each day. He prayed with her, and they read from the little New Testament that he carried. One day they talked about death and dying. "I am terribly afraid," she said, "I've never had time to go to church or anything. What am I going to tell God?"

The minister reached out and took her little work-worn hands. Remembering the long months and years of labor for her family, he said, "My dear, you won't have to say anything. God already knows about you and your life. Just show him your hands."

In the Book of Psalms are recorded these words: "Establish thou the work of our hands . . . ." In large measure, our hands tell the story of our lives. What we do with our hands is up to us.

A number of possibilities are open to us. For one thing, we can sit on our hands. That means doing absolutely nothing. Secondly, we can simply fold our hands. In resignation, we just give up and quit. A third possibility is for us to wring our hands in desperation, "My, oh my, what am I going to do?" Or—would you believe—we can reach out with the two hands God has given us and lay hold on a task waiting to be done.

You know, Judgment Day may be far, far different from the way we generally picture it. It may be that there will be no questions asked at all. The great Judge, who already knows every heart, may only make a simple request: "Show me your hands!"

You Shall Be My Witnesses

"You shall be my witnesses." These are the words of Jesus Christ as recorded in the book of Acts. This is what he wants his followers to be.

In his autobiography, "A Song of Ascent," E. Stanley Jones tells about the first sermon he ever preached. When he told his pastor that he had been called to preach, he invited him to fill the pulpit of his home church on a Sunday evening three weeks hence.

He says that he had the underlying thought that he was to be God's lawyer and plead his case. The little church was filled that evening with relatives and friends, hoping anxiously that the young man do well.

He began on a high key and was doing quite well until he used a word he had never used before in all his life, "indifferentism." When a young college student in the congregation put down her head and smiled, it unnerved him. When he tried to get back to the thread of his discourse it was gone!

His mind was blank. He couldn't think of a thing to say. Finally, he managed to blurt out, "I'm sorry; I have forgotten my sermon!" In shame and confusion, he turned and started down out of the pulpit.

Then it happened. A voice within said, "Stanley, haven't I done anything for you?" Quickly he replied, "Yes, Lord, you have done everything for me." The voice spoke again, "Well, couldn't you tell them about that?"

He came down and stood facing the congregation. "My friends," he said, "I am sorry I forgot my sermon. As you see, I can't preach, but you know what my life was like before my conversion and what it is now. I may never make a preacher, but I do love Christ, and I shall be his witness as long as I live."

After the service, Stanley Warfield, a young friend of his came up and said, "I wish I had what you have found," and there in that little church that evening, the miracle happened in another life. The young man gave himself to Christ and was transformed and changed.

As a lawyer for God, arguing his case, E. Stanley Jones was a failure. As a witness, simply telling what God had done for his life, he was a success. Listen again to the words of the Master, "You shall be my witnesses." Witnesses! That is what we are, if we are. Are we?

Priming the Pump

As Paul was bidding farewell to the church at Ephesus, he charged them to remember the words of the Lord Jesus, how he said, "It is more blessed to give than to receive."

It was Paul's conviction, as it was Jesus' before him, that giving is a prerequisite for receiving. Over and over in the New Testament, we find the keyword to be "Receive." God is not a merchant who sells, he is a father who gives, but he is able to give to us only as we ourselves give.

These are the instructions for getting water from a well beside a seldom-used trail across the desert. The note was written with a stub of a pencil on brown wrapping paper and left in a baking powder can tied to the handle of an old pump. It reads:

"This pump is all right as of June, 1932. I put a new sucker washer on it, and it ought to last for five years, but the washer dries out and the pump has to be primed.

"Under the white rock, I buried a bottle of water, out of the sun and cork end up. There's enough water in it to prime the pump, but not if you drink some first. Pour in about a fourth and let her soak to wet the leather. Then pour in the rest medium fast and pump as hard as you can. You'll get water.

"The well has never run dry. Have faith. When you get watered up, fill the bottle and put it back like you found it for the next fellow. Desert Pete"

At the bottom of the note is this postscript: "Don't go drinking the water first. Prime the pump with it and you will get all you can hold. And the next time you pray, remember that God is like this pump. He has to be primed.

"I've given my last dime away a dozen times to prime the pump of my prayers, and I have fed my last beans to a stranger while saying Amen. It never failed to get me an answer. You have to get your heart fixed to give before you can receive."

Perhaps that is the reason Jesus said that it is more blessed to give than to receive. The only way any of us can receive is through our willingness first to give!

Never Give Up!

It was two days before Christmas in 1972. The Dallas Cowboys had barely made it as a wildcard, playing the San Francisco 49ers who on Thanksgiving Day had beaten the Cowboys 31-10. The morning of the game, Coach Tom Landry asked Billy Zeoli to give the devotional. Billy spoke on the topic, "Never Give Up."

Just before the half, San Francisco was leading 21-6. Alworth took a Morton pass for a 28-yard touchdown to put Dallas back in the game, but in the third quarter, Hill fumbled at the Dallas one-yard line, and the 49ers scored to go ahead 28-13.

The Cowboys had to turn the game around. Coach Landry knew that Roger Staubach had a way of doing just that. With 1:48 on the clock, Roger was sent in.

The Cowboys set up on their own 45-yard line. Staubach hit three passes in a row and Dallas had a first down at the 49ers' 20-yard line. Billy Parks moved downfield, turned inside and took a touchdown pass to make it 28-23 with just 1:10 left. All San Francisco had to do was take the kickoff and run out the clock.

The Cowboys' only hope was an on-side kick. Toni Fritsch nudged the ball. It rolled the ten yards, and a 49er, Preston Riley, grabbed it. As he was falling, Ralph Coleman of the Cowboys hit him, the ball spurted free, and Mel Renfro recovered at midfield for the Cowboys with 1:03 remaining.

On first down, Staubach faded as though to pass and took off running for a 30-yard gain. Then Billy Parks took a pass for 19 yards, stepping out of bounds at the ten to stop the clock. The next play was supposed to go to Parks again, but as the huddle broke, wide receiver Ron Sellers told Staubach that he would be open on a hook route which he ran straight up field and came back for the ball.

The 49ers came with an all-out blitz. There was no time to look for Parks. Staubach threw to Sellers. Ron turned, the ball was there, and he caught it for the touchdown. In the last minute and ten seconds the Cowboys had scored two touchdowns and had beaten the 49ers 30-28.

When I think about that 1972 *game*, I remember Billy Zeoli's devotional, "Never Give Up." I also recall the words Coach Tilmon Kirby used to quote to his charges: "A quitter never wins; a winner never quits."

Pride Goes Before A Fall

Once there was a turtle that lived by a pond. One day two ducks flew in and landed on the pond. The three became good friends. Time passed. "Soon it will be winter," the ducks said, "Before the snow falls, we must fly to our home in the South." "Why don't you come with us?" they asked, "The weather is always warm and delightful, and you would love the reed-filled lake."

"I would like to," said the turtle, "But how can I? I have no wings with which to fly." The ducks thought about it. At last, one of them said, "I know how. The two of us will carry you." The turtle was excited, "Oh, that sounds wonderful. If you will take me with you, I will do anything you say."

The following day, they were ready to begin their flight. The ducks took a stick and held the ends firmly in their bills. They said to the turtle, "Snap on to the middle of the stick and keep your mouth closed. You must not open it until we arrive."

Then the ducks flew up into the air with the turtle between them. The flight was thrilling. For hours they flew over trees and meadows, fields and streams. As they were flying above a village, the townspeople came out to see the strange sight. "How clever!" one of the observers exclaimed, "That is such a brilliant idea! I wonder who thought of it?"

The words of praise thrilled the turtle. The temptation to take the credit was too great. He opened his mouth to say, "I did!" "I" was barely out of his mouth when he felt himself falling through the air to crash upon the ground below.

The book of Proverbs tells us: "Pride goes before destruction, and a haughty spirit before a fall." Simon Peter learned how deadly pride can be. He boasted that though all the other disciples might fall away, he never would.

Then, before the night was over, he denied with oaths even knowing Jesus. Realizing how he had failed, he went out and wept bitterly. It was a hard lesson he never forgot. Years later he wrote: "Clothe yourself with humility, for God opposes the proud, but gives grace to the humble."

The sin of pride steals upon us so subtly. Guard against it at all cost. Remember what happened to the turtle!

In The Beginning God

To look through a telescope is to behold the glory of God. Through it, we look into space so vast that distance is measured in light years, the distance light travels in a year, moving at the rate of 186,000 miles a second.

Our solar system, made up of the sun and the earth and other planets revolving around it, is a part of a huge galaxy, the Milky Way, made up of one hundred billion stars. It is so large it would take light 100,000 years to travel across it.

Today's astronomers tell us that there are as many galaxies in the universe as there are stars in the Milky Way. Sir James Jean once estimated that all the stars of all the galaxies may equal the number of grains of sand on all the seashores of the world.

Nobody knows just how large our universe is. Radio telescopes can penetrate as far as six billion light years into space, and from all indications, this is but the beginning. Outer space appears limitless.

Despite the billions of stars that fill it, space is almost empty. If our sun, which is 860,000 miles across, were the size of the dot over this "i," the star nearest to it would be a similar dot ten miles away. Other stars would be up to the size of a dime, hundreds and thousands of miles apart. Indeed, "the heavens declare the glory of God."

To look through a microscope is to behold the glory of God. Through it we look into the world of cells, molecules, and atoms so small that in order to be seen must be highly magnified.

Everything we know is made up of billions and billions of atoms. Atoms are so tiny they have never been seen. The atom is as small as the universe is large, yet the two are very similar. Like the universe, the atom is made up mostly of empty space dotted occasionally by weightless electrons.

In proportion to their size, these electrons are as far apart as the planets are from the sun. And they move in orbits just as the planets do, whirling around the nucleus billions of times in a millionth of a second.

Such an amazing, incredible, awe-inspiring universe causes one to ask: "Who? What? When? How? The Bible gives us the answer: "In the beginning God . . . ."

Lamentations 3: 22-23

Wait On The Lord!

The twenty-seventh Psalm closes with these words of counsel: "Wait for the Lord; be strong and let your heart take courage; yea, wait for the Lord!"

We get in too big a hurry. A young man rushing to catch a ferry arrived to find it a few feet from the landing. He made a running leap and landed on board. His suitcase came open and personal articles went in every direction. He got up rather pleased with himself. "See that? I made it!" he said to a man standing near. The man looked at him for a moment and said, "You idiot, the ferry was just coming in!" So often our lives are like that. We need to learn to wait.

We need to learn to wait for morning. In the wakeful watches of the night, we can make mistakes in judgment. Many times with the dawn, we see things in a different light. I heard a minister say recently that he had saved several people from suicide simply by persuading them to wait until daylight. The dawn can make a big difference. Wait for the morning.

We need to learn to wait until noon. This is especially true of young people. Wanting to grow up in a hurry, they crowd so much into life's morning hours that life loses its zest.

I knew a student when I was in college who had been around the world three times. At nineteen years of age, there was very little that he had not done. He said to a group of us in the dorm one evening, "If I had it to do over, I wouldn't live so fast. My life is empty, there is nothing to look forward to, I have already used everything up." Don't carelessly run through all life has to offer in the morning. Wait until noon.

Finally, we need to learn to wait before closed doors. Over and over doors slam shut in our faces, and it seems as though they will never open again. It must have seemed so for Paul. When he was imprisoned in Rome, the doors clanged shut with such seeming finality.

It was hard for a man like Paul to wait with patience, but he did, and from that prison came all of Paul's letters we find in the New Testament. Those letters of Paul have inspired millions and changed the world.

You know, quite often when we learn to wait we find that the stops are as valuable as the steps. As you journey through life, remember: "Wait on the Lord!"

The Gospel According to You

V. O. Teddlie was the county agent and advisor for the Future Farmers of America to which I belonged as a boy. At one of our chapter meetings, he told about being assigned to a county in West Texas.

It was at the time trench silos were just coming into use. Knowing what a tremendous asset they could be to the farmers and ranchers, he began promoting them. He held meetings in school buildings all over the county telling about the value of trench silos and giving information urging their construction.

For some unknown reason, cooperation was not forthcoming. An entire year passed without a single silo being built. All of his encouragement seemed to be to no avail. Late at night, he would lie awake wondering what he could do. Then he had an idea. Early the next morning, he went out in the back of his home and set to work building a trench silo.

Neighbors began stopping by to see what he was doing and to ask questions. By the time he had completed the project, people were coming from far and near to see it and get information as to how they could build one of their own.

When Mr. Teddlie was transferred a few years later, there were literally hundreds of trench silos all over the county. They were built, not because of what he had said—all of his talk accomplished nothing. Results were obtained when he went to work, built a trench silo of his own and demonstrated what it could do.

As Christians, we see the world's need for Christ. We spend a lot of time talking about Christ—and talking is good, but I wonder if the world isn't waiting for something more. What a difference it might make if you and I went to work where we are, with what we have, and demonstrated the difference Christ can make in a human life.

This is what Paul had in mind when, writing to the Christians at Rome, he spoke of "my gospel." Paul knew, as we ought to know, that the lives we live say far, far more than our words can ever say.

> You're writing a gospel, a chapter each day,
> By the deeds you do, and the words you say.
> Men read what you write, whether faithless or true.
> Say, what is the gospel according to you?

Do It Now!

In the Book of James are found these words of wise counsel: "Be doers of the word, and not hearers only," and over and over, in the gospels Jesus is heard to say, "Go and do . . . ."

In his book, *Letters in the Desert*, Carlo Carretto tells how this great truth came home to him and shaped his life. At the age of forty-four, after a life of intense social involvement with Catholic Action in Italy following World War II, he went to serve in North Africa.

Early in his desert sojourn, he was resting at midday in the shade of some huge rocks. He reached for a blanket and put it under his head. Another blanket by his side, unused, caused him to feel ill at ease.

The evening before, he had passed through the small village of Irafog. There he had seen Old Kada trembling with cold. Cold in the desert? Yes. The Sahara is often called "a cold country where it is very hot in the sun." He thought of giving Old Kada one of his blankets, but decided he needed them himself. When he left the village both blankets were still in the jeep. Now, they were troubling his conscience.

Finally, he fell asleep and had a strange dream. The great boulder under which he lay fell, crushing him to death and pinning him where he couldn't move. He opened his eyes and saw Old Kada shivering in front of him. The blanket was lying unused behind him. He wanted to give it to the poor man, but the stone would not permit him to move so much as an inch.

He understood in a small measure what hell is like—"no longer to have the possibility of doing, what before, one could have and should have done." Carlo Carretto's story is a parable of the possibility that is offered to each of us—not only to hear, but to act; to do what Christ would do if he were here. As one of our poets has written:

> A bell's not a bell
> Till you ring it;
> A song's not a song
> Till you sing it.
> And love in your heart
> Is not put there to stay;
> Love is not love
> Till you give it away.

God's Forgiveness

At the center of the prayer that Jesus taught us to pray is found these words of petition: "Forgive us." They are there for a reason. This is the heartfelt cry of every one of us. This is the deep need of our lives—to be forgiven, to find an answer to our problem of guilt.

Shakespeare, in "The Merchant of Venice," reminds us, "That in the course of justice, none of us should see salvation." Justice is inadequate for our need; it is the mercy of God that our lives require.

The gospel, the good news, is that God loves us and is waiting to forgive us and remember our sins no more. It is to be found in the Psalms. "As far as east is from the west, so far does he remove our transgressions from us."

Have you ever thought about how far that is? If the Psalmist had said, "As far as the north is from the south," it would be from pole to pole, 12,360 miles. If a person goes north, he eventually reaches the North Pole; then, he begins to travel south. North and South meet at the poles,
but when he travels westward and goes straight ahead, he never travels eastward. East and west never meet.

Recently I heard a true story of a young Catholic nun who had a vision of Christ. She was brought before her European bishop to be interviewed to ascertain the validity of her experience.

The bishop asked her, "Sister, did you talk with him?" "Yes," she said, "I did," and the bishop said to her, "All right. If you ever have another vision, would you ask him this question, 'What was the bishop's primary sin before he became a bishop?'?" He knew that only God and the bishop's confessor would know the answer. That way, it could be determined if she had had a real encounter with Christ.

Three months later, when she returned, the bishop inquired, "Did you see our Lord again?" "Yes, I did," she replied. The bishop continued, "And did you ask him, 'What was the bishop's primary sin before he became a bishop?'" "Yes, I did," she said. "And what did our Lord say?" the bishop asked. The young woman answered, "He said he didn't remember."

Our God is a God of infinite mercy who keeps his promise. Listen again to his words: "For I will forgive their wrongdoing and remember their sin no more."

Matthew 5:14

You Can Change the World!

On September 2, 1945, World War II came to a close. The allies officially designated the date as V-J Day.

That evening, a gigantic rally was held in the Los Angeles Coliseum celebrating the end of the fighting. No more lives of our fighting men would have to be sacrificed. Over 100,000 people packed the great stadium for the observance.

The field was laid out like a veritable battleground. The great lights flooding it were extinguished. In the darkness was heard the rumble of tanks, rifles cracked, machineguns blazed their deadly fire, and heavy artillery flashed and roared.

Amid it all, giant bombers swept down with a deafening roar shaking the whole earth, as though to dwarf the crowd into utter insignificance.

Then suddenly all was quiet. From the press box high above the stands, a voice spoke: "The war is over! By the grace of God, America and her allies have won the war. Now we face the even bigger task of winning the peace."

"It is so easy," the speaker continued, "To feel that we have no part in the great undertaking, to say, I am only one person and don't count. But we do count—every one of us. Watch this!" High above the stands, the speaker struck a match and held it aloft. One hundred thousand people beheld its light.

"Do you see what one little light can do? Your life and mine are like that. To be sure, they may be small. One little light is seemingly very insignificant, but who knows how many thousands may be watching that one little light. Now suppose that one little light were multiplied.

What if each of us lighted a match?"

Then in less time than it takes to tell it, matches were distributed to everyone present. At a given signal, they were struck and held aloft. A great "Oh!" went up from the stand as the coliseum was flooded with light.

What a message for every person there! And what a message for you and me! No life is insignificant. You were created by God, and created for a purpose. Just one little life, it's true, but you can change the world!

Establishing Our Priorities

Charles M. Schwab was a great American industrialist. He became the president of the Bethlehem Steel Corporation in 1903. Because of his energies and qualities of leadership, he was an officer and director of boards and corporations too numerous to mention.

Ivey Lee was an outstanding management consultant. One day Charles Schwab confronted him with this unusual challenge: "Show me a method by which I can get more things done. If what you suggest works, I will pay you anything within reason."

Sometime later, Lee came to Schwab with his plan. He handed him a sheet of paper. "Now," he said, "I want you to write down all the things you have to do tomorrow." When Schwab had completed the list, Lee said, "Now go through and number the items in the order of their real importance."

When the list had been numbered according to importance, Lee said, "The first thing tomorrow morning, start working on number one and stay with it until it is completed. Then take number two and don't go any further until it is completed. Then proceed to number three, and so on.

"If you fail to complete everything on schedule, you are not to worry. By following the schedule, you take care of the most important things and you are protected from being distracted by so many things of lesser consequence.

"The secret," Lee continued, "Is to do this at the beginning of every day. Weigh the relative importance of the things you have to get done, establish priorities, determine your plan of action, and stick with it.

"Test it as long as you like. Have the men in your factory try it. When you have decided on its value, send me a check for whatever you think it is worth."

In a few weeks, Charles Schwab sent Ivey Lee a check for twenty-five thousand dollars. Schwab often said that this lesson was the most profitable one of his business career.

The plan works. It will work for you. Just try it. It's free. Jesus used it. He was the greatest priority expert our world has ever known. He counseled: "Seek first the kingdom of God, and his righteousness, and all these things shall be yours as well."

Our God is Able, If—

"Our God is able, if—." At first glance it seems like a blasphemous limiting of the power of God. But it is true to God's Word. How many of God's promises are conditional! God declared to Solomon, "If my people, who are called by my name, shall humble themselves, and pray, and seek my face, and turn from their wicked ways; then will I hear from heaven, and will forgive their sin and heal their land."

Paul wrote to the Romans, "If you confess with your lips that Jesus is Lord and believe in your heart that God raised him from the dead, you will be saved." In the Gospel of John, Jesus said, "If you abide in me and my words abide in you, ask whatever you will and it shall be done for you."

"Our God is able, if—." William Carey, preaching for the first time in his home church, used this text: "Go into all the world and preach the gospel." After worship service the congregation gathered around praising his message. He could endure it no longer. "You tell me it was a fine sermon; that is not what I want. I want you to do something!" So they all went back into the little church, and, before they left, formed the missionary society that was to send William Carey to India. "Our God is able, if—."

During World War I two boys, Bill and Jim, who had grown up together; joined the army together, trained together, and fought together side by side. One day Jim was sent by their commanding officer into No Man's Land on a mission.

Half way there he was cut down by enemy fire. His buddy requested permission to go to his aid. The request was denied. Rescue was impossible his commanding officer explained; he would only lose his own life. But defying orders, Bill broke away, dashed out amid shot and shell to his companion, placed him on his shoulders and started back. They were almost to safety when bullets riddled both of their bodies.

The commander cried, "I told you not to go! It was so useless!" "No, not useless," Bill replied, "Jim was alive when I reached him. As I lifted him, he whispered, "Bill, I knew you'd come. I just knew you'd come."

Even so, God believes in you and me. There is so much to do, and he is depending on us. He has no hands but our hands to do his work. With so much at stake, how can we let him down? "Our God is able, if—."

The Lamb Shall Overcome

The Apostle John was a prisoner on the Isle of Patmos, writing the Book of Revelation, which is probably the most remarkable book in the Bible. It is written in symbols—three hundred of them in the book. He wrote in cryptic language which only the Christians to whom he wrote would understand. He writes about the beast "that was, and is not, and yet is." The beast makes war against the Lamb, and the Lamb conquers.

Just what the total meaning of the writing was to John and the churches, we cannot know for sure; but through the ages, it has spoken to the hearts of Christians in times of persecution and trouble reassuring us that ultimately goodness overcomes evil, love conquers hate.

Joseph Hunter was a Christian Church (Disciples of Christ) missionary on the Island of Formosa. An old missionary on the island told him about his grandfather who had also been a missionary there. Originally, the people of Formosa were headhunters. They believed that without some heads, they could have no crops. The old missionary preached and pled with them to give up the practice. After many years of persuasion and reasoning, out of love for this man of God, they finally agreed.

Then one year there was a drought. It scorched the land, and they were desperate for food. "We must have some heads," they said. "Then the gods will send us rain." Still the old missionary continued to plead with them. Finally, he got them to agree that if they could have one head, they would not kill anyone else. He promised them that the next morning they would find a victim at a designated place.

The morning came, gray and foggy, as characterizes the island at that season. The young men came riding over the hill through the murky darkness at breakneck speed. In the distance, at the pre-arranged spot, seated on a donkey, they saw the figure of a man slouched over. With one swift slash of the sword, they cut off his head and carried it away.

The dawn came. Above the heavy mist, the sun came out. The band brought their steeds to a stop, turned the head around and looked. It was the head of their beloved missionary! Since that day, there has been no more headhunting on the Island of Formosa.

What John wrote is true: "The beast makes war against the Lamb, and the Lamb shall overcome, for he is Lord of lords, and King of kings."

Hidden Treasure

Over the entrance of the state library in Columbus, Ohio are engraved these words: "My treasures are within." How true this is of all life. We know this in our heart of hearts; and yet, for some unknown reason, we seem prone to forget.

There is an ancient legend that tells how after his creation by God, man lay down and went to sleep. As he slept, the gods came and stole away man's soul.

Immediately, they faced the problem as to where man's soul should be hidden. One of the gods suggested that they bury it deep in the ground. "No," said another, "Someday man will dig down in the earth and find it."

"I know," still another said, "Let's sink it in the depth of the ocean." After due consideration, this suggestion was also rejected. "In time," they said, "Man will travel beneath the sea and come upon his soul."

After more thought, they considered carrying man's soul high into the heavens and hiding it on one of the distant planets; but even this plan was scrapped, when one of the wise ones said, "That will not do either. Eventually man will explore outer space and recover his soul."

The controversy went on and on. At long last, however, a decision was reached—man's soul would have to be destroyed. They took it and cast it into the fire. To their consternation, man's soul was not consumed by the flames. When removed from the furnace, it was brighter and more shining than before.

Just when it seemed that every possibility had been exhausted, one of the wisest thought of a plan with which all of them enthusiastically agreed. "Why didn't we think of it before?" he cried, "We will simply hide man's soul within man himself. He will never think of looking there!" and so, it was done.

The old legend speaks great truth. The real values of life are found within, but in our constant search for material things, we act as though the things that matter most are all without.

The Book of Proverbs speaks with great wisdom to all who will give heed, when it counsels, "Keep your heart with all diligence, for out of it are the issues of life."

November 5   **II Corinthians 6: 2**

While Busy Here And There

Once upon a time the devil decided to destroy the people of the world. He called in his helpers for counsel. Anger said, "Let me be in charge; I will set brother against brother. The people of earth will destroy themselves."

Next, Lust offered a plan, "I will defile their minds. Love will disappear, and people will be like beasts." Greed said, "No, let me instill destructive passion. Unbridled desire will wipe out creation."

The twins Gluttony and Drunkenness presented their strategy. "We will disease men's bodies and warp and degrade their minds,", and so it went.

In turn, Envy, Jealousy and Hate made proposals for the annihilation of the world. Idleness felt sure he could do the job better than all the others combined. But somehow the devil still wasn't satisfied.

Then the last assistant spoke, "I shall remind people they are children of God, and urge them to act as such, to be honest, clean and brave." "What in the world are you thinking?" the devil cried.

His assistant calmly continued, "I shall hold up high ideals and worthy spiritual goals. However, I will be clear. There is no hurry. It can all be done tomorrow," and so it was that Procrastination was sent.

He was going to be all a mortal could be, tomorrow.
No one would be braver or kinder than he, tomorrow;
A friend who was worried and troubled he knew,
He could give a lift and he needed it, too,
On him he would call and see what he could do, tomorrow.

Each morning he stacked the letters he'd write, tomorrow,
And thought of the folk he would fill with delight, tomorrow.
Too bad that he was busy today
And hadn't the time to stop on the way.
"More time I will have to give others," he'd say, "Tomorrow."

The greatest of workers this man would have been, tomorrow.
The world would have known him if he'd ever seen tomorrow.
But, in fact, he passed on and vanished from view,
And all that he left here when living was through,
Was a mountain of things he intended to do, tomorrow.

310

Look Up, My Son!

On September 1, 1939, the Germans invaded Poland, unleashing the most destructive of all world wars. It was a dark time in history. A British statesman said, "The lights are going out all over Europe, and I doubt we will see them go on again in our lifetime."

That following Sunday, Dr. Ralph Sockman, minister of Christ Church, New York, preached on the subject, "The Hills of God." He began with Sinai where God gave the Ten Commandments to Moses, moved on to Christ's Sermon on the Mount, and finally a hill outside Jerusalem's walls where Christ was crucified.

Dr. Sockman's sermon that Sunday helped those who heard it to see things in their true perspective.

"I will lift up my eyes to the hills." Is this the source of my help? "No," replies the writer of the 121st Psalm, "My help comes from the Lord, who made heaven and earth." Above and beyond the majesty of nature is the God of nature. He is the source of our strength.

In his memoirs, an old seaman once told how on his first voyage as a boy, he was ordered by the first mate to climb up to the crow's nest high on the mast of the ship.

The command struck terror to his heart, but he had no choice but to obey. He began to climb. All went well until almost at the top he paused to rest and happened to look down. The deck looked like a tiny spot far below with billows rolling high around it. The young lad's head began to spin. Desperately, he clung to the ladder as blackness crowded in.

Then from far below, he heard a voice. It was the voice of the captain calling, "Look up, my son! Look up!" With heroic effort, he raised his eyes from the swirling waters and steadied them on the vast blue sky above. Soon all was well again. He climbed on up to the crow's nest and then back down to the deck.

How often I, upon the sea of life, look down on waves dashed high against my feeble craft! My world goes black and dizzily spins around. I lose my grip, and all my hope is gone.

And just when all seems lost, I hear a voice—the voice of my Captain calling to me above the roar of the storm: "Look up, my son! Look up!"

Don't Die On Third!

What makes baseball the All-American Game? Home runs are exciting. So are double and triple plays. But for many, nothing is as thrilling as a crucial stolen base. Let me tell you about such a steal.

Years ago the Detroit Tigers were playing the Cleveland Indians. It was the bottom of the ninth, the score was tied, there were two outs, and the great George Moriarty was on third. He had singled to first. The next man up sacrificed him to second, and then a long fly advanced him to third, but unless he reached home plate, all of it meant nothing. Every eye in the park was on the man taking the long lead off third base.

Quickly Moriarty sized up the situation: The Cleveland catcher signaled for a high ball. This meant the runner might dive low to the plate while the catcher was reaching up for the ball.

Moriarty knew that a high ball required the pitcher to wind up a certain way. He knew, too, that the pitcher would wind up a different way if he didn't intend to deliver to the plate. In addition, the pitcher was left-handed and couldn't keep his eye on third while winding up.

Mullins was up. His batting average was 250, which meant he got a hit one time in four. If he swung and missed or got a hit and was put out at first, the game would be over, and the Tigers would lose. There was but one thing to do—reach home between the time of the pitcher's windup and the time the ball reached the catcher's mitt.

It was going to be a contest of speed and an unequal contest at that. The runner would have to hurl his body over 90 feet of ground while the tiny baseball was traveling 60.

This was it! The Cleveland pitcher was winding up. Moriarty poised himself. There was yet a split second for the pitcher to recall the throw. Moriarty crouched like a tiger ready to spring. Now! Now!

The Detroit fans, going wild, saw a white streak; then a cloud of dust at home plate. The hands of the umpire flashed out palms down—Moriarty was home. Safe!

In life, reaching home is what counts. In his letter to the Philippians, Paul said it this way: "Forgetting what lies behind and straining forward to what lies ahead, I press on toward the goal for the prize of the upward call of God in Jesus Christ."

Psalms 103: 2

How The Well Works

Thanksgiving is an American tradition. I find it rather interesting that the word "Thanksgiving" is made up of two words, "Thanks" and "giving." The two seem to go together. Because we have received so much, we are thankful, and because we are thankful, we give. Let me tell you a story.

He was lost in the desert. No doubt about it. His car had run out of gas, and he had started walking. Hours passed as he trudged along, nothing in sight as far as eye could see but burning sand.

Now, weak from hunger and dying of thirst, he was making his way slowly on hands and knees. Just as all hope was gone, he saw a wooden structure on the horizon and with his last ounce of energy crawled toward it.

Pulling himself up beside it, he realized it was the curb of a well. Tied to the handle of the old pump was a baking power can and in it, written with the stub of a pencil on brown wrapping paper, was a note:

"This pump is all right as of June, 1932. I have put a new sucker washer on it and it ought to last for another five years. But the washer dries out and has to be primed."

"Under the white rock I have buried a bottle of water out of the sun and cork end up—DON'T DRINK IT! Lost out here, that bottle of water will not be enough to get you to safety. Take the bottle and pour half of the water down the pump and give it time to soak and wet the leather washer. Then pour in the rest and pump like crazy. You will get water.

"This well has never run dry. Have faith. When you are done, fill up the bottle and put it back like you found it for the next fellow. Don't forget to put this note back in the can and tie it to the pump. Good luck and God bless, Desert Pete"

What would you have done with the bottle of water?

The note from Desert Pete was evidence that someone had been there before. He was saying, "This is how the well works." The Bible gives us a lens through which we can see how God created us and how he wants us to live. Listen to the words of the Master: "Give and it will be given to you; good measure, pressed down, shaken together and running over."

The North Star of Eternity

The man said to his minister, "I'm at the end of my rope. I don't know what I am going to do." For years he and his family had been trying to deal with the heartbreaking problem of a cerebral-palsied child and all the anxiety and medical expense that goes with it. During the past year through no fault of his own, reversals seriously hurt his company.

He was having trouble with his teenage son who in the past year had had three encounters with the juvenile authorities and was running wild in spite of all anyone could do.

Now, in the midst of all this, he had just come from the clinic where after a thorough physical examination, his physician had said, "There's an ominous shadow on the x-ray. We suspect a malignant tumor and must do surgery this week."

What do you say to a man in those circumstances? What can you say to anyone when their world goes to pieces like that? Is there any word of guidance and help?

Dr. William H. Hinson was talking to the navigator of an air force plane who had directed flights skirting enemy territory where the slightest deviation in direction would mean disaster. He said, "Jamming devices lead planes into forbidden air space to be shot down. It is a nightmare when you can't see the shoreline and can't depend on the instruments."

"What do you do in such a situation?" Dr. Hinson asked. The navigator replied, "When you can't see the shoreline and you can't trust the instruments, the pilot climbs until you are above the clouds. There the stars are shining and you can determine your direction by them."

In our time, many of the signposts have been blurred and obliterated. Clouds roll in and we are unable to see the lights along the shore. But Jesus Christ is the North Star of Eternity. Rise above your clouds of confusion, fix your position by him and the words of assurance which William Cullen Bryant spoke after observing the waterfowl can be your words of assurance too:

> He who from zone to zone,
> Guides through the boundless sky
> Thy certain flight,
> In the long way that I must tread alone,
> Will lead my steps aright.

A Time For Soul Searching

On November 11, 1918 the Armistice was signed. "The war to end all wars" was a disappointment. Historians tell us that over the past 5,000 years, there have been only 292 years of peace. During that period, there have been something like 14,351 wars waged, at least 3.64 billion people killed, and the value of property destroyed equal to a gold belt 97.2 miles wide and thirty-three feet thick wrapped around the world

In 1995 for six billion dollars, everyone in the world could have been taught to read, 17 billion would have provided healthcare worldwide, 35 billion would have written off all of the Third World debt, 22 billion would have wiped out starvation and malnutrition—all of this for less than one hundred billion dollars. Instead, the planet spent 1.17 trillion dollars on war!

How stupid can we be? It is said that two cities in Italy fought for 27 years over a bucket that didn't get returned from one city to the other. Can you imagine? A bucket! Little things surely get blown up clear out of proportion.

Look at the history of the United States of America. The Revolutionary War took less than 5,000 lives; Viet Nam, 58,000; World War II, 407,000, but during the Civil War, 558,000 American lives were sacrificed—one out of every fifty persons in our nation.

What does that say to us? Infighting is the cruelest and deadliest form of war. Perhaps that is why the Bible doesn't have much to say about wars among nations but has lots to say about wars in our homes, in our schools, in our businesses, in our churches—"quarrels and fighting among you."

Wars among nations will eventually cease. God has promised, "Nation will not take up sword against nation, nor will they train for war anymore." The only question that's left is will the wars that rage within our hearts cease? They will end only when we come to know the true peacemaker, Jesus Christ, in whom justice and mercy blended as one on the cross of Calvary.

Tomorrow we celebrate Veterans Day. Let us, in the words of Abraham Lincoln, "highly resolve that these dead shall not have died in vain—that this nation, under God, shall have a new birth of freedom—and that government of the people, by the people and for the people shall not perish from the earth."

315

A Prayer For America

Today is Veterans' Day. It should be a day for introspection on the part of all Americans. Reports from the Census Bureau are alarming. Americans falling into poverty last year numbered 1.7 million. Today 34.6 million Americans are living in poverty of which 12.1 million are children. There were 43.6 million Americans uninsured, a jump of 2.4 million from the previous year, a powerful symbol of lost jobs, lost overtime, lost health care, and a lost sense of well-being.

Our political campaigns show a total lack of integrity and honor. They have become negative mudslinging affairs. As a result in our last presidential election, only 51 % of the voting age population bothered to cast a ballot. We are losing faith in ourselves as a nation.

We are tossing aside major international treaties. The leadership of our nation has proven that it is eager to go to war, and there is impressive evidence that the war against Iraq was for reasons other than national security.

Conrad Hilton once closed an address with this prayer that we Americans might well make our prayer on this Veterans' Day:

"OUR FATHER IN HEAVEN: We pray that you save us from *ourselves*. The world that YOU have made for us, to live in peace, we have made into an armed camp. We live in fear of war to come. We are afraid of 'the terror that flies by night and the arrow that flies by day, the pestilence that walks in darkness and the destruction that wastes at noon-day.'

"We have turned from YOU to go our selfish way. We have broken your commandments and denied YOUR truth. We have left YOUR altars to serve the false gods of money and pleasure and power. Forgive us and help us.

"Now, darkness gathers around us, and we are confused in all our counsels. Losing faith in YOU, we lose faith in ourselves. Inspire us with wisdom, all of us of every color, race, and creed, to use our wealth, our strength to help our brother, instead of destroying him.

"Help us to do YOUR will as it is done in heaven and to be worthy of YOUR promise of peace on earth. Fill us with new faith, new strength and new courage, that we may win the Battle for Peace. Be swift to save us, dear God, before the darkness falls."

The Prince of Peace

On November 11, 1918, at 11 AM, the eleventh hour of the eleventh day of the eleventh month, the Armistice ended World War I. One elderly man being interviewed about that day in 1918 said, "Celebrating the end of the fighting, we felt sure that there would never be another war."

War and peace stands out as the greatest challenge of our day. As we pay tribute to the men and women of our armed forces, we still dream of the day when the people of our world shall live together in peace and wars will be no more.

In South America there are two countries that are side by side of each other. Argentina lies along the Atlantic; Chile lies along the Pacific. Between the two tower the Andes Mountains.

Years ago war broke out between the two nations over a boundary dispute. You see the Andes are covered with snow the year round. It is almost impossible to tell where the boundary of one country ends and the other begins. Each country thought the worst of the other.

Bishop Benavente of Argentina felt that war was wrong. Fighting and killing was evil even with wicked people, but the people of Chile were their friends.

On Easter Sunday the people crowded the churches. The bishop preached as he had never preached before. Everyone said he seemed inspired of God. Indeed, he was. God was speaking through him to the people.

As a result the rulers of the two countries placed the dispute before the king of England for arbitration. His envoys examined the boundary and found that each country was partly right and each was partly wrong. A new boundary was drawn and peace was restored. What a lesson the two countries had learned. From their guns and cannons they molded a statue of Christ twenty-six feet high.

Today The Christ of the Andes stands at the top of the mountain range on a granite hemisphere. The left hand supports a cross and the right hand is raised in benediction over the two countries.

Engraved at the base of the monument are these words: "Sooner shall these mountains crumble into dust than the people of Argentina and Chile break the peace sworn at the feet of Christ the Redeemer."

AWOL

John recorded in his gospel, "Now Thomas, one of the twelve, called the Twin, was not with them when Jesus came." He should have been; those were his orders, and Christ had promised that he would meet him there along with the rest of the disciples, but Thomas went AWOL (absent without leave) and doing so he missed Jesus when he came.

That very first Easter Sunday evening the disciples were gathered in the upper room behind locked doors. Jesus came, stood among them and said, "Peace be with you," bestowing upon them peace and poise, but Thomas, having gone AWOL, missed it.

Jesus said to them, "As the Father has sent me, I am sending you." Commissioned by Christ to go forth in his name with the gospel, here was new purpose for their lives, but Thomas had no purpose. Having gone AWOL, he missed it.

Jesus breathed on them and said, "Receive the Holy Spirit." It was the gift of power—God working through them to achieve what they could never achieve alone. But there was no new power for Thomas; having gone AWOL, he missed it. "Then the disciples were glad when they saw the Lord." But not Thomas, miserably unhappy, he refused to believe that the other disciples had seen Jesus.

So quick to judge and censor Thomas, we should be aware that we, too, go AWOL. Commanded, "Forsake not the assembling of yourselves together," and promised, "Where two or three are gathered in my name, there am I in the midst of them."

Christ waits to bestow on us peace and poise, purpose and power, but Sunday after Sunday finds us AWOL, away from the gifts we need and that he waits to bestow.

But Thomas wanted to believe and to receive. The next Lord's Day he was there. Christ came, just as he always comes. Thomas found himself face to face with the risen and living Lord; and addressed him as no one else had previously done—"My Lord and my God."

Along with Thomas we, too, have a rendezvous. He has given us the same orders and made us the same promise. This coming Sunday there is an "Upper Room" where you and I will be expected. Of course, it is true, we have a decision to make. We have a choice: We can report to our Commander or we can go AWOL.

November 14   **Philippians 2: 13**

Life Is Like a Mountain Railroad

An old gospel song says, "Life is like a mountain railroad, With an engineer that's brave; We must make the run successful, From the cradle to the grave; Watch the curves, the fills, the tunnels; Never falter, never fail; Keep your hand upon the throttle, and your eye upon the rail."

Up in the northern part of Pennsylvania, there is a railroad known as the Lackawanna Lines. Benny Locke was an engineer for the Lackawanna for nearly sixty years. During that time, he received no mark of demerit. Before each day's run, he prayed for the safety of the train and its crew.

On a crisp, cool day in October, Number 6 was twenty-five minutes late out of Scranton. Benny Locke stepped into the cab and prayed, "Lord, help me to bring her in on time."

The first part of the trip was a stiff climb up the steep grade of the Pocono Mountains, and it never seemed so steep, it seemed to Benny Locke, as when you were late.

They couldn't gain a second on the sheer incline, but after they cleared the summit, things began to break just right. They almost flew down the mountain. The cold wind rushing by was most invigorating, and Benny Locke, seated at the controls, held her steady and let her roll. Finally, the old train shed at Hoboken loomed into view. As they pulled in, Benny Locke looked at his watch. They were right on the dot.

As he stood wiping the perspiration from his face, Benny Locke heard the tap of a walking cane on the outside of his cab. Looking up, there was the superintendent of the railroad, all smiles. He called out, "A good run, Sir! A very good run!"

Later, talking with friends, Benny Locke said, "You know, the words of the superintendent meant more to me than anything in the whole wide world."

He paused for a moment and then in a husky voice said, "Someday and not in the too far distant future, I will make my final run. When I pull into the Union Depot of that Celestial City, New Jerusalem, if I can hear the Superintendent say, 'A good run, Sir! A very good run!' then 'the toils of the road will seem nothing, when I get to the end of the way.'"

Finding Our Strength

"You shall receive power . . . ." That was the promise Jesus made to the disciples. That same promise he makes to you and me. His words became a living reality in their lives. Years later John wrote, "To all who received him, he gave power . . . ."

Years ago Gertrude Behanna spoke one evening at Christ Episcopal Church in Temple. I had the privilege of hearing her. I had read her life story in her book *The Late Liz.* It was, as she wrote, a life that had "too much to drink, too much money, too many men."

After thirty years of hangovers, thirty years of wrong doing, she finally hit rock bottom. Sometimes we speak of skid row bums as being "down and out." Gertrude Behanna had hit skid row, but she was wealthy. She was "up and out."

Then there came to her a climactic experience that brought her face to face with God. Then on the third day of her new life, she found herself facing a crisis. There was a seemingly impossible thing which she had to do. She had to ask the forgiveness of a person whom she had terribly wronged. The very thought of it struck terror to her heart. Finding the courage to even enter the room was hard enough, and that was only the beginning.

Trembling, she closed her eyes and prayed, "Father, this is the hardest thing I have ever tried to do. I don't have what it takes to do it by myself, so please be around to help me."

The several minutes that the struggle went on within her seemed like an eternity. She thought to herself, "It would be so easy not to do it!" But quickly she put the thought out of her mind. Once more she whispered, "Lord, please be there for me." And he was! Gertrude Behanna found the power she so desperately needed to see it through.

That same power can be yours and mine—the power to do whatever we need to do. Wilbur Fowler, a contemporary American poet, expresses it all in this prayer:

> Give me a task too big,
> Too hard for human hands
> Then I shall come at length
> To lean on Thee;
> And leaning, find my strength.

November 16   **Romans 8:10**
                        Called To Be Saints

In his letter to the Romans, Paul uses a salutation that seems very strange
to us today. It reads: "To all God's beloved in Rome, who are called to be
saints." Paul says this is what every Christian is called to be, but it is an
uneasy title for most of us. To be referred to as "a saint" is about the last
thing any of us want.

Douglas V. Steere in his book, *On Beginning Within*, defines a saint as "one
in whom Christ is felt to live again." If this definition is correct, then the
only failure in life is not to be a saint.

Paul is spelling out this definition of a saint when he declares, "It is no
longer I who live, but Christ who lives in me." And for the Christians at
Ephesus, he prays, "...that Christ may dwell in your hearts through faith."
It is through the words and deeds of such saints that Christ is best made
known.

Bishop Francis McConnell used to tell about a missionary who was sent
by his church to Africa. He had an aversion to record keeping and written
reports; he felt that there were more important things for a missionary to
do. After a number of reprimands, the church cut off support. Without
funds, the missionary made his way farther inland and, in time, was
forgotten.

Some years later the missionary board sent a replacement. He came to
the same village telling the story of Jesus to the simple natives. As he told
them about the one who went about doing good, he saw their eyes light
up in recognition. They said, "We know this man of whom you speak; he
is here!"

"No," the speaker said, "You do not understand. You couldn't know him;
Jesus lived hundreds of years ago. There is no way you could have known
him." But the villagers insisted, "Come with us," they said. They led him
to a little hut on the edge of the village where he met the one of whom
they spoke.

It was the former missionary who had come there years before. He had
lived such a life of love and service in their midst that when they heard
the story of Jesus, they immediately identified his life with this one who
was their friend.

A saint is nothing more than one in whom Christ is felt to live again. Saints!
That's what we are—if we are! Are we?

The Look Of Love

"Mommy, what does love look like?" The question came from a little girl of perhaps five years of age and was asked as seriously as any adult might have asked it. Had you been the mother, how would you have answered her question?

Augustine, one of the early church fathers who lived during the fourth century, once described and defined love. He said four things about it, painting a picture not easily forgotten.

First of all, Augustine says love has eyes to see. There is an old adage that says love is blind. Perhaps it is in a way, but that is only a part of the truth. At the height of the Great Depression a neighbor of ours said to my mother, "A lot of people talk about the economy being bad, but I don't think times are so hard." Even as she spoke, in the tenement next door there were men and women out of work, families out of food and no milk for the babies. There was dire need all around. She just couldn't see. Then love opened her eyes.

Second, love has ears to hear. Isn't it strange? A mother, keeping watch beside the crib of her six month old baby who is ill, toward daybreak, drifts off into a light sleep. The clock in the hall strikes six; she sleeps on. The daily paper, thrown by the paperboy lands on the porch with a loud thud; she is oblivious to the sound. An eighteen-wheeler lumbers by; totally unnoticed. Then her little one stirs ever so lightly and she is suddenly wide awake. Love listens and hears.

Third, love has feet to hasten. God is love and he sent his son into the world that we might know what that love is like. The Bible has a lot to say about Jesus, but I think these words of Peter describe him best: "He went about doing good." Love has feet, and they hurry to bring aid wherever it is needed.

Finally, love has hands to help. Recently I watched and listened as a little girl, her eyes filled with love, looked up at her mother and asked, "May I help set the table?" One of our poets has written,

Love ever gives
Forgives, outlives.
And while it lives
It gives.
For this is love's prerogative,
To give, and give, and give.

No Greater Love

It was mid-afternoon on a day in 1965 that a crowd stood beside the highway looking down at the water which filled the ditch. A short time before, a car had gone out of control, plunged over the side, and disappeared below the surface of the water which was ten feet deep.

A burly truck driver looked at the dark waters and rubbed his hands. He sensed that the crowd was waiting for him to take the lead in whatever was done. "You can't expect me to do anything," he said defensively, "I have a wife and three kids at home."

"Anyway," a woman said, "Whoever was in the car is probably already dead by now," and so they just stood there and watched.

Suddenly a rather battered sedan pulled to a stop. The driver was an African American man of twenty-two by the name of Ted Henderson. He had seen the skid marks leading to the water and knew immediately what had happened. In a flash, he was out of his car wading into the roadside pond.

"You can't do anything," the crowd cried to him, "If you try, you will only drown yourself also." Ted Henderson seemed not to hear. Perhaps he was thinking of his young wife who was expecting their fifth child.

He dove down, found the car, and pulled the door open. The pressure of the water was too great. The door slammed shut tearing off Ted's finger. Back to the surface he came, and the crowd cheered in relief. Blood from his finger was everywhere as Ted rushed to the back seat of his car, picked up a heavy wrench, and dove down again.

He smashed out a glass and the water rushed in relieving the pressure. Then opening the door, he lifted out the sole occupant, a seventeen-year-old white nurse.

That young girl is alive today because Ted Henderson acted in Christian love. He risked his life to save the life of someone he didn't even know.

It was Jesus who said, "A new commandment I give to you, that you love one another. By this all men will know that you are my disciples. And greater love has no man than this that a man lay down his life for his friends." Ted Henderson didn't lose his life, but he was willing to lose it, and that is the thing that counts.

Power for Living

"The trouble with you Christians is you are not enough like Christ!" These are the words of Rabindranath Tagore, the great Hindu poet. He had been asked by E. Stanley Jones, "What else can we as missionaries do to further the spread of the Christian faith in India."

"The trouble with you Christians is you are not enough like Jesus Christ," has long been the criticism leveled at Christians. Furthermore this is the criticism that Christians level at themselves. Followers of Jesus Christ are the first to admit that we are not enough like Jesus. There is a hymn we sing which has this line in the chorus: "His power can make you what you ought to be." It is this power which we so desperately need.

We need the power to think as Jesus thought. God's word tells us, "As a man thinks in his heart, so is he." Jesus saw this with clear insight and made it the measure of our goodness before God. It was with the mind of Christ that Paul spoke when after enumerating the qualities which make up the Christian life, he said, "Think about these things."

We need the power to feel as Jesus felt. Being like Christ is a matter of the mind, but even more it is a matter of the heart. When Jesus walked the earth, his heart was constantly going out to people he encountered. How often we read in the gospels, "He had compassion on them," and once he said, "By this shall all men know that you are my disciples, if you love one another."

Above all, we need the power to act as Jesus acted. It simply is not enough to think about, talk about, and preach about Jesus Christ and his great teachings. The acid test is action.

Jesus closed the Sermon on the Mount with the ringing declaration, "Whoever hears these sayings of mine and does them . . . ." Not thinks about them or feels a certain way about them, but does them.

Peter Marshall was right when he said, "Our problem is not so much that we don't know what we should do. We know perfectly well. We just don't want to do it."

This power to think as Jesus thought, feel as Jesus felt and to act as Jesus acted can be yours and mine. In the Gospel of John are found these words: "To all who received him, he gave power . . . ." He still gives power to all who ask.

November 20   Luke 2: 40
                      Someone Is Waiting For You

In his novel, "The Man Who Lost Himself," Osbert Sitwell tells about a
detective who was trailing a criminal in Paris. He felt sure that the fugitive
was staying in a certain hotel.

To find out, he went to the desk of the hotel, gave his own name, and asked
if he himself was registered there. He intended to glance down the page
of the register for the name of the man he was seeking.

Imagine his surprise when the desk clerk replied, "Yes, he is waiting for
you in room 40. I will have the bellboy show you right up." Up in room 40
he found himself face to face with a man of middle age who was his very
image.

The man was older, heavier, but unmistakably the man himself—the man
he would be at the age of forty—twenty years in the future.

Of course, it was only a story, but in a sense it is true for each of us. Out in
the future—ten, twenty, or thirty years from now, there is someone waiting
for you. What will that person be like? It depends on you.

It was Marcus Aurelius who said, "A man becomes what he thinks about."
Be careful with your thinking. Your thoughts are shaping the person you
will meet out yonder tomorrow.

Your habits are determining what that person waiting for you is going to
be like. George Boardman was right when he said, "Sow a thought, and
you reap an act; Sow an act, and you reap a habit; Sow a habit, and you reap
a character; Sow a character, and you reap a destiny."

Project your habits—good and bad—into the future. They are determining
what that person will be like who is waiting for you out yonder tomorrow.

The friends you make are determining what that person will be like.
This is what the Christian faith is all about. The living Christ offers his
friendship to everyone who will receive it. Walking in fellowship with him
day by day, we are changed into his likeness; in time, we become like him.

It is as true for all of us. Day by day your life is being shaped by your
thoughts, your habits, your friends, and out yonder, tomorrow, someone is
waiting for you.

Just Waiting For You

Years ago a wealthy businessman spent a week's vacation in the Bluegrass country of Kentucky. There, he met a very beautiful girl; they fell in love and were married.

For years they were happy; then tragedy struck. The young wife lost her mind. The husband built a home on the edge of town and devoted himself to her care, but to no avail. She grew no better.

On their physician's suggestion, the husband took his wife back to Kentucky, hoping that the surroundings of her childhood might help her to find herself.

So it was that they returned to the old homestead. Together, they walked across the meadow and down to the little stream where she had played as a little girl, but there was no sign of recognition, only a wild look in her eyes that never went away.

On the verge of tears, the husband gathered his wife into his arms and started back to the house. As he walked along, he felt her head drop down on his shoulder. Soon she was fast asleep.

Carrying her up to the bedroom, he laid her on her own bed and sat down beside her. She was breathing deeply; the first natural sleep she had had in months.

Through the long night he watched over her. Dawn broke and as the sunlight came streaming in on her face, she slowly opened her eyes. Looking up, she smiled. "I have missed you so much," she said "Where have you been?" Remembering the long days and months of longing and hoping against hope, he answered, "I've just been waiting for you!"

Living in a world of trouble, turmoil, and strife, facing the fact of man's inhumanity to man, how often we are tempted to ask, "Where is God; why doesn't he do something?"

Seldom do we stop to think and realize that perhaps God is depending on us to do something. It was Gideon, whose story is recorded in the Book of Judges, who blamed God, asking, "Why has this befallen us?" God answered him, "Go in this might of yours and deliver Israel!"

That is God's message to you and me. Our world doesn't need to stay the way it is. Go in this might of yours. God is waiting for you!

Perspective Unlimited

The man had lived all of his life on a little farm that he inherited from his father. His 100th birthday was quite an occasion. The city newspaper sent a reporter out for an interview and to shoot pictures.

The old man was quick to give the reporter what he considered the central fact about his life. It was the same fact he liked to reveal to every person with whom he came in contact: "I was born right here in this very house," he said, "And the ten mile drive into town is the greatest distance I have traveled in all my life!"

I was thinking about this story recently when my curiosity got the best of me. I called Jean Kubala at the Temple Public Library, and she gathered some astronomical facts. Those facts seem to present a very different perspective.

The planet Earth turns 24,853 miles every twenty-four hours or 9,102,924 miles each year. At the same time, the earth is orbiting the sun once each year. That seems slow at first glance, but in a year it travels 583,783,600 miles.

While this is happening, our galaxy is rotating once every 200 million years, or 4,450,231 miles per year, and you must keep in mind the fact that our galaxy is speeding through the Universe at over one million miles an hour. That is 8,760,000,000,000 miles a year.

Adding all these together causes us to reconsider the assumptions of the old man. He had not been in just one small area throughout his 100 years.

Each year of his life he had traveled 8,760,597,336,755 miles! Ten miles had scarcely been the limit of his travels. During his lifetime he had traveled 876,059,733,675,500 miles!

This is one of the pitfalls of reasoning as a mere mortal; one's perspective is very limited. The man was quite certain in his own mind that he had been no more than ten miles from the place of his birth, but all the while he had been whisked by God over distances that are staggering to the imagination.

Even so, you and I can see and understand only a small part of God's plan and all that he is doing in this vast, expanding Universe. God is at work in ways far beyond our ability to comprehend.

November 23

Luke 17: 10

Remaining at Your Post

During World War II, a young American soldier wrote to his father from Italy: "Why should I try to be decent when the whole world is going to hell?" Against that background place this story:

It happened almost two hundred years ago in the midst of the American Revolution. On May 18, 1780, in the midst of a bright sunny day, at midday, it began to grow strangely dark. Chickens went to roost, and bats were flying through the air.

To this day, no one knows for sure what happened. Evidently, it was some kind of meteorological phenomenon. Out in space, something blocked off the light of the sun and night came at high noon. Panic ensued. People thought the world was coming to an end.

In Hartford, Connecticut, the state legislature was in session. When darkness descended, the Lower House broke up in alarm. In the senate, a motion was made to adjourn.

This, it was thought, would allow the members to be with their families as the end drew near. It would afford them opportunity for prayer, so they might meet the Day of Judgment with whatever courage they might manage to summon.

The question was called for, and they were ready to vote, when one of the senators arose to speak in opposition. The speaker was Abraham Davenport from New Haven. He was a graduate of Yale, a judge, and a friend and advisor of George Washington.

"Gentlemen," he said, "I am opposed to this adjournment. The Day of Judgment is either approaching or it is not. If it is not, there is no cause for adjournment. If it is, I choose to be found at my post doing my duty. Therefore, I move that candles be brought in, and that we continue with our work."

During these days of our lives, haunted by doubts and fears, when an all out atomic war might well mean the end of civilization as we know it—it would be hard to find a better example of levelheaded, quiet courage.

In our search for an answer as to the right course to take, Abraham Davenport gives us inspired guidance: "I choose to be found at my post doing my duty. I move that candles be brought in, and that we continue with our work."

November 24   **Psalms 116:17**
Father, We Thank Thee

I look forward to and enjoy Thanksgiving. It brings visions of harvest time, happy family reunions, tables laden with food—a big turkey with stuffing and gravy, casseroles of all kinds, cranberry sauce, pumpkin pie and whipped cream.

At Thanksgiving, I envision one other thing, and I bet you do too—the Pilgrims. Theirs was the first Thanksgiving. Governor William Bradford of Plymouth Colony issued the very first Thanksgiving proclamation.

It happened 382 years ago. The year was 1621. One year before, the Pilgrims had landed at Plymouth Rock. It was a dreadful winter of starvation, sickness, and death. The losses of life sustained were staggering.

Of the 102 passengers who came ashore that bleak December, 7 died during the first month, 8 died in January, 17 died in February, 13 died in March, and 6 more died before summer.

Four entire families perished. Out of 18 wives and mothers who came over on the Mayflower, 14 died. Four cooks prepared that first Thanksgiving dinner, and yet, they gave thanks!

Today we wonder how they managed it. What did they find for which to be thankful? But they did. Governor Bradford's proclamation was the official utterance of their desire to give thanks to God for their manifold blessings. One can't keep from wondering—is our gratitude that great?

Our nation is the richest nation on earth. Our bounty is incomprehensible to the rest of the world. Yet, in this, the richest nation on earth, there are 34 million people who are hungry. Around the world multitudes are starving. Still, as of old, Christ is saying, "You give them something to eat."

Ours is indeed "the land of the free," but millions on our planet live in bondage and fear. America can never be truly free until people everywhere are free.

The greatest blessing of all is our Christian heritage bequeathed to us and exemplified by the Pilgrims. Because we have received so much let us resolve at this season of Thanksgiving to witness and to share our faith with our neighbors—those next door, across our land, around the world.

Two, Four, Six, Eight

Recently I found myself remembering a pep rally yell from my high school days. It went like this: "Two, Four, Six, Eight, Who do we appreciate? Panthers! Panthers!"

Who do we appreciate? That is a good question for each of us to ask ourselves from time to time. It could make a big difference in our lives and in the lives of all the people about us.

The trouble is, we generally practice just the opposite. We are so busy finding fault and criticizing that we have little time to appreciate anyone or anything they do.

At a chamber of commerce banquet one evening, a large crowd heard a handsome young man give an outstanding address, but he didn't stand up straight. As he talked to the group, he hunched over the lectern. The way he drooped one of his shoulders annoyed some of the listeners. After the address, one of the persons from the audience couldn't resist saying to him, "You would be so much more attractive if you would learn to stand up straight."

The young man's head dropped, "I'm sorry," he said, "You see, I was a soldier in the Korean War. I was struck by shrapnel. I was months in healing. I was finally able to walk, but I have never been able to stand up straight."

We help people, not by telling them about their faults—they know about them all too well already—but by recognizing and appreciating their good qualities.

On his way home from school, a little boy of seven came across a classmate in tears. Her scarf had been blown off into a mud puddle. Wading out to get it, his shoes and socks were really messed up. At home, his mother scolded him soundly. That evening at bedtime, at the door of his room, she overheard him as he knelt by his bed in prayer. "Dear God, help Mommy see the good things I do as well as all of the bad things."

If you want to change the world—your world, learn the art of genuine appreciation. You know, there is really a lot of good in people if we will but take the time to look.

Two, Four, Six, Eight, who do YOU appreciate?

The Things That Matter Most

"Whoever seeks to save his life will lose it; but whoever loses his life will preserve it." These words of Christ are strange and paradoxical, but they are sobering words that no follower of his dares to ignore.

A little boy of some four years of age was playing around the house one morning as his mother busied herself with her chores. It was a little too quiet, she thought and went to check on him.

She found him in the front hall. His hand was stuck in a vase he had taken from the hall table. He couldn't get his hand out and was on the verge of tears.

Picking him up, she sat down on the divan and began working to release his hand. It was to no avail; the hand wouldn't budge. Finally, in desperation, she put him in the family car and drove to the emergency room of the hospital. There, the doctor tried to free it, but the little hand was caught tight. It wouldn't come out.

It seemed there was nothing left to do but break the vase, but this they were reluctant to do. The vase was a very expensive heirloom that had been in the family for generations.

However, the value of the vase was of secondary importance. There was great danger that in the process of breaking the vase the little hand could be cut and the lad injured for life.

"Let's try it just once more," said the doctor to the little boy. "Open your hand; hold out your fingers real straight. Keep them as close together as you can and pull. All right, let's try it," but the little boy wasn't at all ready to follow the doctor's instructions.

He protested to his mother, "Mommy, I can't straighten out my fingers. If I do, I will drop my pennies!"

Isn't there a similar problem in your life and mine? Like the little boy, we are so prone to try to hold on to "our pennies." The great difference however, between our situation and that of the little boy, is that we are risking not just a hand but our immortal soul.

We need to wake up and ask ourselves anew where the real values of life lie, lest seeking to save the things that matter, we lose the thing that matters most!

Hebrews 12: 1
Faster! Higher! Stronger!

The Twenty-third Olympics were a stirring experience for all of us. Patriotic fervor filled the stands and swept our nation as the United States claimed 30 bronze medals, 61 silver and 83 gold for a total of 174 medals.

The competition stirred within us patriotism and pride, but it did more. We learned valuable lessons as to what it means to train and compete.

Paul was familiar with the Olympic Games. His letters are filled with sports language—"We wrestle against principalities," "I have finished the race," "You were running so well," "An athlete is not crowned unless he competes according to the rules."

The Olympics taught us that there is no greatness without pain. We can never forget the heart-rending finish of Anderson-Schiess in the Women's Marathon as she struggled across the line and collapsed at the end of the twenty-six mile race. In the words of Paul, "To you it has been given not only to believe in him but to suffer for his sake."

The Olympics taught us never to give up. Little girls all over Temple are dreaming of being like Mary Lou Retton. They can never forget those last two perfect 10.00's. Six weeks before the Games, Mary Lou Retton underwent surgery, and the surgeon told her she was out of the Olympics. Four weeks before the Games, she couldn't even walk, but she was never out of the Olympics. Within a week, she was back on her feet, and in another week, she was tumbling again. The doctors called it a medical miracle.

Such is the Christian's calling. Stand fast. Be strong and of good courage. Be faithful unto death, and I will give you the crown of life.

Many times during the Olympic Games, television cameras panned the Olympic motto: "Citius Altius Fortius." They mean "Faster, Higher, Stronger." The spirit of the Olympics is that records are made to be broken. Year after year, the contests are to be done better. "Faster, higher, stronger!"

The greatest Champion our world has known died at the age of 33. But he gave the human race its greatest dream. Today, he challenges us to look up, to live a better life, to be a stronger person.

CITIUS ALTIUS FORTIUS

Through Christ Who Gives Us Strength

I was visiting with a fellow minister, the senior pastor of a dynamic and growing suburban church. We were talking shop as ministers do when they get together. Somewhere in our conversation, he said to me, "Clyde, I serve a wonderful bunch of people. They will do just about anything I request except calling on prospective members."

I find this to be the case with most of the pastors I know. Yet friendly calling by lay members of the congregation is a vital ministry and the key to church growth. Why the reluctance? A number of reasons, maybe; but the major reason is, as one young man put it, "I don't know what to say."

A number of years ago, I underwent major surgery and spent several weeks as a patient in the hospital. Late one evening, the Rev. Leroy Haenze, one of the hospital chaplains, came by my room. It was rather late, and I knew he had been making rounds. "It's been a long day," he said, as he dropped into a chair and relaxed.

While we were visiting, he received a call from emergency. A man had been struck by a car on an access road on IH 35 and was being rushed to the hospital by ambulance. The chaplain would be needed to be with the man's family.

Chaplain Haenze had prayer with me, and as he was leaving, I said to him, "I am glad the family will have you with them. You will do a good job." He paused at the door as he said, "Clyde, I don't have anything to give in a crisis like this. People need help, and I can't help. They need comfort, and I cannot comfort them. They need hope and reassurance, and I have none to give." He hesitated and then added, "But I go acting as if I did, and when I do, I find Christ there giving me the words that need to be said, helping me do what needs to be done."

His feelings are shared by most of us, are they not? Over and over, going to make a call—especially if it happened to be a call on total strangers— we ask ourselves, "What can I say; what can I do?"

Paul felt this way, I think. Searching for the help he needed, he found a source of unfailing power. Writing to the Christians in the church in Philippi, he shared with them what he had discovered. Listen to his words: "I can do all things through Christ who strengthens me." Realizing our inadequacy, we are driven back on Christ, and he enables us to say what needs to be said, to do what needs to be done.

November 29

Hebrews 12:2

Strengthening Our Faith

It was Paul who said, "We walk by faith, not by sight." This is true of all life. When we drive a car, ride a bicycle, get into an elevator, plant a garden, mail a letter or turn on the TV, we exercise faith.

A certain man came to his minister seeking help. Everything had gone wrong. His whole life seemed to be falling apart. The minister listened with understanding as he told his story. Then he said quietly, "Are you willing to turn your whole life over to God and walk with him in faith?"

The man got up from his chair. "I might have known," he said, "You are giving me the same old stuff—'Just have faith and all of your problems are solved!'" Bitterly, he started to walk away.

"Wait," the minister said, "God isn't going to do everything for you. You are going to do it. There is limitless power all around you, but you are not using it. It is the power of faith." "If I had faith, I would not have come seeking help," the man cried, "I know I need faith, but how do I get it? Where do I find it?"

After the fashion of Jesus, the minister told him this story. There was once a little fish that lived in a lake. One day he overheard a fisherman say to his companion, "Do you realize how indispensable water is? Without water, everything would dry up and die."

The little fish was terrified. "I must find some water at once or I shall die." Away he swam searching frantically. Suddenly he stopped. What was water? He had never heard of it. He asked a perch, but the perch didn't know. He swam out into the river and asked a catfish, but the catfish didn't know.

Panic-stricken, he kept going until he reached the ocean. There he found an old flounder. "Where can I find water?" he asked. The wise old flounder smiled, "Water? Why you are right in the middle of it; you've never been out of it in all your life."

Feeling rather foolish, the little fish thanked the flounder and turned homeward. "I have been searching everywhere for water, and I have had it all the time. I just didn't know it!"

Faith is like that. It isn't something you search for. You don't have to look for it. It is given to each of us by God. All we have to do is use it.

Lord, I Want To Be a Christian

They are the words of an old African American spiritual: "Lord, I want to be a Christian in my heart." I think it is the deep felt prayer of each of us.

To be a Christian is to be like Jesus. It means thinking as Jesus thought. It means living as Jesus lived. But generally, we are so busy daydreaming about the great things we might do that we completely overlook the many little things we could do.

A young girl once wrote to Dr. Albert Schweitzer praising the work he was doing among those in need of medical help in Africa. She felt that she also could live a life of Christian service if she could go to Africa. In his letter of reply, Dr. Schweitzer said, "Africa is merely where I happen to be. God calls us to serve where we are, and we must find our opportunities there."

The truth is if we are not living like Jesus where we are, we wouldn't be like him anywhere else, and we ought to quit kidding ourselves about that.

Keith Miller in his book, *A Second Touch*, tells about a busy business executive who was rushing to catch a train. Because of the great demands on his time, he had just about given up trying to live a "personal" daily life, but on the way to the station, he had resolved that for that day, at least, he would try to be a Christian instead of just talking about it.

By the time he had picked up his ticket, he was late. He heard the last call "All aboard!" As he rushed across the platform, it happened. He bumped into a little boy with his briefcase. The youngster was carrying a new jigsaw puzzle, and the pieces went flying in every direction. The man paused for a moment. The child was on the verge of tears. Then, as his train pulled away, he knelt down to help pick up the pieces.

The little boy watched him intently. As they finished and the business executive stood up, the little boy asked almost in a whisper, "Mister, are you Jesus?"

The man smiled warmly, "No, Sonny; no, I'm not Jesus. I'm just a follower of his." Then the great lesson hit home. He suddenly realized that for a short while that day on a railroad platform, he had been like the Master.

He Saw Only the Parade

We are in the Advent season, the four-week period preceding Christmas. The word advent means coming and refers to the coming of Jesus into the world. These days of preparation will in a large measure determine what Christmas means to you and me.

Once upon a time there was a little boy who lived on a farm. He had no brothers or sisters, so he played alone. One afternoon some men came and pasted pictures of all kinds of animals on their barn.

That evening he questioned his father as to what it all meant. He was told that the circus was coming to town. There was nothing more wonderful and exciting. Yes, he could attend.

And so it was that on a certain day his father gave him a bright silver dollar for admission, and he rode horseback nine miles into town to see the big show.

When he arrived, he found the town crowded with happy people. Excitement filled the air. He hitched his pony and made his way to the main street.

Suddenly there was a burst of music, and down the street there came a sight such as he had never seen before. There were lions and tigers, camels and elephants, zebras and monkeys—wagon after wagon of animals.

Last of all, came the clowns, turning somersaults and doing tricks. The little boy had never laughed so much in all his life. The biggest clown passed right in front of him and paused, smiling. The lad held out his silver dollar and dropped it into the clown's hands. The clown was taken back in surprise for a moment, but then made a regal bow and was gone.

The crowd melted away. With heart running over, the little boy made his way back to his pony and rode home, and it wasn't until that night when he talked with his dad that he learned the awful truth. He hadn't seen the circus at all; he had seen only the parade!

Don't let it happen to you this Christmas. Amidst all the glitter and excitement, let's keep in mind what matters most. Let us remember whose birthday it is that we are celebrating and what the season really means, lest we, too, miss Christmas and see only the parade.

Giving Ourselves With Our Gifts

James Russell Lowell in his epic poem, *The Vision of Sir Launfal,* wrote:

> Not what we give, but what we share,
> For the gift without the giver is bare;
> Who gives himself with his alms feed three,
> Himself, his hungering neighbor and Me.

In a small town in the mid-west, there lived a little boy who had been crippled from birth. His father had died, and his mother earned barely enough for the two of them to live. Their family physician showed great concern and, at a medical convention, discussed the little boy's case with a close friend who was a famous surgeon. He was very interested. "If you will have the boy brought to my clinic," he said, "I will perform surgery. I believe he can be helped."

So it was that on a certain day the little boy and his mother boarded a train to go east. With one hand, the little boy held the hand of his mother. In the other, he held close his dearest possession—a little brown teddy bear. It was quite worn, an eye was out, a leg was off, and an arm was missing, but he loved it dearly.

The operation was performed and was successful. The little boy would run and play like other boys and girls.

When the day came for them to go home, mother and son went by the doctor's office to say goodbye and to thank him again for all he had done for them.

With a heart running over, the mother tried to express how she felt, but words seemed oh so inadequate, and then something very unexpected happened. With total abandon, the little boy held up the thing he treasured most. "I want to give you my teddy bear!"

When the little boy reached home, there was a large special delivery. Inside was the largest and most beautiful panda money could buy.

Today, if you should visit the office of the great surgeon, you would see in his waiting room a glass case containing a little brown teddy bear, soiled and worn, one eye out, a leg off, and an arm missing.

Under the glass top is a card on which is printed these words: "The largest single fee I ever received for professional service."

To Bring You Joy

Robert Peterson tells about Wendy, a little six-year-old he met on the beach. "Hello," she said. He nodded as a sandpiper glided by. "That's a joy," she said, "Momma says sandpipers come to bring us joy." Feeling depressed, he turned away. "My name's Wendy," she said, "I'm six." He kept walking. "Come again, Mr. P," she called, "'We'll have another happy day."

The next few days were very busy, but one then one morning he said, "I need a sandpiper!" and headed for the seashore. "Hello, Mr. P!" a voice called, "Do you want to play?" "Let's just walk," he said. Walking along he asked, "Where do you go to school?" She replied, "I don't go to school. Mommy says we're on vacation."

It was three weeks later. He came to the beach with a heavy heart. When Wendy showed up, he was in no mood to talk. "Look," he said, "If you don't mind, I'd rather be alone." She seemed unusually pale. "Why," she asked. "Because my mother died!" he shouted "Oh," she said, "Did it hurt when she died?" "Of course it hurt!" he snapped. Wrapped up in himself, he had misunderstood.

A month later when he returned she wasn't there. He went up to the cottage. A sad young woman opened the door. "I'm Robert Peterson, he said, "I missed your little girl and wondered where she was."

"Oh yes, please come in," she said, "Wendy spoke of you often. Mr. Peterson, Wendy died last week; she had leukemia; maybe she didn't tell you." Struck dumb, he struggled to catch his breath.

"She loved the beach; so when she asked to come, we couldn't say no. She seemed much better here, and had a lot of what she called happy days." She handed him an envelope. On it was written "MR. P" in big letters. Inside was a drawing of a yellow beach, a blue sea, and a bird. Underneath was printed: A SANDPIPER TO BRING YOU JOY.

Tears welled up in his eyes, and a heart that had almost forgotten to love opened wide. He put his arms around Wendy's mother, "I'm sorry, I'm so sorry!" he whispered over and over, and they wept together.

The little picture is now framed and hangs in his study. Six words, one for each year of her life. They speak of harmony, courage, and undemanding love; a gift from a child with sea blue eyes and hair the color of sand who taught him the gift of love

Language Of The Heart

Paul was writing to the church in Rome. He was concerned about the bonds that bound them together as followers of Christ. He knew the power of joy and happiness. He wrote: "Rejoice with those who rejoice," but he knew that the bond of tears is the strongest. He continued: "And weep with those who weep."

Harold Kushner, in his book, *When all You Ever Wanted Isn't Enough*, relates how when he was a boy a business associate of his father died under tragic circumstances and he went with his father to see the family.
The man's widow was surrounded by learned friends—ministers, and doctors—all seeking to ease the grief. They knew all the right words, but nothing helped. The wife and mother kept saying, "You are right, I know you are right, but it doesn't make any difference."

Then a man walked in, a big burly man in his eighties who was a veritable legend in the toy and game industry. He had escaped from Russia as a youth after having been arrested and tortured by the Czar's secret police. He had come to America illiterate and penniless and had built a tremendously large and successful company.

He was known as a ruthless competitor who drove hard bargains. In spite of his success, he had never found time to read or write. It was a well-known joke that he could write a check for a million dollars, and the hardest part would be signing his name at the bottom.

He had gotten out of the sick bed to come, and his face and walk showed it, but he walked over to the widow and started to cry, and she cried with him. Immediately, the atmosphere in the room changed.

This man, who had never read as much as one book in all his life, had no words of learning to speak, but he spoke the language of the heart. He was able to comfort and help where the doctors and clergy could not.

The human mind is a great thing, but it has its limits. There are some questions—life's most important questions, which it cannot answer. It was Blaise Pascal who said, "The heart has reasons which reason cannot know."

A verse of scripture in the Gospel of John has taken on lots of new meaning for me. It is the account of Jesus coming to be with Mary and Martha when their brother died. The verse reads: "Jesus wept."

Kneeling Before The King Of Kings

In his autobiography Cecil B. De Mille tells the story of what he considered to be the crowning moment of his entire life.

It was the day before Christmas and they were on location, a sound stage in Hollywood, filming "The King of Kings."

They were re-enacting the crucifixion, and he had recruited a ragtag bunch from the bars and slums of the city for the mob scene. They were to cry out, "Crucify him! Crucify him!"

It seemed so strange to everyone gathered there that day. Here they were, looking up at three crosses looming on the barren hillside. It was Christmas Eve, and they were telling about his death! It was hard for them to realize that in less than twenty-four hours they would be celebrating his birth.

On the spur of the moment, he was never sure what prompted the idea, the great producer-director called for silence. Stepping out in front of the camera he called out, "In honor of Christ the King we will take five minutes for meditation and prayer."

Immediately he realized he had made a big mistake. They would all saunter off, smoke, get a drink or just talk. This was no place for prayer and meditation!

But it was too late to remedy the situation; what had been done was done. Ill at ease, Cecil B. De Mille knelt down, bowed his head and closed his eyes.

The next few moments seemed like an eternity, but then it happened. From that admixture crew he heard the sound of voices singing, "It came upon the midnight clear, that glorious song of old."

Opening his eyes, he looked on the scene in amazement. They were all kneeling before the three crosses on the hillside. On their rough, defeated faces he saw tears of remembrance slowly trickling down.

Now I think you can understand why the great producer-director looked upon this event as the greatest moment of his life. How could he ever forget: Christmas Eve on a Hollywood sound set, three crosses on a hillside and a motley crew kneeling before the Son of God, the King of Kings.

December 6

Luke 4: 18

The Little Blind Shepherd

Once upon a time there lived in Palestine a shepherd by the name of Caleb and his wife, Hannah. They loved each other very much, but found it hard to be happy. Their son, Nathan, had been blind since birth; however, Nathan enjoyed life. He spent his days helping his mother and playing with his friends.

One evening in bleak December when Caleb said to his wife, "I must go to build fires to keep the sheep warm," Nathan asked excitedly, "Oh, Father, may I go?" Caleb looked toward Hannah. When she nodded, he said, "All right, you may go, but you will need to put on lots of warm clothing. Your mother will pack extra food for us. You will get quite hungry before the long night is over."

Soon they were there with the other shepherds. Nathan knew his task. He gathered up one of the flock and moved back to the fire. All the others followed.

They were all seated about the fire eating when Jotham called out, "Caleb! Levi! Do you see that great brightness overhead?" Suddenly, there came the sound of music, and an angel said, "Do not be afraid, I bring you good news of a great joy, for to you is born this day a Savior who is Christ the Lord. And this will be a sign for you, you will find a baby wrapped in swaddling cloths, lying in a manger." Then a multitude of the heavenly host shouted, "Glory to God in the highest, and on earth, peace, goodwill among men!"

Levi said, "Come, let us go to Bethlehem and see this thing that has happened, which the Lord has made known to us." At the stable they stood in awe, looking down and then one by one they knelt.

When they arose to go, the little shepherd said, "Please, lady, I am blind and can't see the baby; may I touch him so I may remember him, too?" Mary smiled, "Hold out your arms, and I will let you hold him."

As Mary laid the precious bundle in his arms, Nathan's world grew warm and bright. The little blind shepherd cried out, "I can see . . . with my eyes . . . I can see him . . . I can see!"

Outside the stable, the dawn was breaking—just for Nathan. With hearts overflowing with gratitude for all they had seen and heard and above all for what had happened, the shepherds returned, glorifying and praising God.

I Am Here!

In the Book of Hebrews are found these words which voice a great truth: "God himself has said, 'I will never leave you, nor forsake you.' So we can confidently say, 'The Lord is my helper, I will not be afraid.'"

For our Christmas program on Tuesday, the VA Hospital chaplain, the Rev. W. L. McDaniel, told the story of how each day during the noon hour a little boy of about ten years of age would come to a downtown church.

He would enter the large front door and quietly make his way down the aisle to the chancel. He would kneel for a few seconds, then rise, and make his way out.

One day the pastor was in the sanctuary and saw him come and go, but thought nothing of it. However, as the days went by, the pastor realized that the little boy was coming every day. He started talking with him and, in time, the two became good friends.

One day, as they talked, the pastor said, "You have been coming to the chapel every day at noon for a long time. You kneel as if in prayer, but you stay for only a few seconds. Why do you come?"

The daily visitor replied, "My parents were killed a year ago. They taught me to come to church and to pray. I don't need to stay very long. Jesus knows all about me; what I do, what I say, and what I need. I just kneel at the altar and say, 'Jesus, it is Johnny. I am here.'"

Months passed. One day the phone rang in the pastor's study. A nurse was calling from the hospital. A little boy had been struck by a car and was in critical condition. Could the pastor come? Yes, he would be there shortly.

The patient was his little friend, Johnny. When the pastor called his name, he stirred feverishly, but that was all. The pastor sat down at his bedside and kept vigil the rest of the afternoon and through the long night.

As dawn broke, Johnny slowly opened his eyes. The pastor smiled in relief, "Johnny, you're awake! How do you feel?" Johnny answered, "I'm OK, now. I had a visitor. I saw him standing at the foot of my bed, looking down at me. He was dressed in white, and I heard him say, 'Johnny, it is Jesus. I am here.'"

Footprints in The Mud

Dr. Jesse Truvillion, an African American minister and pastor of St. Peter's Presbyterian Church in Fort Worth, grew up in East Texas and experienced the deep-seated prejudice, so prevalent, even to this day.

It was two weeks before Christmas. Rain was freezing as it fell. Jesse and his family were eating supper when there was a knock at the front door. Jesse went to answer, only to slam the door and return to the table. "Who was it Jesse?" his mother asked. "Aw, it was just one of the Medley girls," Jesse said. The Medleys were a poor white family who lived down the road. The Truvillion children, along with others, would throw rocks at the Medley house before running home.

Mrs. Truvillion hurried to the door. The little girl, in fear, had stepped back off the porch into the freezing rain. When she was brought into the house, (and through the front door!), Jesse's face burned in anger. Not even the Truvillion children were permitted to come in the front door.

She explained that her father had been gone for two days, that her mother was too ill to cook and had sent the daughter to borrow some bread. The little girl was dried off and seated at the supper table. Then Mrs. Truvillion said, "Jesse, go fetch the other Medley children and tell Mrs. Medley I will be down shortly." Reluctantly, Jesse obeyed.

At the Medley's door, he told the children to get their coats and galoshes and follow him, not noticing until later that they had no galoshes. At the Truvillion home, they were dried off and seated at the supper table. Jesse was so angry, he refused to eat.

He went into the den where his father was reading. After a while his father spoke. "Jesse, tell me, what did you see when you went to fetch the Medley children." Jesse thought for a minute. "Well, I saw the trees bent down with ice, the muddy road and freezing rain." Then hesitatingly he added, "I saw that the Medley girls had no galoshes, and I saw their footprints in the mud."

Then his father said, "Jesse, I think some of that freezing rain got in your eyes. I think the cold got in your heart, too. Jesus' footprints were in that mud. Those little girls are God's children, just like you." There was a long silence. Jesse sat with bowed head, tears welling up in his eyes. His father came over and laid his hand on his shoulder. "Why don't you go back, now, and finish your supper; and get some of your mother's blueberry pie that you like so much!"

And Still No Room

In the Christmas story as told by Luke, Jesus was wrapped in swaddling cloths and laid in a manger, because there was "no room for them in the inn." As we move through this Advent time of waiting, we cannot help but wonder why. We find ourselves saying, "Had I been there, things would have been different."

The truth is that after two thousand years, there is still "no room," and the reasons for the crowded inns of our lives today are much the same as they were then.

One of the main reasons there was no room for him then was the fact that they just weren't expecting him. If the innkeeper had only known, don't you know it would have been a different story? And what happened at Christ's birth was true throughout his life. When Jesus returned to his hometown, Mark tells us "he could do no mighty works there." Why? It was because the people of Nazareth expected nothing.

They failed to recognize him when he did come. They were looking for a conqueror coming on the clouds of heaven that would lead them into war against their hated Roman oppressors. But a tiny baby? In a stable? No way!

How often does he come to us unrecognized? Read again Matthew 25. He comes to us today as a homeless man or woman, as a lonely teenager, lost and all at sea, as a child who will have no Christmas this year unless you step in and help.

But the big reason, then and now, he was not wanted. The innkeeper's protest was that there was no room, but he could have made room. We always find or make room for the things that matter most.

What about you and me? Are the real barriers our sin-filled lives? The knowledge deep down that if we made room for him, other things would have to go? It is a lot easier just to say, "No room!"

But if we are saying it humbly, ashamed of the soiled conditions of our lives, then there is hope. Remember, on that first Christmas, he came not to a palatial palace but to a lowly stable, and all through the centuries, he has never despised a humble dwelling.

Soon we will hear again the good news, "Unto you is born this day a Savior." God grant that there will be room when he comes.

Three Little Trees

Once upon a time there were three little trees growing on a hillside. From time to time they talked about what they would like to be when they grew up. "I want to be a treasure chest," said the first little tree, "I want to be covered with gold and filled with precious stones."

The second little tree said, "I want to be a great sailing ship and carry powerful rulers." The third little tree said, "I don't ever want to leave this mountain," he said, "I want to grow lofty and tall and when people look up at me they will look beyond me and think of God."

Time passed, the rains came, the sun shone, and the little trees grew. Then one day woodsmen came and looked over the three trees. One chose the first tree. "This tree is just the one I need for making a feed trough to feed my livestock." "But I don't want to be a feed box," the first tree cried in protest, "I want to be a treasure chest and hold precious gems." But he was made into a feed trough, and on that night of nights that is where Mary laid the baby Jesus. Suddenly the first tree knew that he was holding the greatest treasure in all the world.

Another woodsman chose the second tree. "This one will make an excellent fishing boat." The tree pleaded, "But I don't want to be a fishing boat, I want to be a great sailing ship and carry powerful rulers."
But he was made into a fishing boat, and one night crossing a lake a storm arose and threatened to sink it and all aboard. But one asleep in the stern arose and commanded, "Peace, be still!" The storm stopped and suddenly the second tree knew he was carrying the King of Kings.

The last woodsman said, "Any tree will do for me." The third tree was cut down, cut up into rough beams and stacked in a lumberyard. Then one Friday morning he was roughly yanked from the forgotten woodpile.

He flinched as he was carried through an angry, jeering mob. He shuddered when soldiers nailed a man's hands and feet to him. He felt so ugly, harsh and cruel, but then came the Easter dawn, and the third tree knew that the love of God was changing everything.

Every dream was realized. The first tree was made beautiful, the second tree was made strong, and through all the years as men and women, boys and girls have looked at the cross it has pointed them to God.

The Indwelling Christ

The Apostle Paul writing to the Colossians used this phrase "Christ in you, the hope of glory." As for his own life, Paul declared, "It is no longer I who live, but Christ who lives in me." Jacopone da Todi once defined a Christian as "one in whom Christ is felt to live again." What about your life and mine? Is Christ felt to live again in you and me?

The poet reminds us:

> Though Christ a thousand times
> In Bethlehem be born,
> If He's not born in thee
> Thy soul is still forlorn.

The Christian life is one of doing something; or rather it is allowing Christ to do things through us. It calls for the dedication of head, hands and heart. God's word declares, "As a man thinks in his heart, so is he." The way we think determines what we do and what we become. That is why we are counseled to think on the things that are honest true and just. Christ-like thinking is one of the things we do.

Jesus "went about doing good." Christian thinking must issue forth in Christ-like deeds. Compassion for those who are ill is not enough. They must be visited and ministered to. Pity for those in need is not enough. They must receive food and clothing. With our hands we reach out and lay hold on a task. With our hands we do something.

Jesus once said to his disciples, "A new commandment I give to you, that you love one another, even as I have loved you; love one another." He went on to declare, "By this all men will know that you are my disciples, if you have love for one another." As we love and serve each other, we show forth our love for Christ.

It seems strange, but Christ is constantly hiding himself in the face of a child, in a stranger lost and alone, in a beggar hungry and cold, in a body wracked with pain.

What better time for a deeper dedication to Christ than at Christmas?

> O Holy Child of Bethlehem!
> Descend to us we pray;
> Cast out our sin and enter in;
> Be born in us today."

Questing For The Holy Grail

James Russell Lowell, in his heart-warming poem, "The Vision of Sir Launfal," tells the story of the young knight's search for the Holy Grail—the cup from which Jesus drank at the Last Supper. His golden spurs, his guild mail—all the things he needed were laid out, ready for him to don at break of day. Filled with excitement and anticipation, he lay down to sleep. At dawn, he would begin the quest.

It was spring. The sun rose bright and clear. The drawbridge dropped with a clang, and through the arch, a charger sprang bearing Sir Launfal, his armor glittering in the morning sunlight. Crouched by the gate, a leprous beggar lifted a whitened hand and called out for alms. Sir Launfal shuddered at the sight, and a loathing swept over him. In scorn he tossed a gold coin which fell in the dust at the leper's feet. As he rode away, he noticed that the beggar didn't even pick it up.

It was winter. Sir Launfal, an old gray man, broken and worn, had come home to find his castle taken over by another heir. He had spent a lifetime in search of the Holy Grail, a search that had been in vain.

It was Christmas time. There was snow, and the morning was very cold. Striving to keep warm, he mused of a sunnier clime. Then he saw the gruesome form. It was the leper, standing before him in the desolate horror of his disease. There was no money for the outstretched hand. Sir Launfal divided his last crust of course, brown bread; then, broke the ice on the little stream, dipped up cold water in a wooden bowl, and gave them to the leper to eat and drink.

Suddenly, a dazzling light shone round about the place. The leper stood before him transfigured, tall and fair. A voice that was calmer than silence, said, "You have spent your life searching for the Holy Grail; behold, it is here—the cup that you filled from the stream just now."

All at once, Sir Launfal was awake. He had been dreaming. The vision changed his life. And it can be so for you and me. Sharing with another's need, we find life's greatest treasure. In the words of the transfigured beggar:

> Not what we give, but what we share,
> For the gift without the giver is bare;
> Who gives himself with his alms feeds three,
> Himself, his hungering neighbor, and Me.

Yes, There Is A Santa Claus!

On that first Christmas the angels said to the shepherds, "I bring you good news of a great **joy**. That is what Christmas and Santa Claus is all about. You don't believe in Santa Claus? What utter nonsense! Let me tell you a story.

It all began when Mary's big sister told her, "There is no Santa Claus. Everybody knows that, you dummy!" Mary stood frozen. "No Santa Claus!" Could it be true? Soon she was on her bike hurrying to her grandmother's. Mary could depend on her to set things straight.

"No Santa Claus?" Grandma exclaimed, "Ridiculous! Don't you believe it! That silly rumor has been going around for years. Let me get my purse and you come with me."

At Massey's General Store Grandma handed Mary a ten-dollar bill—that was a lot in those days. "Take this," she said, "and buy something for someone who needs it. I'll wait for you here in the car."

She remembered Bobby. He didn't have a coat. That's what she would buy. "Is this a Christmas present for someone?" the lady at the counter asked as Mary laid down the ten-dollar bill. "Yes, Ma'am," Mary said. The lady smiled as Mary told her about how Bobby really needed a warm coat. She put the coat in a bag and smiled again as she wished Mary a Merry Christmas.

Back home, as they wrapped the coat in Christmas paper, a little tag fell out and Grandma quietly tucked it in her Bible. They wrote on the card, "To Bobby from Santa Claus," and as they drove to Bobby's house Grandma explained that from that time on, Mary was one of Santa's official helpers.

Mary slipped up on the porch, put the present down, knocked, and flew back to the car. In a few seconds Bobby opened the door.

It happened years ago, but for Mary the joy has never dimmed. She has never forgotten the surprise and happiness that flooded little Bobby's face. In that moment she knew beyond a shadow of a doubt that there was a Santa Claus. Mary still has her Grandmother's Bible. Tucked inside is that price tag: $19.95.

Listen again to the words from Luke's gospel: "Behold, I bring you good news of great **joy** which shall come to all people."

December 14   II Corinthians 5: 18-19
                          God Was In Christ

Advent covers the four Sundays before Christmas. The word itself means
"coming." It is a time of preparation for celebrating the birth of Christ—
God coming into the world through his Son.

We are all familiar with the Christmas story as found in Matthew and Luke.
Did you know that there is a Christmas story in the Gospel of John? The
story in the Fourth Gospel reads like this: "The Word became flesh and
dwelt among us."

Once upon a time there was a man who couldn't believe, in the words of
Paul, that "God was in Christ reconciling the world to himself." He said to
his family, "I am not going with you to the Christmas Eve service. I would
feel like a hypocrite." So that evening, they went to church, leaving him
at home.

They had scarcely left when it began to snow. He made himself comfortable
before the fire to read the paper. Suddenly, he heard a thudding sound
against the large picture window, then another, and another.

A flock of birds, caught in the snowstorm, was desperately seeking
shelter. They were trying to come inside. The man realized their plight
was desperate. Unless something was done and done soon, they would
freeze to death.

The barn - that would provide warm shelter if he could direct them to
it. Putting on coat, cap, and gloves, he went out into the whirling snow,
opened the large double doors and turned on the lights.

But the birds wouldn't go in. Food failed to entice them, attempts to catch
them were futile, and when he tried to shoo them into the barn, they
scattered in every direction.

"They are afraid of me," he cried, "If only I could be a bird and mingle
with them, speak their language, tell them not to be afraid, then I could
lead them into the safe warm barn; but I would have to become like one of
them so they could see, and hear, and understand."

At that moment, in the midst of his frustration and despair, he heard the
distant ringing of the church bells. He fell on his knees in the snow. "Now,
I see," he whispered through his tears, "Now, I know why you came as a
little baby."

What Can I Give Him?

Yesterday's newspaper reminded us that there are only 11 more shopping days before Christmas. It's a wonderful season, but amid all the rush and excitement we are in grave danger of forgetting whose birthday it is that we are celebrating.

In her poem, "My Gift," Christiana Rossetti asks herself, "What can I give him?" Have you thought about what you might give to Christ for his birthday? There are lots of wonderful possibilities.

I remember one year close to Christmas receiving a long distance call from a father who put his four-year-old son on the phone to announce the arrival of his baby brother. I can still hear the thrill and excitement in his voice as he shared the good news.

What finer gift could you and I give this Christmas than to tell someone about the Christ, to introduce Jesus to someone who doesn't know him personally?

Two thousand years ago an angel brought the message to shepherds keeping watch over their flocks. "Behold, I bring you the most joyful news ever announced, and it is for everyone!" is the way the Living Gospels translates it. As Christmas draws near, let's tell the whole wide world that Jesus Christ is born.

We can also share the purpose and task for which Christ came as outlined by the prophet Isaiah: ". . . to tell the good news to the poor, to heal the brokenhearted, to tell the prisoners they are free and the blind that they will see again, and to set at liberty those who are oppressed." What wonderful gifts to bring in celebration of the birthday of Christ our King!

Finally, we can make room for him in our hearts. If Christ is to come in, there are some things that must be moved out. Selfishness and greed, jealousy and hate, vanity and pride are a few of the things that can fill our hearts to overflowing and crowd him out.

The Christmas story as told in Matthew never grows old. It tells how the wise men from the East came seeking the one born king. Finding him, they fell on their knees and worshipped him. Then opening their treasures they presented him with gifts.

What are you planning to give Christ on his birthday this Christmas?

December 16   **Micah 5:2**

Getting Ready For Christmas

It is the Advent season. Edwin Markham, in one of his poems, told the story of Old Conrad, a man who almost missed Christ's coming. It happened one day at year's end. In a dream, Christ appeared before him and announced that he was coming to be his guest.

Excitedly, Old Conrad got busy. He strewed the floor with branches of fir, washed the walls, and decorated the rafters with holly. Then he set out milk and honey and wheaten bread.

When he was finished he sat down before the fire and waited for the knock, the opened door, the welcome, the visit, and at last the breaking of bread at the day's end.

As he waited a beggar drenched by the driving rain came by. Conrad invited him in until the rain stopped and as he left gave him a pair of shoes. A short time later an old woman stopped to rest. When she rose to go her way, Conrad gave her the loaf of wheaten bread from his table.

The day was slipping away. Old Conrad wondered if somehow he had misunderstood. Just then he heard a child crying and hurried to the door. There, just outside, stood a little girl who had wandered off and lost her way.

He dried the little girl's tears and gave her the milk that was in the blue pitcher. Soon she was smiling and happy again. Then Old Conrad took her home. Her mother had been frantic with fear.

The sun was going down. The day was coming to a close. Musing by his fire, Old Conrad whispered, "Lord, did you forget? You promised to come." Softly through the twilight, a voice spoke, "I kept my word. Three times I came to your door. I was the beggar without shoes. I was the woman old and gray. I was the little child so lost and all alone."

Then it was that Old Conrad remembered the words. He had read them in The Gospel According to Matthew just the evening before: "As you did it to one of the least of these, you did it to me."

Remember, God does some mighty strange things. Keep awake; stay alert. Don't get so busy preparing for Christmas that you miss the Christ who is to come.

The Spirit Of Christmas

Dr. Roy Angel was for many years was pastor of the Central Baptist Church in Miami. I want to share with you a true story that he tells in his book, *Baskets of Silver.*

It is about a man whose brother had given him a big new car—a Packard, shortly before Christmas. One afternoon, he came out of his office to find a dirty little boy, a street urchin, walking around the car, touching and staring at it in admiration.

The little fellow looked up and asked what a car like that cost? The man replied that he didn't know, because his brother had given it to him. "You mean your brother gave it to you, and it didn't cost you nothing?" The man smiled, "Yes, my brother gave it to me, and it didn't cost me anything."

For a little while the boy appeared lost in thought. Finally he said, "I wish," —the man knew he was going to say he wished he had a brother who would give him a car. But he didn't. He said, "Gosh, I wish I could be a brother like that!"

When we hear a story like that, we are reminded that the true spirit of Christmas is giving. The Gospel of John sums up what Christmas is about in these words: "For God so loved the world that he gave his only Son . . . ."

During these days of Advent, take these words of Harold Cornelius Sandall and ponder them well:

> Love that is hoarded, molds at last
> Until we know some day
> The only thing we ever have
> Is what we give away.
>
> And kindness that is never used
> But hidden all alone
> Will slowly harden till it is
> As hard as any stone.
>
> It is the things we always hold
> That we will lose some day;
> The only things we ever keep
> Are what we give away.

December 18   **Matthew 2: 1-2**
                          The Other Wise Man

We all know about the Three Wise Men who brought gifts to the manger in Bethlehem, but have you heard the story of the Other Wise Man? Henry Van Dyke told the story over a century ago.

Artaban, a priest of the Magi in ancient Persia, decides to go with the caravan of the Three Wise Men following the eastern star to the birthplace of the new born King. He takes with him three precious jewels; a sapphire, a ruby, and a pearl to give in tribute to the Christ child.

But stopping to render aid to a stranger beaten and robbed, he misses the caravan and spends the rest of his life searching. He finds none to worship, but many to help. Most of his wealth is spent helping the poor and unfortunate.

Thirty-three years pass. Now, an old man, tired and weary from his quest, he comes for the last time to Jerusalem. There he is told, "Today, they are crucifying Jesus who says he is the Son of God and king of the Jews." His heart leaps. He will ransom Jesus with his final jewel. But when a little maid, being sold as a slave, throws herself at his feet, begging for help, he gives the pearl, the last of his treasure he had kept for the King, to buy her freedom.

Now, as Christ is dying on the cross, an earthquake rocks the city. The earth shakes and trembles as though the heart of God is breaking. A falling roof tile strikes Artaban on the temple, knocking him to the ground, unconscious. Bending over him the little maid hears a voice in the twilight dim, but she sees no one. The old man answers in a whisper, "Not so, my Lord! When did I see you hungry and feed you, or thirsty and give you drink? When did I see you a stranger and welcome you, naked and clothe you, or sick or in prison and visit you? All my life I have searched for you, but I have never seen you."

He ceases speaking, and the voice sounds again. This time it seems as though the little maid understands the words: "Truly, I say to you, as you did it to one of the least of these, you did it to me."

A calm radiance of wonder and joy lighted the pale face of Artaban. His journey was ended. His treasures were accepted. The Other Wise Man had found the King.

353

Making Room In The Inn

I would like to share with you one of my favorite Christmas stories. It is a true story that happened years ago in the Midwest.

Wallace Purling was nine years old. He should have been in the fourth grade but was only in the second. He was big and clumsy, slow in movement and slow in mind.

Still, Wally was well liked by the other children, all of whom were smaller than he. None of the boys ever wanted the uncoordinated Wally on their team and generally managed to keep him off, but Wally never got angry. He remained helpful and smiling.

The school was planning the annual Nativity Pageant, and Wally wanted to be a shepherd and play a flute. but he was cast as the innkeeper. There were not so many lines to learn, and Wally's size would make his refusal of lodging to Joseph and Mary more authentic.

The large audience gathered for the yearly extravaganza. Wally was caught up in the awe and wonder of the night. He had to be stopped twice to keep him from wandering on stage before his cue.

When Joseph appeared with Mary and knocked on the door, Wally, the innkeeper asked, "What do you want?" Joseph answered, "Sir, we seek lodging." Wally spoke firmly, "Seek it elsewhere; the inn is filled."

Joseph replied, "Sir, there is no place to stay, and we are exhausted." Wally looked straight ahead. Joseph continued, "Mary is expecting our first child, and she is so tired."

The stern innkeeper relaxed. There was a long pause. The prompter whispered, "No! Be gone!" Automatically, Wally repeated the words, "No! Be gone!"

Joseph and Mary started to move away, but the innkeeper didn't go back inside. His eyes filled with tears. Suddenly, that year's Christmas Pageant took a strange turn. The innkeeper called out, "Don't go Joseph!" Wally's face lighted up with a smile, "The two of you can have MY room!"

Some people thought the pageant had been ruined; but there were others—many others—who felt deep in their hearts that somehow that is the way it ought to have been.

No, Never Alone!

It was Taylor Caldwell's most meaningful Christmas. It began on a rainy spring day of the bleakest year of her life. Her marriage had ended in a divorce, and she was looking for work when she found on the city bus a beautiful umbrella with a silver handle. There was a name and address on it, and she decided to return it rather than turn it in.

The owner was quite surprised. Yes, it was hers; her parents had given it to her for her birthday. She invited her in, and over a cup of tea she inquired as to where Miss Caldwell lived, what she did and expressed sympathy for her plight.

The next six months were wretched with only temporary employment here and there. Her last job ended on Christmas Eve. There was 30 dollars rent due, and she had only 15 which she and her little girl, Peggy, would need for food.

Christmas cheer was in the air as she walked to their apartment, but there would be no Christmas for them. Come January they would be homeless, jobless and without food. She had prayed and prayed but there had been no answer, only the cold and dark.

There were two envelopes in the mailbox—bills probably. She opened the door, and her daughter greeted her joyously. Peggy was only six, but she had set the table and put out the last three cans of food. As she struggled to keep back the tears, Taylor Caldwell, for the first time in her life doubted the love and goodness of God.

The doorbell rang, and Peggy went to the door. It was a deliveryman with arms full of parcels. Incredible! They were filled with all kinds of gifts for the two of them. The sender was the lady whose umbrella she had returned almost a year before.

Suddenly Taylor Caldwell had hope again. She could face the bills and all her other problems. Then she remembered to open the two envelopes. In one was a Christmas bonus for $30 from a company she worked for in the summer. Her rent! In the other was the offer of a permanent job with the government to begin two days after Christmas.

In the distance church bells were ringing. People were on their way to the Christmas Eve service to celebrate the birth of the Savior. She heard the voices singing "O come all ye faithful." She whispered her thoughts aloud: "I am not alone. I was never alone."

God's Greatest Gift

Generation after generation, O. Henry's short story, "The Gift of the Magi," has warmed the hearts of countless thousands at Christmas time. I would like to share it with you as we look forward to Christmas.

The card on the door read, "James Dillingham Young." They were newlyweds and very much in love. His salary came to $20.00 a week and $8.00 of that went for rent on the shabby flat where they lived. Christmas was coming, and both James and Della were wondering what they could give each other.

He had no money; trying to save had been futile. Della was more fortunate. She had managed to save $1.87—in pennies and nickels, but it wasn't nearly enough to buy the kind of present she wanted to buy.

There were two things of which the Youngs were proud. James had a gold watch that had been his grandfather's; the other was Della's hair. When she let it down, it fell like a rippling cascade about her shoulders.

And so it was that a few days before Christmas James decided to buy Della two beautiful combs. She had admired them in the show window, but had no hope of possessing them because of the price. That same day Della went to the hair stylist and sold her hair for $20.00 to buy a gift for Jim, a platinum chain for his watch. She paid the jeweler $21.00 and with the 87 cents hurried home.

On Christmas Eve Jim came home and stopped inside the door, his eyes fixed on Della with an expression she couldn't fathom. Then it passed, and in the light of a flickering candle they sat down on the worn sofa to exchange gifts. Della opened her package first. There they were—the combs she had wanted so long. "Never mind about my hair," she said, "It will grow out again in no time."

Then Della watched as he opened his gift. "Isn't it beautiful, darling? Give me your watch; I want to fasten it on." Jim's face was ashen as he managed an answer, "I don't have my watch. I sold it to buy your combs!"

I don't know, but I imagine the James Dillingham Youngs never forgot that Christmas. Because, you see, they had discovered the real meaning of Christmas. It began some 2007 years ago when God gave us his only Son; and we keep Christmas in our hearts by loving as God loved—to the fullest; and giving as God gave—His very best!

The Christmas Angel

Once on Christmas Eve a man had a strange and wonderful dream. Here is the story as it was told by Henry Van Dyke.

It was the hour of rest in the Country Beyond the Stars. The angels were discussing the troubles they had seen among men. "The earth is full of oppression and injustice," declared the Archangel Michael, "If the hosts of heaven could be sent to mingle in the wars of men, the good could be made victorious."

"I do not agree," said the Archangel Oriel; "Often power has been given to the good, and it has been used for evil. The world is filled with ignorant strife for lack of knowledge. If the great King would enlighten the world the peace of God would come."

Then the Archangel Raphael spoke, "Wisdom has been given before," he said, "Remember Solomon? All of his wisdom didn't save him from weariness and despair. The only cure for the evil is love, but how shall the miracle be wrought; how shall men be made like God?"

Then came this voice, "I know. Man shall be made like God because the Son of God shall become a man. I am the Christmas Angel. It is Christmas Day on earth, and I must fly quickly to bring the good news to those chosen to receive it."

As the young angel dropped swiftly toward the earth, the other angels followed. Who had been chosen to receive the glad tidings? Could it be the Emperor of the world, they wondered, but the flight passed over Rome. "It may be the philosophers," they said, but the flight passed over Athens. "Could it be the priests of the temple?" but the flight passed over Jerusalem.

"And there were in that country shepherds abiding in the fields, keeping watch over their flocks by night. And lo! The angel of the Lord came upon them, and the glory of the Lord shone around them and they were filled with fear. But the angel said to them, 'Fear not; for behold, I bring you good tidings of great joy which shall be to all people. For unto you is born this day in the city of David a Savior, who is Christ the Lord.'"

The man said, "I will go with the shepherds to Bethlehem," and a great voice said, "Come!" Then suddenly he awoke. It was Christmas morning, and he knew he had been dreaming, yet it seemed to him that the things he had seen and heard were true.

December 23

Why The Chimes Rang

Luke 21: 1-4

In his Christmas story, "Why the Chimes Rang," Raymond MacDonald Alden tells about a wonderful church that stood on a high hill in a big city. Every Sunday as well as on sacred days like Christmas, thousands of people came to worship in the beautiful sanctuary.

High in the tower was a chime of Christmas bells, the most beautiful in the world, but no one had heard them for years. They were Christmas chimes, you see, and it was the custom on Christmas Eve for people to bring gifts to the Christ-child and when the best gift was offered, there came, sounding through the music of the choir, the Christmas chimes.

A number of miles from the city lived a little boy named Pedro and his little brother. They knew little about the chimes but had heard of the service on Christmas Eve and planned to go to the celebration.

Christmas Eve was bitter cold with snowflakes flying. Pedro and Little Brother left quietly early in the afternoon. Before nightfall, they saw the lights of the city. Suddenly they saw something dark on the snow near their path. A poor woman had fallen in the snow. Pedro knew what had to be done. "You will have to go on alone, Little Brother," he said, "Everyone is at church now, but when you return bring help.

"Please see and hear everything for me; and oh! If you get a chance to slip up to the altar without getting in the way, take this little silver piece of mine and lay it down for my offering when no one is looking. Don't forget where you have left me and forgive me for not going with you."

The great church was a wonderful place that night. The organ played, the thousands of people sang, and then came the procession. So many wonderful gifts! Last of all came the king. A murmur went up as he removed his crown, set with precious stones, and laid it on the altar, but still only the old cold wind was heard high in the tower.

The choir began the closing hymn. Then it happened. Through the night air, ever so softly, came the music of the chimes, rising and falling away up there in the night sky.

The people sat spellbound for a moment. Then they all stood and looked toward the altar to see what great gift had awakened the long-silent bells, but all they saw was the childish figure of Little Brother who had crept softly down the aisle when no one was looking and laid Pedro's little piece of silver on the altar.

A Pilgrimage To Bethlehem

Each year at Christmas, we go back in spirit and re-live the great event that occurred over 2,000 years ago. A star will light the eastern sky, the angel chorus will announce "good tidings of great joy," and with those of old, ours will be the invitation: "Come, let us go to Bethlehem."

On that first Christmas, there were shepherds abiding in the fields. They came with haste and found the babe lying in a manger. A shepherd's life in those days was very hard.

The days were long, and nights were bitter cold. They were very poor, but there was great hope in their hearts and this made them rich. With this hope, they came to Bethlehem.

Wise men came from the East. In all their wisdom and knowledge, they came in quest of the Prince of Peace. They came looking for a way through the problem of man's relationship with man. They found their answer in a little child when they came to Bethlehem.

The soldiers went forth and slew all the children that were in Bethlehem. Their tramping feet drowned out the song of peace on earth, good will toward men.

I was born in the midst of World War I; my son was born during World War II. Must his children know the death and destruction of war? The soldiers came to Bethlehem. They came to kill.

There were others who made the pilgrimage. Multitudes, whose names we do not know. They came and filled the inn. They slept through that night of nights. The star shone, the angels sang, and Christ was born; but they knew it not! They made the pilgrimage; that was all. But was it all? No, they did something more—they filled the inn, and there was no room for Jesus!

Christmas is coming and all of us are pilgrims once again. How will we go this year? The shepherds came with light in their eyes, and hope in their hearts. The wise men came from the East with their dreams of peace. The soldiers came at King Herod's command to destroy and kill. But the throning multitude—theirs was the most pathetic plight of all; they filled the inn to overflowing and crowded out the Christ!

Listen again to God's Good News: "To you is born this day in the city of David a Savior, who is Christ the Lord." Come, let us go to Bethlehem!

What Christmas Is All About

In 1944, in the midst World War II, some 3,500 prisoners of war at Dachau, ten miles from Munich, Germany, made a formal request that Pastor Martin Neimoller be allowed to preach to them at Christmas. Reluctantly, permission was granted.

Had you been in his place, what would you have chosen to preach on to those soldiers confined to a Nazi concentration camp at Christmas time, away from their homes and families? Martin Neimmoller took his text from Matthew's Gospel: "His name shall be called Emmanuel (which means God with us)."

Listening to Pastor Neimoller's Christmas sermon, the soldiers at Dachau realized that Christ was with them there in that concentration camp as never before in their lives.

As Christ was with those prisoners of war at Dachau in 1944, he is with our fighting men and women today in Afghanistan, Iraq—throughout the world and is also present with each of us.

Every Christmas for many years now, our family has watched "A Charlie Brown Christmas." It never grows old. Year after year our hearts are touched by the antics; and tears of joy well up in our eyes when at the very end amidst all the confusion and frustration, Charlie Brown asks in bewilderment, "Does anybody know what Christmas is all about?"

There is total silence. Then Linus steps out and says, "I know what Christmas is all about." He calls out to the crew, "Lights!" And standing there in the blazing spot he speaks:

"And there were in the same country shepherds abiding in the fields keeping watch over their flocks by night. And an angel of the Lord came upon them, and the glory of the Lord shone round about them, and they were filled with fear.

"But the angel said unto them, 'Fear not, for behold I bring you good tidings of great joy which shall be to all people, for unto you is born this day in the city of David a Savior who is Christ the Lord. And this will be a sign to you, you will find the babe wrapped in swaddling clothes lying in a manger.'"

"That, Charlie Brown, is what Christmas is all about."

If Christ Had Not Come

It was the night before Christmas, the one night in the year when seven-year-old Bobby went to bed without being told. But going to sleep was not easy, he was thinking about Christmas morning and all the presents under the tree. It seemed he had barely fallen asleep when a voice shouted, "Get up!" He sat up and opened his eyes. Suddenly he remembered what day it was. With a shout he hurried into his clothes and bounded down the stairs.

On the bottom step he stopped. The house was strangely silent. The Christmas tree was gone and no stocking hung from the mantel. "But I hung up my stocking and I helped decorate the tree." He went to the door. Cars were whizzing by, people on their way to work as usual. "People don't work on Christmas, he thought. But looking down the street he saw that all the stores were open.

Why are the stores open on Christmas?" he asked a woman nearby. "Christmas?" she asked, staring at him blankly, "What's Christmas?" Everywhere it was the same. People were busy. They had never heard of Christmas.

"I know one place where they have heard of Christmas!" Bobby cried, "At my church! There's a special service this morning!" He ran toward the church. This was the right street; at least he thought it was, but the beautiful church with the tall spire was not there, only a vacant lot grown up in weeds.

Just then he heard a groan from the side of the road where a man was lying. A car that hadn't even stopped had struck him. Bobby began calling for help, but no one came. "I'll run to the hospital," he promised, "They'll send an ambulance!" But there was no hospital on the corner, only a billboard with these words: IF HE HAD NOT COME.

Now Bobby was running home. The family Bible—that was the answer. He picked it up to turn to the book of Luke. There was no Gospel of Luke, no New Testament, no Christmas story. No Jesus at all. Bobby fell over on the divan and began to cry.

"Bobby, wake up! It's Christmas morning!" His mother was calling. He bound out of bed. Church bells were pealing out *Joy to the world!* He called out "I'm coming!" Then he paused, his heart running over with gratitude and joy, "You did come!" he whispered, "Oh, I'm so glad you came!"

December 27

Acts 8: 4

The Work Of Christmas

A mother and daughter were packing away things after Christmas when they came upon this cardboard nativity scene. It had been in the family for years and was greatly treasured. After wrapping it the mother went to get bubble wrap to keep it doubly safe.

When she returned she was horrified to find the daughter standing, a knife in one hand and the cardboard nativity in the other, a big hole cut in the back and a big hole in the carpet. She cried, "What have you done? Why would you cut a hole in the nativity scene? The little girl was shocked. She said, "Mama, we were getting ready to wrap it up and put it in a box, and we had to make a way for Jesus to get out!" It is a strange story, but a true story. Have you and I made a way for Jesus to get out of Christmas and into the New Year, into the lives that need him? How do we begin to share the good news with others?

First of all, look **around**. The mission field begins at our door. Did you know that in Uganda a higher percentage of people are Christian than in America? You have a better chance of running into a Christian there than here. Look around at the people God has put in your life that are not Christian—your family, your neighbors, and your friends.

Then look **up**. Pray for those on your list. Ask God to show you what to say and do to reach and win them. One way is to ask, "Where do you go to church?" It offends no one and opens the door for conversation. You don't have to answer all their questions, just answer the main question—tell them what Jesus means to you.

Most people belong to the church because someone invited them, and 9 out of 10 of the un-churched say they would attend if invited. What a wonderful way to let Jesus out of Christmas and into the New Year!

Today people are searching as never before for something to give life meaning. Begin today. Let Jesus out.

In the words of the poet, Howard Thurman:

> When the song of angels is stilled,
> When the star in the sky is gone,
> When the kings and princes are departed,
> When the shepherds are back with their flocks,
> The work of Christmas begins.

Matthew 5:7
                                   A New Beginning

In his novel "Les Miserables," Victor Hugo told the story of a man whose
life was redeemed by understanding, forgiveness, and love.

Late on a cold and rainy afternoon in a little town in France, a man sought
lodging for the night. It would have been difficult to find a person more
wretched in appearance.

The man was Jean Valjean, an ex-convict of four days. He had no money,
and because of his yellow passport, he was turned away again and again.
Finally, exhausted and without hope of anything better, he lay down on a
stone bench.

Just then, an old woman came out of the church across the way. Learning
of his plight, she whispered, "Go to the home of the bishop; he never turns
anyone away."

Knocking on the bishop's door, Jean Valjean told him the truth. The bishop
interrupted, invited him in, and called to his housekeeper to put another
plate on the table.

After supper, Jean Valjean was shown to his room and a bed with clean
white sheets. Exhausted, he fell across the bed dressed as he was and
was soon asleep.

As the cathedral clock struck two, Jean Valjean awoke. His mind went
back to the day he stole a loaf of bread for the sake of his sister's seven
children. It was this that sent him to the galley for nineteen long years. As
the clock struck three he rose, went to the cupboard, gathered the silver
into his haversack, and fled from the house.

Toward daylight, there was a knock at the bishop's door, and he arose to
answer it. Three of the men standing there were policemen. The fourth
man was Jean Valjean.

The bishop spoke quickly to Jean Valjean, "It is you my friend. I am glad
you came back. I gave you the silver candlesticks, also. Why did you go
off without them?" The officers quickly apologized, "He acted like he was
running away. We thought he had stolen the silver."

Jean Valjean was trembling as the bishop took the silver candlesticks from
the mantel and placed them in his hands. "Now go in peace," he said,
"Use this silver to become an honest man."

December 29   Ephesians 4: 22-24
Two Lives for the Price of One

Luther Williams had gone to the basement of his home intent on taking his life, but he couldn't go through with it. He whispered through his tears, "Oh, God, forgive me for what I am. I don't even have the nerve to kill myself."

It all began the day he finally admitted to himself that he was an alcoholic. No one else knew. How could they? He had a good job, a fine home, a wonderful wife, and two beautiful daughters.

But unless he could stop drinking, he knew he was doomed to destroy all he held dear, and now he knew that he couldn't stop.

It was the usual story. His company was constantly entertaining, and there was always plenty to drink. At first it was just to be sociable. He really didn't like the taste.

He held the glass in his hands, taking a sip now and then, but before he knew it, he was hooked. Up to now, he had somehow managed to keep his problem a secret from everyone, but he could feel his life gradually falling apart.

While his wife and daughters slept, he had taken the automatic from the dresser drawer and had gone to the basement. It had to be done, but he couldn't go through with it.

His words were highly reminiscent of the prophet Elijah, who under the broom tree prayed, "O Lord, take away my life!"

Luther Williams sobbed in anguish, "God, I don't have the courage. I can't even kill myself! You do it. Do what I don't have the fortitude to do. Destroy this man. Take away my life!"

And God did! God heard his cry for death and understood. At the point of total surrender, God destroyed the "old man" and gave life to the "new man." With the help of Alcoholics Anonymous, Luther Williams stopped drinking. It was the hardest battle of his life, but with the help of God he won.

The greatest news in the world is that anyone who wants it—really wants it—can have two lives for the price of one. "If anyone is in Christ he is a new creation. Old things are passed away; behold, all things are made new."

John 14: 23

The Church in Your House

In Paul's letter to Philemon is to be found this strange sounding phrase: "The church in your house." Of course, what Paul was referring to was the fact that the Christians of Laodicea met in the home of Philemon to worship.

You see, there were no church buildings until somewhere around the third century. The early congregations simply met together in the home of one of the members, but there is another way of thinking about Paul's words: There is a church of some kind in every Christian home.

Telling about his efforts to rebuild the South following the Civil War, Henry W. Grady, the great editor, wrote, "I began with legislation, but I soon found that legislation didn't work. Then I turned to the schools; perhaps education could achieve what could not be achieved by legislation. That also was a failure.

"Then I turned to the churches, thinking warm emotion might be better than cold intellect. Eventually, I gave up on that also. Gradually, I came to the conclusion that the only place to begin was with the home."

It is in the home, as nowhere else, that the things of God are made real. What is it like—the church in your house? We are all co-workers with God. He has given us our homes and families and said to us, "Make my love and way of life real in that setting." What do you mean to your home? Is it a happier place when you are there? Do the people who live there look forward to your coming home at the close of day? What is it like—the church in your house?

Up in the state of Washington, there is an Indian mission. On the grounds is a beautiful chapel built of native stone. Above the chancel is a stained glass window. It was given to the tribe by their chief.

The window pictures an Indian teepee upon which is superimposed a cross. Says the old Indian chief, "I want my people never to forget that Jesus Christ is the hope of men who live in teepees."

Jesus Christ is the hope of all the people of our world, whether they live in a teepee or a tenement, an apartment or a palace, and he finds his chance through your home and mine.

What is it like—the church in your house?

December 31

The Jericho Road

> "On the Jericho Road
> There's room for just two.
> No more and no less,
> Just Jesus and you."

The Jericho Road is a road in the land of Palestine and also a road that runs through all the coming year and through your life and mine. Some 3,400 years ago, Joshua led his army down that road. Under his leadership, the Israelites captured the city of Jericho.

For six successive days, you remember, they marched around the city's walls. On the seventh day they encircled the walls seven times, a shout went up, the walls came tumbling down and a great victory was won.

There are victories for you and me to win in the coming year. What would you like to do? Move out into the future at God's command. He waits to lead you to victory.

On the Jericho Road, a little man climbed a sycamore tree in order to see Jesus as he passed by. Jesus went home with Zacchaeus that day, and Zachaeus's life was changed forever.

On the Jericho Road, Jesus is ever passing by. If you will invite him in, he can be in your heart this coming year and all the years to come.

A certain man, a Samaritan, was on the Jericho Road in the story Jesus told when he came upon a man who had beaten, robbed, and left for dead. In compassion he dressed the wounds, brought him to an inn, and cared for him. Because of his deed of love, he is remembered as "the Good Samaritan."

You have the opportunity to be a Good Samaritan in the year ahead. Look around you. You will find many in need. Everyone is carrying a heavy load, and it is forever true: "As we lift our brother's load, we find our own made light."

On the Jericho Road the blind Bartimaeus cried out, "Jesus, son of David, have mercy on me," and found a land of light.

On the Jericho Road there is help for everyone. "Sight, riches, healing of the mind, all we need in him we find." On the Jericho Road, there are victories to be won, service to be rendered and life can be changed.

MOVABLE HOLIDAYS:

Martin Luther King, Jr. Day	The third Monday in January
Palm Sunday	The Sunday before Easter Sunday
Good Friday	The Friday before Easter Sunday
Easter Sunday	The first Sunday after the full moon following the March equinox
Mother's Day	The second Sunday in May
Memorial Day	The last Monday in May
Father's Day	The third Sunday in June
Thanksgiving Day	The fourth Thursday in November

Martin Luther King Day

I John 2: 9

The Brotherhood Of Man

Today is Martin Luther King, Jr. Day. In 1967 I was privileged to hear Dr. King speak. His subject: "Beyond Justice—Brotherhood." The brotherhood of man was his dream. We best celebrate his birthday by dedicating our lives anew to helping make that dream a reality.

Living in a world of hatred and misunderstanding, where people as never before fear and kill one another, we need to work for peace and brotherhood.

Some years ago Taylor Caldwell wrote a short story for Good Housekeeping Magazine. In it she told about a man who was walking across a great desolate wilderness at twilight time. His destination was obscure, and he was very much afraid.

Suddenly, in the distance, he saw the form of another creature coming toward him and was filled with terror. There was no place to hide. He had to go on. He was a traveler all alone in the gathering dark.

As he watched, the figure came closer and closer. All at once he saw that it was a man. Now the traveler was even more terrified. Men were more dangerous than wild animals. Men had weapons and were without mercy or compassion.

The traveler stopped. Was it a robber, a murderer? In the distance the figure halted uncertainly; then, came toward the traveler, timidly and with great apprehension.

In the dim twilight, the traveler saw the figure's face. All at once, he cried out with joy and ran toward the shadowy figure, which he had feared. There in the shadows, as darkness fell, they embraced each other with love and great release. "I thought you were a mad animal that would devour me," cried the traveler. "I thought you were a murderer who would kill me! And all the time you were my brother!"

God's Word tells us "He has made of one flesh all men to dwell upon the earth." It was Cain, you remember, who having killed his brother Abel, was asked by God, "Where is your brother?" Cain replied, "Am I my brother's keeper?"

Today, we are asking that question, "Am I my brother's keeper?" Christ answers the question for us, "No, you are not your brother's KEEPER. You are your brother's BROTHER!"

368

Like A Palm Tree

In the Book of Psalms are these words, "The righteous flourish like the palm tree." The palm tree flourishes in the extremely hot desert. It is able to do so, because it grows down as it grows up. The long taproot reaches down into the moisture far below the burning sands. For every inch the palm grows upward, the taproot grows an inch downward.

The taproot of our soul may reach downward also into the source of life that God provides. Through Bible reading and prayer, we are refreshed and strengthened and are able to grow upward, secure, and strong. Other trees grow to maturity and then limb-by-limb begin to decay. It is not so with the palm. It continues to grow as long as it lives. The righteous life is like that. It never stops growing in the grace and knowledge of God.

The secret of such growth is the fact that the palm grows from the inside out. Other trees grow by adding annual rings. The trunk of the palm is a solid mass and its inner life is soft and growing. God's Word tells us "As a man thinks in his heart, so is he," and we are counseled, "Keep your heart with all vigilance, for from it flows the springs of life."

Throughout history the palm has been a symbol of victory. In the year 155, the persecution of the Christians was at its height. One of the great leaders of the church, Polycarp of Smyrna, was arrested and burned alive at the stake.

Before the torch was lighted, he was given a chance to renounce his faith and live. For a moment he was silent. Then he said, "For 86 years I have served Christ. He has never failed me once. How can I fail him now?"

"The righteous flourish like the palm tree." Their souls grow down in order that their lives may grow up. They grow as long as they live, because they grow from the inside out. And victory is sure through Jesus Christ our Lord.

> Build thee more stately mansions, O my soul,
> As the swift seasons roll!
> Leave thy low-vaulted past!
> Let each new temple, nobler than the last,
> Shut thee from heaven with a dome more vast,
> Till thou at length art free,
> Leaving thine outgrown shell by life's unresting sea!

Were You There?

By day and by night I am haunted by the words of an African American spiritual: "Were you there when they crucified my Lord?" "No," I answer, "Of course not. Jesus was crucified nearly two thousand years ago. No, I was not there." Then, as in a dream, I go back across the centuries to a hill outside a city's wall on that Black Friday. Looking into a sea of faces, one by one, I recognize the people there.

That man is Nicodemus. He first came to Jesus by night. Pride and fear of the Jews kept him silent about his discipleship. Finally, when it was too late, he came requesting the body of Jesus for burial.

There is Pontius Pilate. Cowering before the crowd, he whimpers, "What then shall I do with Jesus?" The man on trial was Pilate—not the Christ.

There in the shadows is Judas the traitor. Judas, Judas! Jesus once asked, "What has a man profited if he gains the whole world and loses his soul?" The whole world! But thirty pieces of silver?

I see the disciples, heartbroken. In the hour they were needed most, they counted least. In Gethsemane, as Jesus prayed, first they went to sleep, and then they ran away.

There is a multitude I do not know. They are passers-by. They stop, and stand, and stare, and then move on. Unconcerned, they go their way, and leave the Son of God to die.

"Were you there?" The words of that old hymn jar my reverie. "No, no, I wasn't there." Again, my eyes survey the setting. I see Nicodemus, Judas, Pilate, Peter, James, and John. But most of all, I see the milling mob.

Then suddenly, I see myself! I was there in Nicodemus with his pride. I was there in Judas—"Still, as of old, man by himself is priced." I was there in Pilate—"Silence is not always golden; sometimes it is just plain yellow." I was there in the disciples—sleeping in time of crisis; then running off in fear. There, among the multitude, I hear the words, "Is it nothing to you, all you who pass by?"

Yes, I was there. I was there, and you were there. The entire human race was there when Christ was crucified. And, somehow, we must all go back, because there, at the foot of the cross, is our only hope.

Searching For Reassurance

Helen has gone home at the age of 98 years, 11 months and 16 days. She was 84 when she asked me, "Would you preach my funeral?" I replied, "Helen, how in the world do I respond to a question like that? Do I say, 'I will be glad to?' I probably won't even be around; you will outlive all of us."

We had many enjoyable visits in her home. We talked about the church, her travels, and about her husband who had died years before. Eventually she would ask, "Do you think there is a heaven?"

It isn't an unusual question. Soon or late, we all ask it of others or of ourselves. It is as old as Job who wondered, "If a man dies will he live again?" I got in the habit of saying, "Helen, you and I both know there is a heaven. " Often, I would quote Emily Dickinson: *I never saw a moor, I never saw a sea, Yet I know what heather's like and what a wave must be. I never spoke with God or visited in heaven. Yet certain am I of the spot as if the chart were given.* You know, poetry comes closer to the truth than just about anything.

But what Helen really wanted was something from God's Word. I would say, "We believe because Paul wrote, 'We know if the earthly house of this tabernacle be dissolved, we have a house not made with hands, a building of God, a home eternal in the heavens.' We believe because Jesus said, 'In my Father's house are many mansions. I go to prepare a place for you. And if I go and prepare a place for you, I will come again and receive you to myself that where I am there you may be also.'"

Invariably she always asked, "What do you think heaven is like?" I would answer, "None of us really knows. Jesus was sure about heaven, but he didn't tell us much about it. To him, heaven was so wonderful we are not capable of even imagining what it is like. 'Eye has not seen, nor ear heard, neither has it entered into the heart of man the wonderful things God has prepared for those who love him.'"

Helen would say, "I have always believed there is a heaven. I just wondered." She wasn't looking for proof. She just wanted reassurance, and that is what you and I want too, isn't it?

Helen has gone home now. She knows firsthand and leaves us to wonder, how beautiful heaven must be. She is at home with all those she "has loved long since and lost a while." She is at home with her Father and our Father, her God and our God.

She Never Did Anything

Some years ago, Dorothy Dix wrote an article entitled, "Just Mom." I would like to share it with mothers everywhere.

"The greatness of a mother has never been better told than when an old woman was chosen by her community for a special honor and replied, 'Who, me? I've never done anything but bring up a house full of kids to be descent men and women. That's all.'

"She never did anything, yet she was a soldier who fought her battles as bravely as any general. Eight times, she faced suffering and possible death to bring her children into the world. Her life was always a hand-to hand fight with poverty, ill health, and discouragement, but she never once ran up the white flag.

"She never did anything, yet she was a financier who would have been Secretary of the Treasury if she had gotten her just deserts. Balancing the federal budget would have been easy compared with making her husband's thin pay envelope cover the needs of a big family. Yet, she did it.

"She never did anything, yet she was a jack-of-all trades and did them all well. She had the wisdom of Solomon when it came to settling disputes between her children. She could kiss a bump and make it well. She was a nurse whose hands had healing in their touch.

"She never did anything, yet she was the character builder who held before her children high ideals and made them the kind of men and women who are the glory of our nation.

"She never did anything, yet she was a laborer who had no union hours and no forty-hour weeks. She had no holidays, no vacations, not even a Saturday afternoon off, because there was always too much work to do for that.

"She never did anything, yet for years and years she slaved and pinched pennies and denied herself even the medical attention she knew she needed so her sons and daughters might have the education that would forever put them out of her class.

"She never did anything; no, of course not. She was 'Just Mom,' and even her children never knew how truly great she was."

II Corinthians 5: 1

No Doubt About It!

"If a man dies, shall he live again?" That haunting question comes to all of us. Let me share with you a true story.

It was without doubt the most trying moment of the young minister's life. What could he possibly say to the little blue-eyed fellow who had just come to ask, "What happens to you when you die?" I don't know! Neither did he!

A car had struck the little boy's puppy, and he had witnessed it. His grandmother whom he loved had died two months before and now this whole thing about death was bothering him. His mother had dropped him off at the minister's study and there it was, plain as day, "What happens to you when you die?"

The young minister had no real good eight-year-old response. He didn't have a good twenty-five-year-old response either. As the two of them sat and talked it occurred to him that he did have a way of answering his little friend that could at least get them started. He didn't know who wrote it, but this is what he read to his little friend:

"I am standing upon the seashore. A ship at my side spreads her white sails to the morning breeze and starts for the blue ocean. She is an object of beauty and strength, and I stand and watch her until at length she hangs like a speck of white cloud just where the sea and sky come down to mingle with each other. Then someone at my side says, 'There! She is gone!'

"Gone where? Gone from my sight—that is all. She is just as large in mast and hull and spar as she was when she left my side, and just as able to bear her load of living freight to the place of destination. Her diminished size is in me, not in her; for just as someone at my side says, 'There! She is gone!' there are other eyes watching her coming, and other voices ready to take up the glad shout, 'There she comes!' And that is dying."

The little boy looked up as he squeezed his teddy bear. Past a single tear, he said, "Do you think my little dog and Grandma are on that boat?"

Remembering his father, his grandma, and so many, many others who had touched his life and then joined the communion of saints, the young minister said, "No doubt about it! No doubt about it at all!"

Father's Day

A Message For Fathers

Fathers, listen up; this is for you:

A certain mother, to teach her daughter to save, gave her two quarters. One was to be put in the bank; the other could be spent. The quarter to be saved was immediately put in the piggy bank, but the other quarter—what to do with it?

That was something to be carefully considered. While the daughter was mulling it over, without thinking, she started to put the coin in her mouth. Mom quickly said to her, "Honey, don't do that!" Startled, she asked, "Why?" The mother explained, "Well, first of all the quarter is dirty. You don't know who has had it. Second, because it is probably covered with germs. Third, because you could choke on something that small, and it could kill you."

The little girl was quite impressed. After a moment, she asked, "Mommy, where did you learn all that stuff?" With a smile, mother replied, "Honey, all mommies know things like that. It is on the mommy test. If you don't know things like that, they flunk you and you don't get to be a mommy." Totally unfazed, the little girl took about two seconds and then asked, "And if you flunk the mommy test, then do you have to be a daddy?"

That's the low opinion many people have about fathers. Commercials portray dads as sofa-sitting, beer-swigging, incompetent idiots. TV sitcoms show them as bungling, bigoted bozos incapable of understanding the complexities of family life. Seventy-five percent of adults believe that the family unit is weaker today than thirty years ago.

Is there hope for today's fathers and families? Yes, there is. A recent study by *Homemade* shows that if neither father nor mother goes to church, only 6 % of their children will. If Mom goes to church alone, the figure rises to 15 %. But fathers, if you bring your children to church, the number rises to 55 percent. And if both mother and father attend worship the figure rises to 75 %.

Fathers, God has given you children. You have a God-given task. On this Father's Day, give yourself anew to Christ. Set the example. Let your children see you read the Bible. Let them hear you pray. Be a father worth having.

Be the father God wants you to be!

Who Is Thankful For You?

Someone has said, that the all-important question to be asked at Thanksgiving is not, "For what are you thankful?" but rather, "Who is thankful for you?"

If it is true that charity begins at home, then perhaps we should begin there at Thanksgiving. Two little girls were playing when one asked the other, "Does your father have a den?"

"Oh, no," replied her playmate, "He just growls all over the house." It's hard to be thankful for someone who growls all the time.

Not long ago, a man said to me, "I don't know what I would do without my wife. During my long illness, in spite of the bad weather and all she had to do, she didn't miss coming to the hospital a single day." It's easy to be thankful for someone like that.

A wife says with a warm light in her eyes, "I have such a wonderful husband; he is one in a million!" Or a boy remarks to his companions, "My dad is the greatest!" At your house—who is thankful for you?

At Thanksgiving we are thankful for the church and for our Christian faith. How thankful is the church for you? One of our church families moved to another community.

Later, when I talked with the minister about them, he said, "They are a wonderful Christian family. I wish you would send us ten more families like them!" What about your life and faith, is the church thankful for you?

At Thanksgiving, we pause in gratitude for our country and our heritage of freedom. Ours is indeed, "One nation under God." It was "conceived in liberty and dedicated to the proposition that all men are created equal."

What are you doing to make real the great American dream? Is the United States of America thankful for you?

At Thanksgiving, we pause in gratitude to give thanks to our heavenly Father for our families, our faith, and our freedom.

But remember: the all-important question is not "For what are you thankful?" but "Who is thankful for you?"

I appreciate receiving feedback from my readers. You can reach me at 5309 Whistle Stop Drive, Temple, Texas 76502, or at my email address, cmnichols44@hot.rr.com. I answer all my emails.

Made in the USA
San Bernardino, CA
31 August 2018